D0596150

FRACTURED STATES

THE SECURITY CONTINUUM
Global Politics in the Modern Age

A series published in association with the Matthew B. Ridgway Center for International Security Studies and the Ford Institute for Human Security

CHILD SOLDIERS IN THE AGE OF FRACTURED STATES

EDITED BY SCOTT GATES AND SIMON REICH

UNIVERSITY OF PITTSBURGH PRESS

Published by the University of Pittsburgh Press, Pittsburgh, Pa., 15260
Copyright © 2010, University of Pittsburgh Press
Manufactured in the United States of America
Printed on acid-free paper
10 9 8 7 6 5 4 3 2 1

Library of Congress Cataloging-in-Publication Data

Child soldiers in the age of fractured states / edited by Scott Gates and Simon Reich.
    p.   cm. — (The security continuum: global politics in the modern age)
  Includes bibliographical references and index.
  ISBN-13: 978-0-8229-6029-4 (pbk. : alk. paper)
  ISBN-10: 0-8229-6029-X (pbk. : alk. paper)
    1. Children and war—Developing countries. 2. Child soldiers—Developing countries. I. Gates, Scott. II. Reich, Simon, 1959–
  HQ784.W3C487 2009
  303.6'6083091724—dc22   2009024340

CONTENTS

ACKNOWLEDGMENTS

Most work on child soldiers has been done by activists and practitioners. Surprisingly, little academic attention has been brought to bear on the issue. The idea behind this project from its genesis has been to bridge these two communities to mate the theories and rigor of academic research with the deep knowledge and experience of the policy community. We invited participation from policy makers representing the national governments of Canada, the United States, and Norway; international organizations such as the United Nations Office of Children and Armed Conflict, UNICEF, UNESCO, and the World Bank; nongovernmental organizations, including the Red Cross, Human Rights Watch, Save the Children, the Coalition to Stop the Use of Child Soldiers, the Norwegian Refugee Council, Norwegian People's Aid, and the International Crisis Group; think tanks that include the International Peace Research Institute, Fafo, Norwegian Institute for International Affairs, the Brookings Institution, U.S. Institute for Peace, Institute for Reconstruction and International Security through Education, International Crisis Group, and the Human Security Centre; and academics from National University of Colombia, Norwegian University of Science and Technology, University of Oxford, University of Pittsburgh, Wake Forest University, Columbia University, Randolph-Macon College, Rutgers University, RTI International, George Mason University, and the University of Oslo.

The initial phase of this project consisted of two workshops, one held at the International Peace Research Institute, Oslo (PRIO), and a second at the University of Pittsburgh in 2006. From the beginning a good rapport was established between members of the different groups. Indeed, there was probably more heated debate among the academics than between policy makers, nongovernmental organization representatives, and the academics. This volume only reflects one aspect of the rich dialogue established during the two work-shops. In its entirety, the project pushed us all toward a better understanding of the issue of child soldiers.

We have many to thank for their help, including the Research Council of Norway, the Norwegian Ministry of Foreign Affairs, and the Carnegie Foundation of New York for financing this project. For their support and assistance, we thank Radhika Coomaraswamy, UN Special Representative of the Secretary General for Children and Armed Conflict, and Alec Wargo of the Office of Children and Armed Conflict at the United Nations. Karen Sham Poo, former deputy executive director of UNICEF, gave the keynote address at the Oslo meeting and participated in the Pittsburgh meeting. Betty Bigombe, from the World Bank and renowned for her work with child soldiers in Uganda, was also featured in the Oslo meetings. Ragne Birte Lund (Norwegian ambassador for children and youth) played an instrumental role in organizing and helping finance the Oslo meeting. Steve Del Rosso, program officer at the Carnegie Foundation, was invaluable in his support of the Pittsburgh meeting. Ingeborg Haavardsson was the main organizer of the PRIO meeting. Vera Achvarina served as her assistant while she was a visiting researcher at PRIO and helped organize both meetings. Elizabeth Jareg, from Save the Children, Norway, provided invaluable advice. Sandy Monteverde, Jessica Hand, and Penelope Nelson all assisted in either organizing the meeting at the University of Pittsburgh or dealing with logistics in its aftermath. Martha Snodgrass and Andrew Feltham at PRIO helped to keep the project moving after the workshops.

The second stage of our project was to publish an edited volume. We cannot thank enough Bill Keller, coeditor of the Security Continuum Series at the University of Pittsburgh Press, for his support, encouragement, advice, and editing of this volume. Stathis Kalyvas and Chris Blattman at Yale provided valuable comments. Sigurd Ziegler, Kristian Hoeschler, and Lars Seland Gomsrud at PRIO provided tremendous help putting order to each contributor's citation style and filling in myriad missing references. Lynn Nygaard and Lars Seland Gomsrud also helped with the editing. We also thank Monica Phillips for her editing of the final manuscript for the University of Pittsburgh Press.

In addition, Scott and Simon would like to thank Ingeborg, Christine, Alexandra, and Caroline, and Ariane, Jamie, Melissa, and Amanda for bringing a sense of joy to life and serving as a constant reminder of what is valuable.

Finally, this book is dedicated to Olara Otunnu, someone who has dedicated his life to protecting children in war.

ABBREVIATIONS

ANGOLA

UNITA   National Union for the Total Independence of Angola

JURA   Angolan Youth Movement (youth wing of UNITA)

COLOMBIA

AUC   United Self-defense Forces of Columbia

ELN   National Liberation Army

EPL   Popular Liberation Army

FARC   Revolutionary Armed Forces of Colombia

COTE D'IVOIRE

APWé   Patriotic Alliance of the Wé

FAFN   Armées des Forces Nouvelles

FN   Forces Nouvelles

FLGO   Front for the Liberation of the Great West

MILOCI   Ivorian Movement for the Liberation of the West of Cote d'Ivoire

UPRGO   Union of Patriots for the Resistance of the Great West

DEMOCRATIC REPUBLIC OF CONGO

ADFL   Alliance of Democratic Forces for the Liberation of Congo-Zaire

RCD-ML   Rally for Congolese Democracy–Movement for Liberalization

LIBERIA

AFL   Armed Forces of Liberia

LPC   Liberian Peace Council

LURD   Liberians United for Reconciliation and Democracy
MODEL   Movement for Democracy in Liberia
NPFL   National Patriotic Front of Liberia
SBU   Small Boys Unit
ULIMO   United Liberation Movement for Democracy

MYANMAR

KNLA   Karen National Liberation Army

SIERRA LEONE

RUF   Revolutionary United Front

SRI LANKA

LTTE   Liberation Tigers of Tamil Eelam

SUDAN

SPLA   Sudanese People's Liberation Army

UGANDA

LRA   Lord's Resistance Army

Part I

Overview

INTRODUCTION

Scott Gates and Simon Reich

ALTHOUGH THIS VOLUME FOCUSES ON CHILD SOLDIERS, it is not limited to children brandishing a gun. It also examines the roles of children, many of whom are preadolescent, linked to armed groups with a variety of functions. As such, child soldiers work as spies, cooks, porters, messengers, sex slaves, and, indeed, as both armed and unarmed combatants who serve in government armies, militias, and nonstate groups.[1] The authors in this collection analyze the phenomenon of child soldiers, examine what has been done to address it, and explore what remedies exist, if any.

Dating from the signing of the United Nations (UN) Convention on the Rights of the Child nearly two decades ago,[2] the number of international protocols, treaties, and conventions intended to shield children from the worst excesses of armed conflict has proliferated.[3] Many of these initiatives focus explicitly on the protection of children (under eighteen years) from recruitment into armed groups. In 1996, the landmark *Graça Machel Report* on child soldiering led to the establishment of the Cape Town Principles. A decade later, the anniversary of this report was notable for a UN-organized conference in Paris where fifty-eight countries signed what has been referred to as the Paris Commitments. These governments agreed to act against the unlawful recruitment and use of children by governments and rebel forces.

There is little evidence that these measures have been effective. One strategy, "naming and shaming," has frequently been used by the UN and nongovernmental organizations (NGOs) against transgressors of the norm. Advocates privately argue that this approach has had some effect on some governments, such as Colombia and Britain, although there is scant evidence to support their claims. In 2006, the United Kingdom banned the use of seventeen-year-olds in combat. Colombia has suspended the enlistment of child soldiers and now treats doing so as a war crime. Whether public calls played an important role in those decisions is unclear.

Nevertheless, many states still seem impervious to public pressure. Myanmar provides the most egregious example, with tens of thousands of children reputedly members of the armed forces.[4] Moreover, ten of the twelve signatory nations to the Paris Commitments appear on the UN blacklist of countries that recruit child soldiers. They are Burundi, Chad, Colombia, Ivory Coast, the Democratic Republic of Congo, Nepal, Somalia, Sudan, Sri Lanka, and Uganda. The remaining two offenders, Myanmar and the Philippines, neither attended the conference nor signed the document.[5]

The worst forms and largest degree of child soldier recruitment are now generally carried out not by governments but by nonstate actors, insurgency groups, and government-supported militias.[6] Public pressure appears to have little effect on these nonstate actors, with few examples of success. Naming and shaming has little influence in shaping the behavior of armed groups that depend heavily on children as combatants, such as the Lord's Resistance Army (LRA) in Uganda. Rebel groups care little about external organizations, the media, or the United Nations. For the international community, translating words into action, therefore, has proven elusive thus far.

The campaign against child soldiering seems to be exceptional in terms of its limited success. In other celebrated campaigns, such as those aimed at human trafficking or the ban on land mines, the efforts of NGOs have brought tangible results. Fewer states use landmines and more have enforced the criminalization of trafficking. But attempts to highlight and address the human rights abuses of children—who are simultaneously engulfed in conflict as both perpetrators and victims—seem to have exerted little influence on the behavior of belligerents. Across Asia, Africa, and Latin America there are high and sustained rates of noncompliance with child protection agreements that often have the status of international law. Armed groups use children as direct combatants with little concern about the consequences.

Moving beyond formal protocols, and possibly in response to the failure of moral suasion, the international community has shifted its focus to criminalizing the recruitment of children for combat in what Tonderai Chikuhwa terms an "era of application." As the first case to come before the International Criminal Court (ICC), Thomas Lubango Dyilo's celebrated trial is the most palpable attempt to constrain the use of child soldiers.[7] But the trial foundered on 2 July 2008 when judges ordered his release on the grounds that he could not receive a fair trial because evidence had been withheld from the defense.[8] Despite the attempt to prosecute Lubango, it is premature to judge whether such prosecutions will prove to be a deterrent. The leaders of armed forces most strategically reliant on children, and thus the worst offenders, are unlikely to release these children if they calculate that doing so will result in their defeat. Furthermore, if rebels are interested in negotiating a peace agreement, they may be less likely to lay down their weapons and stop fighting if they fear postwar prosecution. Many rebel leaders still believe they can negotiate an amnesty as part of a peace agreement, granting them immunity from postconflict prosecution. Indeed, a government interested in securing peace may be willing to incorporate amnesty with a peace agreement to buy off rebels and end the violence.

In Uganda, the Lord's Resistance Army overwhelmingly relies on children to make up its military force.[9] For any peaceful resolution to the conflict, the Ugandan government must negotiate with its leader, Joseph Kony. Yet Uganda, as a signatory to the Paris Commitments and a member of the ICC, is expected to abide by the principles and rules of both. Such commitments are therefore potentially in tension with Uganda's need to negotiate a peace agreement with Kony, whom the ICC has declared to be a criminal suspect in abrogation against its prohibition on the use of child soldiers. Criminalization may therefore prove an obstacle to peace in the absence of consistently applied enforcement mechanisms, leaving little reason for optimism that deterrence will work unless the risks of using children outweigh the rewards—and the prospects of prosecution are significantly increased. Without a greater capacity to implement new enforcement measures, deterrence and the force of law have limits.

In many ways the fundamental problem is armed conflict itself. Certainly there have been significant efforts to address the issue of children in armed conflict, including a variety of measures taken by diverse UN agencies and NGOs. The number of children active in armed groups is clearly nominal when compared to the millions of children who do not participate directly as soldiers but are profoundly affected by war. Nonetheless, this group is a tangible, visible, and dramatic example of the deprivation of the human rights of children. Clearly, boys and girls with bloated bellies, no parents, and bruised and broken bodies present a compelling image of victimhood. But as demobilization, disarmament, and rehabilitation (DDR) programs reveal, child soldiers suffer in several other dimensions. They are subject to intense psychological trauma associated with their participation in or witnessing of atrocities associated with combat. They are frequently humiliated and abused. And they are typically unable to reintegrate into their former communities.

The humanitarian aspect of child soldiering is a subject of publicity in Europe and North America. Popular books by former child soldiers (such as Ishmael Beah's [2007], which was sold at Starbucks across the United States) offer compelling narratives by the victims and have become the foundation for public advocacy campaigns on their behalf. Yet, the humanitarian aspect is only one of a series of components of the problem of child soldiers.

The contributions by Chikuhwa and McMahan discuss the issue of culpability, as well as authority and redress. Such issues have implications for postconflict justice. The movement toward the criminalization of international law, whereby culpability shifts from governments to individuals, could have profound implications for guaranteeing the rights of children who have been members of armed groups, as well as protecting those who might be in the future.

The issue of ethics also bears on the question of the rules of engagement for professional military personnel when they encounter child soldiers. Currently there is no consistent policy, and few countries have explicit rules of engagement. Those that do differ considerably in their content.

Meanwhile, child soldiers are now involved in terrorism and insurgency as direct participants. For example, in Sri Lanka, the territories of the Palestinian Authority, and Iraq, children have been reputedly used as suicide bombers.[10] In Afghanistan, a fourteen-year-old was responsible for the first killing of a NATO soldier, and sporadic reports claim that the Taliban's forces comprise a notable number of child soldiers.[11]

Once demobilized, former child soldiers suffer from a lack of educational and vocational skills that dramatically reduces their earning potential and enhances the possibility of intergenerational violence (Blattman and Annan 2007). They are more at risk of gang membership, violent behavior, and (re-)recruitment in combat forces than other children, a point discussed by McClure and Retamal.[12] This reality is not surprising given that the factors that led to their participation in an armed group are likely to persist after the termination of hostilities. Criminal leaders often play a significant role in the dynamics of armed conflict, motivated by the drug trade or the control of natural resources. They have comparably easy access to arms. As a result, it is often functionally difficult to distinguish urban youth gangs from armed groups that recruit children.

The activities of a variety of violent groups thus contribute toward ensuring that countries experiencing civil war—or at risk of doing so—remain in a perpetual state of insecurity. The failure or incapacity to address these problems sows the seeds of future war and criminality—what Paul Collier et al. (2003) has called "the conflict trap." As in the case of Guatemala, postconflict societies are sometimes as violent as they were when at war as rates of criminal activity soar. This lawlessness serves to foster a host of both economic (poverty, lack of education, and lack of employment opportunities) and social (domestic and sexual abuse) problems that drive child recruitment.

Child soldiering provides an interesting and potentially rewarding avenue into understanding the dynamics of political and economic development and civil conflict. Since children (especially young children) are rarely employed by military groups in peacetime, it is obvious that the major immediate cause of the employment of children as soldiers is conflict itself. Thus, in order to comprehend the threats posed to children in armed conflict, we must understand the dynamics of civil war. Recent works by Jean Paul Azam, Stathis Kalyvas, Scott Gates, and Jeremy Weinstein feature the dynamic qualities of civil conflict, focusing on issues such as the targeting of violence, recruitment, and the organization of rebellion.[13] Child soldier recruitment forms a part of this mosaic.

One of the theoretical components of this work concerns economic factors, which play a particularly important role in explaining the onset and continuation of civil conflict.[14] Indeed, children are much more likely to be directly engaged in the types of wars associated with low gross domestic product levels and low growth rates (Collier et al. 2003). In societies where child labor is common, it is not so surprising that armed groups also recruit children. Moreover, the opportunity costs of joining are likely to be lower in poor countries (Collier and Hoeffler 2002, 13–28; Collier and Hoeffler 2004, 563–595; Collier and Sambanis 2005a, 2005b). Christopher Blattman, drawing on interviews with rebel leaders and surveys of 462 conscripts associated with the LRA in northern Uganda, demonstrates how the benefits and costs of recruits varied systematically with age, and that adolescent (twelve- to fourteen-year-old) recruits yielded the largest expected net gain to the rebel leader. While adults were generally regarded by the leadership of the armed group to be more skilled as guerrilla fighters, they were also more likely to desert. Adolescents and younger children were more easily indoctrinated and disoriented, and thus likely to stay, but were relatively ineffective as fighters.

Gross domestic product is more indirect. It tends to accompany inefficient governments, which are associated with a high risk of civil conflict (Hegre et al. 2001, 33–48; Fearon and Laitin 2003, 75–90). Dysfunctional governments caught in the conflict trap, moreover, tend to have long-lasting wars with small-scale fighting organizations (Hegre 2004, 243–252). These are precisely the types of conflict that are characterized by the recruitment of children to armed groups.

Historically, Kalyvas demonstrates that small wars fought with rudimentary technologies are nothing new (Kalyvas 2001, 99–118). What may be new is an increase in the number of small wars and the relative accessibility of efficient small arms (e.g., AK-47s). These wars involve relatively little direct combat among belligerents. Rather, most violence is directed against unprotected and unarmed civilians (Azam 2002, 131–153; Kalyvas 2003, 475–494; Kalyvas 2006; Weinstein 2007). The dynamic created, in terms of large-scale flows by vulnerable populations, is marked. Jean-Paul Azam, for example, offers the novel observation that the targeting of a leader's own civilian supporters, and their coerced movement, may be part of a broader strategy aimed at achieving specific strategic goals. He argues that military leaders often target their own supporters for violence and forced migration in an attempt to consolidate the geographic breadth of their support as well as their manpower and material resources (Azam 2006, 53–73). Colombia provides an example of this pattern.

Where these populations settle is nonetheless undetermined. Self-settlement in cities, towns, and villages is often eschewed by the displaced in favor of camps for internally displaced persons (IDPs) and refugees for practical reasons, particularly the promise of food aid and security. In practice, the camps may serve as bastions for militarization, recruitment, and abduction by government forces, militias, and rebel groups, as the chapters by Achvarina and Reich and by Lischer demonstrate.

Children become especially vulnerable under these circumstances. The breakdown of traditional extended familial, communal, and broader societal structures has a severe impact on them, given their greater dependence. In theoretical terms, the literature, although increasingly sophisticated, has failed to note the centrality of this issue. This volume seeks to contribute to an understanding of this problem.

Another theoretical aspect is the linkage between war and criminality in the context of civil wars. Parts of the literature on violence have discussed the similarities between the behavior of warlords and the leadership of criminal gangs. In his discussion of the former Yugoslavia, John Mueller (2003, 507–518) draws a comparison between the motives of and methods used by differing ethnic groups both during a war and after the cessation of military conflict. This includes an emphasis on intimidation, coerced membership of the group, racketeering, and robbery. It also has much to say about the construction of identity and group solidarity (Gates 2002, 111–130). In the Balkan wars, for example, criminal elements were explicitly recruited and even released from prison in order to enlist. These soldiers were among the most violent and may have been recruited for that very quality. As rebel and militia groups operate outside the law, they often act in ways more often associated with common crime (extortion, trade in illicit drugs, smuggling, etc.) in order to fund their operations, as the Revolutionary Armed Forces of Colombia's (FARC) heavy involvement in the coca trade in Colombia illustrates.

The study of children in armed conflict thus has significant analytic value in linking economic factors with the prevalence of small arms, the dynamics of population movements, and the use of force targeted against civilian populations. Many of the chapters that follow feature these linkages. Child soldiering thus constitutes a template through which the conjunction of sociological, economic, and political influences can be studied.

The issue of child soldiering also poses a puzzle to those interested in the influence of norms and international sanctions on actor behavior, particularly with regard to postconflict justice. In theoretical terms, consolidation of the norm should be of interest to scholars working on the issue. The evidence contained in these chapters challenges the idea that child soldiering is a product of either ancient or modern hatreds. Nor is it one of embedded cultural views of childhood (Kaufman 2001). Different countries with similar ethnic compositions vary enormously in their propensity to use child soldiers; there is no evidence that child soldiers are consistently employed in a particular country across different conflicts over time, with the possible exception of Liberia; and those countries where child soldiers compose a high proportion of troops are spread around the globe. In sum, there is no cultural or historical thread that links the use of child soldiers to particular national cultures or a set of historical experiences. Using child soldiers is not, for example, "an African thing," nor is it to be found where genocides have recently occurred. Neighboring countries vary enormously in their propensity; Rwanda suffered from a mass slaughter but is not notable for its use of child soldiers.

From a human security perspective, where the focus is on the human rights of the individual, both the children themselves and the communities from which they are drawn are part of the broader conundrum of vulnerable populations whose lives are at risk in countries across the globe. The international community—composed of policymakers and NGOs—has worked extensively to address the problem. Yet, realistically, they have made limited headway, perhaps as a result of a lack of credible data and, in part, due to a lack of systematic analyses across cases.

The contributors to this volume remain modest in their claims. Nonetheless, drawing together such an experienced and qualified multidisciplinary group to participate in this project may contribute to the development of a credible, foundational basis for the promotion of novel, feasible policy proposals. Indeed, analyzing child soldiering may have policy implications for the larger population of civilians at risk from direct physical violence. Education can also play a significant role in mitigating the problem of child recruitment by military groups, as discussed in the chapters by McClure and Retamal and by Vargas-Barón. Education is particularly relevant for demobilization, disarmament, and reintegration programs.

Collier et al.'s work (2003) claims that nearly 60 percent of the countries that have experienced a civil war experience it again. Failure (or an inability) to attend to the problems that lead to the onset of civil war in the first place sows the seeds of future war. While it is true that the number of civil conflicts has fallen dramatically since 1992, the world experiences between twenty-eight and thirty-three armed conflicts per year, with many experiencing low-intensity conflict that varies from year to year. Such countries are hard pressed to sustain even modest levels of economic growth. They are caught in a trap in which the conditions that lead to the onset of armed conflict are maintained by the conflict. Poor countries with low rates of growth are more likely to experience civil war, which in turn slows economic growth and keeps them poor (Collier et al. 2003).

The logical conclusion of this pattern is sobering: those countries currently or recently engaged in conflict are most likely to be engulfed in war again. It is these future conflicts that presage a higher and higher proportion of wars fought with children. Moreover, there are increasing reports of child soldiers in areas where they were once rare, such as Central Asia and the Middle East. The best policy to prevent child soldiering is to ensure that peace settlements remain robust and vibrant, to move societies from civil war to civil peace. If such efforts fail, however, it is helpful to think about alternative strategies regarding recruitment and demobilization.

In this collection, we move from methodology to how the international community, particularly the United Nations and The Hague, has dealt with the issue of children in armed conflict. Several theoretical chapters feature different aspects of the phenomenon of recruiting children to organized armed groups. Case studies are drawn from sub-Saharan Africa, Asia, and Latin America. Contributions on education policy show how schooling can work to mitigate the risk of child soldiering in the first place and how it can play a central role as the reintegration part of a demobilization, disarmament, and reintegration policy.

Barry Ames addresses questions of methodology, noting that child soldiering as a subject suffers symptomatically from the problems encountered by policy fields overwhelmingly populated by advocates rather than more impartial analysts. Inferences are extrapolated from limited numbers; conclusions are drawn from skewed samples; and guesstimates are often inflated to draw attention to otherwise legitimate issues. The result is that myths get circulated and reproduced to the point that they take on the status of facts and become the foundation for policy. The very issue of the global number of child soldiers illustrates the problem well. Reputedly (although not verifiably), the figure of 300,000 was calculated by a group of NGO representatives looking for a convenient number to use in their public campaigns over a decade ago. Whether there was any attempt to form a substantive basis for the claim or if it was simply chosen for its dramatic effect is unclear. What is clear, however, is that the number has never been justified in terms of hard data, has no clear basis in fact, was arguably never accurate, and is now certainly wrong.[15] Yet few reports, academic or otherwise, begin without reference to the figure, even though it has been used for years and multiple wars have begun, ceased, or been renewed since it was introduced.[16] Recently, some reports have cited a new figure of 250,000 to account for the cessation of hostilities in a number of major conflicts where child soldiers were involved in large numbers—for example, Angola, Sierra Leone, and Liberia—but this figure is also not based on hard evidence. Ames addresses the central question of how to compensate for the inherent problem of the limitations of data collection in a policy area such as child soldiering by still employing reputable and reliable methods of data gathering and analysis.

The problem of recruitment is linked to ethical, legal, and international organizational issues. Jeff McMahan examines the moral dilemma of those who are faced with fighting child soldiers, asking under which conditions it might be permissible for adults to use force. His analysis exposes the inherent difficulties that war theory encounters when confronted with child soldiers who, by virtue of their age, may have diminished moral agency and/or diminished personal responsibility for their actions.

Tonderai Chikuhwa, who works in the UN's Office for Children and Armed Conflict (CAAC), analyzes how the debate between the Office of the Secretary General and the members of the general assembly on how to enforce norms on the ground has been played out since the CAAC was created over a decade ago. Progress toward an era of application of human rights norms for children has involved walking a tightrope between the protection of children and a series of political sensitivities. Nonetheless, the pattern is encouraging, particularly in the increasing integration of CAAC concerns into the international peace and security agenda of the UN Security Council.

Peter Singer focuses on the globalization of small arms in explaining the growth of child soldiering since the end of the cold war. In particular, he examines the interplay of a shifting socioeconomic environment, the technological advancements of the small arms industry, and the immorality of the leadership of military groups in explaining why child soldiers are now used in conflicts around the world despite a historical precedence against their use coupled with greater international efforts at prohibition. These three factors, Singer suggests, have combined to strip away the normative protections children have traditionally enjoyed, as the benefits and ease of using children as expendable military assets currently far outweigh moral qualms of military leaders.

Simon Reich and Vera Achvarina focus on the significant variance in the use of child soldiers in African conflicts over the course of the last decade.

Their chapter assumes that demand is constant and that the real constraint lies in the supply of children in refugee camps, arguing that the degree of access that belligerent parties have to IDP/refugee children is the principal determinant of their likely use as child soldiers. Their finding is not only more robust in explaining the varied use of child soldiers in Africa, but also provides a potential foundation upon which policymakers can implement a practical solution to address the problem in a short time frame.

Jens Christopher Andvig and Scott Gates develop a more generalizable model drawn from theories of organizational behavior and labor economics. They demonstrate that variation in the demand for child soldiers (in conjunction with supply factors) accounts for the tremendous variation across groups in the proportion of child soldiers. This demand, they argue, is influenced by the motivations of the leadership of the military group and by the type of resource endowments available to the organization.

Sarah Kenyon Lischer takes up the theme of camp protection, militarization, and vulnerability in her study of the Democratic Republic of the Congo. Building on Achvarina and Reich's chapter, she illustrates how the dangers of displacement for IDPs and refugees can make living in refugee camps almost as desperate as those in the conflict they hoped to escape, especially for children. By viewing the militarization and enhanced insecurity of displaced populations as two major facets of recruitment, Lischer identifies camps as ideal breeding grounds for child soldiers. State capability, international backing, and porosity of international borders are key factors in a camp's vulnerability to recruitment.

Jo Becker's study of three Asian cases further develops the theme of vulnerability. In Nepal and Sri Lanka, Becker finds that quota systems obligate families in rebel-controlled territories to "volunteer" one family member to their cause. In Burma/Myanmar, forced child conscription is the primary method of recruitment. Becker argues that political indoctrination plays a role in these cases and that schools aid in propaganda and forced recruitment in Nepal and Sri Lanka.

Francisco Gutiérrez Sanín's examination of Colombia and James Pugel's survey research on Liberia both employ elements of Andvig and Gates's model. Gutiérrez argues that some specific characteristics of military organizations may carry a strong allure for minors, such as the opportunity for a different life. He counters the presumption that children and adults have identical incentive-based motivations for joining military organizations, and addresses the question of why a military organization may recruit children based on its structure and the characteristics of the general population with which it interacts. James Pugel's study of Liberia supports these findings, comparing motivational factors that drive recruitment of child and adult soldiers through the analysis of a data set of ex-combatant samples differentiated by both faction and age. Disaggregating the data in this way highlights disparities that would not have been otherwise visible. Rationales, Pugel finds, differ significantly depending not only on age but also on which faction was joined.

Michael Wessells utilizes child psychology theory to study the roles of Angolan girls in conflict. His findings substantiate that girls are recruited for a variety of reasons and that they are often left out of postconflict reintegration programs. Additionally, their distinctive gendered needs are not addressed, creating greater difficulties and stigmatization in postconflict life. Overall, Wessells found research on girls was generally underexamined, even though females constituted a significant proportion of child soldiers.

Maureen McClure and Gonzalo Retamal also use child psychology in their study. They link education strategies to broader social contexts to address the question of why some children become child soldiers. Highlighting the advantages and disadvantages of fugitive literature, they advocate using community-level programs to address recruitment deterrence. The authors note that although these programs can be effective, the international community has done little to specifically target children with these local-level partnerships.

Emily Vargas-Barón focuses on efforts to protect displaced children through the use of preventative education measures intended to thwart recruitment and break the cycle of re-recruitment. With a focus on community-level education reform and conciliation measures—as well as the development and maintenance of basic services wherever possible—Vargas-Barón recognizes the push-and-pull factors that make child soldier recruitment a multifaceted, difficult, and complex problem to tackle.

Andrew Mack focuses on the trends in global human security and children in armed conflict, dispelling myths about the nature of armed conflict, child soldiers, and children as a special dimension of human security.

In the conclusion we discuss why the policies currently employed by the international community have failed so profoundly at curbing the recruitment and abduction of child soldiers. Integrating the findings of the other chapters with broader research on trends in civil conflict, we demonstrate why the problem of children in armed conflict is unlikely to recede. Indeed, it is a phenomenon that likely will be characteristic of more civil conflicts around the globe. Taking these trends into account, we prescribe policy measures to mitigate them while addressing the special needs and vulnerabilities of children in war zones.

CHAPTER 1

METHODOLOGICAL PROBLEMS IN THE STUDY OF CHILD SOLDIERS

Barry Ames

CHILD SOLDIERS MAY BE THE MOST DEPRESSING TOPIC in the field of international conflict, and the elimination of child soldiering is a completely laudable goal. But the methodological principles promoting good scholarship are still crucial. A more precise understanding of why children join violent conflicts, why irregular armies recruit and abduct children, why children leave irregular armies, and what problems they face after leaving will help craft policies to reduce child soldiering.

Much of the literature on child soldiers comes from advocacy groups. Not only would it be unrealistic to expect such advocates to jump into complex statistical analyses; it would also be counterproductive. Advocacy groups are valuable precisely because they awaken readers to the horrors of child soldiering. The research of advocacy groups, nevertheless, can be informed and guided by the theoretical models and rigorous statistical techniques of the scientific community.

This essay adopts an extremist methodological perspective. Scientific inference, in this view, depends not only on what one knows but also on recognizing what one does not know—that is, on recognizing the gap between the data one has and the data one wants. This does not mean that the real limitations of data availability should be ignored; rather, the consequences of the inevitable compromises imposed by limitations of time and money should be explicit.

Research on child soldiers falls into four arbitrarily defined categories. Perhaps the best known is work based on compiling reports on ex-combatants in multiple countries. A good example is Ilene Cohn and Guy Goodwin-Gill's monograph, *Child Soldiers: The Role of Children in Armed Conflict* (1994). Cohn and Goodwin-Gill use data from Sri Lanka, Guatemala, El Salvador, Liberia, and the Israeli-occupied territories. Qualitative single-country (quasi-ethnographic) studies include Sebastian Brett's *You'll Learn Not to Cry: Child Combatants in Colombia,* published in 2003 for Human Rights Watch.[1] Quantitative studies focusing purely on child soldiers in individual countries seem nonexistent, but quantitative studies of ex-combatants in general (both children and adults) include Humphreys and Weinstein's important papers on Sierra Leone (2006a, 2006b).[2] Multiple-country quantitative projects have two subtypes. *Child Soldiers Global Report 2004*, a worldwide compilation of facts, laws, and protocols sponsored by the Coalition to Stop the Use of Child Soldiers (CSUCS), is essentially a data fact book. The only quantitative large-N (multicountry) project of which I am aware is Achvarina and Reich's "Why Do Children 'Fight'? Explaining the Phenomenon of Child Soldiers in African Intra-State Conflicts" (2006b).

How we do research usually depends on the substantive questions we ask. Here I focus on the most commonly asked question: Why do children (typically defined as persons younger than eighteen) participate in armed conflicts? Sometimes guerrilla and paramilitary groups abduct children; sometimes children join voluntarily; sometimes they are sold into combat groups by relatives. Note the vagueness of these categories. There may be little distinction in practice between coercion and seemingly voluntary enlistment. And the data used to measure children's participation may take the form of an aggregate rate (how many children in a given population participate) or an individual decision to join or not to join.

A cursory reading of the qualitative literature on participation produces a common set of explanations. Grievance factors include poverty, loss of parents, lack of economic opportunity, abuse at home, ethnicity, political belief, and so on (Brett 2003). Inducement factors include pay, glory, and promises of future material gains. Solidarity factors include group cohesion, village networks, and friends (Petersen 1993). Accessibility factors include the presence and vulnerability of refugee camps (Achvarina and Reich 2006b).

These factors may be thought of as competing, but all might be true—indeed, all probably are true—at least under specified and varying circumstances. The task is to assess the causes of children's participation and to determine the relative importance of various causal factors. Because ultimately only statistical modeling can make such assessments, I focus on large-N comparison.[3] My suggestions, specific as well to the particular problem of child soldiers in civil wars, come in only a small measure from the single large-N study so far undertaken (Achvarina and Reich 2006b). To a larger degree they come from the kinds of explanations, explicit and implicit, found in the ethnographic literature surveying ex-combatants. Though I focus on large-N quantitative comparisons, the suggestions developed here also apply to the qualitative, quasi-ethnographic undertakings of advocacy groups in single or multiple-country settings.

The Unit of Analysis

In political science, most large-N statistical comparisons of aggregate data are based on nation-states. Sometimes nations are grouped into dyads, as in the study of interstate conflict; sometimes individual countries are maintained as units, as in the study of conditions favoring democratization. In either case, we take for granted that the nation-state is the unit of analysis.[4]

In studies of child soldiers, I suspect that taking the nation as the unit of analysis is almost always a mistake. If the object of explanation (the dependent variable) is an attribute or behavior of a fixed political or geographical entity (as in studies of levels of democratization), then that entity, typically a nation, is the appropriate unit of analysis. And if all we care about is predicting some outcome, such as an election winner, a nationwide sample ignoring spatial variation may work quite well. But in studies of child soldiers we seek to understand whether or how many children become part of irregular forces, and we hope we can intervene in some of the variables identified as central to recruitment.[5] The nation-state is an inappropriate unit if such predictive factors vary across the national space. Of course in analyses of child soldiers the predictive factors nearly always do vary spatially. Conflicts are localized within particular communities, ethnic groups, or regions. Even in cases without ethnic conflict, such as Colombia, rural areas are much more likely than urban areas to be involved.

Suppose, as one indicator of grievances, we want to assess the effects of poverty on the willingness of children to join irregular forces. Poverty rates are likely to be quite a bit higher in areas contested by guerrillas and government forces, because conflict destroys assets and disrupts agricultural activities. By taking the national poverty rate as an indicator of poverty, its observed effects will inevitably appear weaker than its true effects. Similarly, it is expected that children are more likely to become child soldiers if one or both parents are dead. But the percentage of children missing one or both parents is much higher in disputed areas (areas contested by rebels, paramilitaries, and/or government forces) than in the nation as a whole.

Whether kids are abducted by irregular forces or they join more or less voluntarily, local context matters. Children join because their friends join (Brett 2003); guerrillas abduct because they have already penetrated a village; and the presence of other parentless children affects individual parentless children. Contextual effects need to be assessed at the appropriate level. Sometimes the appropriate level is the faction, as in Pugel's discussion of four factional groups in Liberia (this volume), and sometimes it is the village or group of closely related villages. Researchers must, in addition, take particular care with post hoc explanations or rationalizations provided by ex-combatants who have left irregular forces.

People in Context

In the early years of public opinion surveys, two perspectives, the Michigan school and the Columbia school, competed. The Michigan model, represented by the Institute for Social Research and the Interuniversity Consortium for Political and Social Research (ICPSR) at the University of Michigan, focused on national surveys. Because such surveys are nationally representative, they are very good at predicting the results of national elections. The Columbia (University) model, represented by the work of Lazarsfeld, Berelson, and Gaudet (1968) was more sociological. Its surveys frequently limited themselves to communities and neighborhoods. Such surveys could not be generalized to the national level, but they were better at illuminating the processes leading people to change their opinions and behaviors. In the end, the Michigan model dominated, in part because its surveys were better able to predict broad electoral outcomes and in part because a model assuming an atomized citizenry fit twentieth-century American society.

The places where children fight are worlds away from late industrial society. No television, no air-conditioning, no bedroom suburbs; these are places where face-to-face contact is the primary mode of persuasion, where ideas move through dense social networks.[6] And it is exactly here that surveys of smaller ecological units, surveys that include respondents' neighborhood and workplace contacts, may be better able to reveal the deeper motivations of adults and children as they confront irregular forces.

Selection Bias

Surveys of children as ex-combatants typically (perhaps always) suffer from a simple form of selection bias, because they fail to interview noncombatants.[7] Some children join irregular forces; most children do not. Guerrillas and paramilitaries offer selective incentives to children; only some accept. Only by comparing combatants to noncombatants can we assess what makes them more likely to respond to incentives.[8]

Another form of selection bias comes from focusing solely on children. Recruitment of children may be no different from recruitment of adults. Moreover, the way irregular forces treat civilians affects the recruitment of children.

If the relevant population is not merely children and not merely ex-combatants, a given population then consists of noncombatants, volunteers, and victims of abduction.[9] Both volunteers and victims of abduction may be further subdivided into the various factions and subfactions with which they may be involved. At the level of the individual, through survey responses, the appropriate methodological technique is then some sort of multinomial logit—that is, a statistical technique allowing the simultaneous comparison of distinct, nonordinally related categories.[10]

Finally, large-N studies need to include cases in which intrastate conflict did not result in the utilization of child soldiers. In terms of the factors that induce recruitment of children, whether by guerrilla, paramilitary, or governmental forces, exclusion of no-recruitment cases leads to an underappreciation of the forces leading different kinds of organizations to decide to include or exclude children (see Gutiérrez Sanín, this volume).

The Centrality of Time

Cross-sectional surveys cannot provide a basis for inference unless we assume that the variables included in the model are stable over time. In most political science research this assumption is questionable, but the temporal variation is often random and simply produces noise.[11] In research on child soldiers, however, time variation is an inherent and systematic problem.

Suppose each conflict contributes one data point (one observation, in a large-N study) where the observations are regions, villages, or other relevant units of analysis. These single data points, however, may represent very different stages in a civil war. Brett (2003, 20) notes that the use of children by paramilitaries and guerrillas in Colombia only began in the 1990s, while fighting—and the emergence of paramilitaries—began long before. Recruiting changed, including the initiation of forcible abductions, because conditions in the countryside changed. Poverty for children increased, and the guerrillas needed manpower from both boys and girls. In Mozambique, Renamo began recruiting children after 1979, when Rhodesia ceased to be its main source of funds and support (Weinstein 2005, 612). And in Sierra Leone, the Revolutionary United Front (RUF) rebel movement, once dominated by university students, began recruiting unemployed youths and urban marginals after the collapse of its student base. Not only did the nature of the recruits change, but the kinds of incentives provided to them changed. Looting, for example, became more prominent.

Collecting data from ex-combatants is obviously very difficult, and it would be foolish to mandate the use of panel surveys. But coding schemes can be time-aware. At the individual level, this means including variables measuring the stages at which respondents joined and left conflicts. For aggregate data (where the object of explanation might be the percentage of some community's child soldiers who joined or left irregular forces), researchers might be able to project or impute data at parallel stages of a conflict. Humphreys and Weinstein (2006a, 15), in their surveys of ex-combatants in Sierra Leone, asked respondents to give their location and faction membership for seven designated time periods "marked by major events in the history of the conflict." Interviewers then asked about one of these periods of activity, chosen at random.[12] Other, perhaps simpler, schemes to build time-awareness into surveys are possible; what is not acceptable is to ignore the problem.

Model Interactions

In terms of grievances, broadly defined, most ethnographic studies stress the same factors for why children join irregular forces. In Colombia, for example, Brett (2003) notes that most recruits come from poor homes, have dropped out of school, and have suffered abuse at home. But in the areas where irregular forces recruit, almost everyone is poor and most children refuse to enlist. Does this mean that poverty really has no impact? In a linear additive model, poverty might drop out (as it does in Achvarina and Reich [2006a]). But stories about poverty, lack of opportunity, and abuse are really stories about interactions— that is, about conditions working jointly. We hypothesize that abuse, for really poor people, may trigger the kind of hopelessness that leads to abandoning the community and joining irregular forces. For middle-income people, abuse may not trigger such enlistment, because more social support is available from relatives and friends. Similarly, poverty may have different consequences for different ethnic groups, because some groups engage in more communal sharing of resources, thus cushioning individual-level poverty.

Scholars should consider every independent variable in conjunction with every other independent variable, asking whether the effects of one variable might depend on the level of another. If so, interactive tests are appropriate. Modern statistical software makes this simple; all the major statistical packages (Stata, SAS, etc.) allow easy calculation and graphing of interaction terms (Gary King's Clarify program is very user-friendly).

Impute Missing Data

In large-N analyses of child soldiering, missing data are almost a given. Earlier generations of scholars were trained simply to delete cases listwise—that is, to drop entire cases if a measurement on any variable was missing. Such deletion is no longer acceptable, because it is now understood that the biases introduced by deletion can seriously distort inference (King et al. 2001). Because data are rarely missing purely randomly, deletion biases results.

Listwise deletion is not always the wrong strategy. When the cases dropped are only a small portion of the data set, and when they are representative of the whole data set—that is, a truly random sample—then deletion can work. But "representative" means that the chance an observation is missing does not depend on any data values, whether observed or missing.

Researchers should first ask why data are missing. Suppose we are modeling weight (Y) as a function of gender (X).[13] If some respondents refuse to give their weight, Y will have missing values. There may be no particular reason why some respondents give their weights and others do not. Thus the probability that Y is missing may have no relationship to X or Y. Such data are missing completely at random (MCAR). One gender may be less likely to report its weight. Thus the probability that Y is missing depends only on the value of X. Such data are missing at random (MAR). Heavy (or light) people may be less likely to disclose their weight. In this case, the probability that Y is missing depends on the unobserved value of Y itself. Such data are not missing at random (NMAR). This is the problem of non-ignorable missing data.

In the study of child soldiering, missing data are especially unlikely to be missing completely at random (MCAR). Conflicts attracting less international attention are likely to be those with more missing data. International advocacy groups with limited resources naturally concentrate on the biggest conflicts. Smaller conflicts, conflicts further back in time, conflicts initiated closer to the data collection point, conflicts involving political rather than ethnic grievances; all these will attract less attention.[14] But in all these cases, if we are trying to explain child soldier recruitment rates, the missing data can be modeled as a function of various independent variables (such as political rather than ethnic grievances). Hence these are all examples of missing at random (MAR) data.

Recall the earlier discussion of units of analysis or observation. It is easy to see that they impact data availability. Though imprecise, estimates for variables predicting grievances or material inducements may exist at the national level. If such indicators have to be specified for multiple, smaller units of observation, the likelihood of variables with missing observations is quite high.

Awareness of the problem is a first step toward its amelioration. If nongovernmental organizations (NGOs) working on child soldiers understand that deleting cases because of missing data hinders inference, they will pay more attention to gathering complete data at appropriate observational levels in the first instance. It is always more difficult to go back and fill in data gaps than to structure a data-gathering design correctly in the first place. For scholars working in large-N context with previously gathered data, and the data are MCAR or MAR, the best solution is some kind of imputation. Analyzing data one does not have may seem bizarre, but imputation has become standard practice in statistics (Allison 2001; Little and Rubin 1987).

All forms of imputation create values for missing data by modeling the relationships between the variables of interest (including those with no missing data at all). But we cannot simply replace a missing value with a value generated by an equation involving the other variables in the model, because we have less confidence in the imputed values than in the nonmissing values. In other words, inserting single values for missing data would result in estimates of variances that are too small. Multiple imputation techniques address this by modeling our uncertainty, both in the parameters generating missing values (since these are generated in part by the missing values) and in the values themselves.[15] With modern software packages, this is much less difficult than it sounds.[16]

In studies of child soldiers at the individual level, nonignorable missingness might result when modeling the postcombat propensity of child soldiers to commit violent acts, because the most violent ex-combatants might be reluctant to admit to violent acts. At the aggregate level nonignorable missingness would occur if cases with the highest rates of child recruitment are reluctant to allow researchers to enter their territories.

One approach to nonignorable missingness is to impute values based on data otherwise external to the research design. Race, for instance, can be estimated with census block data associated with the address of the respondent. Another approach is the use of expert information, including the judgments of country and regional experts. This approach should be particularly useful in time series cross-sections (TSCS), or the analyses of a large number of cases over time. In these TSCS analyses, we might be missing an estimate of the number of child soldiers for a case in a single year, but we have data for the years before and after. If experts on the conflict know that a spike (up or down) was likely or unlikely, that information can be used to constrain (and thus improve) the imputation model. Likewise, if the poverty level is missing for a year characterized by a famine, that information helps to estimate the missing poverty rate. Honaker and King (2006) have recently discussed, with some interesting African examples, new techniques for analyzing situations of nonignorability.

Judging Explanations

In the words of King, Keohane, and Verba (1994, 19), a social science theory is a "reasoned and precise speculation about the answer to a research question, including a statement about why the proposed answer is correct." Theories generate testable hypotheses. From Achvarina and Reich's argument about refugee camps (this volume), one can derive the following theoretical statement: If refugee camps are unprotected, guerrilla groups will use them as a base for the recruitment of child soldiers. This hypothesis is inductively derived in the work of Achvarina and Reich, but it now takes on the status of a research finding and can thus be evaluated in new settings as part of a broader explanation of child recruitment. Their hypothesis has some fundamental characteristics: it may be falsified, it has observable implications, it is concrete.

Some theories begin with findings from prior work on the same broad problem but then emphasize new explanatory variables not previously examined. Jo Becker's chapter on child soldier recruitment in Sri Lanka, Nepal, and Burma (this volume) stresses factors unique to these nations, including political indoctrination and past government abuses. The next logical research step is the evaluation of Becker's factors in Africa, the setting of the original research.

In this volume, three chapters stand out as self-consciously theory driven because they present comprehensive causal arguments derived from prior research. Jens Christopher Andvig and Scott Gates's "Recruiting Children for Armed Conflict" emphasizes the economics of child labor as well as the psychology of children. For example, research on child behavior finds that children underestimate low probability risks when associated with losses, even if the risk of loss is fairly high. Children underestimate risks more than adolescents. Of course, the world of child soldiers is unlike a Western laboratory setting, but this result provides some support to the idea that it may be easier for guerrilla organizations to employ children than adults, given the inherently high risk-reward ratios of these conflicts.

Francisco Gutiérrez Sanín's "Organizing Minors" stresses organizational factors. Within a given country, some armed forces recruit children while others do not. Noting that rational choice arguments are inherently limited—no rational calculation of costs versus benefits would lead anyone to volunteer for a guerrilla force—Gutiérrez Sanín points to the differences between rent-seeking bands (as in Sierra Leone) and armies with a consistent political ideology and minimal rent seeking, such as the Revolutionary Armed Forces of Colombia (FARC). The FARC was too big and too serious to rely on selective incentives, hence its leaders were forced to develop socialization mechanisms promoting gregariousness and a sense of the collective in its recruits. The organization learned this after several military disasters. Gutiérrez-Sanín's analysis suggests that political armies, those whose objectives transcend rent seeking, either begin with mechanisms for socializing young recruits, develop such mechanisms in response to military debacles, or eventually cease to recruit young soldiers altogether.

James Pugel's "Disaggregating the Causal Factors Unique to Child Soldiering" demonstrates that eliminating one form of selection bias—by comparing child combatants to adult combatants—helps refine arguments about recruitment, because it turns out that certain factors thought to be unique to children are also present for adults. When Pugel disaggregated the warring groups in Liberia by faction and age of soldier, it turns out that the reasons cited by children for their participation in armed groups—money, family protection, and abduction—were the same as those cited by adults.

Summary

This essay began by defending a principled methodological perspective, laying out the data requirements and analytical techniques necessary for rigorous scientific testing of theories predicting whether and under what conditions children will participate in irregular forces. Questions of data requirements and statistical methodologies are interwoven, because the statistical techniques suggested here usually require more and better quality data. Given the limited budgets of child soldier researchers, it would be naive to think that this principled perspective will be adopted wholesale. Where should researchers compromise?

Individual research groups (mainly sponsored by NGOs) have skills and resources linked to particular conflicts. Instead of seeking to mount multiconflict research designs (especially designs in which a handful of ex-child soldiers are interviewed from each conflict), it should be cheaper and easier to focus on carefully selected units of observation within particular conflicts. This means, of course, a loss in generality, but the gain in the accuracy of the theoretical argument should easily compensate. At the same time, the various NGOs interested in child soldiering could coordinate their research (through conferences like the PRIO–Ford Institute workshop), so that their research questions are the same and their methodologies mutually consistent.

If we accept the importance of the social contexts in which potential child combatants live, we ought to be able to enrich the analyses of these contexts. One possibility is to interview enough people at the level of the community or neighborhood so that the aggregate opinion—political and social—of the social unit can be measured. Another possibility is to develop snowball samples, samples in which respondents provide information identifying their immediate social contacts. These contacts are in turn interviewed, and the resulting network constitutes the real social group encouraging or discouraging children from abandoning their communities to join irregular forces. Because interviewers are likely to be on the ground in the community already, such techniques can deepen an understanding of the forces impinging upon children without dramatically increasing the cost of research.

Part II

Ethical, Legal, and International Dimensions

CHAPTER 2

AN ETHICAL PERSPECTIVE ON CHILD SOLDIERS

Jeff McMahan

MORAL PHILOSOPHY OBVIOUSLY HAS NOTHING TO SAY about the urgent practical problem of preventing unscrupulous recruiters from forcing children to fight their unjust wars for them. That is a question of political and legal policy on which philosophers have no special competence to pronounce. But the problem of child soldiers does have a normative dimension and raises questions that philosophers are specially qualified to address. Do conditions of ignorance and duress in which child soldiers normally act ever make their action morally permissible, even if the war in which they are fighting is unjust and even if they commit war crimes? Even if their initial action in fighting is wrong, is it permissible for them to kill in individual self-defense when they are threatened? Or is their action somehow exempt from moral evaluation altogether? Might it be that even though they act wrongly, they are fully exculpated by their nature as children, in conjunction with the conditions in which they act? Can they be seen as morally responsible agents at all? Can they deserve punishment or blame? Perhaps most important, how do the answers to these questions bear on how morally conscientious adult combatants should fight against them? Is there a moral requirement to exercise restraint in fighting them? Should adult combatants, for example, accept greater risks to themselves in order to minimize the harm they inflict on child soldiers?

The Orthodox Theory of the Just War

To address these questions, it would be helpful to have some guidance from moral theory. Many of the resources needed are available, but they cannot be found in the theory of the just war in its currently orthodox form. According to this theory, the *jus in bello* requirement of discrimination holds that while it is impermissible for combatants intentionally to attack noncombatants, all enemy combatants are legitimate targets, irrespective of whether they have a just cause for fighting and irrespective of whether they can be held morally responsible for their action. For the currently orthodox theory of the just war follows the international law of war in treating combatant status as the ground of liability to attack, though it offers a different and supposedly deeper rationale for distinguishing between combatants and noncombatants.

In international law, the rationale is primarily pragmatic. Given the inevitability of war, it is necessary to have a neutral rule that grants all combatants the right to attack certain targets and assures them that if they confine their attacks to those targets, they will not be held criminally liable for the harm they cause and will be treated well if they are captured. Both in granting combatants the right to attack other combatants and denying them permission to attack noncombatants, international law aims to limit and contain the destruction of war, insulating ordinary domestic life from the effects of war to the greatest degree possible.

Just war theory, by contrast, grounds the significance of the distinction between combatants and noncombatants in a certain conception of the right of self-defense. In this view, when a person poses a threat to another, he thereby makes himself liable to defensive attack. It is therefore because combatants pose a threat to others that they are legitimate targets of attack; and it is because noncombatants threaten no one that they are not legitimate targets. This view is reflected in the language of just war theory, which endorses the venerable principle that it is wrong intentionally to kill the innocent, but interprets innocence in accordance with the etymology of the term. In Latin, the innocent are those who are not *nocentes*—that is, they are not those who are injurious or threatening.[1]

Because child soldiers pose a threat in exactly the same way that adult combatants do, they have combatant status and are therefore legitimate targets of attack according to contemporary just war theory. Whether they are morally responsible for the threat they pose is irrelevant, as is the fact that they are children. It is permissible to fight against them in exactly the same way one would fight against adult combatants.

I think the orthodox theory is right on three points: The principal justification for killing in war appeals to the idea that the target of attack is *liable* to attack. Liability is individual rather than collective. And—a closely related point—liability derives from individual action and not merely from membership in a group. Yet I think the orthodox theory has the wrong account of the basis of liability to attack in war. The right account, as the orthodox theory recognizes, has to be grounded in the morality of individual self- and other-defense. But when applied at the individual level and outside the context of war, the orthodox theory's criterion of liability to defensive violence is plainly unacceptable.

Suppose that someone attacks you without justification. The attack is malicious and culpable. You will be killed unless you kill the attacker in self-defense. Most of us think that you are justified in fighting back. But according to the orthodox theory, if you do fight back you will pose a threat to the attacker and will thus be morally liable to attack by him. On this view, merely by fighting back you lose your moral right not to be attacked by the culpable aggressor. But that cannot be right; you cannot lose your right not to be killed by an unjust assailant merely by defending yourself against his unjust attack. For you are morally *justified* in attacking your attacker, who will not be *wronged* by your action, even if you kill him.

Perhaps, therefore, the criterion of liability to attack is posing an *unjust* threat—or posing a threat of unjust or *wrongful* harm. This explains why one would be justified in killing an attacker in self-defense, though the attacker would not be justified in killing the victim, *even* in self-defense. I think, indeed, that this is right as far as it goes—that is, that it is not the posing of a threat but only the posing of an *unjust* threat that can make a person liable to defensive violence. If this is right, then this a view that is radically in conflict with the orthodox theory of the just war—namely, that in general the only combatants who are morally justified in fighting are those who fight for a just cause in a just war.

The Relevance of Moral Responsibility

Yet, while merely posing a threat is neither necessary nor sufficient for liability to defensive violence, posing an *unjust* threat, or a threat of unjust harm, is also neither necessary nor—though this is quite controversial—sufficient for liability to defensive violence. Suppose that I put a drug into a person's drink that causes him to lose all control of himself, so that he ceases to be responsible for his action. And suppose that, for a brief period, it also causes him to become wholly and uncritically suggestible; it makes him do whatever he is told to do. Suppose that during this brief period, I direct him to kill some innocent person and, because of the effect of the drug, he sets out to kill this person. At this point he ceases to be suggestible, and I lose the power to control him. He will continue to try to kill the potential victim until the drug loses potency.

Suppose, finally, that for some fantastic reason characteristic of hypothetical philosophy examples, the potential victim can save herself either by killing me or by killing him. What ought she to do?

The drugged person poses a threat of unjust harm but is not responsible for his action. I do not pose a threat to the innocent person but am morally responsible for the unjust threat she faces from the drugged person. Normally, of course, posing an unjust threat and being morally responsible for the unjust threat coincide: those who pose an unjust threat are normally responsible for doing so. But when responsibility for a threat and proximate causation of the threat diverge, as in this case, responsibility seems more important. If asked whether the potential victim ought to kill the drugged person, kill me, or allow herself to be killed, virtually everyone would answer that she ought to kill me, or at least that she ought to kill me rather than him.

This shows that most people think that moral responsibility for an unjust threat is, on its own, a sufficient basis for liability to defensive violence. It is not necessary that one also be the agent who poses the threat. I go further, however, and make a stronger claim. I claim that merely posing an unjust threat, without being in any way morally responsible for doing so, is not a basis of liability at all. In the case I just sketched, the drugged person is in no way morally responsible for the threat he poses. I call such a person a *nonresponsible threat*. In this case, the drugged person *acts*, but not as a morally responsible agent. This person's action is wholly nonvoluntary. And it seems true, and may indeed be a necessary truth, that only voluntary action can generate liability. This is true even of strict liability. Only when a person has voluntarily acted in a certain way—constructed a building, manufactured a product—can she become strictly liable for events that are entirely beyond her control. She has to take a certain action voluntarily in order to place herself within the scope even of strict liability. There has to have been some point at which, by avoiding acting in some way, she could have avoided the possibility of becoming strictly liable.

The main reason for accepting that a nonresponsible threat cannot be liable for the threat he poses derives from a requirement of consistency. Most of us believe that it is not permissible to kill an innocent bystander as a means of self-preservation. The innocent bystander—perhaps as a matter of conceptual necessity—has done nothing to make himself liable to be killed as a means of saving someone else's life. Unless, therefore, there is some morally significant difference between an innocent bystander and a nonresponsible threat—a difference that would explain why the nonresponsible threat is liable while the innocent bystander is not—a nonresponsible threat cannot be liable either.

It is true, of course, that a nonresponsible threat is causally involved in the threat to the potential victim, whereas this is not true of an innocent bystander.

This means that a nonresponsible threat can be killed in self-*defense*, whereas an innocent bystander cannot be. But this is just a fact about the nonresponsible threat's location in the local causal architecture. The nonresponsible threat's causal position is such that it is necessary for the potential victim to kill him in self-defense in order to survive. But notice that something similar is true of the innocent bystander: his causal position is also such that it is necessary for the potential victim to kill him in order to survive. The difference between them is only one of causal position. The nonresponsible threat finds himself, through no fault or voluntary choice of his own, on the causal path of the threat itself, while the innocent bystander, also through no fault or voluntary choice of his own, finds himself on a possible causal path to averting an equivalent threat. How can this mere difference in the positions they occupy in the causal architecture constitute a difference in personal liability to be killed?

It is tempting to claim at this point that the relevant difference is that the nonresponsible threat is about to violate the potential victim's rights, whereas this is not true of the innocent bystander. But the response here is the same, for the conditions for the violation of a right are the same as the conditions of liability. The drugged person in my example does not threaten to violate the innocent victim's rights; he is merely a threat to her life. Rights can be violated only through morally responsible agency. Neither a falling rock nor a charging tiger can violate a right; neither, therefore, can an individual whose capacity for voluntary agency has been eliminated by a drug.

Some people argue that if a person who is in no way responsible for his action threatens your *life*, it is permissible for you to kill him simply on the ground of self-preference. If you and the person who threatens you are both equally innocent and you must choose between your life and his, surely you are permitted to give priority to yourself. But this will not do, since it would also justify the killing of an innocent bystander in self-preservation. Few people would disagree that if I can save my life or a stranger's but not both, I am permitted to give priority to myself. But personal partiality functions differently in a choice of whom to save from the way that it functions in a choice between allowing oneself to be killed and killing another.

The upshot of my argument here is not that it is never permissible to use violence in defense against a nonresponsible threat who poses a threat of unjust harm. It is instead that if there is a justification for defensive violence against a nonresponsible threat, then that justification will not be that the nonresponsible threat is morally liable to be attacked. There may be other forms of justification—for example, a lesser-evil justification—for defense against a nonresponsible threat, and even for the defensive killing of a nonresponsible threat. But if there is no morally significant difference between a nonresponsible threat and an innocent bystander, then in general a threatened person is permitted to do in self-defense against a nonresponsible threat only what he or she would be permitted to do to an innocent bystander in self-preservation.

This conclusion is contrary to commonsense intuition. The commonsense intuition, which I share, is that it is permissible to kill a nonresponsible threat if that is necessary to prevent oneself from being killed by him. But I have come to believe that there is no justification for this intuition, that the intuition itself is indefensible. It is, I suspect, the product or our tendency to overgeneralize the robust core of our beliefs about the permissibility of self-defense.

The Moral Status of Child Soldiers

Suppose it is right that there can be no liability without some element of responsibility. What are the implications for conduct in war? One question, of course, is whether combatants in war are ever really nonresponsible threats. There are at least a couple of serious possibilities. One derives from epistemic considerations. Suppose that certain combatants are fighting in a war that is objectively unjust but that all the evidence accessible to them supports the belief that the war is just. Suppose, in other words, that they are epistemically justified in believing that their unjust war is just. In an earlier time it would have been said that they suffer from "invincible ignorance." Because of this, although they pose an unjust threat, or a threat of unjust harm, they are not morally responsible for doing so. Because their beliefs are reasonable in the circumstances, they either act permissibly in fighting in the objectively unjust war or are fully exculpated for their participation. Either way, it seems that they would be nonresponsible threats and would not, on the assumption that liability presupposes responsibility, be liable for their objectively wrongful action.

Another possibility is that some combatants who fight in an unjust war are not morally responsible agents at all. It is, of course, rare to find adult soldiers so mentally defective or disturbed as to be incapable of morally responsible agency. But child soldiers put the assumption that soldiers must have the capacity for moral agency under pressure.

There is certainly a case to be made for the claim that in many or most child soldiers, the capacity for moral agency is absent or has been systematically subverted. Here is a sketch of a case that, although hypothetical, is not atypical. A group of armed men enter a village and, through a credible threat to kill him or his parents, force an eight-year-old boy to kill his best friend, in view of the entire village, including the victim's parents. The boy is then abducted and taken to a camp where he is further brutalized and also indoctrinated. His having killed his best friend not only makes him feel irredeemably tainted, and therefore helps to blunt his conscience, but has also effectively severed him from his previous community, making him thereafter dependent on his captors. (In his final reflections on the Nazi concentration camps, Primo Levi wrote of those prisoners who became collaborators with the Nazis that "the best way to bind them [was] to burden them with guilt, cover them with blood, compromise them as much as possible, thus establishing a bond of complicity so that they [could] no longer turn back" [Levi 1989, 43]. It is surprising how naturally accessible to otherwise ignorant and psychologically insensitive men this one piece of knowledge of human psychology seems to be.) Several years later, when the boy has been fully indoctrinated and trained, he is given a light automatic weapon and administered drugs that further anesthetize his conscience and subdue his fears and is then sent to fight for an unjust cause. Can this boy, now aged eleven or twelve, be reasonably held morally responsible for the wrongful action in which he is engaged?

If, given his age and all that has been done to him, this child lacks the moral resources to resist the command to fight, then he is, in the circumstances, a nonresponsible threat. If I am right that a nonresponsible threat cannot be *liable* to defensive attack, the justification, if there is one, for attacking this child must, it seems, appeal to the idea that attacking him is dictated by necessity: the necessity of averting a much greater evil—for example, the greater evil that would be involved in the success of his leaders' unjust cause. (If child soldiers are fighting for a just cause, there cannot be a justification for fighting against them at all, according to the account of the morality of war that I have sketched. But it would seem that the causes for which child soldiers are mobilized are usually unjust, and I will restrict the discussion in this chapter to cases in which this is so.)

Such a lesser-evil justification, if it succeeds at all, seems to impose on those who fight against child soldiers a requirement of restraint. If child soldiers are nonresponsible threats, then in fighting against them, just combatants must exercise restraint, accepting greater risks to themselves in order to minimize the harm they inflict on the child soldiers. The commander of a force fighting against a unit of child soldiers might be morally required to order his own soldiers to fight in a way that would predictably cause them to suffer greater casualties, and even a greater number of deaths.

There are, however, reasons for resisting the claim that child soldiers, or at least very many child soldiers, are actually nonresponsible threats. Even if they are cognitively and emotionally immature, and even if they have been brutalized and brainwashed, they are still, it might be argued, sufficiently morally responsible to be able to recognize that indiscriminate killing is wrong. And in the areas of the world in which child soldiers are found, and especially in the types of conflict in which they are deployed, much of the business of warfare does in fact consist in killing the innocent—for example, while destroying villages for purposes of terrorization, intimidation, or forced relocation of populations.

The idea that even terribly abused children can be morally responsible for their action is not implausible. Human children beyond a few years of age are, after all, vastly more highly developed psychologically than any animal. And all parents regard their own and their neighbors' children as morally responsible to a degree. If one's own child or the neighbor's child torments the cat, one regards it very differently from the way one regards the dog's efforts to harm the cat.

A child's responsibility is often regarded as diminished, often greatly so. But the generally recognized age at which childhood officially ends and adulthood begins is eighteen (thus in law the category of child soldiers includes all those below the age of eighteen), and those of us who accept that most adult human beings are morally responsible agents will find it impossible to believe that all or even very many seventeen-year-olds are wholly lacking in the capacity for morally responsible agency. After all, many of the combatants in properly constituted armies are between the ages of eighteen and twenty, and in most cases there is very little difference with respect to the capacity for moral agency between a seventeen-year-old and a nineteen-year-old, certainly not enough to make it a reasonable presumption that the one lacks the capacity for moral agency while the other is a morally responsible agent.

What seems most reasonable is to view child soldiers, in general, as people who have a diminished capacity for morally responsible agency and who act in conditions that further diminish their personal responsibility for their action in war. If, as I suggested earlier, moral responsibility for an unjust threat is the basis of liability to defensive violence, and if liability is a matter of degree and varies with the degree of a person's responsibility, then child soldiers may be liable to attack in war but to a significantly diminished degree. This view contrasts sharply with that of the orthodox theory of the just war, which holds that the criterion of liability to attack in war is all-or-nothing: a person is either a combatant or a noncombatant and there are no degrees of combatancy.

To some it may seem puzzling to say that child soldiers are liable to attack but to a diminished degree. It may seem that either it is permissible to attack them or it is not. In fact, however, the way in which the degree of a person's liability affects what it is permissible to do to him in war is through the proportionality constraint. Suppose that there are two combatants fighting in an unjust war, one who is responsible to a high degree for the unjust threat he poses, and another who is only minimally responsible for the threat he poses. A goal that might be sufficient to justify attacking the highly responsible combatant might not be sufficient to justify attacking the minimally responsible combatant; a degree of harm that it would be permissible to inflict on the highly responsible combatant to achieve a certain end might be an excessive or disproportionate degree of harm to inflict on the minimally responsible combatant for the same purpose; and risks that one would be required to take in order to reduce the harm one would inflict on the minimally responsible combatant might be ones there would be no reason to take for the sake of the highly responsible combatant.

The last of these points is of considerable practical significance. For the claim is the same one I made in connection with the lesser-evil justification—namely, that if the liability of child soldiers is, in general, diminished relative to that of most other unjust combatants, there should be a requirement to exercise restraint in fighting against them. Just combatants are in general required to accept greater risks to themselves in fighting against child soldiers, in an effort to minimize the harm inflicted on them. The idea that there is a moral requirement to exercise restraint in fighting against those who are not culpable has precedents in the history of thought about the just war. For example, in a passage in his work "On the American Indians," Vitoria argued that if the "barbarians" attack the Spanish out of unfounded but excusable fear, "the Spaniards must take care for their own safety, but do so with as little harm to the barbarians as possible, . . . since in this case what we may suppose were understandable fears made them innocent. . . . This is a consideration which must be given great weight. The laws of war against really harmful and offensive enemies are quite different from those against innocent or ignorant ones" (Vitoria 2006, 303).

There is, however, an objection to the idea that variations in the degree of a person's liability *always* affect the proportionality constraint in this way. Perhaps the best way to see this is to consider an example of individual liability outside the context of war. Suppose that instead of my putting a drug in your drink, you take a drug that you believe will just make you pleasantly high but that turns out to be a drug that causes you to begin hallucinating and to lose control of your behavior. As a result, you begin to attack an innocent person. You will kill him unless he kills you in self-defense. You may ordinarily be a very kind person and your mistake may have been one that anyone in your situation might easily have made; but the fact that you are responsible, even if only to a slight degree, for the fact that either you or the innocent person must die makes you liable and arguably makes it permissible for him to kill you in self-defense. Even a slight asymmetry in responsibility can be morally decisive when the outcome is all-or-nothing. (If the harm could somehow be divided between you, the innocent person might be obliged to accept some nonlethal harm in order to avoid killing you.)

Extending this conclusion to the case of child soldiers, it seems that in a situation in which either a certain number of minimally responsible child soldiers must be killed or they will kill a certain number—perhaps a lesser number—of just combatants, there is no requirement for the just combatants to sacrifice themselves for the sake of the child soldiers. Indeed, if third parties could intervene, it seems that they would be required by considerations of justice to intervene on the side of the just combatants and against the child soldiers. If the child soldiers are morally responsible even to a minimal degree for the unjust threat they pose, and if the just combatants are in no way at fault for the threat they face, then it does not seem that justice could require even one just combatant to allow himself to be killed in order to spare the life of a child soldier.

This is a harsh doctrine, which clashes with my intuition that just combatants ought to fight with restraint against child soldiers. But it may well be that the source of that intuition is not that child soldiers are nonresponsible threats but simply that they are *children*—that is, individuals who have hardly had a chance at life yet and who, in this case, have already been terribly victimized.

Just combatants have reason to show mercy and restraint, not because child soldiers are altogether lacking in responsibility for their action, but because they are owed leniency because of their special vulnerability to exploitation and loss. Just combatants should show them mercy, even at the cost of additional risk to themselves, to try to allow these already greatly wronged children a chance at life.

I am reluctantly compelled to conclude inconclusively. The reason that just combatants have to exercise restraint in fighting child soldiers may in some cases be a requirement implied by the proportionality constraint. But in other cases—for example, a case in which there is an unavoidable trade-off between the lives of just combatants and the lives of child soldiers—proportionality may not require self-sacrifice by the just combatants. Their reason to show restraint in such cases is not a requirement of *justice*. It is a reason of *mercy*, which may not rise to the level of a moral requirement. These are cases in which our higher ideals may demand the surrender of our rights. I know of no formula for the resolution of such conflicts.

CHAPTER 3

THE EVOLUTION OF THE UNITED NATIONS' PROTECTION AGENDA FOR CHILDREN

Applying International Standards

Tonderai W. Chikuhwa

> One boy tried to escape [from the rebels], but he was caught. . . . His hands were tied, and then they made us, the other new captives, kill him with a stick. I felt sick. I knew this boy from before. We were from the same village. I refused to kill him, and they told me they would shoot me. They pointed a gun at me, so I had to do it. The boy was asking me, "Why are you doing this?" I said I had no choice. After we killed him, they made us smear his blood on our arms. They said we had to do this so we would not fear death and so we would not try to escape. . . . I still dream about the boy from my village who I killed. I see him in my dreams, and he is talking to me and saying I killed him for nothing, and I am crying.
>
> —**Susan, sixteen, abducted by the Lord's Resistance Army in Uganda**

THE HORRORS THAT ARE BEING VISITED ON CHILDREN in the context of war is a blight on the conscience of humankind. Today, in so many of the conflicts around the globe, children are being brutalized in unimaginable ways. Not only are civilians, particularly children, women, and the elderly, increasingly the primary targets and victims of atrocities, but children are also becoming some of the worst perpetrators of brutalities against their own families and communities. They are being forced to give expression to the hatreds of adults. Ironically, at the same time as the situation on the ground deteriorates for children, we are witnessing an unprecedented elaboration and strengthening of international child protection norms and standards. The central dilemma that confronts the international community is not the lack of protection standards but rather the prevailing culture of impunity of those who commit grave violations against children. The critical challenge of the moment is to bridge the gap between existing standards and the catastrophic situation of children on the ground. The United Nations secretary-general has referred to this as embarking on an "era of application" of international standards and norms to end impunity for grave child rights violations.

This chapter traces the evolution of the United Nations protection agenda for children affected by armed conflict (CAAC) since the publication in 1996 of the seminal report of Graca Machel entitled "The Impact of Armed Conflict on Children" (Machel 1996).[1] This report was so profoundly disturbing in its articulation of the plight of children in situations of armed conflict that it galvanized the resolve of member states of the United Nations to address this problem in a more concerted and systematic manner. As a step toward this end, in 1997 the general assembly accepted one of the key recommendations of Graca Machel to establish the mandate of a special representative of the secretary-general for children and armed conflict as the convening focal point for the United Nations protection agenda for CAAC.[2] This essay highlights some of the notable progress that has been registered for CAAC in the ten years since the Graca Machel report, focusing in particular on the strategic engagement of the Security Council on CAAC. The systematic engagement of the council has led to a powerful momentum toward an era of application of international norms and standards for the protection of children on the ground and has generated both energy and pressure within the United Nations system to address the issue of CAAC in a more purposive and strategic way. The Security Council resolutions, as well as the annual report of the secretary-general, on CAAC have evolved into a centerpiece of the protection agenda. These tandem instruments of a regime engender compliance of parties to conflict with international standards. There are a number of significant developments that illustrate an unprecedented resolve and orientation toward the protection of CAAC by key policy-level entities.

There are presently more than thirty situations of concern where children are suffering severe and systematic abuses. It is conservatively estimated that over 2 million children have been killed in situations of armed conflict in the last decade, while six million children have been permanently disabled or injured. Over 250,000 children continue to be exploited as child soldiers, and tens of thousands of girls are being subjected to rape and other forms of sexual violence. Abductions are also becoming more systematic and widespread. Since 2003, over 14 million children have been forcibly displaced within and outside their home countries, and between 8,000 and 10,000 children are killed or maimed every year as a result of land mines.

The 2006 annual report of the secretary-general to the Security Council on Children and Armed Conflict (United Nations 2006b) documented grave violations against children in twelve situations of concern, including Burundi, Côte d'Ivoire, the Democratic Republic of the Congo, Somalia, Chad, the Sudan and Uganda, Colombia, Myanmar, Nepal, the Philippines, and Sri Lanka. Furthermore, the report explicitly cited forty parties, both state and nonstate actors, for commission of grave violations against children.

In order to reverse the trend of abominations against children in the context of armed conflict, the international community must now begin to deliver on the paper promises that have been made to children. There is an urgent need for a redirection of focus and energy from the elaboration of international protection norms and standards to their application on the ground.

In the development of the United Nations protection agenda for CAAC, advocacy efforts have focused on four elements that define the era of application campaign: systematic monitoring and reporting of grave violations against children as a basis for action to end the impunity of those committing abuses; mainstreaming of CAAC concerns into the policies, priorities, and programs of the entities and institutional processes of the United Nations and beyond; strategic advocacy, awareness raising, and dissemination of CAAC norms and standards; recognition, support, and enhancement of local civil society actors, organizations, and networks who represent the front line of protection and rehabilitation of CAAC.

Significant energy has been directed toward the structuring of a monitoring, reporting, and compliance regime as the cornerstone of the era of application. The central challenge in this project has been to negotiate an effective balance between acute political sensitivities and constraints and the imperative of ensuring the highest threshold of protection for children. The political dimension of the agenda has extended beyond the realm of member states of the United Nations to the often vexed internal political dynamics between United Nations agencies, departments, funds, and programs. The agenda has also balanced the critical engagement and politics of nongovernmental organizations (NGOs) as important stakeholders and partners. The monitoring, reporting, and compliance regime may be disaggregated by reviewing the conduct of parties to conflict, resulting in the systematic naming and listing of offending parties for grave child rights violations; initiating dialogue with parties to conflict in order to prepare and implement action plans to halt grave child rights violations; establish a monitoring and reporting mechanism to provide systematic and reliable information on violations and compliance as a basis for action; and take concrete action both at national and international levels to stop the commission of grave violations against children.

In spite of the dire circumstances for children in many situations of armed conflict, the past several years have nonetheless seen significant advances in the development of the protection agenda. This progress is beginning to coalesce into tangible protection for children on the ground.

Developing and Strengthening Norms and Standards

The elaboration and strengthening of the international normative infrastructure for the protection of children has included the adoption of the Optional Protocol to the Convention on the Rights of the Child, as well as far-reaching standards and instruments such as the Rome Statute for the International Criminal Court (ICC), which classifies war crimes against children; the African Charter on the Rights and Welfare of the Child, the first regional treaty establishing age eighteen as a minimum age for all recruitment and participation in hostilities; International Labour Organization Convention 182, which defines child soldiering as one of the worst forms of child labor and sets eighteen as the minimum age for forced or compulsory recruitment; and six resolutions of the Security Council on CAAC.[3] As paper promises for children, these standards represent a remarkably high threshold of protection. The emphasis of the era of application campaign is to make good on these commitments to children by engendering compliance with the norms by parties to conflict.

Children's issues are increasingly being reflected in peace negotiations and accords, on the premise that the inclusion of their concerns in these critical processes at the peace-making phase carries significant implications for the provision of adequate attention and resources for intervention programs for children in the aftermath of conflict. Examples include the explicit inclusion of children's concerns in the Good Friday Agreement in Northern Ireland in 1998, and in the 1999 Lomé Peace Agreement for Sierra Leone. Most recently, child protection provisions have also been included in the New Comprehensive Ceasefire Agreement for Darfur, adopted in May 2006. In addition, child protection considerations are being integrated more systematically into specific initiatives of the United Nations, such as the recently established and innovative United Nations Peacemaker Databank, which has been designed to strengthen the mediation infrastructure and capacity of the organization.[4] It is anticipated that the analysis of child protection provisions in existing peace agreements, combined with the specific child protection guidelines for mediators contained in the UN Peacemaker will facilitate more systematic inclusion of children's concerns in peace negotiations and accords.

In the past several years, the United Nations system has made considerable progress in mainstreaming the issue of children and armed conflict into entities of the organization, as well as key institutional processes convened by the United Nations system, such as the Consolidated Appeals Process for Humanitarian Emergencies or the Poverty Reduction Strategy Papers framework for multilateral donor assistance to postconflict countries. Increasingly, children's issues are reflected in relevant cross-cutting thematic activities across the United Nations system. Concerted advocacy has led to the UN senior management's increased commitment to and promotion of concerns relating to children affected by armed conflict, as well as to a more consistent integration of children's concerns into policies, priorities, and programs. In-house knowledge, expertise, and training to inform policies, strategies, and day-to-day operations are also increasing.[5] However, it is important to stress that these gains remain fragile and could weaken and dissipate unless they are consolidated and institutionalized.

One of the most tangible examples of more fundamental mainstreaming of CAAC in important areas of work of the United Nations is the increasing orientation of United Nations peacekeeping mandates and operations toward child protection. Since 2001, the United Nations has deployed child protection advisors to peacekeeping operations to advise the special representatives of the secretary-general in the mainstreaming of children's concerns across civilian, military, and police components and to support the advocacy and programs of national governments, child protection agencies, and NGOs on the ground (see United Nations 2005b). The impetus for this practice derives from the resolutions of the Security Council on CAAC, which explicitly request the secretary-general to systematically assess the need, number, and role of child protection advisers in preparation of each United Nations peacekeeping mission, and for their deployment to peacekeeping operations on a case-by-case basis (see United Nations 2001b, 2003b, 2004a, and 2005c). The engagement of UN peacekeeping on CAAC has also led to important conversations within the UN system about complementarity of efforts, more effective collaboration, and delineation of division of labor on children's issues, which legitimately cross-cut into the mandates and spheres of responsibility of multiple UN actors.

Regional organizations and groupings have also begun to incorporate CAAC concerns more systematically into their agendas, policies, and programs, including in the area of postconflict reconstruction and rehabilitation. The most notable examples include the European Union's adoption of guidelines on children and armed conflict (European Union 2003) and the Economic Community of West Africa's (ECOWAS) establishment of a child protection unit within its secretariat (*Accra Declaration* 2000). Other multilateral groupings such as the Human Security Network have also consistently included CAAC on their agendas.

Increased Global Awareness and Advocacy

The past several years have also seen a significant increase in overall coverage on CAAC, as well as a more sophisticated treatment of the issue particularly by the media. This awareness and publicity of the plight of war-affected children has been an important factor in maintaining the pressure on the UN system and other important policy-level institutions to undertake concrete actions and initiatives on behalf of CAAC.

Civil society organizations are also engaging in CAAC concerns. NGOs in particular have played a critical role in the development and advancement of the agenda, and in recent years there has been a more direct exchange between civil society and key UN entities such as the Security Council.[6] The role of academia is crucial as well, particularly to ensure that the significant gaps in knowledge concerning CAAC issues are systematically addressed. These gaps include a lack of basic data, including the global number of child soldiers and the impact of child recruitment, and significantly hamper effective advocacy and program response.[7]

Placing children firmly on the international peace and security agenda has represented the central strategic imperative of the special representative of the secretary-general for CAAC, working in concert with UN partners, member states, and NGOs. The most impressive aspect of progress on the CAAC agenda has been the concerted, purposive, and systematic engagement by the UN Security Council on this issue since 1999. The council's involvement has generated high momentum toward an era of application of international standards and the end of impunity for those committing grave violations against children. It has also raised the stakes considerably on all sides of the issue.

From the perspective of state and nonstate parties committing grave violations, the perceived and actual risk level for abusing children has risen appreciably as the Security Council has moved closer to adopting sanction measures against them in successive resolutions. There are clear signs that this is beginning to affect their behavior. From the perspective of UN system actors, the Security Council's involvement has resulted in a new sense of urgency and pressure within the system, to reevaluate and redirect priorities, to coordinate better, to define more clearly territories for collaboration on CAAC, and to determine and agree to divisions of labor to deliver protection for children on the ground. As the rigor and sophistication of the Security Council's engagement on this issue have increased, so have the levels of outside interest, understanding, and scrutiny of the work of the council in this area. Concerted action for children is increasingly perceived by the Security Council as a matter of its credibility. The CAAC agenda has opened the door for more systematic engagement of the Security Council on a number of other critical thematic human rights concerns, such as women, peace, and security and protection of civilians in armed conflict. It is clear that the evolution of the CAAC agenda will have a direct bearing on the development and advancement of other thematic agendas in the Security Council.

The Political Dimension of the CAAC Agenda in the Security Council

The engagement of the Security Council on a thematic human rights issue such as CAAC has necessitated the negotiation of both practical and political considerations. The council tends to take a situation-specific approach, focusing primarily on country situations of concern. To be included on the council's agenda, a situation must be considered by the members as a legitimate threat to international peace and security. Hence, the Security Council has on its present agenda some of the worst situations of conflict and instability, including Sudan, Cote d'Ivoire, the Democratic Republic of the Congo, Somalia, Iraq, Afghanistan, and Haiti. Yet, it is clear that what makes it onto the formal agenda and what does not is also a political determination by Security Council members. Thus, for instance, it is conspicuous that a number of grave situations where there has been protracted conflict over many years and where those conflicts also have significant international dimensions and implications are not formally on the agenda of the Security Council, such as Colombia, Sri Lanka, Nepal, and Uganda.

The engagement of the Security Council on the thematic issue of children and armed conflict must be viewed against this political backdrop. When the council adopted the first resolution on CAAC—SCR 1261 (United Nations 1999a)—it signaled that the situation of children in situations of armed conflict constitutes a legitimate threat to international peace and security that belongs on its agenda. The practical implication of this decision is that the council is now increasingly compelled to focus on all situations of concern where children are being abused in the context of armed conflict, including situations such as Colombia, Sri Lanka, Nepal, and Uganda, which are a focus of the secretary-general's CAAC agenda. Therefore, the central political preoccupation and concern within the council, and more broadly among many member states of the United Nations, is that thematic issues such as CAAC may be used to slip specific country situations onto the agenda of the Security Council.[8] This has been a concern, for example, for Colombia (which has otherwise been actively supportive of the CAAC agenda), as well as for permanent members of the Security Council, such as the United Kingdom and the Russian Federation, as the CAAC agenda has focused on the commission of violations by paramilitary groups in Northern Ireland and by Chechen rebels.

This central political dilemma has become an increasingly vexed question as the CAAC agenda has evolved and the Security Council moves closer to adoption of sanction measures against violators. It is a testament to the political will of all stakeholders, particularly member states, that these significant political considerations have so far been overridden by a broad-based consensus on the imperative to protect children in situations of armed conflict.

At the same time, it should also be noted that the proactive engagement of the Security Council on CAAC has exacerbated the inherent tension between the council and the United Nations General Assembly, which views the work of the Security Council on any thematic human rights issue as a fundamental encroachment on its mandate and terrain. There are many voices in the General Assembly that would wish to see the issue of CAAC move out of the sphere of the Security Council altogether, which has represented a constant and underlying political challenge of the mandate of the special representative of the secretary-general for children and armed conflict.

Security Council Resolutions

The six Security Council resolutions on children and armed conflict since 1999 represent an important pillar in the international normative protection infrastructure for children, and they should be understood as instruments to compel parties to conflict to adhere to international child protection standards.

Security Council resolution 1261 marks the entry point of the council on CAAC. It represents the first resolution of the Security Council on a thematic concern and affirms that the protection of children in situations of armed conflict constitutes a legitimate threat to international peace and security. The resolution outlines a broad framework for the protection of children and may be read alongside Graca Machel's report "The Impact of Armed Conflict on Children" (Machel 1996). The resolution essentially draws out the major themes and priorities outlined by Machel as the broader framework of engagement of the Security Council on CAAC. It should be noted that the five subsequent resolutions do not add any significant new elements, but rather focus on and refine critical aspects of SCR 1261. In this sense, the first resolution may be viewed as the cornerstone of the council's formal engagement on CAAC.

The subsequent resolutions have sought to advance the CAAC agenda of the council by strategically identifying critical substantive elements and orienting them toward concrete measures on behalf of children. Even though the resolutions have dealt with multiple aspects of the agenda, such as inclusion of child protection in peacekeeping mandates, responsibility and engagement of regional groups, importance of explicit programs for disarmament, and demobilization and reintegration of children, the central emphasis has been to structure a monitoring, reporting, and compliance regime. Thus, SCR 1314 provides a more specific plan of action for child protection, calling for an end to impunity for those who abuse children, including through their exclusion from amnesty provisions; for intensified efforts to obtain the release of abducted children; and for the inclusion of child protection advisers in United Nations peacekeeping operations. The key feature of SCR 1379 (United Nations 2001b) was to formally establish the practice of monitoring, reporting, and compliance by mandating that the secretary-general prepare and publish, as an annex to his or her annual report to the Security Council on CAAC, a list of parties that recruit or use children in situations of armed conflict. SCR 1460 (United Nations 2003b) endorses the secretary-general's call for an era of application and broadens the scope for monitoring and reporting by calling on parties identified in the secretary-general's list to provide information on steps they have taken to halt the recruitment and use of children, with the expressed intention of the Security Council to consider taking appropriate steps where insufficient progress has been made.

Resolution 1539 (United Nations 2004a) outlines the key elements of the monitoring, reporting, and compliance regime introduced in previous resolutions. The Security Council requested the secretary-general to provide information on progress and compliance by parties named in the annexes to annual report, taking into account information concerning other violations and abuses committed against children. Broadening the focus to other grave violations has been critical, because hitherto the council's formal engagement had been pegged to the issue of recruitment and use of child soldiers as a violation of international law. SCR 1539, for the first time, articulates other categories of grave violations against children, thereby expanding the protection framework.

The Security Council requested that the secretary-general devise action plans to end grave violations for which parties to conflict have been cited,[9] as well as an action plan for a systematic and comprehensive monitoring and reporting mechanism. The council also considered imposing "targeted and graduated measures" against parties to conflict who commit grave violations against children, which may include, among other things, "a ban on the export or supply of small arms and light weapons and of other military equipment and on military assistance, against these parties if they refuse to enter into dialogue, fail to develop an action plan or fail to meet the commitments included in their action plan" (United Nations 2004a, 3). Finally, the Security Council formally assigned the primary responsibility of follow-up to the heads of the United Nations—namely, the special representatives of the secretary-general and United Nations resident coordinators.

Even as it advances the protection of children in a number of crucial respects, perhaps the most significant added value of SCR 1612 (United Nations 2005c), adopted in July 2005, is that it mandates an infrastructure for monitoring and reporting grave child rights violations and compliance with international child protection standards. In this resolution, the Security Council requested that the secretary-general monitor and report six grave violations committed against children, as specified in the 2005 report of the secretary-general to the Security Council. It also requested that heads of the United Nations initiate contact with the parties to conflict listed in the secretary-general's report to halt the recruitment of child soldiers and other grave abuses. In addition, the Security Council established the Working Group on Children and Armed Conflict to review reports on violations and action plans by parties to conflict and to make specific recommendations to the Security Council and other policy-level bodies for action. Finally, the council mandated that the secretary-general continue reporting specific information on grave violations against children and prepare monitoring lists naming offending parties.

Security Council Working Group on Children and Armed Conflict (SCWG-CAAC)

The central import of the SCWG-CAAC is that it further deepens and systematizes the engagement of the Security Council on CAAC. Hitherto, the council's seasonal engagement has been inadequate in responding to the immediate protection needs of children and the rapidly evolving situations on the ground. The SCWG-CAAC provides a vehicle for child protection practitioners to seize the attention of the Security Council on an as-needs basis throughout the year.

On 2 May 2006, the SCWG-CAAC formally adopted its terms of reference.[10] The key features of these terms are that the SCWG-CAAC now consists of all the members of the Security Council, and it meets formally at least every two months (with additional meetings on an as-needs basis). The terms of reference provide for a regular exchange between the SCWG-CAAC and any relevant authority, and the group reviews information from the secretary-general, as well as any other relevant information presented to it. The group also reviews progress on the action plans of parties to conflict, which are named by the secretary-general. Based on its review of information, SCWG-CAAC makes recommendations to the Security Council on measures to promote the protection of children. SCWG-CAAC also addresses requests for the protection of children to other bodies within the UN system. And, importantly, the group ensures transparency of its engagement.

The Secretary-General's Report on CAAC

In understanding the evolution of the United Nations' protection agenda for CAAC, and particularly the monitoring, reporting, and compliance regime aspect, it is important to appreciate the relationship between the reports of the secretary-general on CAAC and the resolutions of the Security Council. The report of the secretary-general defines the United Nations' substantive agenda for children and armed conflict. The specification of the agenda is based on the imperative of establishing the highest possible threshold of protection for children. The Security Council resolutions respond to the policy recommendations contained in the secretary-general's annual report, and on the basis of these recommendations the council has in turn played a leading role in determining the direction and pace of the agenda. Thus, the secretary-general has challenged the Security Council with far-reaching recommendations on CAAC. In turn, the council has responded vigorously through proactive engagement, challenging the UN system, NGOs, and other key stakeholders to act more effectively within the purview of their own mandates, roles, and responsibilities.

The conversation between the United Nations secretariat and the Security Council through the vehicles of the secretary-general's report and Security Council resolutions has been the primary mode for advancing the CAAC protection agenda. In this sense, the secretary-general's report may be understood beyond its narrative account of the plight of children, as an instrument to bridge the gap between the reality on the ground for children and the norms and standards for their protection. The report, therefore, serves a dual function of raising the level of substantive engagement on the key aspects of the CAAC problematic while progressively evolving into a more focused monitoring and compliance report—the so-called report of record—on commission of abuses against children.

Therefore, it is important for the secretary-general's report to be crafted in a specific way to facilitate action by the Security Council and other policy-level actors. The report must represent the different aspects of the CAAC problematic; enhance the UN system's understanding of CAAC; direct and maintain the Security Council's attention on parties to conflict committing violations; ensure the council concentrates on situations beyond its country-specific agenda; specifically cite violators in order to take action; forge a consensus on what grave violations constitute the basis for monitoring and reporting; offer viable means for a monitoring, reporting, and compliance regime; and provide unimpeachable reliability, accuracy, and timeliness.

The fifth report of the secretary-general to the Security Council on Children and Armed Conflict (United Nations 2005a) represents the culmination of a graduated strategic process since 1999 to build in all of these features, and to develop a compliance report of record on the commission of grave violations against children. The report outlines a structured mechanism to monitor and report on grave violations against children in situations of armed conflict. The product of extensive consultations since 2001 among UN system entities, NGOs, national governments, regional organizations, and civil society in conflict-affected countries, the mechanism operates at three levels: country, which includes information gathering, coordination, action, and report preparation; headquarters, which includes coordination, scrutiny, and integration of information and report preparation; and destinations for action, which includes using report information to ensure compliance, particularly by national governments, regional organizations, the Security Council, the General Assembly, the Commission on Human Rights, the International Criminal Court, the Committee of the Rights of the Child, United Nations Country Teams, and United Nations Peacekeeping Operations.

The monitoring and reporting mechanism will also monitor the following six grave abuses against children in the context of armed conflict: killing or maiming children; recruiting or using child soldiers; attacking schools or hospitals; raping or otherwise gravely violating children sexually; abducting children; denying humanitarian access for children.

The momentum that has been generated on CAAC, especially as a result of the purposive engagement of the Security Council, has begun to make a qualitative difference for children in situations of armed conflict. The international community is orienting itself increasingly toward an era of application of international child protection standards. Following are examples of significant developments over the past year.

On 18 March 2006, the chief prosecutor of the International Criminal Court, Luis Moreno-Ocampo, issued a statement announcing the indictment of Thomas Lubanga, founder and leader of a militia group in Ithuri, in the Democratic Republic of the Congo. He was indicted for committing war crimes—specifically, conscripting and enlisting children under the age of fifteen and using children to participate actively in hostilities. In his statement, the prosecutor stressed that "this is the first case, not the last. The investigation is ongoing, we will continue to investigate more crimes committed by Thomas Lubanga Dyilo and we will also investigate other crimes committed by other groups. This is important, it's a sequence. We will investigate crimes committed by other militias and other persons—this is the first case, not the last. . . . We are totally committed to staying in Congo—to make sure justice is done" (ICC 2006).

On 19 March 2006, Major Jean-Pierre Biyoyo became the first person to be convicted in a national judicial process for recruiting child soldiers. He was sentenced to five years imprisonment by a military tribunal. The case establishes an important precedent in that it represents the first time that a court of the Democratic Republic of Congo has tried and convicted a soldier for recruitment of children (Agence France Presse 2006).

Charles Taylor, former president of Liberia, was transferred into the custody of the Special Court for Sierra Leone on 17 March 2006, indicted on eleven counts of war crimes and crimes against humanity, including "conscripting or enlisting children under the age of 15 years into armed forces or groups, or using them to participate actively in hostilities" (Special Court for Sierra Leone 2003). The case sets an important precedent by indicting, for the first time, a former head of state for recruitment and use of children. It should also be noted that the recruitment of children has been included in the list of counts against all eleven individuals who have so far been indicted by the special court.

In November 2005, the Force Nouvelles, one of the parties listed by the secretary-general for recruitment and use of child soldiers in Cote d'Ivoire, submitted an action plan in the context of dialogue established under the framework of SCR 1612. In it the group commits to taking measures to prevent recruitment of children and to the release of all children associated with their fighting forces. The pressure exerted on Force Nouvelles also opened the possibility of child protection dialogue beyond the issue of recruitment and use of children. For example, the top leadership of the Force Nouvelle, at the behest of the United Nations, issued a Command Order to its forces in April 2006. It ordered the release of all children in detention in the northern half of Cote d'Ivoire, which is under rebel control, and stopped the practice of detaining children. The issue of juveniles in detention has been a major child protection concern in rebel-controlled and administered territory given the nonexistence of functional justice systems (UN Department of Peacekeeping Operations 2006). The 2006 report of the secretary-general to the Security Council states that the Forces Armées des Forces Nouvelles (FAFN) has made all efforts to comply with the action plan of 2005. Furthermore, FAFN agreed in 2006 to establish an independent verification commission with UNICEF to ensure compliance with the action plan (United Nations 2006b). In September 2006, four of the main pro-government militia groups, FLGO, MILOCI, APWé, and UP-RGO also committed to action plans to prevent recruitment of children and to identify and release all children associated with their forces.

On 7 February 2006, the Security Council Sanctions Committee for Cote d'Ivoire, established pursuant to resolution 1572, approved a list of individuals subject to specific sanction measures, including travel ban and attachment of financial assets. Martin Kouakou Fofie of Force Nouvelles, commandant of Korogo Sector, was listed in this regard, under the citation that forces under his command had engaged in recruitment of child soldiers, abductions, and sexual abuse and exploitation. It is important to note that these sanction measures were not adopted in the framework of resolution 1612 on children and armed conflict, but it signals the willingness of the council to consider imposing sanction measures for violations against children under the frame of existing sanctions regimes.

On 19 April 2006, the secretary-general's panel of experts on Sudan issued the following recommendation:

Recommendation 11. The Security Council should request the Committee to consider information on children and armed conflict presented to the Council by the secretary-general under the monitoring and reporting mechanism established in Council resolution 1612. The Committee would then use this information to assist in the deliberations on possible designation of individuals who commit violations of international humanitarian or human rights law as being subject to the measures in subparagraphs 3(d) and 3(e) of resolution 1591. (United Nations 2006c)

Subparagraphs 3(d) and 3(e) of Security Council resolution 1591 refer to sanction measures as follows:

3(d) that all States shall take the necessary measures to prevent entry into or transit through their territories of all persons as designated by the Committee pursuant to subparagraph (c) above, provided that nothing in this paragraph shall obligate a State to refuse entry into its territory to its own nationals;

3(e) that all States shall freeze all funds, financial assets and economic resources that are on their territories on the date of adoption of this resolution or at any time thereafter, that are owned or controlled, directly or indirectly, by the persons designated by the Committee pursuant to subparagraph (c) above, or that are held by entities owned or controlled, directly or indirectly, by such persons or by persons acting on their behalf or at their direction, and decides further that all States shall ensure that no funds, financial assets or economic resources are made available by their nationals or by any persons within their territories to or for the benefit of such persons or entities.

Most significantly, the recommendation illustrates an increasing cohesion of various frameworks of the Security Council and reinforces the assertion that the council is prepared to consider sanction measures against those parties who commit grave violations against children under the framework of existing country-specific sanctions regimes.

Since the initiation of the working group pursuant to SCR 1612, the secretary-general has for the first time presented to the council country-specific reports on the situation of children and armed conflict in the Democratic Republic of the Congo, Sudan, Burundi, and Cote d'Ivoire, with reports to the working group on Nepal, Sri Lanka, and Somalia. In response to these reports of the secretary-general, the working group recommended to the Security Council, among other specific conclusions, the referral of continued grave violations against children by parties in the Democratic Republic of the Congo and Cote d'Ivoire to the existing Security Council Sanctions Committees established for these two situations.

Although the plight of children in many situations of armed conflict around the globe remains grave and unacceptable, collaborative efforts over the recent years among UN entities, governments, regional organizations, NGOs, and other civil society groups have resulted in notable progress and have created a strong momentum for the protection of children on the ground. These advances include the elaboration and strengthening of international norms and standards for the protection of children; more fundamental mainstreaming of CAAC concerns in the UN system and beyond; and, increasingly, the broadening of the global circle of stakeholders and action on behalf of CAAC. Perhaps most significantly, the systematic and purposive engagement of the

Security Council has raised the stakes considerably on this issue, not only for those committing grave violations, but also for the UN system and other actors charged with advocacy and program interventions for CAAC. There is now a turning of the tide for children as commitments translate into concrete action for their protection. However, it is also evident that so far the progress remains fragile and may dissipate if not consolidated and reinforced. Even higher levels of commitment and collaboration by the international system will be required to achieve the era of application of child protection standards.

Part III

Alternative Explanations of Child Recruitment

CHAPTER 4

NO PLACE TO HIDE

Refugees, Displaced Persons, and Child Soldier Recruits

Vera Achvarina and Simon Reich

REPORTS OF TALIBAN RECRUITMENT OF CHILDREN as insurgents and possible suicide bombers surfaced in the U.S. media in August 2005 (CNN 2005). Estimates at the time suggested that the insurgent forces in Afghanistan may have comprised up to 8,000 children (IRIN 2003a). To many in the West, this was a surprising revelation, but it should not have been. Children participated in the Israeli-Palestinian conflict and had been used as soldiers by the Taliban against Soviet forces in the 1980s.[1] Many of the current adult insurgents in Afghanistan came from the ranks of these former child soldiers (Center for Defense Information 2001). News of their use in Afghanistan has only added a new strategic security dimension to the growing list of consequences of the rapidly increasing numbers of child soldiers across the globe.[2] No longer does this phenomenon simply represent a moral dilemma or a problem whose consequences are geographically confined to belligerent forces in fragile or failed states.

Added to this increased complexity is the growth in the volume of child soldiers. One UN source suggests that their number grew from 200,000 to 300,000 between 1988 and 2002;[3] by the latter date they served in seventy-two government or rebel armed forces in about twenty countries (Coalition to Stop the Use of Child Soldiers 2004, 13–17). A rough approximation of 300,000 is now clearly outdated and potentially underestimates the gravity of the current problem. Evidence drawn from individual conflicts since 2002 suggests that new wars are often characterized by an extensive use of child soldiers.[4]

This growing use of child soldiers flies in the face of the claim that international norms and laws are exerting an increasing influence on the behavior of state and nonstate actors (Bell 2002; Finnemore 1996, 158; Jepperson, Wendt, and Katzenstein 1996, 45). Indeed, a plethora of global protocols, agreements, and declarations attempting to protect children from both forced and voluntary recruitment have been flagrantly ignored since the end of the cold war.[5] The historical taboo against the use of child soldiers thus seems to have decisively broken down and the problem has become geographically widespread (Singer 2005, 15, 38). With the Lord's Resistance Army in Uganda as an extreme illustration of the problem,[6] child soldiers have become a principal component of military forces across Africa, Asia, and Latin America, and are playing an increasing strategically important role in the Middle East (UNICEF 2002a, 8).

It is tempting to assume that this numeric growth is a product of the breakdown of state control: that rebel forces, not states, recruit child soldiers. The evidence drawn from African cases is far more ambiguous. Our data for the Liberian conflict of 1989–1995 does indicate an overwhelming proportion of child soldiers among the ranks of rebels and not the state's military, but other conflicts demonstrate a contrary trend toward a larger use of child soldiers by governments. The second Liberian conflict of 1999–2003, for example, had a 70/30 split between rebel and government forces.[7] The Sudanese civil war of 1993–2002 had a 64/36 split between rebel and governmental forces, but that majority was reversed to a 24 (rebel) and 76 (government) distribution by 2004 (CNN.com 2001; Save the Children, n.d.; CSUCS 2004a). The data we compiled for the Angolan conflict, although not definitive, suggest that children have made up between 24 and 33 percent of the government's forces since the war against the rebels began in 1996.[8] In that case, abduction has been a major method of recruitment, with both sides estimated to have seized forty thousand children in total by 2003.[9]

In considering the underlying causes of child soldiering, we examine nineteen cases drawn from African conflicts over the last three decades. Since 1975, Africa has become the epicenter of the problem, providing the largest concentration of both conflicts and child soldiers. By the late 1990s, fourteen out of the forty then ongoing or recently concluded armed conflicts in Africa included significant numbers of child soldiers.[10] Estimates suggest that 120,000 children, 40 percent of all child soldiers, were soldiering in Africa at the beginning of the twenty-first century (CSUCS 2000; Twum-Danso 2003). East Asia and the Pacific ranked a distant second, with approximately 75,000 child soldiers

(UNICEF 2002a.). Furthermore, Africa has experienced the fastest growth in the use of child soldiers in recent years.[11] More disturbing, the average age of the children enlisted in some African countries is declining—from their teen-age years to as low as nine or ten.[12] Although a question remains regarding the degree to which African conflicts are representative of child soldiering, there is little doubt that it is the most chronic location for the problem.

The literature on the use of child soldiers is fairly sparse, and a heavy pre-ponderance of it is written by members of the think tank and civil society com-munities rather than by academics. Although he offers no formal tests, P. W. Singer in *Children at War* provides several possible explanations for the growth in the number of child soldiers that have currency among activists and scholars working on the issue, including high poverty levels, rising orphan rates, and technological innovation in—and the global sale of—smaller and lighter arms (Singer 2005, 38, 55). These arguments point to structural features that may in-deed contribute to this global growth in the number of child soldiers. But their focus on world trends is not helpful in explaining the significant variation in child soldier rates across countries.

In this chapter, the key factor in explaining child soldier recruitment rates is the degree of access to refugee and/or internally displaced persons (IDP) camps gained by the belligerent parties (both government and rebel forces) in conflicts.[13] The prospect of escaping from poverty may lure potential child recruits; high orphan rates may make these recruits more vulnerable to ei-ther incentives or threats; but it is the degree of vulnerability of children in refugee/IDP camps that ultimately explains their participation rates. They gather in such camps in great numbers. According to a UN High Commis-sioner for Refugees (UNHCR) 2001 report, children constitute 57 percent of the inhabitants of refugee camps in the UNHCR-mandated facilities in Africa. Whether orphans or not, children conveniently amassed in large groups are of-ten so vulnerable that they are too tempting a target to pass up for armed forces seeking recruits in the absence of a sufficient deterrent. We therefore argue that child soldiers will constitute a larger percentage of belligerent forces where camps are relatively vulnerable to infiltration or raiding. Protection from ac-cess by belligerents is therefore crucial. A lack of it provides an incentive that will likely increase the probability of successful raids by armed factions seek-ing recruits.

Of all the possible explanations for the recruitment of child soldiers, no other systematically or empirically examines the potential importance of the access of belligerents to either refugee or IDP camps. Barnitz does mention that "children who are in refugee camps or in orphanages are particularly vul-nerable to joining armed organizations when conflict erupts" (Barnitz 1999, 4). But she does not address the issue of raids by belligerents as factors. Cohn and Goodwin-Gill also suggest in passing that refugee children are vulnerable to political exploitation and are possibly being primed to use guns (Cohn and Goodwin-Gill 1994, 32). But, again, they do not focus on assaults on camps designed to recruit children.

While the existing literature on refugees does include a discussion about the possible militarization of refugees (whether voluntarily or through forced conscription) (Stedman and Tanner 2003, 1–15), it does not concentrate on the issue of children. And, although some studies do mention the need to protect refugee/IDP camps, they do so only with regard to the delivery of aid.[14] Little has been written on whether children in these camps are an especially vulnerable group prone to joining armed organizations when conflict erupts.[15]

IDP and refugee camps, if unprotected, form an important resource pool for child soldiers—whether conscripted or voluntary. The image of children plucked off the street or out of the fields may have some relevance. But it is an inefficient way for belligerents, already shorn of sufficient manpower, to recruit soldiers and is unlikely to account for relatively high participation rates. For government and rebel forces, rounding children up at unprotected IDP or refugee camps presents a far more attractive source of fresh recruits (CSUCS 2004a, 31, 33).

Historically, such camps are supposed to be protected under international laws and protocols (Terry 2002, 28). They are supposed to be off limits to belligerents and generally assumed to be under the protection of a legitimate judicial authority, whether a sovereign government, a regional entity, or an international organization. But protection is often, in practice, uneven or nonexistent. Reaching a refugee or IDP camp does not ensure either personal security against outside forces or relief from hunger. Often, it is little more than a place for those in danger to congregate, particularly children.[16]

The practical result is that a high-risk pool of potential recruits is created. As one UNICEF official reported to us in interviews, "Recruitment in refugee camps is relatively widespread. It is an area one ought to research a little bit more because we always have the sense that displaced children, whether they are refugees or internally displaced, particularly I would say displaced children, are more at risk of recruitment as they are more at risk of other human rights violations. . . . As such, it can be imagined that young boys and young girls who are in the age of fighting are at-risk of being recruited in that context . . . . IDP camps are wonderful places where people are regrouped and propaganda can be conducted quite easily. . . . I think there's clear factual anecdotal evidence when you go in refugee camps that it's happening."[17] As an official from Save the Children pointedly suggested, "There is a recruitment that happens directly in refugee camps too. There is usually no fence or a wall surrounding camps, and people can slip in."[18]

Armed factions, therefore, infiltrate camps and often become indistinct from the civilian population so that they can recruit them. They enlist or seize inhabitants (including children) through the use of coercion or propaganda—a phenomenon referred to as "refugee manipulation and militarization"—from within the camps. According to the UNHCR, about 15 percent of refugee crises "foment refugee militarization" (Stedman and Tanner 2003, 3, 4). In other instances, however, the lack of physical protection of camps incites insurgencies and attacks by both rebels and government militias. So, we anticipate that the larger the number of instances of camp militarization or outside incursions, the higher the number (and thus ratio) of child soldiers.

Methodology: Data Samples and the Dependent Variable

We confine our data analysis to cases involving intrastate conflicts in Africa between 1975 and 2002.[19] We have chosen to examine only intrastate conflicts because according to one UNICEF report, "The conflicts that involve child soldiers are usually relatively small, internal struggles. Rather than fighting in international wars, children serve in civil wars, which have bitter religious or ethnic enmities and create social pressures to fight" (Model United Nations of the University of Chicago 2003, 5).

Research revealed that child soldiers were reported as present or absent in conflicts. Of those, twelve had confirmed reporting of child soldier numbers, enabling the calculation of positive child soldier ratios.[20] For seven conflicts, reports had confirmed that there was no use of child soldiers.[21] These conflicts varied in duration. There seemed to be little relationship between duration and the use of child soldiers.[22]

Table 4.1 provides information on the twelve cases where we could identify

TABLE 4.1   Child soldiers: Countries, conflicts, and percentages

Country and conflict	Number of child soldiers	Number of combatants	Percentage of child soldiers
Angola (1975–1994)	8,000	194,000	4
Angola (1996–2002)	20,000	72,500	28
Burundi (1993–1993)	5,000	50,000	10
Burundi (1995–1999)	14,000	45,000	31
DRC (1996–2001)	20,000	72,000	28
Liberia (1989–1995)	17,500	60,000	29
Liberia (2000–2002)	21,000	40,000	53
Rwanda (1990–1995)	17,500	70,000	25
Sierra Leone (1991–2000)	10,000	45,000	22
Sudan (1993–2002)	15,700	40,000	39
Uganda (1994–2002)	16,000	74,000	22

reliable estimates on child soldier recruitment. It includes the duration of the conflict, the total number of combatants, the number of child soldiers in each conflict, and the ratio of child soldiers in each case. We calculated the ratio by dividing the number of children recruited by all armed factions (including governmental forces) in each intrastate conflict by the number of all combatants participating in the conflict at some stage. The data revealed that in all twelve cases both government and rebel forces engaged in child recruitment, with approximately the same distribution of numbers, except (as previously mentioned) in Uganda, where rebel forces recruited disproportionately more children, and Mozambique, where the obverse was the case.[23] The column in table 4.1 listing the percentage of child soldiers demonstrates the variation in our dependent variable, bearing in mind that the percentage was zero for seven additional cases.

Our data suggest that substantial poverty rates say little about whether a country is likely to have child soldier participants in armed conflicts. We use the percentage of population estimated below the poverty line as the measure of national poverty, defined by the World Bank as the minimum standard required by an individual to fulfill his or her basic food and nonfood needs (World Bank 2005, 42).[24] The evidence we have generated questions whether poverty rates explain the enormous variations in child soldier rates.[25]

In figure 4.1 we plotted a simple regression line between poverty and child soldier rates. For the relationship between the two to exist, the cases would approximate the slope from bottom left to top right, with a corresponding increase in poverty rates and child soldier ratios. None is evident according to these data; the results suggest no systematic relationship between the two.

We adopted a measure of child orphans from a Joint United Nations Programme on HIV/AIDS report on orphan estimates in order to evaluate the relationship between orphans and child soldiers' participation in conflicts (UNAIDS-UNICEF 2002). Figure 4.2 shows the lack of proximity to the imaginary trend line. There seems to be little discernable relationship between orphan rates and child soldier participation rates.

We argue that the larger the number of instances of camp militarization or outside incursions, the higher the number (and thus ratio) of child soldiers. In testing this argument, we operationalized the independent variable of access as a ratio. By an "instance" we mean occurrence of camp attack or camp militarization event(s) during a given year by parties to the conflict in question. Our approach leaves unaddressed the question of whether there are key distinctions between refugee and IDP camps, access to the former, for example, being contingent on the additional factor of either a host government's collusion or its inability to halt assaults by government or rebel forces. Regardless, the effect is the same: a lack of protection for refugee camps.[26]

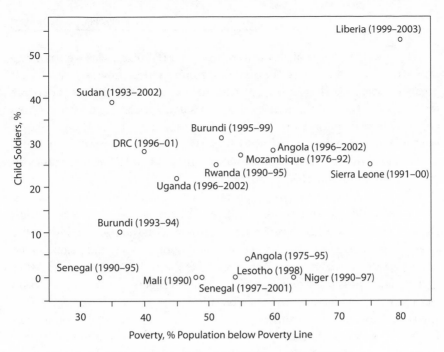

FIG. 4.1. The relationship between poverty and child soldier rates (1976–2003)

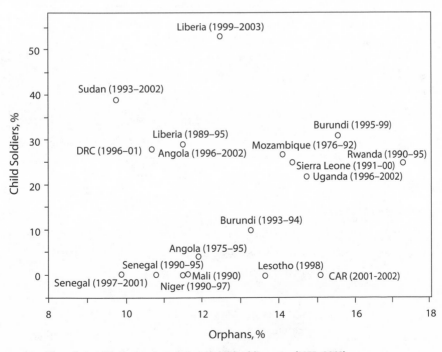

FIG. 4.2. The relationship between orphan and child soldier rates (1975–2003)

To assess the degree of access to refugee and IDP camps, as well as camp militarization, we employed the qualitative information provided by relevant organizations, as well as reports, papers, and news articles. The major source for our calculations of the access variable is a data set compiled by Sarah Lischer for the years between 1987 and 1998 (Lischer 2000).[27] For the years after 1998, we relied on data from the yearly reports of the U.S. Committee for Refugees as our main source of the information. The data on IDP camps came primarily from the Global IDP Database country reports.[28]

Figure 4.3 adds support to the proposition that access to refugee and IDP camps and child soldier rates are correlated. With relatively limited variations, the figure shows a rise in access rates consistent with the rise in child soldier rates. The clustering and location of the cases along an imaginary slope in figure 4.3 appear far tighter than in figures 4.1 and 4.2. This suggests, at least as a "first cut," a possibly stronger causal relationship between camp protection from access by belligerents and child recruitment rates.

To evaluate the relationship between access to camps and child soldier rates further, we performed a multiple regression test on nineteen observations for which the data on the third independent variable (access) and the dependent variable (child soldier ratios) were available, excluding three cases where the

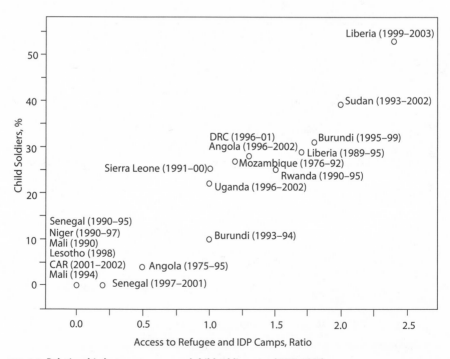

FIG. 4.3. Relationship between access and child soldier rates (1975–2003)

data on poverty were unavailable.[29] In conducting a multiple regression test, we assessed the impact of our three independent variables—poverty, orphan rates, and access to refugee and IDP camps—on the dependent variable.[30] The general model to be estimated is written as:

$$Y = a + \sum_{k=1}^{K} \beta_k X_k + \varepsilon$$

where K is the number of our independent variables. Our model is specified as follows:

$$CS = a + \beta_1 Poverty + \beta_2 Orphans + \beta_3 Access + \varepsilon$$

where CS stands for child soldier ratios.

The coefficients of correlation between our independent variables are presented in table 4.2. They suggest that none of the independent variables is significantly correlated with any other one.[31] Therefore, collinearity is not a problem (Hill, Griffiths, and Judge, 2001, 190).

The regression results, summarized in Table 4.3, demonstrate that only access is significantly related to child soldier ratios. The coefficient value predicts that every single unit increase in access is matched with a twenty-unit increase

TABLE 4.2   Pearson correlation coefficients for independent variables

	Poverty	Orphans	Access
Poverty			
Orphans	.194		
Access	.212	.108	

***Correlation is significant at the 0.01 level (2-tailed).
**Correlation is significant at the 0.05 level
*Correlation is significant at the 0.1 level

TABLE 4.3   Multiple regression results

Independent variable	Coefficient estimates
Poverty	.156 (.081)
Orphans	−.472 (0.497)
Access	20.536** (1.406)

Notes: N=16, R^2=0.976, adjusted R^2=0.953; the dependent variable is child soldier ratios. Unstandardized coefficients are reported because they convey the true information about the magnitude of the effect on the dependent variable. Mutual comparisons of standardized coefficients are not necessary here since only one is statistically significant. Standard errors are in parentheses.
*** Coefficient is significant at the 0.01 level (2-tailed).
** Coefficient is significant at the 0.05 level.
* Coefficient is significant at the 0.1 level.

in child soldiers. The coefficient values on orphans and poverty are insignificant, implying that there is no statistically significant association between poverty and child soldiers or between orphans and child soldiers. The findings of this test further reinforce our contention that access to camps is the key determinant of child soldier rates.

Illustrative Case Studies: Liberia 1989–1996 and 1999–2003

We have chosen two Liberian cases because they constitute crucial tests. The 1999–2003 case is important because it offers the highest ratio of child soldiers recorded in our nineteen cases. If an explanation focusing on the denial of access for government and rebel forces to camps were not clearly sustainable in such a case, then it would seriously weaken our argument. Being able to sustain it, in contrast, reinforces our claims—given that Liberia is typically poor, representative of orphan rates, and yet has such variance in proportionate and absolute terms over the course of two proximate conflicts. By focusing on the relative amount of protection given to refugees and IDPs, we seek to build upon our finding that the degree of access to refugee/IDP camps is crucial. Comparing the two Liberian cases allows us to hold many variables constant because factors such as culture, ethnicity, and poverty rates remained largely unchanged; even orphan rates altered only marginally between the two periods.

The civil war began in 1989 with rebel leader Charles Taylor's invasion of Liberia from the neighboring Ivory Coast (Armed Conflicts Events Data 2003). Taylor's National Patriotic Front of Liberia (NPFL) forces were intent on deposing the existing regime (the People's Redemption Council), led by Samuel Doe and his National Democratic Party of Liberia. The NPFL rebels terrorized both border and refugee communities in neighboring countries (UNHCR 1994) and then carried out a series of executions and gross human rights abuses.[32] By 1990, Doe was captured and subsequently executed.

Yet the war lasted until 1996, and the intervening years were marked by attacks on border communities within Liberia, notably by the NPFL, and the fragmentation of control (UNHCR 1994). From 1990 onward, the Economic Community of West African States (ECOMOG) deployed Nigerian-led peacekeeping mission troops, which established order only in and around the capital of Monrovia (Norwegian Refugee Council 2005, 5). The force initially consisted of 2,700 soldiers. Nonetheless, the conflict continued elsewhere, "characterized by brutal ethnic killings and massive abuses against the civilian population" (Human Rights Watch 2004b, 7). To protect Monrovia, the ECOMOG forces were increased by 3,000 men, and a limited offensive military capability enhanced their capacity as they shifted their mission from traditional peacekeeping to one of sustaining law and order there (Howe 2001, 139–140).

First, they pushed belligerent forces out of the capital. Then they enlarged their area of operations. In the words of Collin Scott, "As the NPFL rebellion drove people across international borders or toward the security in Monrovia, ECO-MOG deployed outward to create a security zone, protecting the bulk of the internally displaced" (Scott 1998, 114).

A shaky cease-fire agreement followed. In Monrovia, "protection was effectively ensured by the presence of ECOMOG forces" for most of the war (Norwegian Refugee Council 2005, 36). However, only Monrovia and the surrounding security zone constituted an effective safe haven (Howe 2001, 143–144). Control of the rest of Liberia was divided between Taylor's forces and a number of factions that proliferated over the years (Human Rights Watch 2004b, 6). Fighting was sustained in these areas despite the presence of regional peacekeepers and a United Nations military observer mission (Human Rights Watch 2004b, 15). As a result, thousands of people were trapped inside conflict zones with no access to humanitarian organizations (Human Rights Watch 2004b, 6). "Lacking physical security, Liberian displaced persons and refugees in shelters were vulnerable to physical abuse, and fell prey to torture and massacre. The AFL, the NPFL, the United Liberation Movement for Democracy (ULIMO), and the Liberian Peace Council (LPC), engaged in human rights abuses and massacres of displaced persons and refugees in camps or shelters."

Fifty-nine percent of Liberia's population of 2.6 million was displaced as they headed for refugee and IDP camps (Scott 1998, 113). By the end of 1994, the total number of Liberian refugees in neighboring countries exceeded 800,000 (Human Rights Watch 1995b).[33] Of these, more than 500,000 were estimated to be located in Guinea, 318,000 in the Ivory Coast, 20,000 in Ghana, 6,000 in Sierra Leone, and 4,000 in Nigeria (Human Rights Watch 1995a). The refugees were not guaranteed safety, however, and had to rely on host government protection.

Estimates suggest that by 1996 "there were approximately 750,000 IDPs in Liberia. Of these, 300,000–500,000 were located in shelters in and around Monrovia" (Human Rights Watch 1995b, 15). The rest were distributed in IDP camps throughout the country. In sum, protected areas became overburdened as unprotected areas emptied. Displaced people, seeking to escape from the ongoing fighting, swelled the "greater Monrovia" security zone, estimated to contain more than a million people (114). ECOMOG's presence, in this regard, was crucial: "Although ECOMOG never had explicit humanitarian objectives, it did reduce hostilities and atrocities, and by establishing order in greater Monrovia it set up a safe haven for thousands of displaced Liberians" (105).

As the war progressed, however, even the IDPs located in Monrovia were no longer well protected. Despite the presence of ECOMOG troops, they could not spare the capital from the "engulfed violence and horror" in the final stages of the conflict (Norwegian Refugee Council 2005, 10; Scott 1998, 108). By that time, approximately 46 percent, some 361,880 of the estimated 780,000 inhabitants of Monrovia, had to abandon their homes. Of these, 30 percent moved into shelters—completely dependent on the international community for their basic needs and protection (Norwegian Refugee Council 2005, 15). Children were left vulnerable to the war's ravages and, seemingly, none were spared from its horror. The child population can be divided between those who were victims as civilians and those who were victims and perpetrators as child soldiers.[34]

Taylor's NPFL became infamous for the abduction and use of boys in war dating from the start of conflict in 1989. According to one Human Rights Watch report (1994, 26), many children were told, "You join us or we'll kill your family." Another noted that many of these children had been forcibly recruited after soldiers had killed their parents (Human Rights Watch 1990). From this pool they formed the infamous Small Boys Unit of the NPFL (Howe 2001). Some reports claimed that children were also assigned to a special bodyguard unit designed to protect NPFL ministers (Human Rights Watch 1994, 22–23). But still others were used elsewhere as cannon fodder on the front lines.[35] Children also formed an integral part of other Liberian armed factions, such as ULIMO (Human Rights Watch 1994, 24).

One United Nations High Commissioner for Refugees (UNHCR) report made clear the authors' views on the role of children in the conflict at the time: "The civil war in Liberia has been a children's war. All factions except the AFL have used many thousands of soldiers under the age of 18, including some as young as eight or nine. . . . It is indeed true that many children have witnessed their families being killed with the utmost brutality. However, in many instances children have been forcibly recruited and compelled to take part in atrocities" (UNHCR 1994).

In the early years of the war, ECOMOG forces were able to protect children in Monrovia and the surrounding security zone from these factions. But a number of reports suggest that this was not the case outside the security zone. As Scott described at the time, in these areas, "children have been co-opted or coerced into the armed factions, where they have been subjected to violence both as victims and as forced perpetrators" (1998, 114). By 1996, children inside Monrovia and the security belt were no longer protected and had become the targets of an increasing number of factions.

As the war drew to a close, and the ECOMOG forces withdrew their protection, the inhabitants of Monrovia were as vulnerable as those IDPs and refugees elsewhere, in an environment of unmitigated violence. In total, about 17,500 children were engaged as child soldiers in the seven-year armed conflict, constituting approximately 29 percent of all combatants.[36] Only the presence of ECOMOG soldiers, in a country where child soldiers were readily recruited, had kept the figure down to this (albeit significant) level.

Charles Taylor ruled for three years before the armed faction of the Liberians United for Reconciliation and Democracy (LURD) launched attacks on his regime. This conflict lasted until early 2003, when the rebels were joined by another opposition faction based in the Ivory Coast, the Movement for Democracy in Liberia (MODEL).[37] A negotiated cease-fire resulted in Taylor's departure from office, and a subsequent deployment of regional and later international peacekeepers brought an end to major hostilities (Human Rights Watch 2004b, 8).

In contrast to the prior conflict, the international community's universal antipathy toward Taylor's human rights record in the aftermath of the 1997 elections, coupled with a belief that his regime was backing armed insurgencies in neighboring countries, resulted in UN Security Council sanctions being tightened on his regime in March 2001. These measures were designed to curb arms trafficking to the Revolutionary United Front (RUF) in Sierra Leone. Two months later, further sanctions followed, including travel restrictions on senior government officials and a ban on diamond and timber exports (Norwegian Refugee Council 2005, 7).

Distrust of Taylor was so great that local journalists accused him of manufacturing a humanitarian crisis (Norwegian Refugee Council 2005, 14). This time, the international community refused to send troops to quell the growing disorder. In their absence, IDP protection fell under the jurisdiction of Liberia's ministry of justice, while the government's refugee agency (LRRRC) was supposed to oversee the management of camps and coordination of relief. Both, however, lacked the expertise and resources to discharge their respective functions, suffering from limited technical, financial, and logistical capacities (UN 2001, 106). The government's inability to protect citizens was consistently reported and linked, for example, to the practices of sexual exploitation of girls in refugee and IDP camps (Norwegian Refugee Council 2005, 78). Donor antipathy forced nongovernmental organizations to scale down their activities and to reduce the level of support they had been providing to IDPs and other vulnerable populations (Norwegian Refugee Council 2005, 115). Meanwhile, a lack of resources and access to the critical locations of the conflict hampered international humanitarian operations (Norwegian Refugee Council 2005, 7). The consequences were predictable for IDP camp inhabitants: "Their total lack of protection from increasingly widespread human rights abuses carried out not only by Liberian security forces but by LURD combatants as well" (Amnesty International 2002, 60). "As a result, growing numbers of IDPs continue[d] to concentrate in camps around Monrovia" (Norwegian Refugee Council 2005, 37).

By 2002 the Liberian government had restricted aid agencies to the greater Monrovia area while blocking IDPs from entering the capital, thus denying the agencies any contact with the vast majority of IDPs. "In the absence of any protection, the plight of these IDPs, and of refugees (mostly those located in camps in Guinea) was a desperate one, with numerous reports of substantial raids being carried out against them by both government and rebel forces."[38]

Meanwhile, Liberian authorities attempted to close borders, trapping prospective refugees between the cities and the borders, and leaving them exposed to forced recruitment. Indeed, British and French intervention in Sierra Leone and the Ivory Coast, respectively, "drove the most intractable combatants [from those countries] into Liberia," bringing additional instability and greater insecurity for the displaced population of Liberia. Both IDPs and refugees, therefore, lived in terror and consistently, though unsuccessfully, moved to avoid raids.[39] UN attempts to encourage self-protection in IDP camps proved no panacea, as "most displaced were crammed into camps that afford[ed] little security or managed to settle in the sordid suburbs of the capital" (Jezequel 2004, 162–163).[40] One report at that time, furthermore, claimed that "government forces conducted conscription raids within neighborhoods in Monrovia" (Human Rights Watch 2004b, 8).

Neither in Monrovia nor in rural areas could IDPs or refugees find safety. The LURD's movements and governmental retreat forced the population of villages and IDP camps to flee, either in anticipation of attacks or in response to them (Jezequel 2004, 169). All factions made the recruitment of children in newly captured territory a central pillar from the outset of the war (Human Rights Watch 2004b, 9). According to Human Rights Watch, "both of the opposition groups as well as government forces which include militias and paramilitary groups widely used children when civil war resumed in 2000. In some cases, the majority of military units were made up primarily of boys and girls under the age of eighteen. Their use and abuse was a deliberate policy on the part of the highest levels of leadership in all three groups" (Human Rights Watch 2004b, 1). When denied protection in the refugee and IDP camps, many of the children who had fought in the previous conflict were easily re-recruited when fighting resumed in 2000, because "according to participants, forced recruitment has been a standard practice in Liberia's recent history" (Norwegian Refugee Council 2005, 46).

The initial stage of the war centered primarily in the gold- and diamond-rich area close to the borders of Liberia, Sierra Leone, and Guinea—from where children were recruited (Norwegian Refugee Council 2005, 6). For example, Guinea-based LURD recruited children among Liberians living in refugee camps there. MODEL, operating from a base in the Ivory Coast, recruited children from refugee camps in that country (Human Rights Watch

2004b, 17). Taylor's militia groups also included numerous child combatants from RUF, which he had supported since its inception in 1991.

IDP children were just as vulnerable. Without protection, the forced recruitment of children became relatively easier to implement as the plight of IDPs became increasingly desperate. The massive movement of IDPs described earlier left a large pool of children unaccompanied and unprotected in IDP camps—and therefore highly vulnerable to recruitment. As one report suggested, "Many families have become separated during their flight from Lofa country and there are large numbers of unaccompanied women and children in IDP camps" (Norwegian Refugee Council 2005, 43). Elsewhere it noted, "The virtual collapse of most of the family structures and the limited capacity of families to provide adequate care has exacerbated the situation of children, both in IDP camps and in war-affected communities. . . . SCF [Save the Children Fund] has documented over 6,000 cases of child separation as a result of new displacements in Lofa County. . . . At present, there are an estimated 20,000 separated children in Liberia and neighboring countries" (Norwegian Refugee Council 2005, 67).

This time, however, Monrovia was not spared. Children were regularly taken by government forces in their raids on the IDP camps near Monrovia in 2002 and 2003. As a result, parents learned to keep their children inside when the government forces visited the camp to avoid their being taken away to fight (Norwegian Refugee Council 2005, 15). All sides looked to large camps for their child recruits. "By mid-2003, an estimated one in ten of children in the Montserrado camps were being recruited into government forces" (CSUCS 2004a, 77). More children became involved as combatants in the attacks on Monrovia between June and August 2003 (Human Rights Watch 2004b, 9).

We estimate that 21,000 children were soldiers in the Liberian war between 2000 and 2003, constituting 53 percent of all combatants. This represents an increase of 24 percent from the 1989–1996 Liberian conflict in terms of the proportion of child soldiers to all belligerents, as well as approximately a 20 percent increase in absolute terms of the total number of children involved in comparison to the first conflict. In essence, as adults were killed or fled, both sides became more reliant on children—and took advantage of their greater availability in the absence of international or domestic soldiers to protect them.

A Superficial Comparison

The rates of child soldier involvement in Liberia's two wars are very high by historical standards, at 29 percent and 53 percent respectively. Yet, the degree of protection provided to children in the two conflicts varied significantly. In the first war, IDPs had the option of heading for Monrovia and the protection of ECOMOG forces.

No such domestic protection existed during the second war. Nor was fleeing abroad any longer an option. The international community did not offer refugee assistance in either case. Liberians representing all factions in the conflict clearly had a predilection for the use of children in war. That predilection was unhindered and unmitigated by any opposition and resulted in an escalation of numbers beyond that of the first conflict. UN efforts to encourage camp self-protection proved a fruitless option for IDPs and refugees who were geographically concentrated, subject to constant terror, unarmed, and largely unfed. This resulted in the increase of child recruits in both absolute and relative terms.

The comparison of these two cases thus supports our general argument. The pressure to use child soldiers may have arguably increased in the context of two wars so proximate in time. But it was not the demand for children that was the key factor; it was the supply of children that distinguished the two cases. Children were available in far greater numbers in the second conflict because unprotected IDPs and refugees had nowhere to seek safety.

Poverty in war is often offered as the primary reason for the advent of child soldiers. Our results suggest that although poverty may remain a necessary condition by possibly having a threshold effect, it does not offer an effective causal explanation for child soldier rates. Even the threshold claim is weak, because while richer countries may not use child soldiers in intrastate conflict, child soldiers do not serve in all intrastate conflicts in poor countries.

A large pool of orphans is another factor often discussed as a cause for relatively high child soldier rates. Yet again, our work suggests that there is a relatively weak relationship between the rates of orphans and the ratios of child soldiers. Orphans may be vulnerable, but this does not mean that they are inevitably employed by belligerents in war.

In contrast, our evidence suggests a relatively robust relationship between the capacity for access to refugee and IDP camps and the rate of child soldier participants. Presumably, children (whether or not they are orphans) are not as susceptible if well protected in camps. But large numbers of children congregated together in easily identifiable locations, if left unprotected, make an easy target as recruits for belligerents. Here there is a potential parallel between the issue of child soldiers and food aid; belligerents often steal aid intended for camp refugees. A debate therefore rages about whether force should be used to ensure that food reaches the intended recipients. Likewise, there is seemingly little point in gathering children together in camps if they are not protected from preying governmental and nongovernmental-armed groups. Indeed, doing so may further imperil their lives. The implications, at least potentially, seem evident. As former Pentagon spokesman Kenneth Bacon noted in an interview with the authors of this article, children have now often started to avoid unprotected IDP or refugee camps for fear of being recruited as child soldiers.[41]

We hope that this preliminary work provides helpful insights concerning both the utility of different explanations and the need to protect camps, while serving as a useful foundation for further research. Our principal finding is that access to camps (and the level of their protection) is the greatest determinant of child soldier rates, and if those rates are to fall, then children need to be both fed and protected. How to do so effectively therefore becomes a central logistical and military conundrum.

APPENDIX 4.1   Child Soldiers Presence in African Conflicts

Positive with figures (Reports identified numbers of child soldiers)	Positive minor (Reports identified child soldiers as a minor problem)
Angola (1975–1995)	Guinea-Bissau (1998–1999)
Angola (1996–2002)	Comoros (1989)
Burundi (1993–1994)	Comoros (1997)
Burundi (1995–1999)	Guinea (2000–2001)
Democratic Republic of Congo (1996–2001)	Ethiopia (1974–1991)
Liberia (1989–1995)	South Africa (1966–1978)
Liberia (1999–2002)	Congo–Brazzaville (1993–1994)
Mozambique (1976–1992)	Chad (1989–1990)
Rwanda (1990–1995)	Chad (1991–1994)
Sierra Leone (1991–2000)	Chad (1997–2002)
Sudan (1993–2002)	
Uganda (1994–2002)	
Positive substantial (Reports identified child soldiers as a substantial problem)	**Negative** (Reports identified child soldiers not present in a conflict)
Rwanda (1998–2002)	Senegal (1990–1995)
Sudan (1983–1992)	Senegal (1997–2001)
Uganda (1981–1988)	Niger (1990–1997)
Uganda (1989–1991)	Mali (1990)
Djibouti (1991–1994)	Mali (1994)
Somalia (2001–2002)	Lesotho (1998)
Ethiopia (1996–2002)	Central African Republic (2001–2002)
Algeria (1991–2002)	
Congo–Brazzaville (1997–1999)	
Congo–Brazzaville (2002)	
Ivory Coast (2002)	
Somalia (1981–1996)	
South Africa (1979–1988)	
South Africa (1989–1993)	

APPENDIX 4.2   Poverty and Child Soldier Rates

Case	Child soldiers (%)	Population below poverty line (%)
Angola (1975–1995)	4	56
Angola (1996–2002)	28	60
Burundi (1993–1994)	10	36.2
Burundi (1995–1999)	31	52
Democratic Republic of Congo (1996–2001)	28	40
Senegal (1990–1995)	0	33
Senegal (1997–2001)	0	54
Lesotho (1998)	0	49
Liberia (1999–2003)	53	80
Mali (1990)	0	48
Mozambique (1976–1992)	27	55
Niger (1990–1997)	0	63
Rwanda (1990–1995)	25	51.2
Sierra Leone (1991–2000)	25	75
Sudan (1993–2002)	39	35
Uganda (1996–2002)	22	45

APPENDIX 4.3   Orphan and Child Soldier Rates

Case	Child soldier ratios (%)	Orphans (%)
Angola (1975–1995)	4	11.90
Angola (1996–2002)	28	10.70
Burundi (1993–1994)	10	13.25
Burundi (1995–1999)	31	15.55
Central African Republic (2001–2002)	0	15.10
Democratic Republic of Congo (1996–2001)	28	10.65
Lesotho (1998)	0	13.65
Liberia (1989–1995)	29	11.50
Liberia (1999–2003)	53	12.50
Mali (1990)	0	11.60
Mozambique (1976–1992)	27	14.10
Niger (1990–1997)	0	11.50
Rwanda (1990–1995)	25	17.30
Senegal (1990–1995)	0	10.80
Senegal (1997–2001)	0	9.90
Sierra Leone (1991–2000)	25	14.35
Sudan (1993–2002)	39	9.75
Uganda (1996–2002)	22	14.75

APPENDIX 4.4   Access to Refugee/IDP Camps

Case	Militarization of refugee camps	Attacks on refugee camps	Attacks or militarization of IDP camps
Angola (1975–1995)[a]	Angolans in Zambia (1 year); Zairian in Angola (2 years)	Angolans in Zambia (1 year)	No reports
Angola (1996–2002)	Angolans in Zambia (3 years); Zairian in Angola (1 year)	Zambia (1 year); Congo (4 years at least); Angolans and Namibians in Namibia (5 years)	Sites protected by the government
Burundi (1993–1994)	No reports	Rwandans in Burundi (2 years); Unconfirmed attacks on Burundi refugees in Rwanda (1 year), not included	No reports
Burundi (1995–1999)	Burundi camps in Rwanda (1 year); Burundi camps in Zaire (1 year); Burundi camps in Tanzania (4 years)	Rwanda camps in Burundi (1 year); Burundi camps in Tanzania (1 year); Fears of attacks on Burundi refugees in Zaire (1 year)	No reports, government protection
Central African Republic (2001–2002)	No reports	No reports	No reports
Democratic Republic of Congo (1996–2001)	Angola (1 year); Rwanda (1 year); Tanzania (2 years); Zambia (1 year)	Rwanda (2 years); Burundi (1 year)	No reports, camps since 2002–2003
Lesotho (1998)	No reports	No reports	No reports
Liberia (1989–1995)	Cote d'Ivoire (1 year)	Sierra Leone (2 years); Guinea (3 years); Cote d'Ivoire (3 years); Liberia (2 years)	Monrovia region (1 year)
Liberia (1999–2003)	No reports	Sierra Leone refugees in Liberia (4 years); Liberian refugees in Guinea (3 years)	Attacks reported for 5 years
Mali (1990)	No reports	No reports	No reports
Mali (1994)	No reports	No reports	No reports
Mozambique (1976–1992)[b]	Zimbabwe (2 years); Zambia (1 year)	Malawi (1 year); Zimbabwe (1 year); Zambia (1 year)	No reports
Niger (1990–1997)	No reports	No reports	No reports

continued

APPENDIX 4.4   Access to Refugee/IDP Camps, continued

Case	Militarization of refugee camps	Attacks on refugee camps	Attacks or militarization of IDP camps
Rwanda (1990–1995)	Rwandans in Uganda (3 years); Rwandans in Tanzania (2 years); Rwandans in Burundi (1 year); Rwandans in Zaire (2 years)	Burundians in Rwanda (1 year)	No reports
Senegal (1990–1995)	No reports	No reports	No reports
Senegal (1997–2001)	Guinea-Bissau (1 year)	No reports	No reports
Sierra Leone (1991–2000)	Sierra Leone camps in Liberia (4 years); Sierra Leone camps in Guinea (3 years)	Sierra Leone camps in Guinea (3 years)	No reports, camps protected
Sudan (1993–2002)	Kenya (1 year); Central African Republic (1 year); Ethiopia (1 year); Uganda (1 year)	Dozens of rebel attacks on camps in Uganda (1 year); Ethiopian settlements in Sudan (2 years); Sudanese People's Liberation Army (SPLA) attacks on camps in Zaire (6 years); Attacks by Sudanese rebels in Kenya (3 years); SPLA raid on camp in Central African Republic (2 years); Attack on Eritrean refugees by Sudanese factions from Eritrea; Skirmishes between Ethiopian refugees and Sudanese troops (1 year)	Attacks started in 2003 with Darfur crisis
Uganda (1994–2002)	No reports	Attacks on Sudanese refugees in Uganda (8 years); Attacks on Ugandan refugees in Congo (1 year)	No reports before 2003

[a]For Angola, the data for years 1975–1987 was missing. Altogether, the data was obtained for eight years and was missing for thirteen years.

[b]For Mozambique, the data for years 1976–1987 was not available. Altogether, the data was collected for five years and was missing for twelve years.

APPENDIX 4.5.   Child Soldiers and Access to IDP/Refugee Camps

Case	Child soldier ratios (%)	Access ratio
Senegal (1997–2001)	0	0.2
Senegal (1990–1995)	0	0
Niger (1990–1997)	0	0
Mali (1990)	0	0
Mali (1994)	0	0
Lesotho (1998)	0	0
Central African Republic (2001–2002)	0	0
Angola (1975–1995)	4	0.5
Burundi (1993–1994)	10	1
Uganda (1996–2002)	22	1
Rwanda (1990–1995)	25	1.5
Sierra Leone (1991–2000)	25	1
Mozambique (1976–1992)	27	1.2
Democratic Republic of Congo (1996–2001)	28	1.3
Angola (1996–2002)	28	1.3
Liberia (1989–1995)	29	1.7
Burundi (1995–1999)	31	1.8
Sudan (1993–2002)	39	2
Liberia (1999–2003)	53	2.4

APPENDIX 4.6   Multiple Regression Assumptions Tests

One-sample Kolmogorov-Smirnov test

	CS ratio	Poverty	Orphans	Access
N	19	16	18	19
Kolmogorov-Smirnov Z	.944	.529	.627	.810
Asymp. Sig. (2-tailed)	.335	.942	.827	.528

This table summarizes the results for normality of distributions of the multiple regression variables. All the variables confirm to normality.

APPENDIX 4.7   Child soldier ratio

The model linearity assumption appears satisfied due to the symmetry of the scatterplot below along the horizontal axis. The data display a slight degree of heteroscedasticity, but this will not prove fatal for the analysis (Mertler and Vannatta 2001, 34).

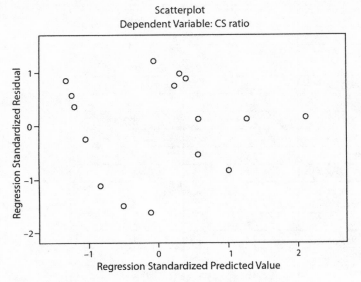

Scatterplot
Dependent Variable: CS ratio

Note: Multicollinearity was found not to be a problem (min. tolerance = 0.910 > 0.1 cutoff value, max. VIF = 1.099 < 10 cutoff value) (Mertler and Vannatta 2001, 169).

CHAPTER 5

RECRUITING CHILDREN FOR ARMED CONFLICT

Jens Christopher Andvig and Scott Gates

DATA ON CHILD RECRUITMENT IN SUB-SAHARAN AFRICA collected by Achvarina and Reich (2006) and Becker's comparison of Sri Lanka, Nepal, and Burma in this volume demonstrate that the proportion of child soldiers varies considerably from one group to another. A wide variety of case studies from around the world also suggests that the welfare of the children employed by violent groups varies across organizations. In this chapter we focus on this variance and examine the patterns of recruitment across different kinds of violent organizations. We also seek to answer the general puzzle of why a group would recruit children to be soldiers.

The Demand and Supply of Child Soldiers

Discussing the demand and supply of child soldier labor may seem callous, but it provides a useful way to think systematically about why an armed group would recruit young adolescents. As detailed in a number of the other chapters in this volume, a variety of factors are associated with the phenomenon of child soldiers. We can categorize these factors as they relate to the supply or demand for children in armed groups.

One structural phenomenon that has altered the demand for child soldiers is the wide availability of new technologies to exploit this especially odious form of child labor. Cheap, easily available weapons, such as the AK-47, as outlined in the chapter by Peter Singer, diminish the inherent advantages of an adult soldier compared to a child soldier. In this way, new, lighter (but more powerful) weapons increase the ability of an armed group to substitute adult labor with child labor.

Material and nonmaterial incentives play an important role in recruitment and retention in any organization. The chapters by Gutiérrez Sanín, Wessells, Singer, and to some extent Pugel, focus on the way groups recruit and maintain their armies. As these authors point out, some groups determine that children may be easier (through coercion, intimidation, or persuasion) to recruit than adults, given the strategic ambitions of the group. Certainly, groups lacking a clear ideological basis may find it easier to maintain the loyalty, and participation, of children. Desertion is a potential problem facing any army, and children often find it harder to desert than adults. To discourage desertion further, some groups force children to commit atrocities in their home village, thus severing former bonds and limiting the child's options. Clearly, demand-based factors play a major role in the variation across countries. Similar contextual factors affect the supply of children available for recruitment or abduction. Achvarina and Reich demonstrate in their chapter that such supply-based factors—for example, the level of poverty and the number of orphans in a population—poorly explain the variance in the incidence of child soldiering across sub-Saharan Africa. The protection and securitization of civilian populations (especially children) prove to be more significant factors. Indeed, as the chapter by Lischer shows, refugee and internally displaced persons (IDP) camps are prime recruiting grounds for armed groups. Children are particularly vulnerable to the siren call of life outside the camp "fighting the good fight," as well as to forced abduction.

Factors such as poverty, education, war, refugee camp securitization, religious or ethnic identity, family or its absence, and friends all play a role in determining the supply of children available for recruitment (Cohn and Goodwin-Gill 1994; Brett and Specht 2004; Achvarina and Reich 2006a; Singer 2006). The dynamic interaction of a rebel group and the government may also affect supply, particularly when government actions provoke grievances and a desire for retribution. Such supply factors are indeed important, but they neglect demand. To understand the demand for child soldiers, we must look more closely into civil wars and violent organizations, as well as understand what motivates the children themselves. Many of the factors that shape supply are rather invariant across many of the conflicts; demand is what determines the actual number of children who are ordered to kill.

Child Soldiering and Child Capabilities

Analysis of child labor in the context of households and farms indicates that (young) children and adults are likely to be employed as complementary goods, while adults' unskilled labor are substitutes. (Informally, a complementary good is one that should be consumed with another good; for example, a printer and an ink cartridge. A substitute good can stand in the place of another good, such as butter and margarine.) The differentiation of task between younger children and adults indicates a complementarity between child and adult labor in a military organization. Classic historical examples of the employment of complementary child labor in a military organization are evident in the squire (attendant to a knight) in feudal Europe or the many young midshipmen who served actively aboard naval vessels in the age of sail.

The main difference between these historical examples and contemporary employment of child soldiers regards the proportion of child soldiers recruited by armed groups. Historically, children constituted only a small share of total soldiers. Today, as other chapters in this volume demonstrate, a large number of groups rely to a high degree on child recruits. Such large proportions of young children indicate that they are employed as substitutes for adults and not as complements. Our central puzzle revolves around why this shift has occurred.

Evidence of physical maturation of children and their (in)ability to fight effectively is incontrovertible. Whether children fundamentally differ with regard to decision-making ability, emotional maturity, and psychological stability is more difficult to assess. Officers of an armed force that employs children assess the relative capabilities of children and adults both in their recruitment and when allocating tasks (these decisions will vary across cultures and the context in which the organization operates). And in some respects, children may be viewed favorably. A Congolese rebel officer summarizes the three main reasons why children make very good soldiers: "they obey orders; they are not concerned with getting back to their wife and family; and they don't know fear" ("Children under Arms" 1999, 22). Indeed, these three characteristics come up again and again in the studies of child soldiers.

When possessing sufficient physical strength, children may in a technical sense substitute for adults to a degree that is surprising given Western attitudes toward and expectations about childhood. The degree to which they may substitute clearly depends on the nature of the tasks to be solved and decisions to be made. In most countries, children must shoulder adult work responsibilities at an earlier age than is accepted in the West. Iversen (2005, 11), based on his research on child migration in India, reaches a fairly clear conclusion: "boys aged 12–14 regularly made labor migration decisions independently of their parents and often without the consent or even informing the parents about their departure." Despite many cultural differences, it is also at about this age that children may seek military employment on their own and solve many of the simpler military tasks independently if employed. Before this age, we may assume that children will be more dependent on older soldiers to conduct more complicated tasks and, more significantly, less able to desert. In this regard, children across cultures follow similar patterns despite widely differing cultural and economic conditions.

While children generally lack the physical capacity of grown men, evidence from Blattman (2007) and others indicates that they exhibit certain tendencies that some military leaders unconstrained by any normative concerns might find appealing. If we treat child soldiers as a labor issue, children beyond a certain age can be regarded as substitutes and not as complements to adult labor.

The Context of Children in Armed Conflict

To Clausewitz's famous adage that "war is nothing but a continuation of political intercourse with the admixture of different means" (1976, 605), one could also add "social and economic relations." Wars where children have become active soldiers now typify the wars of today—"a stalemated guerrilla war confined to a rural periphery of a low-income, post-colonial state" (Fearon 2005). These are also areas where children are engaged in all kinds of adult economic activities. In sub-Saharan Africa, the more rural a country is, the higher the child labor participation rates tend to be.

Based on detailed observations from several long field stays, Shepler (2004) documents that many of the specific ways children are employed in violent organizations of present-day Sierra Leone can be traced back to traditional age group organizations, West African child fosterage traditions, secret societies, and so on. Her presentation gives a most detailed description of how established social and economic forms may have impact on the violent organizations and generate prescriptions for how many and in what way children could be used.

What the extensive economic participation of children in rural areas does explain in the broader sense, however, is that children are more likely to become potential recruits when commanders from their own experience are used to seeing children do the household and farming tasks. This is reinforced by the tendency of the violent organizations to emulate the dominant patterns for organizing economic activities in their neighborhoods and families. The most visible manifestation of the copying of family-based organization is a tendency of the male commanders (and often also soldiers) to acquire "wives" in many of the conflicts.[1] Nonetheless, to explain the variation in the proportion of child soldiers in any given conflict, we need to examine more specific mechanisms, which are most likely found in the violent organizations themselves. Each organization is likely to have its own ways of adapting the established customs regarding child/adult task allocations when recruiting children. Manners of recruitment and socialization vary from group to group. The dramatic variation in child/adult soldier ratios even for a number of African conflicts all taking place in countries dominated by rural populations is reflected in the figures reported in Achvarina and Reich (2006). How can such large variation be explained?

Violent Organizations and Their Demand for Children

A violent organization's guiding aims (not necessarily its professed ones) in many ways define the behavior of the group, including its reasons for recruiting children and its ways of treating them. Since every organization operates under some form of financial constraint, such organizations should only substitute children for adults if they are cost effective. The only formal theoretical discussions of the recruitment of child soldiers we are aware of are Gates (2004) and Blattman (2007). Gates develops his ideas about child recruitment by means of a principal agent model. Put simply, agents of a military organization (that is soldiers) when recruited on a voluntary basis have to receive sufficient utility by joining that they do not run away (the participation constraint). Furthermore, the leadership (the principal) must be able to find a way to reward the soldiers so that they choose to act in a way that will produce the maximum increase of the probability of winning (or sustaining a "profitable" conflict) with the lowest financial costs (incentive compatibility constraint). Hence the leadership may employ children if they are sufficiently cheap to compensate for their (potentially) lower military efficiency.

In another article, Gates (2002) makes the point that nonpecuniary benefits can be used to meet the compatibility and participatory constraints. Indeed, all groups distribute benefits that exhibit a mixture of pecuniary and nonpecuniary rewards. Pecuniary rewards consist of wages, one-shot monetary rewards (often associated with loot), and other tangible rewards such as drugs or alcohol. Indeed, drugs have played a large role in several civil wars (e.g., Liberia and Sierra Leone). A nonpecuniary reward can come in the form of the satisfaction associated with performing a given task. In a military organization, such functional rewards can come with participating in the "good fight." At the other end of the moral spectrum, groups may appeal to the sadistic tendencies of certain elements of any population (thugs and hooligans) by giving them license to commit acts of extreme violence. Rituals, uniforms, and even dark glasses can aid in creating an altered state, enhancing this sense of toughness, which in turn can promote violence (Slim 2008). But it is also a reality that military fighting might be experienced as exciting, particularly when the most likely alternatives are either boring idleness or drudgery. When asked why they became soldiers, 15 percent of the children selected for interviews in the Democratic Republic of Congo, Congo, and Rwanda who had joined one of their violent organizations said fascination with the military was their main reason (ILO/IPEC 2003, 29).

Nonpecuniary benefits can also be seen in the comradeship shared by members of an armed group. Spending day and night together in life-threatening situations can create strong bonds between fellow soldiers. Identity-based groups (i.e., organizations based on ethnicity or religion) also tend to be characterized by higher solidarity preferences than other types of groups. Religious mystical groups such as the Lord's Resistance Army (LRA) in Uganda (Veale and Stavrou 2003, 27) and expressive violent organizations (the Revolutionary United Front [RUF] in Sierra Leone) employ mixes of functional and solidarity benefits.

The extent to which a group can rely on pecuniary benefits depends on the group's resource base. Nonpecuniary benefits, alternatively, can be created by the group and can be used to motivate members instead of material benefits. Leaders have an incentive to inculcate a sense of membership and solidarity and thereby construct an identity for their organization. Indeed, all effective militaries depend on nonpecuniary rewards. Indirect evidence from child psychology indicates that nonpecuniary benefits may be more influential for children than adults (Harbaugh and Krause 1999). It may take less effort on the part of the organization to create solidarity norms for children due to their greater tendency toward altruism and bonding to a group (Blattman 2007).

If children's outside options are sufficiently bad such that they will accept a lower compensation in order to join (and stay), this model predicts that a group would focus its recruitment energy on children. For example, André and Platteau (1998), who happened to collect land tenure data from a Hutu village just before the genocide in Rwanda, demonstrate that adolescents were receiving very little land (against established traditions), while older landholding males were overrepresented among the villagers killed. Richards (1996) also notes that an important reason for the recruitment of youths to rebel organizations in Sierra Leone was their lack of access to land (although absolute scarcity of land was less pronounced than in Rwanda). Given the lack of economic opportunities, the children recruited to these conflicts had less to lose in joining the rebel army. Alternatively, if children are easier to supervise such that fewer resources are needed to maintain some aspect of a command structure, this model again predicts that a group would recruit relatively more children than adults. Members of a military group are kept attached to the organization through three forms of incentives: force, nonpecuniary benefits (which are often linked to ideology, religion, or ethnicity), and economic incentives.

All forms of incentives may in principle be present at the soldier level whatever the forms of leadership motivation. When force is applied in recruitment, force will, of course, be one of the incentives for staying, but both nonpecuniary and pecuniary incentives may be applied to some degree in order to reduce the desertion rate. Here children and adults may possibly differ. From experimental evidence we know that children bond more tightly to a group (Harbaugh and Krause 1999). As a result of this reframing, children may "forget" more quickly that they were recruited by force. Socialization and indoctrination thus play a fundamental role in maintaining allegiance to a group that recruits forcefully (Blattman 2007).

Military activities are in the end decentralized activities where both the final killing and the organizational infrastructure around it need to be improvised. Centralized monitoring is difficult because of classical asymmetric information issues. The risks of death and molestation in battles make it rational for the individual to exit before the battle begins. If many do so, the organization will lose and the remaining members will be exposed to larger risks of death. The incentive to exit for an individual will increase with the number of others exiting, hence the sudden switch from collective fighting to collective exiting when it becomes clear that one's side is losing the battle.

The use of economic incentives to manage a violent organization in any precise way is hampered by strong versions of the classical problems of asymmetric information, collective action, and adverse selection: if recruiting soldiers on the basis of expected economic gain, the organization has a higher risk of getting a mix of members who will tend to run away before a battle or during it with any setback of winning prospects; asymmetric information makes it difficult to reward efforts. Result-oriented selective rewards that may avoid battle desertion imply looting, a risky strategy since the organization will lose local support. To prevent severe collective action problems, the use of force to prevent desertion is obviously necessary and remains necessary even when most soldiers are recruited on an ideological, ethnic, or religious basis and they possess a strong sense of solidarity. In general, nonpecuniary rewards motivate actions when motivation is needed, and they are relatively inexpensive to distribute once an organization is endowed with social factors that promote solidarity and functional benefits. By reducing the severe collective action problems involved in actual fighting, functional rewards and solidarity norms can substantially reduce the need for harsh physical punishment.

But as pointed out by Frey (1997) in a general context (and by Weinstein as applied to violent organizations) both external force and economic rewards may crowd out and destroy intrinsic motivation. Moreover, organizations are not able to choose their incentive mix freely. The ability to create or inculcate intrinsic motivations is severely limited. Ethnic, religious, and ideological

identities from which it is much easier to sculpt solidarity are difficult to create. A group, particularly those that are ideologically or religiously based, may
develop sophisticated socialization mechanisms that inculcate a fierce loyalty
and allegiance to a social movement. Force and economic rewards, however,
may be both managed and more easily combined.[2] Hence, one may expect
significant differences across organizations as to their mix of pecuniary and
nonpecuniary rewards and with respect to how incentives are combined with
harsh punishment to prevent disintegration.

The predictions of Gates's (2004) model follow: more children will be recruited if their military efficiency increases relative to adults', if children's income possibilities outside the organization decline compared to the adults'
outside options (for example, increasing land scarcity may block children's access to land while adults remain holding the land), or if for some reason the
relative cost of monitoring children compared to adults decreases. This will
happen, for example, if the fighting is moving farther away from the soldier's
homestead, since children have lower geographical mobility. The difference
naturally will be larger for younger children. Moreover, if child soldiers are
added to a contest function (modeling the conflict between the rebel group
and the government), they are by implication (when properly weighed for their
lower efficiency) perfect substitutes for adults. Hence, a wide variation in its
adult/child composition would not be surprising—for example, caused by
shifts in their respective participation constraints.

In this chapter we extend Gates's (2004) work, recasting the focus on military organizations' demand for child soldiers to explaining the extreme variance in the use of child soldiers across groups, even within similar economic
and cultural contexts. In particular, we examine the role of force as it is used
to abduct recruits and prevent desertion, topics not fully developed by Gates
(2004).

Motivations, Group Endowments, and the Demand for Child Soldiers

A dominant theme in conflict research during the last decade or so has been
the role of economic factors in causing violent conflicts. For some time this
led to a rather fruitless debate over whether greed or grievances served as the
chief motivation for groups to take up arms against the state.[3] The general
problem is that professed motivations (and alleged motivations) do not necessarily coincide with "real" or ultimate motivations. This is a hermeneutic problem. Can we ever know whether politics or religion provides the fundamental
motivation for groups in Chechnya or in the Middle East? Equally difficult is
deciding whether money or politics provides the fundamental motivation for
other groups, which finance their operations through lootable resources such

as opium, cocaine, or diamonds. Also difficult to determine is whether professed goals are for a broad public who are not members of the military group or for the group members themselves. As in other contexts, the actors may have good reasons for trying to misrepresent their goals (and those of their adversaries). Religion may be a pretext for politics, and politics a pretext for money. The hermeneutic issue is how to impute motivations when statements about motivation may themselves be motivated.

While we may not be able to uncover the ultimate motivation for a group (or at least its leadership), groups do exhibit behavioral tendencies, and we can make assumptions about such motivations on the basis of the resource endowment of a group, which will affect the ability and the form of rewards a group allocates to its subordinates. Weinstein (2007) examines two types of leadership motivation and asks how they may arise and be sustained. He points out that if a rebel movement initially has access to large economic endowments (easy looting, control of diamonds, and so on) compared to social endowments (shared identities, ideology, and social networks) it may drive out political altruism in the organization, a kind of rebellion's natural resource curse. The chapters in this volume by Gutiérrez Sanín and Pugel point to the kinds of variation across groups in these regards.

Selective economic incentives are expensive and most rebel organizations are poor even when their violence activities are the most individually remunerative in the neighborhood. Hence, their leaders will try to restrict the number of members allowed to share in the net income. Again physical punishment is useful to restrict access, but there are also reasons to expect that children are more easily kept away from sharing; thus organizations that rely on economic incentives have more to gain financially by employing children. In Mozambique, for example, Renamo made extensive use of economic incentives when they were receiving substantial economic support from South Africa. When that support disappeared, Renamo began to rely on forced recruitment and to recruit children, some very young. Almost 9 percent of the recorded, demobilized Renamo soldiers were ten years old or younger (Weinstein 2007). In Northern Uganda, where LRA was relying on forced recruitment, the leadership appears to have preferred very young recruits since the average abduction ages increase at the later stages of the war when prospective abductees were more difficult to catch (Blattman 2007).

Both economically and socially endowed organizations may apply force in order to recruit members, but on average one would expect that voluntary recruits of socially endowed organizations would be motivated by nonpecuniary benefits and voluntary recruits of economically endowed organizations would be motivated by material rewards. Indeed, the underlying motivation of an organization is likely to affect a group's demand for children. Different groups are likely to recruit children for different reasons and to treat them differently once they have joined.

In the preceding discussion we have presented the possibilities in terms of dichotomies, as does Weinstein. There is, however, no inherent reason that a group must distribute material rewards at the expense of nonmaterial benefits. Pecuniary and nonpecuniary benefits are often jointly evident, as when a child defends his own right to his homestead as part of his tribe's control of the right of the land to which his homestead is a part. Moreover, socialization can serve to overcome the nature of a group's resource endowment.

Nonetheless, if economic endowments do serve to crowd out nonpecuniary social benefits as proposed by Weinstein (2007), after a while greed-based organizations may reveal themselves as such and will receive fewer ideologically committed recruits. The fraction that has to be recruited by force will tend to increase over time. While not empirically well documented, children who are recruited by force may have lower desertion rates than adults recruited the same way. This applies more clearly for younger children. It is more difficult for them to desert. Hence, we expect the fraction of child soldiers in small-scale, economically endowed violent organizations to increase over time.

Considering the relative costs of recruitment, the fraction of child soldiers should be considerably higher than in socially endowed organizations. Pecuniary rewards (i.e., money, loot, or other material selective incentives) are often used to entice and to maintain participation (Gates 2002, 2004; Humphreys and Weinstein 2006a; Olson 1971). Moreover, given extensive hunger, poverty, youth unemployment, and the absence of educational opportunities, joining an armed group may be a relatively attractive opportunity, thereby reducing the material incentives required (e.g., Brett and Specht 2004; Honwana 2006; ILO/IPEC 2003; Machel 1996).

In some African countries the main grievances are actually held by the older children and youth, who may have lost traditional access to land and marriage (André and Platteau 1998; Richards 1996). Hence we may expect a large share of children among the grievance-motivated recruits and even among the commanders. In the extreme case of Mindanao, where whole families are actively engaged (Cagoco-Guiam 2002), the share of children may also be quite high (but not in command), reflecting the demographic state of the area, but presumably the younger children will be kept away from the most risky tasks.

In either case, the scale of the fighting is also likely to be important for the share of children to be recruited. If heavy, expensive, and complex weapons or the disciplined coordination of large units of soldiers are necessary, children are less useful. Research on child labor in general suggests that children have rarely been given responsibility for technically complex and expensive equipment. There is no reason to believe it will be otherwise in child soldiering. Indeed, when a group does possess advanced technologies, children are not put in charge. Kids do not pilot helicopters. Furthermore, if the group is engaged in a low-intensity guerilla war, it is easier to organize consumption in the military units in the same way as in ordinary households, so they will include many tasks that are ordinarily performed by children and will demand more children for noncombatant tasks.

Organizations that have developed sophisticated socialization mechanisms are likely to handle collective actions better and therefore to rely less on force as long as the members stay strongly motivated. That motivation embraces not only direct military task solving, but also the motivation to monitor and discipline the other members. Decentralized monitoring is essential in many military situations that are uncontrollable from the command center. The resulting discipline appears to be essential for the welfare of the child soldiers (and women soldiers). Children and youth tend to be at least as strongly motivated as the communities from where they have joined. The leadership would on average need to treat their members at an acceptable level, including the children. In addition to internal reasons for it, some of the political costs of bad treatment and forced recruitment of children will be internalized. The strength of political motivation is fickle, however, and may quickly decline. As pointed out already, these organizations would also need to apply extensive force in order to keep its collective action problems within bounds and to recruit new manpower. The case of Sri Lanka substantiates this point. Internal fighting between northern and eastern Tamil factions has caused the Liberation Tigers of Tamil Eelam (LTTE) forces to lose legitimacy, and they are now applying more force when re-recruiting children, evidently expecting a new outbreak of the civil war (Becker 2004b).

Organizational Structure and the Welfare of Child Soldiers

To gain a better understanding of differences in organizational culture, we examine the application of force as a selective incentive. A violent organization must produce violence as a major part of its output. When the violence apparatus is already there, it is tempting to apply it for other purposes. It may be used both for recruitment of soldiers and as a (negative) incentive for controlling the behavior of the members after recruitment. It is selective in the sense that it is meted out to individuals, but it has also important spillover effects by creating general fear either among members or the population at large. While the spillover effects may reinforce the original selective effects, they are obviously imprecise. The fear may make soldiers more obedient or make them desert. Fear may break resistance against recruitment or increase the efforts of potential recruits to hide.

In his exceptionally well-documented research from northern Uganda, Blattman (2007) examines how the benefits and costs of recruits varied systematically with age. He finds that although adult recruits were generally regarded by the leaders of the LRA to be better soldiers ("more skilled as guerrilla fighters"), "adolescent (twelve- to fourteen-year-old) recruits yielded the largest expected net gain to the rebel leader." One of the principal problems was that adults were more likely to desert. Moreover, "adolescents and younger children were more easily indoctrinated and disoriented (and thus likely to stay) but were relatively ineffective as fighters" (Blattman 2007, 1). Blattman's field research in northern Uganda demonstrates that children respond differently from adults to forced recruitment.

As pointed out in Wiles (1977, 15–16), to make threats of force effective, there must be some form of restraint on physical mobility. It is much easier to run away from a military organization operating in an unclear or divided area of control than it is from a jail or an area under strict control. The lack of mobility of young children relative to adults makes force more efficient in their case. Forcing children to perform abhorrent public killing against, and in front of, former neighbors is one way to restrain mobility.

Mutual monitoring induced by the shared negative consequences of desertion is a further barrier. Organizations such as the RUF in Sierra Leone established a buddy system, in which children are paired. If a child's buddy deserts, the remaining child is punished, with the penalty often being death. A violent organization needs to consider the effects of any given mix of incentives and its recruitment mechanisms when choosing its child soldier ratio.

Another important organizational variable is the degree to which the structure of the organization is personalized. Children may more easily adjust to the latter form of management, which may be one of many reasons why child soldiering is mainly observed in poor countries where a personalized management style is still quite common. As pointed out by Weinstein (2007), violent organizations with high social endowments are likely to use it to greater advantage and receive a higher share of voluntarily recruited children. Shepler (2004) describes how personal ties to commanders were important both in the recruiting and management of children in Sierra Leone. Children's need for security, to have someone to love and respect, may be transferred to military commanders.

An obvious factor is the nature of war and the kind of violence the children become involved in personally. "Indoctrination into the LRA was a complex process of spiritual training, misinformation, and the strategic use of fear and violence" (Blattman 2007, 18). Shepler describes a similar process in the RUF in Sierra Leone (2004). Further, as a means of breaking down the recruit's

psychological defenses, adolescent recruits are often forced to engage in violence, particularly in their home community, thereby foreclosing an option of
escaping and returning home (Honwana 2006; Singer 2005). While the study
on Central Africa did not ask in a systematic way about the punishment the
children were exposed to in case they disobeyed, a regime of harsh punishment and fear among the children evidently prevailed. Fear was both a cause
for staying as well as for joining.[4] When the children from Mindanao, on the
other hand, were asked what happened if they did not follow orders, 62 percent
answered nothing would happen. Their participation was voluntary. Indeed,
the atmosphere in Mindanao appears strikingly different than in Uganda, as
does the welfare of the children who joined. Since the children who joined the
Mindanao movement could stay in their home area most of the time, they did
not lose contact with their family and could also even (with some interrup-
tions) continue their studies at school.

The Market for Child Soldiering

To best understand why there are so many children participating in some military organizations and few or none in others, we need not only look at demand
and supply in isolation but also examine how supply and demand interact. Children's voluntary supply and the area characteristics—the ease with which they
may be recruited by force—constitutes the supply side. While Gates (2004)
presupposes an equilibrium solution, even though the supply side of his model
is extremely rudimentary, such an equilibrium condition may not exist. Given
the possibility of forced recruitment as well as the high child unemployment
rates in many areas in which the violent organizations operate, the child soldier
ratio may not be an equilibrium outcome, although that is certainly a possibility. Indeed, while it is possible that the market for child soldiers is efficient, it
is unlikely.

  Situations of pure excess demand occur when a violent organization tries
to get more recruits than it is able to acquire of both adults and children. Here
the supply side should determine the child/adult rate.[5] If, for some reason, a
violent organization refrains from the use of force when recruiting both adults
and children, then the child/adult ratio will be determined by the voluntary
supply functions. The supply of child soldiers relative to adults will be affected
by the distribution of landownership and prospects of inheritance for children,
the stock of orphans,[6] family cohesion, child poverty levels (which will be influenced by differential birth rates by different sectors of the population), child
unemployment rates, and so on. In addition, children's expectations about
their welfare after joining the violent organization are important and may also
differ from those of adults. Excess demand situations may also arise in the final

days for a military force that is losing. Nazi Germany and the American Confederate army both employed child soldier volunteers as well as senior citizens in the final days of those odious regimes.

Excess demand may be resolved through forced recruitment, but an organization still may be unable to obtain all the recruits it demands (when forced recruits are not paid, demand may increase). In such a case, the child soldier ratio will be influenced additionally by the characteristics of the accessibility of recruits, including the proportion of usable children versus adults in the area; the ease of capturing a child compared to an adult; and the existence of exceptionally good "fishing grounds," such as refugee camps or secondary schools. Even in this case the perceived excess demand will be influenced by the nature of the military contest. For example, in the face of losing battles, an organization is likely to experience excess demand.

For groups with well-developed socialization mechanisms and with the ability to meet participatory and compatibility constraints through the distribution of functional rewards and solidarity norms, a condition of excess demand will also mean that supply conditions dictate. We expect to see no significant differences between socially and materially endowed groups under conditions of excess demand.

Under conditions of pure excess supply situations, the characteristics and the policy of the violent organization will determine the child soldier ratio. The leadership's view about the desirable ratio will be instrumental. Let us again look at a couple of cases. When a violent organization relies only on voluntary recruitment methods and the distribution of economic incentives, excess supply means that at the going rates the organization may recruit as many children and adults as it wants as long as it is able to meet the participation and compatibility constraints of the recruits. Hence, the leadership decides the number of children (and, by implication, the child/adult ratio) on the basis of the expected profitability (taking into account the chances of victory in military contests) of their numbers and their mix. The child/adult ratio in this situation is based on cost and efficiency. Assessing the relative cost efficiency of assigning children or adults to a range of tasks would be critical. Fighting would constitute only one of these tasks.

The case when a violent organization also recruits forcibly is in many ways quite similar. One may of course question the use of the term "excess supply" in cases when force is used. The idea is that the recruitment area contains such rich fishing grounds that it is always able to catch the desired proportion of either adults and/or children and could acquire more on the same terms if the group so desired. The size of the organization may be constrained either by a lack of capital (especially with regard to the ability to acquire weapons) or by the nature of the war (especially with regard to its intensity and duration). The choice of the desired ratio is also in this case determined by the cost effectiveness of children compared to adults, but the ratio is likely to be different. Furthermore, the optimal child soldier ratio will be higher in forced recruitment situations for the reasons outlined above regarding the general differences between children and adults, confirmed by the Uganda case.

When a group decides on a recruitment method, the possible interference on the cost efficiency between the methods should also be considered.[7] In any case, the observed child soldier ratio will be determined as a kind of average of the forced and voluntary rates of recruitment.

For groups with well-developed socialization mechanisms in a situation of excess supply, recruitment is more selective. Under such conditions, ideological, ethnic, and religious criteria may be imposed in addition to a soldier's ability to engage in violent activity. Children are likely to be viewed as second-best labor and fewer of them will be recruited. Forced recruitment is also unlikely to be employed. Such organizations operating under conditions of excess supply will tend to have low child/adult soldier ratios.

If a group is richly endowed both socially and materially, Weinstein's argument that material endowments will crowd out social endowments is unlikely to occur under conditions of excess supply. Because groups can be picky, they will choose those soldiers most positively predisposed toward certain nonpecuniary benefits (while taking into account the soldiers' abilities). Identifying which individuals are more positively predisposed toward solidarity norms and functional benefits will be easier for identity-based groups in which the criteria for selection is based on already belonging to a particular ethnic or religious group. For purely ideological groups, candidates may have to demonstrate their commitment to the cause, particularly through sacrifice.

When supply and demand reach equilibrium, marginal conditions dictate recruitment patterns. Equilibrium may occur under different child/adult soldier ratios depending primarily on the nature of the war being fought. Military organizations engaged in direct competition with many battles will favor adults over children regardless of the nature of their resource endowment. Groups will also distribute a mix of pecuniary and nonpecuniary benefits to ensure that members' participatory and compatibility constraints are met. These conditions follow more directly from Gates (2004), such that the child-soldier ratio will increase as children's military efficiency increases relative to adults', children's income possibilities outside the organization decline relative to adults' outside options, or the cost of monitoring a child relative to an adult decreases.

Summary

In order to understand the phenomenon of child soldiers, we also must understand the nature of the market for soldiers in general for both governmental forces and for groups fighting against the state.

Most research on the phenomenon of child soldiers has focused on factors that affect the supply of child soldiers (i.e., the relative proportion of children available for recruitment). The main argument of this chapter is that to understand the great variation in the child/adult ratios across military organizations, we must look at the demand for child soldiers in addition to supply factors. This point is echoed in the chapters by Gutiérrez Sanín and Pugel. Several variables play a key role in determining violent groups' demand for child soldiers. The organizational structure of the military group is especially important. Groups based on personal leadership are more likely to have a higher child/adult soldier ratio. The nature of a group's resource endowment is also an important factor, especially under conditions of equilibrium and excess supply. If a military group is unlikely to engage another army militarily, the physical differences between adults and children are minimized and they become substitutes for one another.

We do not mean to imply that contextual factors are irrelevant; however, such variables may not impact the child/adult soldier ratio directly. As described by Fearon (2005), long-lasting low-intensity conflicts fought by violent organizations operating in rural neighborhoods are explained by a variety of political and economic variables. Moreover, the contextual factors highlighted by the chapter by Achvarina and Reich, such as the orphan rate and the level of poverty in the area, dictate the supply of children that can be recruited voluntarily by a military group. These conditions, however, do not vary much from one war zone to another (though refugee and IDP camp securitization does). Indeed, supply factors alone cannot explain the big variance in child-soldier ratios across violent organizations operating in similar areas. Moreover, the fluctuations in the fortunes of war can cause strong shifts in supply and demand (when losing, the demand goes up and supply down). Ultimately though, the child-soldier ratio is determined mainly by the policies and characteristics of the organizations themselves, not by the characteristics of the areas in which they operate.

CHAPTER 6

THE ENABLERS OF WAR

Causal Factors behind the Child Soldier Phenomenon

P. W. Singer

WHILE WARFARE HAS LONG BEEN THE DOMAIN OF ADULTS, juveniles have been present in armies in a number of instances in the past. For example, young pages armed the knights of the Middle Ages and drummer boys marched before Napoleonic armies. Child soldiers even fought in the U.S. Civil War, most notably when a unit of 247 Virginia Military Institute cadets fought with the Confederate army in the battle of New Market in 1864. More recently, U.S. forces fought against small numbers of underage Hitler Jugend (Hitler Youth) in the closing weeks of World War II.

However, these were the exceptions to what the rule used to be, that children had no place in war. Throughout the last four thousand years of war as we know it, children were never an integral, essential part of any military forces in history. But the rules of war have changed. The participation of children is now not a rarity, but instead a growing feature of war.

The practice of child soldiers is far more widespread, and more important, than most realize. There are as many as 300,000 children under the age of eighteen presently serving as combatants around the globe. Their average age is just over twelve years old. The youngest ever was an armed five-year-old in Uganda. The youngest terrorist bomber was a seven-year-old in Colombia. Roughly 30 percent of the armed forces that employ child soldiers also include girl soldiers. Underage girls have been present in armed groups in fifty-five countries.[1]

Children now serve in 40 percent of the world's armed forces, rebel groups, and terrorist organizations and fight in almost 75 percent of the world's conflicts; indeed, from 2002 to 2007, children have served as soldiers on every continent but Antarctica. An additional half million children serve in armed forces not presently at war. The children are often abducted to fight and participate in all the full horrors of war; indeed they are sometimes forced to carry out atrocities that adults shy away from.

With the global deployment of U.S. forces after 9/11, from Afghanistan to the Philippines, child soldiers are present in every conflict zone U.S. forces now operate in. Indeed, the very first U.S. soldier killed in the war on terrorism was a Green Beret killed by a fourteen-year-old sniper in Afghanistan. At least six young boys between the ages of thirteen and sixteen have been captured by U.S. forces in Afghanistan in the initial fighting and were taken to the detainee facility at Guantanamo Bay, Cuba. They were housed in a special wing entitled Camp Iguana. As the Pentagon took more than a year to figure out whether to prosecute or rehabilitate them, the kids spent their days in a house on the beach converted into a makeshift prison, watching DVDs (their favorites were *Castaway* and *Call of the Wild*) and learning English and math. In Iraq, the problem has grown to great concern. U.S. forces have fought children in at least seven Iraqi cities, including during house-to-house fighting in Falluja, in which Marines talked about the difficulty of "fighting kids armed with assault rifles." More than two hundred kids were held at the notorious Abu Ghraib prison.

The result is that war in the twenty-first century is not only more prevalent, but also more tragic. With children's involvement, warlords, terrorists, and rebel leaders alike are finding that conflicts are easier to start. In turn, wars are harder to end, such that the wars drag on, consuming societies and childhood itself for literally hundreds of thousands of children. A particularly troubling aspect then is not only what happens during the fighting, but also the legacy it leaves for children after the fighting is done. That is, recovery from the traumas of war is hard enough; it is all the more difficult when the soldier in question is a child.

The Rules against Recruiting Child Soldiers

The recruitment and employment of child soldiers is one of the most flagrant violations of the norms of international human rights. Besides being contrary to the general practices of the past four millennia of warfare, there are a number of treaties that attempt to prohibit it today.

At the international level, these treaties have been codified into law. They include the 1945 Universal Declaration of Human Rights, the Geneva Conventions of 1949, the 1977 Additional Protocols to the Geneva Conventions, and the 1989 Convention on the Rights of the Child. Additionally, the UN Security Council, the UN General Assembly, the UN Commission on Human Rights, and the International Labor Organization are among the international bodies that have condemned the practice. There has also been a global grassroots effort against it, embodied in the Coalition to Stop the Use of Child Soldiers, an umbrella group of NGOs based in over forty countries. At the regional level, the Organization for African Unity, the Economic Community of West African States, the Organization of American States, the Organization for Security and Cooperation in Europe, and the European Parliament have also denounced the use of child soldiers.

In May 2000, the UN General Assembly adopted a new optional protocol to the 1989 Convention on the Rights of the Child, further illustrating the growing global sentiment against the use of child soldiers. This measure specifically targeted the phenomenon by formally raising the minimum age of recruitment and use to eighteen years old (the old convention limit was fifteen, which most armed groups would still be in violation of anyway). It has since been signed by more than one hundred states.

Unfortunately, the growing and global practice of child soldiers illustrates just how extensively this long list of conventions and laws is ignored. The recruitment and use of child soldiers is a deliberate and systematic choice currently being made the world over. Simply put, children fighting on the battlefield has become normal practice in current warfare. Thus, rather than compliance these prohibitive norms have been turned inside out. That is, going by actual behavior, child soldiering is the new standard rather than its ban.

The underlying causes behind these deliberate violations of international standards are complex. They involve three critical factors that form a causal chain: (1) social disruptions and failures of development caused by globalization, war, and disease have led not only to greater global conflict and instability but also to generational disconnections that create a new pool of potential recruits; (2) technological improvements in small arms now permit these child recruits to be effective participants in warfare; and (3) there has been a rise in a new type of conflict that is far more brutal and criminalized. These forces have resulted in the viability of a new doctrine of how to operate and succeed in war, particularly in the context of weakening or failed states. Conflict group leaders now see the recruitment and use of children to be a low-cost and efficient way for their organizations to mobilize and generate force. The rules against child soldiers be damned.

The Lost Generation

The desperate position in which many children around the world find themselves is almost unimaginable. While positive in some terms, the developments of globalization that dominated the last quarter century have left many behind, as well as rending traditional societies and mores. The developed world saw great prosperity from the opening of economies, but this certainly did not produce a homogenous world economy or culture with affluence for all. Indeed, three billion people, roughly half the world's population, presently subsist on two dollars a day or less, over 1 billion live in countries in civil war, 800 million have insufficient food, and 1.3 billion lack access to clean water (Collier 2003; Population International Institute 2003; Renner 1998, 275; UN Human Settlements Program 2003).

The brunt of these socioeconomic problems has fallen on the youngest segments of the population as we are now in the midst of the largest generation of youth in human history. Unprecedented numbers of children around the world are undereducated, malnourished, marginalized, and disaffected. Almost a quarter of the world's youth survive on less than a dollar a day. As many as 250 million children live on the street; 211 million children must work to feed themselves and their families; and 115 million children have never been to school (U.S. Department of Labor 2003; UNFPA 2003).

These desperate and excluded children constitute a huge pool of labor for the illegal economy, organized crime, and armed conflicts. In describing the concurrent risks, Juan Somavi, secretary-general of the World Social Summit, notes, "We've replaced the threat of the nuclear bomb with the threat of a social bomb" (Renner 1998, 273).

As the world population continues to swell from the present 6 billion to 9 billion by 2025, these pressures will worsen. With the depletion of nonrenewable energy stocks, high-quality agricultural land, water resources, and fisheries, resource scarcities are growing at the same time demand is rising by greater amounts. For example, estimates are that, by 2025, two-thirds of the world's population will face severe shortages of water (Population International Institute 2003). As these social, economic, environmental, and political problems come together, some analysts worry that the problems will feed off of each other. They fret about a cascading breakdown of our increasingly complex ecological, political, and economic systems, and have even come up with a new term for it, "synchronous failure" (Homer-Dixon 2003). While this may be the ultimate nightmare scenario, it is clear that the disconnection between growing population needs and supplies sharply increases the general demands on state and society while simultaneously decreasing their ability to meet them. Research indicates that the result is invariably socioeconomic fragmentation, a weakening of the state's legitimacy, and ensuing violent conflict (Homer-Dixon 1994; Nichiporuk 2001; Platteau and André 1996, 1–39). Conflict groups are well aware of these gaps and sometimes seek to exploit them. They can widen the gap by intentionally undermining social stability or even seek to gain strength and support by serving as surrogates for the social services that healthy societies and capable governments would normally be able to deliver. For instance, in war-ravaged Lebanon, the Hezbollah group has taken over the entire realm of social services, from hospitals to schools, creating a reliance on the armed group.

Other catastrophes, such as famine and disease outbreaks, underscore this broad trend of disconnection and distress among growing numbers of youth around the world. Of particular worry is the enduring nature of the AIDS epidemic in the developing world, particularly sub-Saharan Africa. Determinedly, this is where the center of the child soldier phenomenon lies (Singer 2002). The disease is altering the very demographics of the region, with terrifying consequences for both stability and security.

AIDS does not strike with equal weight across age groups. In a "unique phenomenon in biology," the disease actually reverses death rates to strike hardest at mature, but not yet elderly, adults.[2] The consequence is that population curves shift (eliminating the typical middle-aged hump), almost directly opposite to the manner of previous epidemics. Such a shift in demographics is worrisome. Recent research has found a strong correlation between violent outbreaks, ranging from wars to terrorism, and the proportion of young males to the overall population (Mesquida and Weiner 1999; Morin 2001; *Profiles* 1999). Once the ratio of young males grows too far out of balance, violent conflict tends to ensue. AIDS will likely cause this in several states already close to this dangerous threshold.

This process is known as "coalitional aggression." Young men, who are considered psychologically more aggressive, naturally compete for social and material resources in all societies. When outnumbering other generations, however, there are inevitably more losers than winners among the youth in this process. Moreover, the typical stabilizing influences of elders are lessened by the overall mass of youth. These lost youths are more easily harnessed into more pernicious activities that can lead to conflict. For example, demagogues, warlords, and criminals all find it easier to recruit when a large population of angry, listless young men fill the street. Riots and other social crises are also more likely. In a sense, it is conflict caused from the bottom up, rather than the top down. While such a correlation is certainly a simplistic explanation of violence, the disturbing fact is that the pattern has held true across history. Outbreaks of violence from ancient Greek wars to recent societal breakdowns in Rwanda, Yugoslavia, and the Congo were all presaged by similar demographic patterns.

At the same time, the factors that disconnect the children from the structure of society also debilitate the very institutions needed to solidify the state and prevent conflict. For example, estimates of HIV infection rates among regional armies in Africa include 50 percent in Congo and Angola, 66 percent in Uganda, 75 percent in Malawi, and 80 percent in Zimbabwe (Bisseker 1998). This devastates their ability to maintain the peace or resist new rebel and warlord groups. Similar hollowing-out is occurring in many other government agencies and parts of the economy in AIDS-hit regions.

Added to these socioeconomic trends is the continuing prevalence of global conflict; the result is an often-dangerous mix. While many hoped for a new world order after the end of the cold war in 1989, the real order that came about was that of peace in the West, war for the rest. About half the ongoing wars in the world are entering their second generation of prospective fighters. In such extended conflicts, children have grown up surrounded by violence and often see it as a permanent way of life. These children are also valued as a potential source of new recruits. For example, the head of a Karen rebel training camp in Burma describes how he brought his own twelve-year-old son into the fight. "I took him out of school in the third grade to turn him into a military man. I thought that if he studies now, he'll just have to fight later. Better to fight now, and learn later when there is time for it" (Anderson 1992, 161).

In addition to witnessing fighting and bloodshed, children who grow up in the midst of war usually lack basic necessities (schools, health care, adequate shelter, water, and food), face disrupted family relationships, and even experience increased patterns of family violence (Smith 2001). The totality of this environment makes it difficult for communities to foster healthy cognitive and social development. A weakened social structure is then generally unable to steer their children away from war.

Children are also typically forced from homes and stable environments during fighting. The UN High Commissioner for Refugees (UNHCR) estimates that there are some 25 million uprooted children in the world, having become either cross-border refugees or internally displaced persons (IDPs). Each day, 5,000 more children become refugees (UNFPA 2003, 8). Children tend to remain in this situation an average of six to seven years, making them highly vulnerable to recruitment (Save the Children Fund UK 2000).[3]

It is estimated that one out of every 200 of the world's children suffers from a war-related psychological malady (Save the Children 2000). The impact of this is only starting to be understood. War is thought to have an all-encompassing impact on child development. It envelops children's attitudes, relationships, moral values, and the framework through which they understand society and life itself (Jacobs 1991, 6). Having been exposed to horrible violence during key developmental stages of their life, many children come to accept it as a perfectly normal part of their existence. As one child in Northern Uganda describes, "If you are under 20 and living here, you have known virtually nothing else your whole life but what it is like to live in a community enduring armed conflict—conflict in which you are a prime target" (Women's Commission for Refugee Women and Children 2001, 8).

All this gives a new meaning to the moniker of "the lost generation." The overwhelming majority of child soldiers are drawn from the poorest, least educated, and most marginalized sections of society, who have been forced to grow up in what one writer called a "roving orphanage of blood and flame" (Bergner 2003, 45).

Children who are forcibly recruited are usually from special risk groups: street children, the rural poor, refugees, and others displaced (those most vulnerable to efficient recruiting sweeps). Those who choose to enlist on their own are often from the very same groups, driven to do so by poverty, propaganda, and alienation. The combination of unimaginable misery many children face and the normalization of violence in their lives can lead them to search for a sense of control over their chaotic and unpredictable situations. Research on child development indicates that they will then be more likely to seek out and join armed groups that provide protection or adhere to ideologies that provide this sense of order, regardless of the content (Punamäki 1996). Those who find themselves to be victims often construct their identity along such lines. Such "victim motivation" can also become a motivation to commit acts of violence of their own, in a bid for preemptive protection or revenge (Stichick and Bruderlein 2001). The tragic result is that these coping strategies place children in further danger and feed further cycles of violence.

The Advantages of Small Arms Weaponry

Concurrent with this trend of socioeconomic disconnection has been the proliferation and technological advancement of personal weaponry. This development is a key enabler, without which the earlier trend would not matter. Technological changes are what allow this broadened pool of potential recruits to be turned into able soldiers.

When thinking about military operations, we typically focus on the most complex and expensive weapons systems, such as missiles, tanks, and aircraft carriers. For most conflicts around the globe, however, this picture is inaccurate. Instead, the weapons that shape contemporary warfare the most are the ones that are the simplest and least costly.

These "small arms" or "light weapons" include rifles, grenades, light machine guns, light mortars, land mines, and other weapons that are "man-portable"(a term often used by the military). Even though they represent less than 2 percent of the entire global arms trade in terms of cost, small arms are perhaps the most deadly of all weapons to society (Salopek 2002; Smith and Stohl 1999). They are the weapons most often used both in battle and in attacks on civilians and have produced almost 90 percent of all casualties in recent wars (Klare 1999). In just West Africa alone more than 2 million people were killed by small arms in the last decade (Neild 2000). Indeed, modern small arms can rend the fabric of civil society like no other weapon; with them, a small, relatively weak group can easily turn a peaceful country into a man-made humanitarian disaster.

Technological and efficiency advances in these weapons now permit the transformation of children into fighters just as lethal as any adult. For most of human history, weapons relied on the brute strength of the operator. They also typically required years of training to master. This was obviously prohibi-tive to the effective use of children as soldiers. A child who was not physically mature could not bear the physical burdens of serving in the phalanx of the ancient Greek hoplites or carrying the weight of medieval knight's armor, let alone serve as an effective combatant. Even until just a few generations ago, personal battlefield weapons such as the bolt action rifles of World War II were still heavy and bulky, limiting children's participation (Center for Defense In-formation 1997).

However, there have been many recent improvements in manufacturing, such as the incorporation of plastics. This now means that modern weapons, particularly automatic rifles, are so light that small children can use them as easily and effectively as adults. They are no longer just man-portable but are child-portable as well. Just as important, most of these weapons have been sim-plified in their use, to the extent that they can be stripped, reassembled, and fired by a child younger than ten. The ubiquitous Russian-designed Kalash-nikov AK-47, which weighs ten and a half pounds, is a prime example. Having only nine moving parts, it is brutally simple. Interviews reveal that it generally takes children around thirty minutes to learn their use. The weapon is also de-signed to be exceptionally hardy. It requires little maintenance and can even be buried in dirt for storage (something guerilla groups often do as a sort of insur-ance policy, in case a cease-fire breaks down).

At the same time as these improvements in simplicity and ruggedness, vast strides have been made in the lethality of personal weapons. The weapons that children can now fire with ease are a far cry from the spears of the phalanx or the single bolt rifle of the GIs. Since World War II, there has been a steady and multiplicative increase in the destructive power of small arms. With just one pull of the trigger, a modern assault rifle in the hands of a child can release a burst of thirty bullets that are lethal more than four hundred yards away. Or, they can shoot off a rocket propelled grenade, whose explosions can tear down buildings. Thus, a handful of children now can have the equivalent firepower of an entire regiment of Napoleonic infantry. When targeting unarmed civilians, the results are doubly devastating. Hence, with only a few hours' training, a youngster can be taught all he or she needs to know in order to kill or wound hundreds of people in a matter of minutes.

Not only have these weapons become easier to use and far more deadly; they have also proliferated in number, to the extent that there is almost a glut in the market. There are an estimated 500 million small arms present on the global scene, one for every twelve persons on the planet (Cobb 2001). The consequence is that the primary weapons of war have also steeply fallen in price over the last few decades. This has made it easier for any willing organization to obtain them and then turn children into soldiers at a minimal cost.

The irony is that this proliferation of small arms partially resulted from the cold war's "peace dividend." After the fall of the Berlin Wall, millions of weapons were declared surplus. Instead of being destroyed, however, it was cheaper to dump them on the world market. For example, when the two Germanys combined in 1990, the entire weapons stock of the East German army was auctioned off, much of it to private bidders. The result was literally tons of light weapons available at cut-rate prices. Light machine guns went for just sixty dollars, land mines for nineteen dollars, and pistols for eight dollars (Bonn International Center for Conversion 1997). These stocks were added to the masses of weapons that had already been given to superpower proxies during the cold war. Moreover, many ended up in the hands of arms brokers and gunrunners who had no compunctions about their final destination or use. The result is that as much as 40–60 percent of the small arms around the world are now in the hands of illicit organizations (Cobb 2001).

Even with this dump of weaponry, however, manufacturing has continued apace for the past few decades, as weapons industries, particularly in the former Soviet bloc, have tried to stay afloat. The result is that there is no place around the globe where small arms are not startlingly cheap and easily accessible. More important, they tend to be concentrated in the most violence-prone areas. This phenomenon was so particularly evident with the Soviet AK-47 type assault rifle and its knock-offs that one analyst even coined the phrase "Kalashnikov Age" to describe how the 1990s saw their spread around the world and impact on global conflict levels (Klare 1999). For example, in just postwar Mozambique there were around 6 million AK-47s for a population of roughly 16 million (Aird 2001). For a period of time, they were even used as a form of currency (Stavou and Stewart 2000). In Uganda and Sudan, an AK-47 can be purchased for the cost of a chicken; in northern Kenya, it can be bought for the price of a goat (the equivalent is about five dollars) (Smith and Vines 1997). In South Africa, AK-47s are just slightly more expensive, valued on the market at twelve dollars each.

The outcome of this proliferation is that not only can any group readily obtain the arms necessary for war; the general presence of combat weapons is now a pervasive part of daily life in many parts of the world. The effect is a militarization of many societies, which further places children at risk of being pulled into the realm of war. As even one Afghan warlord lamented, "We have young boys that are more familiar with a gun than with school" (Stohl 2002, 281).

While the weapons themselves are not the direct cause of conflict, their proliferation and cheapening is an enabler. It allows any local conflict to become a bloody slaughter. Moreover, an abundance of arms within society takes away certain barriers to civil war. The range of politically relevant actors literally multiplies, and any sort of dissent within society can now easily become a violent one.

This dynamic also reworks the leadership structures within many societies—to dangerous ends. Power and control over the tools of war once tended to accrue with age. In many cases where weaponry has become pervasive, though, it has begun to devolve to what are called "youth elders." These are often impetuous, armed children no longer constrained by the age groupings that limited who could participate in warfare and who gained the rewards that went with them. Instead, these youths now dictate the rules to the former heads of their tribes, by the sheer dint of their new weaponry. With this new authority has not come responsibility, and violence levels have risen. As one Kenyan analyst describes the alteration of tribal warfare in Africa, "Somehow, the seat of authority has moved from the elders to the youth, and that has some very, very bad consequences for managing conflict" (Sam Kona as quoted in Vick 2001).

Finally, this trend is representative of the general weakening of the state (Lock 1998). States' control over the primary means of warfare was once fundamental in their formation (Kaiser 1990). With the proliferation of small arms and their centrality in much of warfare, this is lost. Small groups can not only mobilize disaffected children, but also turn them into a force that can quickly overwhelm the capacity of many states in the developing world. The easy availability of inexpensive small arms thus has the potential to rework the local balance of power and further the risks of failed states. Even after the fighting has ended, the very presence of these weapons also makes it harder for war-torn societies to recover and war easier to reinitiate (Wood and Peleman 1999).

Postmodern Warfare

The context in which these developments have occurred matters as well. The decision whether to implement a doctrine that uses children now takes place within a period of transformation in warfare. In many of the ongoing wars around the globe, the traditional political and strategic rationales behind the initiation, maintenance, and continuation of war are under siege (termed a "breakdown in the warrior's honor") (Ignatieff 1998). While the large-scale military operations carried out by the Western powers have become more technological, this is not the only face of warfare. At the same time, in the majority of conflicts carried out in the developing world, warfare has become messier and criminalized. In many cases, the private profit motive has become a central motivator, equal or greater to that of political, ideological, or religious inspirations (Berdal and Malone 2001; Makarenko 2003). Or, as one military analyst put it, "With enough money anyone can equip a powerful military force. With a willingness to use crime, nearly anyone can generate enough money" (Metz 2000a, 24).

Today, the fighting in a number of conflicts around the globe lacks any sort of link to a broader political or religious cause. Instead, they are driven by a simple logic of appropriation, from seizing mineral assets and protecting the drug trade to simple looting and pillaging. As World Bank expert Paul Collier writes (2003), "The key characteristics of a country at high risk of internal fighting are neither political nor social, but economic."

The new rule of insurgency appears to be that if conflict groups want to survive, they have to find their own financial resources (Collier and Hoeffler 2000). In many cases, there is a direct link between the fighting and ready commodities that groups can sell directly. These provide willing conflict entrepreneurs with the incentive to quickly seize what they can (Collier 2000a). In Sierra Leone, the key matter in their ten-year war was not over who was in place in the capitol, but who had control over the country's diamond fields. Similarly, in the war in the Democratic Republic of the Congo (DRC), foes and allies alike have battled over coltan mines. Coltan is a little known mineral that is drawn from mud but is now a key ingredient for the circuit boards used in almost all cell phones, laptops, and pagers. In short, as one local observer noted, "People are fighting for money. Everything that happens, it's about money" (Harden 2000). This stands in sharp contrast to the traditional understanding of war. The classic military philosopher Clausewitz (1976, 75), writing in the early 1800s, believed "politics is the womb in which war develops." Today, for much of contemporary warfare, economics plays at least as much a part in nurturing and shaping conflict.

Whether the groups evolved from cold war organizations or were new entrants into conflict, income generation (pure plunder, the production of primary commodities, illegal trading, etc.) thus has become an essential activity in many wars. A particularly lucrative area has been the international drug trade. For example, 70 percent of opposition groups' funds in Tajikistan are from drug income. The estimates are even higher in Colombia, where 90 percent of the cocaine in the United States originally comes from. The rebels and their paramilitary opponents are thought to pull as much as 80 percent of their funding from the cocaine trade. Of this estimated $800 million a year, only 10 percent goes to the war effort, while the other 90 percent enriches the individual commanders (Kaldor 2001, 102; Wilson 2003). Other activities are utilized as well. In the Philippines, Abu Sayyaf funds itself through kidnapping, while the Tamil Tigers in Sri Lanka run a worldwide shipping conglomerate. In Uzbekistan, Kosovo, and Afghanistan, militant groups profit by running protection rackets for opium traffickers (Dao 2002).

Many of these bands continue violent activities long after the original rationale for their formation has lost meaning.[4] They may have started out with some ideological or popular goals, often related to the cold war, that has fallen by the wayside as they struggle to survive. Far from being irrational or a breakdown in a system, war then becomes an end not a means. As such, war making serves as an alternative system of profit and power (Duffield 1999). The combination of these criminal goals and increasingly less professional, soldierless forces also leads to a variation in strategies toward civilians. While traditional insurgency strategy is to "swim among the people as a fish swims in the sea" (as elucidated by Mao Tse-tung, the Chinese communist leader and master of guerilla warfare), these new or reconstructed groups aim at terrorizing and pillaging the population rather than winning hearts and minds.

In short, while economics has always played a role in conflict, the last two decades have seen a new type of warfare develop, centered on profit-seeking enterprise. Conflicts around the globe are increasingly characterized not as temporary outbreaks of instability, but rather as protracted states of disorder. Within these wars, resource and population exploitation, rather than mass production, drive the new economy of war (UNICEF 2002b, 3). It may be organized mass violence, but it also involves the blurring of distinctions between traditional conceptions of war, organized crime, and large-scale violations of human rights (Kaldor 2001, 1).

The New Child Labor Problem

These trends of socioeconomic dislocation of children, technologic simplification of weaponry, and the broader changes in the nature of much of contemporary warfare were necessary factors to the emergence of child soldiers as a global phenomenon. They created not only the mass availability of child recruits but also the new possibility that they could indeed serve as effective combatants. They also underscored their utility in the changing context of warfare. In conflict after conflict, this has led to the implementation of a new doctrine of war, one that prescribes the recruitment of children and their use on the battlefield. The key is that this is not something that just happened; it has repeatedly involved deliberate choices among the leaders of local armed organizations. Children would not be used as combatants if the organizations they fight within did not see them as useful.

The strategy of using children as an alternative source of fighters has proved appealing to many groups, not only because it is cheap and easy to implement but also because the costs so far are outweighed by the benefits. It provides an easy means for organizations, even the most weak and unpopular, to generate significant amounts of force with almost no investment. On the other side of the equation, the costs of using children in this manner are considered quite low. Moral opprobrium is the only major risk to a group that uses child soldiers. However, any group that contemplates using children as fighters has already shown itself unwilling to be limited by prevailing moral codes. The lesson from this is that prohibitory norms are quite weak whenever they are not underscored by substantive penalties for violating them.

It is within this changing context of warfare that the perception of children and their role in warfare also has begun to change. With their ready availability and easy transformation into combatants, children now represent a low-cost way to mobilize and generate force when the combatants do not generally care about public opinion. This creates the doctrine of child soldiers, a new way of enacting violence that prescribes the methods and circumstances of children's employment in battle.

This new doctrine is particularly well-suited within the situation of weak or failed states, which have become ever more prevalent because of the trends described earlier. During the cold war, state failure was not as much of a problem as the two superpowers competed to prop up their weaker allies and undermine their opponents. However, this created the precursors to today's problems. Fragile postcolonial structures never solidified, and by the end of the period many Third World countries were states in name only. They lacked any semblance of good governance and were instead shells of what a functioning government should be. In general, they were underdeveloped, financially fragile, patriarchally structured, and without proper systems of accountability and civil-military controls (Young 1998, 114). Despite military aid, most developing militaries remained notoriously weak and brittle, incapable of carrying out any sustained military operations. Their forces were also comparatively small in relation to their overall populations (Metz 2000b, 11).

Thus, by the end of the cold war, maintaining internal order became a near impossible task for many of these weak states. It is no coincidence that many of the client states, who had received massive amounts of small arms, were the very same states that then failed when their patron's support evaporated

(Clapham 1996, 156). As these countries degenerated into violence, often ethnic scars reopened and state assets went up for grabs. An opening was created for new conflict actors who could hijack the chaos.

Many of the warlords and "conflict entrepreneurs" that emerged had no great political or military background. They were distinguished only by their willingness to break old norms and mobilize force to their own ends. Foday Sankhoh in Sierra Leone was a former cameraman; Charles Taylor in Liberia was an escaped convict; Joseph Kony in Uganda was just the young relative of a tribal shaman who had never held a job; and Laurent Kabila in Congo was a little-known guerilla leader who had been irrelevant for the previous thirty years. However, these men, and many like them, realized that arming children could serve as a means to gaining military capacity. Their comprehension of this not only sucked children into war but also led to the spate of civil wars and state failures that shaped much of global politics after the cold war.

Highly personalized or purely predatory armed groups, such as warlords, which are focused on asset seizure, are particularly dependent on this new doctrine of using children. Small fringe groups that would have found it impossible to mobilize—and thus been marginalized in the past—now can vastly expand their power by using children. In short, they can make children into soldiers and thus transform an insignificant force into an army. As an illustration, the Lord's Resistance Army in Uganda has a central cabal that numbers as few as 200 men and enjoys no popular support among the civilian populace. But through the abduction and transformation of 14,000 children into soldiers, the LRA has been able to engage the Ugandan army in a bloody civil war for almost two decades ("They'd Make You Kill Your Parents," 2000).

Regardless of the ideology behind a conflict, in wartime situations there is always some motivation to assemble added military force. It may be for political or strategic reasons or simply because of the high attrition rates among soldiers fighting in tough situations, such as in disease-ridden jungles. Children now provide a new alternative to adult recruiting pools. State regimes fighting unpopular wars, such as in El Salvador or Guatemala, and highly outnumbered rebel or ethnic groups that do not enjoy broad support, such as in Myanmar or Nepal, find this new pool particularly useful. They often first seek to tap it when the adult pool runs dry. In Sudan, for example, it was after a recruiting drive for adult males fell flat on its face that the Khartoum regime began targeting children. For two years (1993–1995), it tried to conscript all young men between the ages of eighteen and thirty-three. However, because of the unpopularity of the war the regime was fighting with the South, only 26,079 of the nearly 2.5 million men in that age bracket actually turned up for training. As a result, the government began to recruit street children to fill out its forces (Human Rights Watch 1995a). Likewise, the Liberation Tigers of Tamil Eelam (LTTE) in Sri Lanka began using children in the nine to twelve age range after it faced a manpower shortage in battles against the Indian peacekeeping force in the late 1980s and could not pull in enough adults because it had lost local support (University Teachers for Human Rights 1995; Cohn and Goodwin-Gill 1994).

An added incentive is that children are recruits that come on the cheap. While adults usually desire to be paid for their roles, even if they believe in the cause, children rarely are. One survey of child soldiers in Burundi found that only 6 percent had ever received any sort of remuneration. In the Eastern Congo (DRC), only 10 percent had ever been paid (ILO/IPEC 2003, 26). This can make children very attractive recruits, inducing a turn to child soldiering not just in emergencies but also as an alternative, low-cost supply of recruits. For example, in the 1990s, the Colombian Revolutionary Armed Forces of Colombia (FARC) faced the rise of competitive paramilitary groups who paid $350 a month. Thus, the FARC (which paid no salary) had to find a means to keep pace in the recruiting wars. Its solution was to increase the role of children, and their numbers in the group doubled (Otis 2001).

Children no longer enjoy any of the traditional protections stemming from their underage status. Instead, children are increasingly recruited because of the very fact that they are young. Groups that use child soldiers view minors simply as malleable and expendable assets whose loss is bearable to the overall cause and quite easily replaced. Or, as one analyst notes, "They are cheaper than adults, and they can be drugged or conditioned more easily into violence and committing atrocities" (Reuters 2001). Thus, the synergy of these three broad, and often interrelated, dynamics led to both the emergence and rapid growth of the child soldier phenomenon. Socioeconomic changes, technological developments, and base avarice within the changing contexts of war have created the circumstances, the opportunity, and the motivation for children to be turned into soldiers.

Where once children and battlefield weapons were incompatible, now they combine to create a completely new pool of military labor. Stemming from the combined trends of socioeconomic disconnection and technological efficiency gains in small arms, children now represent an easy and low-cost way to mobilize armed force. The only remaining ingredients required are groups or leaders without scruples. They must only be willing to connect these trends and pull children into war. As the payoffs can be huge, many take this immoral plunge. It is only until we find a way to end this cycle, through amending the causes and changing the cost versus benefit analysis that leaders go through, that the child soldier doctrine will be put into the dustbin of history.

CHAPTER 7

CHILD RECRUITMENT IN BURMA, SRI LANKA, AND NEPAL

Jo Becker

THE NUMBER OF CHILD SOLDIERS IN ASIA IS SECOND ONLY to that in Africa. Although precise figures are impossible to establish, the number of child soldiers in the region is likely to exceed 75,000. Child soldiers have participated in several of the region's ongoing armed conflicts, including those in Afghanistan, Burma, the Philippines, and Sri Lanka, and the recently ended conflict in Nepal.

As in other regions, myriad factors contribute to the recruitment and participation of children in Asia's armed conflicts. These include poverty, displacement, and a lack of schooling or work opportunities, separation from family, or an abusive family environment. In most situations of child recruitment, multiple factors are at play and often overlap.

While all of these factors contribute to child recruitment in Asia, three recruitment mechanisms are particularly dominant: forced recruitment, indoctrination, and the role of government abuses in fueling recruitment by armed opposition groups. Specifically, this chapter examines these mechanisms in relation to child recruitment by the Liberation Tigers of Tamil Eelam (LTTE or Tamil Tigers) and the Karuna group in Sri Lanka, the Communist Party of Nepal (Maoists) in Nepal, and the Tatmadaw (national army) and armed ethnic opposition forces in Burma (Myanmar).

Forced recruitment, indoctrination, and government abuses fuel child recruitment in many of the world's armed conflicts. For example, Gutiérrez Sanín (this volume) finds in his examination of child recruitment in Colombia that over 40 percent of former child soldiers identified at least one of these factors as a key reason for joining the guerillas.[1] However, in several respects, the characteristics of these child recruitment patterns differ notably in Asia compared to other parts of the globe.

Forced recruitment of children in Burma, Nepal, and Sri Lanka is particular to the region in at least two respects. First, in Nepal and Sri Lanka, forced recruitment by armed opposition groups has often been characterized by quota systems, rarely seen in other conflicts, where families are forced to supply one member for the "cause." Second, forced recruitment in most conflicts is generally practiced by armed opposition groups; therefore, the widespread and systematic forced recruitment by government forces in Burma is somewhat anomalous.

Indoctrination during the recruitment process may play a stronger role in many Asian conflicts because of the political sophistication and clear political agenda that characterize many of the opposition forces found in Asia. As a consequence, child recruitment by these groups often is marked by a strong element of political indoctrination, as armed groups endeavor to convince children that it is their duty to join the armed struggle. Political indoctrination has been practiced by armed opposition groups in all three countries, and particularly by the Tamil Tigers in Sri Lanka and the Maoists in Nepal. One form of indoctrination widely practiced by the Maoists prior to the 2006 ceasefire— short-term abduction for indoctrination sessions—is not utilized by any other known armed group.

Human rights abuses by government forces are a third factor that significantly fuels recruitment by opposition forces in all three conflicts. Attacks against civilians, arbitrary detention, displacement, extrajudicial executions, sexual violence, and other abuses against members of family or community members are cited by child soldiers in all three conflicts as a reason for joining armed opposition groups.

This chapter relies principally on interviews conducted during Human Rights Watch field investigations between 2002 and 2006. In each of the three countries, between twenty and thirty-five former child soldiers provided in-depth accounts of their recruitment, training, and participation in armed groups and forces.[2]

The former child soldiers were identified for interview by several methods. Many were known to local nongovernmental organizations, including both human rights and humanitarian groups working with war-affected populations. The majority of former child soldiers interviewed in Sri Lanka, and some of those interviewed in Nepal, were participating in rehabilitation programs for former child soldiers or children affected by armed conflict. Many of the former Burma government soldiers interviewed along the Thai-Burma border were identified by armed ethnic opposition groups; many of these former child soldiers had surrendered to the groups after deserting government forces. In Nepal, a significant number of former child soldiers were interviewed while in government detention following their capture from Maoist forces.

The former child soldiers were between the ages of eleven and seventeen at the time of their recruitment. Their length of service with armed groups or forces ranged from several weeks to ten years. The former child soldiers interviewed in Sri Lanka were primarily girls;[3] in Nepal they included both boys and girls; and in Burma they were exclusively boys.[4]

The Extent of Child Recruitment

The conflicts in Sri Lanka, Burma, and Nepal have each been marked significantly by the recruitment and participation of children. In Sri Lanka, the LTTE have used children as combatants and in other roles throughout most of the twenty-year conflict (see Human Rights Watch 2004c). Children were initially recruited into a "baby brigade," but later integrated into other units. Assessments of LTTE soldiers killed in combat in the 1990s found that between 40 and 60 percent of the dead fighters were children under the age of eighteen (Gunaratna 1998). The total number of children recruited by the LTTE is unknown, but an extensive monitoring system established by UNICEF just prior to the 2002 ceasefire agreement documented 6,098 cases of child recruitment by the LTTE between January 2002 and the end of March 2007.[5]

In 2006, reports emerged of child recruitment by forces led by V. Muralitharan, a former LTTE commander known as Karuna. Karuna had between 4,000 to 6,000 forces under his command, including some 2,000 child soldiers, when he broke off from the LTTE in March 2004 (Human Rights Watch 2004c, 2007c).[6] The LTTE attacked and defeated his forces, which quickly disbanded. In 2005, however, Karuna began to rebuild his forces and fight against the LTTE. By the end of March 2007, UNICEF had received 285 reports of child recruitment by Karuna forces but estimated the actual total may have been three times higher.[7] In numerous cases the Sri Lankan government, including local security forces, had knowledge of child abductions from government-held territory yet failed to intervene or secure the release of the children (Human Rights Watch 2007b).

In Burma, children have been recruited by both national armed forces as well as myriad ethnic opposition groups (Human Rights Watch 2002c). During the 1990s, the number of children in government armed forces increased significantly as the government doubled the size of its military and recruiters increasingly targeted children for forced recruitment to compensate for a lack of adult volunteers. Former child soldiers from government forces interviewed by Human Rights Watch in 2002 reported that up to 20 percent of those in their units were children under the age of eighteen, and that 35 to 45 percent of new recruits may have been children.[8] Given the size of Burma's military—an estimated 350,000 troops—these accounts suggest that tens of thousands of children are serving in the national army.

Many of Burma's ethnic armed opposition groups similarly include children. In 2002, Human Rights Watch estimated that nineteen of the armed resistance and insurgent groups had a combined total of 6,000 to 7,000 child soldiers, making up 10 to 20 percent of opposition forces. The overall numbers of child soldiers in opposition forces declined considerably during the 1990s as most of these groups lost military strength and many reached ceasefire agreements with the government. At the time of our research, we estimated that approximately 10 percent of Burma's child soldiers were found in opposition forces, while government recruitment accounted for the vast majority of the country's child soldiers. Later research conducted in 2004 and 2005 concluded that rates of child recruitment by government forces had not changed significantly (Human Rights Education Institute of Burma 2006).

During Nepal's eleven-year civil war, which ended in 2006, Maoist forces recruited children into their ranks and also abducted large numbers of children for brief periods of indoctrination. Most children recruited by the Maoists served in support roles as porters, cooks, guards, spies, and to assist with political mobilization, but some were given military training and used as combatants. According to one estimate, the Maoists recruited 2,000 to 4,000 children between 1996 and 2004 (Coalition to Stop the Use of Child Soldiers 2004a, 191). In 2003, the Asian Human Rights Commission estimated that about thirty percent of Maoist forces were children between ages fourteen and eighteen (Asian Human Rights Commission 2003). In 2006, government security analysts estimated that children made up 30–40 percent of Maoist forces and believed that the total number of Maoist forces was 10,000 to 12,000.[9] Children's rights organizations estimate that to date over 30,000 children and teachers have been abducted by Maoists forces. While the vast majority are released after brief periods of indoctrination, some children are retained as soldiers (Child Workers in Nepal 2006).

Forced Recruitment

Forced recruitment has been commonly practiced in all three conflict situations, particularly by the LTTE and Karuna group in Sri Lanka, the Maoists in Nepal, and the Burma army. Both the Maoists and the LTTE have conducted campaigns claiming that every family is obligated to provide a son or daughter for the cause. The LTTE typically targets boys and girls between ages fourteen and fifteen, but they have taken children as young as eleven. LTTE cadres routinely visit Tamil homes, particularly in the east of Sri Lanka, seeking a member of the family to join the struggle. Families that resist are harassed and threatened. Parents are told that their child may be taken by force if they do not comply, that other children in the household or the parents will be taken instead, or that the family will be forced to leave the home. If after several visits the family still refuses to provide a child, LTTE cadres may come to the home in the middle of the night and take a child by force or abduct a child on his or her way home from school. Some children initially reported to Human Rights Watch that they volunteered to join the LTTE, but when probed further it became clear that they were persuaded that the family had a duty to provide one member. They believed that if they did not step forward, then one of their siblings would be taken instead.[10] LTTE recruiters also target children attending Hindu temple festivals for forced recruitment. Temple festivals are typically attended by large numbers of Tamils, and adolescents often congregate together during the events. These children are easily targeted by recruiters, who may force groups of children into vans and take them to LTTE camps.[11]

Some accounts suggest that during the ceasefire period between 2002 and 2006, as government abuses in Sri Lanka abated significantly, the LTTE found it much more difficult to find volunteers and increasingly resorted to forced recruitment. Without an active armed conflict, and without active assaults on their communities by government forces, many children and their families did not see a need to join the Tigers. Of the thirty-five former child soldiers interviewed by Human Rights Watch in 2004 (two and a half years into the ceasefire), fewer than half a dozen said they had joined of their own accord. The remainder was recruited by force or coercion (Human Rights Watch 2004c). As hostilities between the government and the LTTE escalated in late 2005, some parents informed international NGOs that the LTTE had threatened them that unless they provided a child for LTTE forces, the LTTE would not provide them with security when war broke out (Hogg 2006, 10).

In 2006, the Karuna group also began forcibly recruiting children to fight against the LTTE.[12] Typically, a group of at least six men, usually armed with assault rifles, would arrive in a village and take children and young men from their homes, workplaces, temples, playgrounds, public roads, and even weddings. The armed men often knew who they were looking for, suggesting they had intelligence about the local population (Human Rights Watch 2007b).

Children interviewed by Human Rights Watch in Nepal in early 2006 described a "one family one person" campaign in Western districts of the country. Maoists visited villages and homes, saying that one person from each household had to join. Although the campaign was not specifically targeted at children, in many cases children joined because there was no available adult (Human Rights Watch 2007b). For example, one seventeen-year-old girl reported that she had to join because her father was working in India and her mother had to stay at home to care for her five-year-old sister. She indicated that from her district the Maoists took about one hundred people during their campaign. Most of them were between fifteen and nineteen years old.[13]

In another case in Nepal, a girl reported that the Maoists first took her fourteen-year-old younger brother. He escaped, and after reaching home he refused to return to the Maoists, saying that he would rather be beaten. The girl recalled, "so we had to decide between us in the family whom to send—otherwise the Maoists would have locked our house. I had to go."[14]

In Burma, forced recruitment is practiced primarily by the Tatmadaw, the national army, despite national laws prohibiting the practice. Following a violent 1988 government crackdown against pro-democracy demonstrators in Burma, the government began a rapid expansion of its armed forces, doubling the size of its army in large part to control the civilian population. Child recruitment increased, not only because recruiters were under increasing pressure to bring in new soldiers, but also because adults—increasingly alienated from the government—were less willing to volunteer. In his chapter on factors behind the use of child soldiers, Singer also discusses the recruitment of children by unpopular regimes, citing a similar example of Sudan, which began recruiting child soldiers after its conscription campaign of adult men failed to yield sufficient troops.

While armed groups in Nepal or Sri Lanka frequently approach children in their homes and through their families, recruiters for Burma's army most often target unaccompanied boys in public places, such as bus, train, and ferry stations, marketplaces, the streets, and festivals. They typically approach boys between the ages of twelve and seventeen and use threats and intimidation to coerce them into joining the military. The most common technique is to ask a boy for an identity card. Because few boys have official identification cards, they often are unable to produce one. The recruiter may then use the lack of identification as a pretext to threaten the boy with either a long prison term or enlistment in the army. Boys who try to resist may be subjected to beatings and/or detention until they agree to enlist (Human Rights Watch 2002c).

Once recruited, the boys are usually taken to a recruitment holding center where they are registered and kept until they are sent to training camps. In numerous accounts given to Human Rights Watch, boys are asked their age during the registration process, but when they truthfully give an age younger than eighteen, they are told, "No, you must say eighteen." Registration officials thus collude with recruiters in facilitating the recruitment of underage soldiers (Human Rights Watch 2002c).

In Burma, recruiter incentives play a significant role in fueling the forced recruitment of children. Recruiters are often given bags of rice or cash in exchange for new recruits. The payout varies by battalion and region, but usually includes between 1,000 and 10,000 kyat (equivalent to one week to three months' income for an average person) and fifteen to fifty kilograms of rice per recruit. Age documentation is routinely ignored or forged, and underage recruitment is almost never prosecuted. As a result, recruiters often prey upon children to meet their quotas, since children are less able than adults to withstand intimidation and threats, and less likely to be able to pay the bribes that may win their release (Human Rights Watch 2002c).

Forced recruitment appears to be the primary method by which Burma's army recruits children. Of twenty former child soldiers with the government army interviewed by Human Rights Watch, all but two had been forcibly recruited. One was forcibly recruited at age fourteen and deserted several years later. He rejoined because he was afraid he would be caught in his village. The other, a fourteen-year-old boy, initially joined as a volunteer, but only five days later he changed his mind and tried to escape.[15]

Andvig and Gates (this volume) note that armed forces that recruit through coercion must also induce compliance among their unwilling soldiers, often through the threat of violent punishment. This is well-illustrated in Burma, where trainees caught trying to escape are typically forced face down on the ground and then are beaten by each of the 250 members of their training group. In some instances, children reportedly have died after such punishment.[16]

With the exception of the United Wa State army, few of Burma's armed ethnic opposition groups rely on forced recruitment, even though some recruited forcibly in the past. Most groups have significantly declined in numbers in recent years, as the groups have either reached cease-fire agreements with the government or have appreciably decreased the size of their forces. In recent years, most of these groups have maintained force strength primarily through volunteers.

Indoctrination

Both the Maoists in Nepal and the Tamil Tigers in Sri Lanka rely heavily on indoctrination as part of their recruitment strategy. Both groups routinely target children with messages glorifying their cause and participation in their ranks and utilize schools as a prime recruitment ground. In their chapter on education in refugee camps, McClure and Retamal acknowledge the potential of schools for propaganda purposes and for protective spaces.

In Nepal, primarily in poor, rural areas, the Maoists conduct cultural programs in schools and villages to entice schoolchildren to join. These programs generally consist of singing, dancing, and speeches. Children are told that the

Maoists are fighting for the people, fighting against government corruption, and that they must support the cause (Human Rights Watch 2007b). Often those presenting the programs are children similar in age to those they are trying to enlist. In some areas, these programs are presented somewhat infrequently—for example, once a month. But in others, the programs may take place nearly every day and last for several hours. One sixteen-year-old boy told Human Rights Watch that the Maoists began visiting his class regularly when he was in grade 6. By grade 9, the vast majority of his classmates had joined. He decided to join too. He said, "I was impressed by their speeches and very influenced by what they said about fighting for the people and fighting corruption" (Human Rights Watch 2007b, 26–31).

Among forces using child soldiers, the Maoists seem to be unique in abducting children solely for the purpose of indoctrination. Children are often taken from their schools to another site where they may be forced to witness cultural programs like those already described. These sessions may last a couple of days, a couple of weeks, or even longer. At their conclusion, most abductees are allowed to return home. Presumably their indoctrination experience will make them more likely to join the Maoists later or support the Maoists through donations or other means. However, after their initial abduction, it is not unusual for some children to choose or be forced to remain and become members of the Maoists. The Maoists often use deception as a way of retaining children, telling them that they are to participate in a mobilization campaign for a month or two, but in reality forcing them to stay indefinitely.

In Sri Lanka, the LTTE employs systematic propaganda campaigns in schools to gain recruits. LTTE cadres often visit schools to speak about the LTTE's struggle for an independent Tamil Eelam or to show films that portray LTTE service in a positive light and highlight LTTE "heroes." In some areas, the LTTE has provided area teachers and principals with exams on the history of the LTTE to give to their students. UN officials familiar with these history lessons called them propaganda campaigns.[17]

Outside of the schools, the LTTE regularly expose Tamil children to special events honoring LTTE heroes, parades of LTTE cadres, public displays of war paraphernalia, and speeches and videos. Families of LTTE heroes are afforded special respect. Children are repeatedly told of discrimination and abuses the Tamil people have experienced, and they are told that the LTTE is fighting on their behalf for a separate state. One boy, who left school at age fifteen to join the LTTE, said that he did so because he "wanted a separate Eelam."[18]

Similar to the cultural programs put on by the Maoists in Nepal, the LTTE also use street dramas as a way to recruit children (and to win the support of their parents). One person described a drama they had witnessed that depicted a father, mother, and two children. One child is shot and killed by government security forces. The remaining child, who is still in school, then decides to join the LTTE. In the drama, the mother resists and begs the child not to join, but the father ultimately convinces the mother that the correct thing to do is to give their remaining child to the LTTE.[19] Although such dramas are performed for people of all ages, children are a key target audience.

As noted by Wessells in this volume, the use of girls by armed groups is prevalent in many armed conflicts. Both the Maoists in Nepal and the Tamil Tigers in Sri Lanka recruit significant numbers of girls. In Sri Lanka, 40 percent of the children recruited into the LTTE are girls, one of the highest percentages of girl soldiers of any country in the world.[20] In some Maoist strongholds in Nepal, one-third of Maoists are reportedly female (Gautam, Banskota, and Manchanda 2003, 94). Both the Maoists and the LTTE portray the recruitment of girls as a reflection of the group's commitment to gender equality. For example, the LTTE claims that the recruitment of girls and women is a way of "assisting women's liberation and counteracting the oppressive traditionalism of the present system" (CSUCS 2001, 342).

The Maoists also portray participation in their struggle as a positive alternative to the gender inequality experienced by many women and girls, including limited opportunities for education, arranged marriages, and lack of property rights. For example, one seventeen-year-old girl said that the Maoists initially convinced her to join their campaign by explaining that as a woman she would never be able to achieve anything, even if she continued her studies. She said, "I had finished sixth grade by then. They were saying that young girls like me should join them because in Nepal there was no point in studying, since in any case I would not be able to get a job."[21]

In their chapter, Andvig and Gates discuss the role of ideological incentives in the recruitment process, but note that ideology alone is often insufficient to develop a strong enough bond with the armed group to avoid high rates of desertion. They argue that force is often used in addition to nonpecuniary benefits (linked to ideology, religion, or ethnicity) and economic incentives. This bears out in the cases of the Maoists and the LTTE, which both use indoctrination in combination with force to recruit and maintain children in their forces.

Indoctrination plays little role in child recruitment practices in Burma. The government makes little if any effort to persuade children to join the army of their own accord, relying instead on forced recruitment. Most children who were forced into the army did not want to join, having heard stories from others about the difficulty of life in the army. Most of the former government child soldiers interviewed by Human Rights Watch had no idea of why they were fighting. Some reported that their commanders tried to motivate them with propaganda about the ethnic opposition groups—for example, describing abuses (often fictitious) by these groups against Burmese monks or the elderly.

However, most said they received little or no information from their superiors about the army's objectives or the nature of their enemy (Human Rights Watch 2002c).

At least in recent years, most ethnic opposition groups in Burma have not used indoctrination to any significant degree, as the severity of government abuses fuels the groups' limited need for new recruits.

Government Abuses

In nearly all conflicts where children participate, human rights abuses by government forces play a role in encouraging children to join opposition forces. In her chapter on displacement and child recruitment, Lischer discusses the impact of witnessing atrocities against family members or peers in the decision to join an armed group. Children may be seeking revenge for abuses committed against members of their family, or they may believe that their participation in the struggle is needed in order to protect their community. In this respect, recruitment patterns in Asia are similar to those in other parts of the world.

Prior to the 2002 ceasefire, children in Sri Lanka routinely experienced or witnessed government abuses against Tamils. Abuses by government forces included unlawful detention, torture, execution, enforced disappearances, and rape. A 1993 study of adolescents in Vaddukoddai in the North found that one-quarter of the children studied had witnessed violence personally (Somasundaram 1993). In response, many children joined the LTTE, seeking to protect their families or to avenge real or perceived abuses.

One boy told Human Rights Watch that he joined the LTTE when he was sixteen. He explained that the army burnt his house and raped women in his neighborhood. "They tortured us," he said. It became clear during the interview that the events that he described took place years before, when he was only three years old. Although he may not have remembered the events directly or understood their meaning at the time, they became an important part of his family's narrative and heavily influenced his decision to join the LTTE years later.[22]

Another girl recounted how the Sri Lankan army had killed her father and four of her uncles as suspected LTTE cadres when she was eight years old. She described being very angry at government forces, and when she was sixteen she decided to join the LTTE.[23]

In Burma, government abuses also play a significant role in the participation of children in the myriad ethnic opposition groups that have long fought the government. The military regime has been responsible for displacing hundreds of thousands of people from the ethnic minority areas, burning villages, using children and adults for forced labor, and retaliating against civilians in areas where opposition groups are active. Children interviewed often identified such abuses as an impetus for them to join opposition groups. For example, one boy who joined the Karen National Liberation Army (KNLA) at age fifteen said, "I decided to fight the Burmese soldiers because they'd burned and destroyed our village. I hate the Burmese soldiers."[24] Another boy said that he joined the KNLA because the army had killed his mother when he was six years old.[25]

In Nepal, government abuses against civilians were common during the country's ten-year civil war. Over 13,000 people were killed, the majority civilian. More than 1,700 people disappeared; and in 2003 and 2004, Nepal recorded the highest number of new cases of disappearances in the world (Human Rights Watch 2005, 1). The vast majority of these disappearances—approximately 1,300—have been attributed to the government. The government is also known to have carried out torture and killings of suspected Maoists, rape of women and girls, and arbitrary arrests and detention (Human Rights Watch 2005).

Although Human Rights Watch interviews suggested that forced recruitment and indoctrination played a more significant role in child recruitment by Maoist forces, government abuses also influenced some children to join. For example, one seventeen-year-old girl was taken by the Maoists for a two-week indoctrination session. When she returned home, she discovered that the army had killed two people from her area who had participated in the Maoists' mobilization. She said that incident influenced her to stay with the Maoists.[26]

Another girl reported that she began experiencing harassment by members of the government army when she was nine years old. The army sought information about her older brother, a member of the Maoists, and suspected her of being a Maoist informer. She said that the army repeatedly came to question her at her home and school. Twice they detained her in army barracks for torture and questioning, once for five days and once for a week. During these periods of detention, she said that she was blindfolded, beaten twice a day, and given little food. She said that this mistreatment by the army influenced her increasing involvement with the Maoists as a member of a cultural troupe. She participated as a singer and dancer in Maoist cultural programs over a two-year period but also learned to use a range of weapons—including magnums, rifles, grenades, socket bombs, and pressure-cooker bombs—and performed some military support duties.[27]

Policy Directions

Forced recruitment, indoctrination, and government abuses are all significant factors underlying children's participation in Nepal's, Sri Lanka's, and Burma's armed conflicts. In all three countries, forced recruitment is a dominant strategy used to recruit children, with the exception of most ethnic opposition groups in Burma. Indoctrination plays a significant, though lesser, role in Nepal and Sri Lanka, but is nearly absent in the Burmese context. Human rights abuses by government forces also influence the participation of children in all three countries' opposition groups, particularly in Burma and in Sri Lanka prior to 2002.

The relative strength of each factor not only varies between countries but also within individual countries, based on the ebb and flow of the conflict itself. For example, in Sri Lanka, the influence of indoctrination and government abuses was dominant prior to the 2002 ceasefire, but with the cessation of hostilities in 2002, forced recruitment became much more prevalent. As hostilities escalate in 2007, recruitment through indoctrination and as a result of government abuses may again become more common. The recruitment factors explored here, including their particular manifestations in these conflict situations, suggest a number of policy directions and prevention strategies.

Incidents of forced recruitment can be reduced by removing any financial or professional incentives that recruiters may enjoy for securing children as new recruits, as well as employing effective sanctions against recruiters found to be recruiting children in violation of national laws or the stated policies of armed groups. Both government and nongovernmental armed forces should be encouraged to adopt clear policies and codes of conduct governing recruitment practices that comply with international law and incorporate appropriate safeguards against underage recruitment, including verification of age, clear sanctions, and criminal prosecution for recruiters who violate minimum age standards. The inclusion of such codes, as well as implementation and verification mechanisms, should be part of any action plans to end child recruitment that are developed in cooperation with the United Nations. (See Chikuhwa's chapter in this volume regarding the UN protection agenda and measures, including action plans, requested by the UN Security Council.) In addition, any military training for government or nongovernmental armed groups, whether conducted by the UN or by individual countries that provide training for foreign troops, should actively promote such codes and practices.

Indoctrination, for the purposes of child recruitment, can be mitigated by restricting the access of armed groups and forces to schools, as sites for propaganda campaigns, and by conducting countercampaigns to educate children and their families regarding the realities of military service. UN agencies such as UNICEF, international nongovernmental organizations, and donor governments can all play an active role in working with local community groups (including parents, religious leaders, educators, and local elders) to develop and support public education campaigns and identify measures that are appropriate to the local context to limit recruiter access to schools. McClure and Retamal's chapter on education in refugee camps outlines a number of programmatic interventions and strategies to develop a school's potential to protect children from recruitment.

Child recruitment by opposition armies can be decreased if government forces scrupulously adhere to international humanitarian law and avoid human rights abuses against civilian populations that may engender a desire for revenge among children. Governments should ensure that soldiers in their armed forces are trained in international humanitarian and human rights standards. This can be done through developing or strengthening their own training programs or utilizing training from the International Committee of the Red Cross, the United Nations, or third-party governments. As mentioned, clear penalties should be established, clearly communicated throughout the chain of command, and, most important, applied to any soldier found to commit human rights violations. The application of sanctions against violators is essential to fostering good discipline and eliminating the culture of impunity that prevails in many armed forces.

CHAPTER 8

ORGANIZING MINORS

The Case of Colombia

Francisco Gutiérrez Sanín

PRACTITIONERS AND RESEARCHERS HAVE THOROUGHLY examined an ample set of push factors that cause minors to join nonstate armed organizations in Colombia, ranging from poverty to the provision of weapons. Pull factors and the interaction between push and pull, however, also play a crucial role.

Prima facie, recruiting minors does not seem such a good business for an irregular force. Indeed, having children in an armed group may provide several strategic advantages. There are clear disadvantages though. Children can be undisciplined; their bodies and psychology are not prepared for the sustained hardships of war; and they do not stand a chance when confronting an adult force. The motivation behind recruiting children would not be such a serious puzzle if, as Collier (2000a) assumes, taking power and fighting were not an objective of the rebels. They are not armies but rent seekers. Collier's blithe assumption, however, does not hold in Colombia.[1] There is quite a bit of fighting going on, and it has increased both in absolute terms and in other forms of violence. This applies with particular force to the main guerrilla group, the Revolutionary Armed Forces of Colombia (FARC), a point that is corroborated by governmental reports, which show that the risk of being killed in the guerrilla

group is quite high (Pinto, Andrés, and LaHuerta 2002) and that in the last
four years the combat activity of the FARC has risen sharply. The FARC is indeed a rent seeker; but it is also an army that has to solve all the technical issues armies face. Colombian evidence suggests that a very high percentage of
children enlist voluntarily (given the caveats discussed earlier). In Colombia,
it may be the case that no more than 20 percent of the minors are forced at gunpoint into the groups (see table 8.1). In their excellent study, Brett and Specht
(2005) remind their readers that children get involved in war because war exists. As such an obvious factor, this strong point is frequently glossed over. But
it certainly does not explain all cases (such as the massive presence of minors in
the British army), nor does it address the age specificity issue. We are troubled
about the presence of minors in armies because we feel that they should be doing other things instead of fighting. The treatment of the issue in Colombia is
complicated by the high presence of female combatants in the FARC, ranging
from 20 to 30 percent, according to available evidence. There are some motivations in youths that seem to be gender specific in many cultures—the allure of
guns, for example (Brett and Specht 2005). In many peasant societies, girls are
raised to organize domestic life, not to participate in the most strenuous and
risky forms of public engagement. In some cultures, girls are relatively immune
to certain motivations and are not educated for war; nonetheless, they heavily
populate the FARC ranks.

Using children in war can be quite problematic. And the younger and more
inexperienced the child, the more problematic it can become. Therefore, groups

TABLE 8.1   Basic data of the demobilized up to 2002

Membership	FARC-EP, 83%
Age	Between 13 and 17 years: 44%; 17 years or more: 56%; 82% joined the guerrillas between 10 and 17 years
Gender	92% male
Education	84% did not complete primary studies; 8% no formal schooling at all; 8% incomplete secondary studies
Marital status	88% unmarried
Reasons for joining the guerrillas	Forced recruitment, 20%; the allure of weapons and uniforms, 20%; false promises (salary, good treatment), 16%; belief in the cause, 12%; fear or vengeance (regarding the army or the paramilitaries), 10%
Reasons for leaving the guerrillas	Ill treatment (37%); lack of salary (19%); lack of freedom, 17%; false promises, 16%

N=316 interview subjects.
Source: Pinto et al. 2002, 8.

have to transform them into warriors. It seems likely that such a transformation is heavily colored by the nature of the respective group.

Chronology of the Colombian Conflict

Researchers and practitioners disagree as to the origin of the Colombian conflict. Some have asserted that there has been a continuous state of violence in the country since 1940. There have been two distinct waves of confrontation, one that started in the late 1940s and concluded in the early 1960s, and another one that began only in the late 1970s and has lasted until today. Though they are linked and share some characteristics (for example, they are both agrarian confrontations), I am concerned here with the most recent.

Indeed, Colombia—like many other Latin American countries—had revolutionary guerrillas in the 1960s, but their role was quite marginal. They were very small groups waging an "imaginary war" (Broderick 2000). For example, the FARC, which for decades has been the main guerrilla force, had no more than 780 combatants in 1978 (Ferro and Uribe 2002; see table 8.2, which briefly describes some of the main denominations in the conflict in the past

TABLE 8.2   Colombian illegal armed groups

Name	Acronym	Characteristics
Fuerzas Armadas Revolucionarias de Colombia	FARC	1964– Started as a force related to the pro-Soviet Communist Party; by the late 1980s and early 1990s became totally independent; currently has between 13,000 and 20,000 members
Ejército de Liberación Nacional	ELN	1966. Castroist organization almost completely destroyed in 1973; came back to life in the 1980s; currently has fewer than 5,000 members
Movimiento 19 de Abril	M-19	1973–1991. Nationalist-populist organization; negotiated a peace agreement with the government and became a successful political party
Ejército Popular de Liberación	EPL	1966– Started as a Maoist force; in 1991 negotiated a peace agreement but was crushed by the FARC; some remainders have maintained armed activity (completely independent from the FARC) until today
Paramilitaries/self-defenses	Several; main denomination is the AUC (Autodefensas Unidas de Colombia)	Began in the early 1980s as antisubversive force; some death squads developed into big regional organizations; in late 1990s built a national federation that did not last long; in 2002 began a peace process

forty years). The FARC had little influence in national politics, and the other groups—Castroist National Liberation Army (ELN) and Popular Liberation Army (EPL), among others—were even smaller and more vulnerable. The ELN was practically wiped out in the Anorí operation in 1973.

In the early 1970s, though, a new guerrilla force appeared of nationalist hue: the Movimiento 19 de Abril (M-19). Contrary to its predecessors, it was capable of "nationalizing the war"; this, plus the very fast and strong development of the narco-economy in the second half of the 1970s pushed the problem of widespread violence to the center stage of political life. If the M-19 was the great innovator of the Colombian conflict, then the guerrilla force that was most favored by the hike in its intensity was the FARC. In the 1980s a full-fledged internal conflict was being fought in the country, with some extremely brutal events taking place. The guerrillas became deeply involved in the narco-economy, but also in a wide range of criminal economic activities, the main one being kidnapping. Counterinsurgents responded in kind (though with their own idiosyncratic repertoire). The Colombian government claimed that an explicit alliance between *narcos* and *guerrilleros* had taken place.[2] Certainly, in the second half of the 1980s the narcotraffickers had declared a terrorist war against the state. This other war was waged by planting bombs in the country's main cities, blowing up a plane full of passengers, kidnappings (more often than not followed by assassinations), and shooting state officials, policemen, and politicians. But while attacking the state, narcos were also enthusiastically funding paramilitary groups.

In the meantime, the paramilitaries were growing even faster than the guerrillas. Following the standard strategy of such groups in Latin America of drying the pond so as to catch the fish, they exercised systematic terror against civilians.[3] They routinely massacred the peasant population, triggering huge displacement waves. The paramilitary groups expressed a de facto coalition in the field that included army officers, cattle ranchers, agro-industrialists, and big-time criminals (Gutiérrez and Barón 2005; see also Medina Gallego 1990 and Romero 2002). Their murderous activities continued during the 1990s, probably achieving a peak in the 1998–2002 administration, when they carried out an offensive against civilians through quotidian massacres to create a climate of terror and sabotage the peace talks between the FARC and the government. Since 2004, however, the paramilitary has been in a process of demobilization, though as different academics and independent observers have witnessed, they are a deeply criminalized force.

The Colombian war has ranged from low to medium intensity (Pizarro 2004). Perhaps, for classificatory purposes, it is more helpful to observe that, contrary to the first wave of Colombian violence, this one has not caused a massive civilian polarization (Posada-Carbó 2006). More precisely, the overwhelming majority of the Colombian population strongly rejects both the guerrilla and the paramilitary forces and condemns some of their main criminal practices. There is evidence of long social networks associated with some of the practices of those groups (Gutiérrez and Barón 2005), but the war does not divide the population in more or less equivalent politicized rival portions.

Age and Gender in the Colombian Conflict

If the Colombian conflict has evolved, the conceptions of role and gender in it have changed as well. The Colombian state incorporated minors in its ranks—both in combat and desk activities—but the 1991 constitution gave child defenders the tools and arguments to exert strong pressure against such practice. After several ups and downs, it was banished, but some analysts maintain that it has been revived in different forms. Something similar can be said about the penal status of minors. There are two types of legal pressures in this regard. On the one hand, a liberal trend: Colombia has engaged in international agreements that demand special treatment for child offenders. On the other, a pragmatic one: the legal unaccountability of minor offenders has become an incentive for their recruitment by criminal or subversive groups, and a real problem for anticrime policies. The debate has resurfaced cyclically in recent years.

The guerrillas have had their own trajectory. By the mid-1960s the ELN was a very small, wholly male, and probably entirely adult force. It was famous for its machismo, and its commanders reserved themselves the right of picking out women from the (very small) peasant base that sympathized with it (Medina Gallego 1996). Clearly, this was an affair of youngsters, which is natural if it is taken into account that this was a force composed of university students and peasants that joined the labor market very early (see the narrative of the commander Nicolás Bautista "Gabino" in Medina Gallego [1996]). However, it does not seems to have been massive, as the extreme hardships, ideologization, and marginal character of the ELN, summed to its brutal internal purges, were not a friendly environment for minor participation. Not only was it a fragile experience; it simply was not fun.[4] The ELN ranks were populated by peasants and university students, and at least the latter were mainly young adults. When after the Anorí debacle it was rebuilt in the 1980s, the ELN had suffered a deep transformation. The blood baths due to internal conflicts disappeared, doctrinarism relaxed, resources—due to kidnapping and, eventually, rent extraction from the mining economy—increased by several orders of magnitude, and volunteers joined their ranks in large numbers.[5] This process probably feminized the ELN and lowered its age averages.

The FARC has deep roots in the previous cycle of violence: its immediate antecedent was a peasant self-defense group, initially composed of Liberal families that escaped the Conservative government harassment and fell under communist influence. At the beginning, they were more of a roaming community than a proper guerrilla force. They were an association of households, with women dedicated to domestic labor and raising children, and the men switching between cultivating the land and fighting. Some children participated in combat. The familial structure was technically not sustainable, and when the FARC was formally created in 1966 it had already become much more guerrilla-like. As stated earlier, despite its grand discourses—past and present—it was very marginal. By 1978, it had, according to its own reports (Ferro and Uribe 2002), no more than 800 members, and acted in removed and very poor territories (Vélez 1999). At the same time, it was much more efficient and result-driven than its counterparts. I also believe it was subject to a much earlier process of feminization than any other Colombian irregular force, perhaps due to its family-based origin. Then the FARC made two crucial decisions. In 1978, after a strong internal debate, it agreed to participate in the coca economy, first as a rather timid regulator, later in a full-blown fashion (Ferro and Uribe 2002). And in 1982, it declared itself a popular army (FARC-Ejército del Pueblo) and sketched a strategic plan for the next years, which it approximately accomplished, at least until the mid-1990s. As in the case of the ELN, the FARC received, from the early 1980s on, a sustained stream of supporters. Based on governmental reports about casualties of and desertions from the FARC, and taking into account that in the last two decades it has risen to a membership of between 15,000 and 20,000, it seems reasonable to conjecture that in that period it has accepted between 3,000 and 5,000 members each year. This is quite impressive, taking into account not only the idiosyncrasies of the FARC but also the fact that its mass base is weak. Opinion polls and other evidence attest to a strong rejection of the FARC in Colombian public opinion.

As stated above, of that flow a significant percentage, between 20 and 30 percent, are women who participate directly in combat as well as minors. Women are very important in the FARC, but they hit a glass ceiling; their presence at the higher ranks is scarce. Minors may account for up to 40 percent of the FARC. For example, almost half of the respondents of table 8.1 joined the guerrillas when they were younger than seventeen years old. The FARC leaders have stated explicitly that they will not stop enlisting them (Ferro and Uribe 2002).

The paramilitaries were created in the 1980s as death squads, but sometimes they were not devoid of a social base (for the early experience of the Magdalena Medio, see Medina Gallego [1990] and Gutiérrez and Barón [2005]). A sector of its leadership strived to transform this cloud of localist, heterogeneous units into a national antisubversive army. By 1997 a national federation, the Autodefensas Unidas de Colombia, was formed. But the original project—to evolve

TABLE 8.3   Rebel group member profiles

Membership distribution	FARC, 1,115; ELN, 271; ERP, 16; ERG, 6; EPL, 17; paramilitary (United Self-defense Forces of Colombia), 607
Entry age	FARC, 15.93; paramilitary, 16.15; ELN, 15.85
Education level (in years)	FARC, 3.9; ELN, 4; paramilitary, 5.22
Females	FARC, 33.68%; ELN, 32.47%; paramilitary, 14.66%.[a]

[a]Differences between both guerrillas and paramilitary significant at 0.01 level.
Source: ICBF.

toward an armylike structure—was infeasible; centrifugal forces were too strong (Gutiérrez and Barón 2005). In 2002 the federation was dismantled, and in 2004 it started a negotiation process with the government. As a whole, the paramilitary are a male, paid force, in which social and military hierarchy overlap, with a short organizational ladder to climb and lax discipline. Women— possibly many of them ex-guerrillas (Lara 2000)—appear occasionally as social activists, but there is strong evidence that in military activities proper they appear in significantly less proportion than in the guerrillas (see for example table 8.3). Regarding minors, the situation seems rather complicated— and woefully understudied. There have been journalistic reports about massive abductions of children by paramilitary groups, especially in the south of the country, but we know little about the magnitude and stability of the practice. In the reinsertion process only a few minors appeared, but this may respond to a conscious legitimizing strategy. It must be remembered, additionally, that the paramilitaries operate on very lax networking principles. Openly criminal groups that engage voluntarily scores of children swarm at the outskirts of these networks. It is hard to tell if they belong to the paramilitary proper. Subjectively, a portion of children that owe allegiance to such gangs appear to believe that they are paramilitary cadres as well.

In January 2001, the Colombian press reported that the army had finished the Berlin operation, targeted against a FARC column—the Columna Móvil Arturo Ruiz—that in a few days had marched rather spectacularly from the south of the country to the northern department of Santander. It was a resounding success for the governmental forces. They mopped up the column, killing and injuring several of its members and forcing almost all of the others into surrender.

Such a crushing defeat is rarely seen in the Colombian conflict. The event hit the headlines not because of its strategic value, but rather because a huge proportion of the members of the Arturo Ruiz column were children. Despite the huge meaning of the incursion, and its financial costs, the FARC secretariat showed it was willing to take its chances with child soldiers.[6] It failed miserably, both in the military and the political sense. Public opinion was outraged by the massive utilization of underage combatants. Few people failed to express their repulsion. All insiders expressed their astonishment that the FARC, a militarily savvy group, made such a blunder.

There is another side to the story. In national wars, the participation of children (and women) in war has been seen as a sure symptom of mass support and social inclusion—also, indeed, as one of the highest forms of heroism. *Cuore,* the sentimental juvenile literature classic by Edmundo D'Amicis written 120 years ago, with which millions of boys were reared in the twentieth century, is the hagiography of the fortitude of children ready to offer their lives for the sake of Lombardy. This nationalist lullaby is only one example of a very long thread that still manifests itself quite vigorously today. For example, in his recount of the Nicaraguan revolution, the poet Ernesto Cardenal focuses on one important event, the insurrection of Monimbó, claiming proudly: "Boys played a very important role in the insurrection" (Cardenal 1999, 70). "Adolescents and children [he continues] also fought in that war. I hear that one was shooting with a pistol, and when it broke he started to cry. Humble old women with their *ponchos* went from house to house with baskets distributing homemade [*de contacto*] bombs. Women threw boiling water from the roofs on the heads of the guards" (63). A man offers his testimony in the following terms: "I have seen young lads defending a position to allow the others to escape. And they knew that they were going to die. Brother! Now I understand what it is to be Christian" (123). Further on, a child declares, with the obvious approval of the author, "I was recruited by my mom" (131).

Naturally, Colombia is not unfamiliar with such tradition. An epitome of national indomitability is early-nineteenth-century Policarpa Salavarrieta, a young woman who sacrificed her life during the Spanish invasion.[7] After independence, the participation of children in several of the country's civil wars is documented in numerous testimonial works.

To summarize, D'Amicis, Cardenal, and others feel strongly that the participation of children and women in organized violent resistance is a huge moral and political victory. Their participation symbolizes the capacity of a group to motivate new social layers into the public space. It should also terrify its enemy, because it is morally difficult and politically costly to face children and women. This contrasts sharply with the outcome of the Berlin operation.

The Tensions behind Recruiting Minors

Concerning drafting age, there is a lower boundary that military theorists and practitioners identify easily. The line is to be drawn precisely at the moment a child becomes an adult. Napoleon, for example, stated with the utmost clarity: "We need men and not boys. No one is braver than our young people, but lacking fortitude they fill the hospitals and even at the slightest uncertainty they show the character of their age. Eighteen year old boys are too young to wage war . . . far from home . . . Being too young, none should be sent to the field army. Instead, they should remain in France, where they will be clothed, armed, and drilled" (Napoleon 1999, 2). Note that he did not reject the recruitment of minors, only their participation in combat. When he identified the limits of "boys" as soldiers, he was not referring to the physical hardships of war but to their psychological fragility and immaturity.[8]

In several polities there is the widespread perception that war is an affair of (young) *adult* men. The reality may be different, but the perception is strong. The fact that other demographic categories decide to risk their lives, or are pushed into doing so, is a political highlight. Since war is always brutal, involving children and women appears as an obvious denaturalization, a transgression of deep-seated norms about age and gender (Honwana 2006). In Colombia, the fact that the government has suspended—or at least limited severely—the enlistment of children in the armed forces, and that increasingly such practice is considered a very serious war crime, has sharply aggravated its risks. It is possible that the growing governmental self-restriction regarding minor recruitment has prompted the guerrillas and the paramilitaries to establish limits themselves in an effort to restrict judicial vulnerability and public disrepute. Even so, engaging children in war has justly earned a wealth of criticism and odium from citizens, stakeholders, and civil society spokesmen.

Determining the benefits of recruiting children is necessary since illegal armed groups, particularly the FARC, still indulge massively in child recruitment. Potentially, there are several benefits, but almost all are problematic—at least when confronted with the empirical data about the Colombian conflict. Precisely because some sociodemographic categories have been historically separated from war, and sometimes are surrounded by special protections, they can have great strategic value. In many wars, including the Colombian conflict, children are routinely used as informants and messengers. This does not explain their utilization in combat, which is the focus of this chapter; however, a first contact as an informant may trigger a process that ends in recruitment proper.[9] In this version, child enlistment is a by-product of child part-time utilization given a system of incentives that favors it (the unaccountability of minors from a legal standpoint). However, the evidence I have at hand—autobiographical recounts, fieldwork by other researchers, press clips, judicial proceedings—suggests that this path is one among many, actually not the most overcrowded. Minors tend to join directly, frequently after a very brief training course (Ferro and Uribe 2002). Closer to the point may be the malleability of children. Since the motivations to join an armed illegal group are so varied, the recruits have to be thoroughly transformed into useful soldiers.[10] Children can be more easily induced into false beliefs before joining and more easily molded when they have already become members. It may be the case as well that the guerrillas simply have no alternative. A sustainable rebellion has to be able at least to replace its casualties and desertions with a fresh stream of admissions.

Colombia is a highly urbanized country, with a hardly viable rural economy and a huge displacement problem (between 2.5 and 8.0 percent of its population).[11] Furthermore, as mentioned, it is intensely rebuked by the majority of the population. So the pool of potential recruits may be small. It might be speculated that the guerrillas prefer any recruit to none, resulting in a very low average age and mixed gender composition. The problem of this explanation is that it is difficult to know if it holds; if anything, the guerrilla recruiters boast that they can allow themselves the luxury of selecting among the hundreds of applications they get (Ferro and Uribe 2002). This sounds exaggerated but not plainly absurd, at least in some regions.

The problem probably should be reinterpreted through the lens of the interaction between the organizational blueprint and the motivation of the children in a given population. I suggested that there was a purely technical, military "Napoleonic boundary" concerning the recruitment of children: below a certain age they do not fight very well and, even worse, they break down easily. Actually, the FARC has its own limit, which it states explicitly: fifteen years (Ferro and Uribe 2002). There is no serious reason for doubting that this limit is more or less respected. For example, in a Colombian Family Welfare Institute (ICBF) database of minors captured or deserted between 1999 and 2004, among the more than 1,115 FARC entries there are 166 cases, or 14.4 percent, that reported having joined when they were under fifteen.[12] This shows that the fifteen-years-old rule is used implicitly or explicitly in practice.[13] As highlighted by Napoleon's quotation, this is not a normative but a strictly rational behavior.

There is a political "Napoleonic drive" as well. Napoleonic wars were national in the sense that they were driven not only by national themes but also an aspiration for universal coverage and inclusivity. Napoleon believed this implied adult male enlistment—a mirror of adult male enfranchisement. Clausewitz argued that such a mass mobilizing strategy was *politically* invincible and could only be countered by a symmetrically opposed mass mobilization. The ulterior national wars of the nineteenth and twentieth centuries in this sense only pushed the Napoleonic impulse to its logical consequences, increasingly involving more and more socio-demographic categories in the conflict. This applies even to cultures that have entrenched conceptions about age or gender. Even today, some wars and groups clearly show the imprint of the Napoleonic drive. A good example is the LTTE in Sri Lanka.

In the military sense, the more armylike and combat prone the group is, the more it needs real military proficiency to survive. In the political sense, the more armylike and nationalistic the more it will tend to include socio-demographic categories other than young male adults. But some of these categories, like children, are not fully endowed to carry on combat activities.[14] The FARC has resolved this tension by tracing its own lower boundary and including those new categories as combatants, but not in the leadership, where of course no child but also no woman is to be found. This allows it to broaden the pool of potential recruits and thus the quality of those who are ultimately chosen. I would conjecture that all this works because of the peculiarities of the new categories: women have more motives to escape than men, and children are more easily victims of false beliefs, have shorter time horizons, and are more vulnerable to peer pressure. In other terms, the FARC is a minority, politically marginal force, but it can resolve the tension because of both the strength of the push factors and its recruitment strategies.

The answer to why rebel forces recruit children lies in the interaction between the organizational needs of the given group and the characteristics of the population.[15] For the FARC, the wider the recruitment pool the better. If it has the liberty to choose, it can pick better fighters and can form a reserve disposed to go into action at any moment. On the other hand, child recruitment is an act of social inclusion, which unequivocally shows the massive character of its cause (Ferro and Uribe 2002). At the same time, the recruitment of minors creates real technical problems that are apparent from time to time, as in the Berlin operation.[16] The FARC generally fights with mixed forces—gender- and age-wise—which helps assimilate some of the shortcomings of children as warriors.[17]

Comparing Systems of Incentives

The main differences between the three main illegal organizations that participate in the Colombian war—the FARC, the paramilitaries, and the ELN—are synthesized in table 8.4.[18] The explicit objective of the FARC is to build a "popular army." It emphasizes discipline and combat capacity. It has built a strong line of command, which is extremely centralized. Its members do not receive a salary (Gutiérrez 2004; Human Rights Watch 2003c; Ferro and Uribe 2002).[19] There is hardly a case of individual looting by FARC members,[20] and they do not have access (as individuals) to rents. The FARC members can handle huge resources coming from narcotrafficking and kidnapping, but it is always clear that this money belongs to the organization. From time to time (once or twice a year) a commander escapes with a pot of money. But overwhelmingly, the general rule is that soldiers get their equipment and no more; indeed, a major reason for desertion is the absence of salary (Human Rights Watch 2003c).

The FARC internal discipline is extremely harsh. Restrictions are widespread, and a high level of self-sacrifice is demanded from the rank and file.

TABLE 8.4   Comparison of the FARC, the ELN, and the paramilitaries

Criterion	FARC	ELN	Paramilitaries
Structure	Centralized	Federalized	Localistic
Incentives			
Pay	Very seldom	Very seldom	Yes
Access to individual benefits	No	No	Yes
Relation with civil society	Low	Medium	Strongly integrated
External risk	High	High	Low to medium
Recruitment	Mainly but not only voluntary, provision of both genuine and false information	Mostly voluntary	Voluntary and forced, depending on region
Exit	Death or desertion	Death, desertion, negotiation	Death, desertion, negotiation
Discipline	Very severe	Medium-low	Medium-low, but with high internal risk
Ideology	Organizational culture	Christian militancy	Self-defense

Verticalism and the obsession for control, or simply open arbitrariness, are present in all domains of life. The fighter's day is meticulously planned, and in all steps of quotidian life it is stressed that the organization's interests are above those of the individual. For example, superiors can order the separation of well-established couples, responding to the imperatives of war or to their own desire, for example, to get rid of the husband and take his place (Molano 2001a, 2001b). Pregnant women have to abort or surrender their babies to a relative (see Ferro and Uribe 2002). Several transgressions—stealing, raping, and looting—are punished with the death penalty. "The Farc-Ep prohibits unruly conduct by its fighters, especially when they are among the civilian population. Robbery, extortion, threats, sexual abuse, and the irresponsible use of firearms can be capital offences" (Human Rights Watch 2003c, 69). Even petty offenses to FARC's military regulations, like falling asleep during a night guard, can produce a tragic outcome. These brutal strictures harm mainly the underage members of the organization.

The FARC is very inward looking. Though it has an ideological life of its own, which should not be ignored, the cement that unites it is its strong "organizational culture"—that is, its capacity to build links between an individual and the organization. Since its combat activity is high, members develop "platoon solidarity," one of the most powerful human gregarious sentiments. But there is much more. Since there is a high percentage of females, couples are formed mainly within the organization.[21] FARC members develop all their private and public life on an organizational stage. They develop practices and learn skills that will be useful in the FARC. There is also a coercive element. Deserters are killed. Desertion is perhaps the worse conceivable offense. The official position of the organization is that by joining one makes a lifelong commitment. Only very rarely is a member allowed to leave.

FARC officials claim that they always warn potential recruits about the meaning of the step they take when they join the organization (Ferro and Uribe 2002), but deserters dispute this. Since both sides have a high element of self-interest—to boost the image of the organization, on the one hand, and to decline responsibility, on the other—it is hard to discern the truth. My impression is that the FARC creates many false beliefs, or at least allows for their creation, with the hope that after joining the recruit will be transformed into a loyal, resilient soldier. From the point of view of the FARC, it is worthwhile to lie. For example, a potential recruit (A) wants to join because she has wrong beliefs (she thinks that in the FARC she can take revenge against someone or earn some money). The FARC tells A she will in effect get a salary, so she joins. Then she discovers that her beliefs were wrong, but in the meantime (a few weeks or months) she has been transformed and integrated, so she is not excessively unhappy. If this method works in a large number of cases, then lying is preferable to abducting or coercing.[22] In certain regions, the FARC is an attractive alternative in its own right and receives a steady stream of applications. Its link with the civil society is weak, or rather almost completely mediated by coercive-regulatory practices (weapons, policing, and market regulations). Thus, the FARC accepts children without parental consent, an option that cannot be easily implemented by the ELN, for example.[23]

The distinctive features of each organization are clearly reflected in the recruitment process. All three groups resort to forced recruitment, but this does not account for the bulk of new entries. The FARC leaders provide a very reasonable explanation for their attachment to free will: unwilling soldiers are bound to shoot their superiors in the back, and they have the ideal conditions to do so in an irregular war (Ferro and Uribe 2002).

The enlistment blueprint of the FARC has three outstanding characteristics. First and foremost, it is a lifelong engagement. Recruits do not have the right to leave, and this is common knowledge. FARC officers do not miss the opportunity to stress this point,[24] especially during the two- to three-month trial period before enlistment becomes irreversible. Second, the organization implies that recruits should break their ties with society. Life as the recruits once knew it is left behind. Family contacts are reduced to a minimum for security reasons—and, I suspect, to preserve internal discipline. Regular contacts with the population are seen as a serious security problem and are discouraged. Indeed, judicial proceedings show that as soon as fighters return to their normal background they engage in practices—such as drinking and partying—that make them more vulnerable. Third, the organization is based on very tight control. As discussed, no salary is paid, and gifts from the family pass through the hands of the guerrilla authorities before (at least in theory) they are redistributed.[25] Personal objects, especially gold chains and other jewelry, are confiscated. FARC leaders have an obvious concern about the effect that money may have on discipline and morale.

For different reasons, the ELN and the paramilitaries allow much more latitude for the advancement of individual interests. In the past, the ELN killed or threatened deserters, particularly prominent ones, but it has long abandoned such practice. People can leave and return, a grave offense that FARC members would never permit. The ELN's routine is much less military driven than FARC's. The ELN is much more ideological than the FARC regarding compensation, at least in the conventional sense.

The paramilitaries offer economic selective incentives and generally do not demand the fighters leave home. The authorities support or turn a blind eye to the activities of the group, and the local elites back them solidly. Therefore, there is no question of starting a new life from scratch, like in the guerrilla groups, nor of leaving behind the system. Egalitarian rules that seem strong both in the FARC and the ELN are nonexistent in the paramilitaries. Control mechanisms, in sum, are much more lenient than in the guerrilla groups. At the same time, the probability of bloody internecine feuds is high.

Joining a guerrilla or the paramilitary group is risky, and the probability of losing one's life grows sharply after entry. Table 8.5 compares the violent death probability of a "typical" noninsurgent Colombian and that of a guerrilla member (the numerator is the dead of the respective category; the denominator is the total count of the category). The result is a 1:70 ratio. Naturally, the actual working ratio may be different. On the one hand, children must be subtracted from the total population's denominator; but, at the same time, those engaged in high-risk activities (such as police, military, and members of narcotrafficking networks), whose death toll is also unusually high, should be removed from the numerator. On the other hand, in some regions the risk of "conventional" citizens may be very high, which could be associated with unusually high rates of recruitment; but risk-averse people can migrate, which they do massively. All in all, not joining a guerrilla group increases one's chance of survival between one and two orders of magnitude.

Even though between 2000 and 2002 the FARC and the government held peace talks, the number of casualties grew. More than one guerrilla member is killed for each soldier, and it is much worse for the ELN.[26] It is not rare that members are killed by members of their own organization (in the early ELN

TABLE 8.5   Probability of violent death for guerillas and Columbian citizens

Year	Guerrilla members (%)	Average citizens (%)
1995	4.81	0.07
1996	5.61	0.07
1997	5.44	0.06
1998	4.76	0.06
1999	4.82	0.06
2000	4.45	0.06

Source: Pinto et al. 2002, 9.

there were frequent internal purges; in the present-day FARC even small transgressions can be punished with death).

Guerilla Motives

Currently, the most accepted interpretation of the motives of guerrilla recruits is still Collier's, along the lines of his famous "greed or grievance" dichotomy. Collier claimed that people joined the guerrillas searching for a job that they did not find in the legal sector. Guerrilla members were the "rebel's workforce." War, then, offers an economic solution to the leaders (rent-seeking) and to the soldiers (salary). Thus, Collier's profile of the typical illegal armed group member is male, young, and unemployed. I do not believe this description is adequate in general, and it does not fit the Colombian case.

Collier has not taken into account that someone who has not found employment in the legal market has many options. A nonnormative Colombian has many choices if he decides to work illegally. He can engage in narcotrafficking, which is both more profitable and less risky than being a guerrilla. Or he can become a paramilitary, which offers pay above the Colombian minimum salary. Because there is no ethnic or religious segmentation in the country, not even a sharp territorial one,[27] any rational expected value calculation should imply avoiding the FARC and choosing any other alternative.

Moreover, the socio-demographic composition of the FARC does not correspond to what Collier himself called his fundamental prediction. The percentage of women is high. The members of the FARC tend to be young, but they can hardly be called "unemployed," even excluding all legal definitions.[28] According to the evidence I have gathered from judicial proceedings, the vast majority of FARC members had a job *before* joining and earned *above* the national average. Of course, this result does not come from a representative sample, but it is nonetheless logical. After the mid-1980s, the FARC strongholds have been coca-growing regions and/or regions rich in other natural resources (Vélez 1999), so one would expect its peasants to be better off than the rest of the population. In summary, a set of peasants—proportionally quite small, but not negligible—joins an organization that offers much worse material conditions than what they had previously, critically high levels of risk of losing their lives, severity, and hardship. In particular, thousands of children join the FARC rather than other groups.

Organizational Pull

The only way to understand the irrationality of those who join the FARC is to consider both pull and push factors. The recruitment strategy of an armylike illegal group *must* be different from the strategy of another kind of group—precisely at the very point at which the economic metaphor finds its limits. Big military organizations cannot be built solely on economic selective incentives. Armies intent on looting or plain mercenaries do not fight well, a fact well acknowledged by every respected military analyst since Machiavelli, because a key feature of a good soldier is the capacity to choose the collective interests in life-and-death situations. Particularly in defense, collective survival may depend on individual sacrifice. Conversely, the hubris of a vindictive warrior, the individualistic drive of a greedy type, or the discipline of a strictly presentist soldier can be self-defeating, as several episodes of the Colombian war have clearly demonstrated (see Jaramillo, Ceballos, and Marta 1998).

Warriors must be taught social values. Once again, this is not a normative but a rational, technical concern. The leaders create a system of incentives that evolves through conscious or imperceptible adjustments. This evolved incentives system leads to important discoveries—that is, successful technological innovators that take a bigger share of the entrants and mold them into efficient warriors—for example, the early discovery by the FARC of the importance of funneling the spoils of combat to the treasury of the organization (Alape 1989), or the requirement of life militancy, which increased its firepower and organizational cohesion. But at the same time, warriors are transformed by the very experience of war. They create strong social ties and develop the knowledge that survival depends on the precision and adequacy of collective tasks.

People who join and remain inside the FARC do so because the FARC actively recruits and tries to turn them into good soldiers. In contrast, the paramilitary offers a real possibility of financial gain, but it never quite forms an armylike force. It is not accidental that, despite the success of paramilitarism in Colombia as a social phenomenon, it was an organizational failure.

Reasons for Fighting

Motivations of recruits are the micro mechanisms that link social structures with preferences and decisions. They are variegated and complex. Several serious qualitative studies have identified, through systematic interviews with retired or active combatants, some of the main ones. Despite the contextual differences, there is a wide area of intersection between them. For example, for Brett and Specht (2005) and Honwana (2006), the main push factors are poverty, unemployment, vengeance, avoiding violence from the rival group, and the allure of the military life. Colombia is prone to this syndrome. Twenty percent of the interviewed assert that they were forced to join at gunpoint, but many others cited the prestige of a military career, false economic promises, conviction, and vengeance as their reason for joining the guerillas (see Gutiérrez 2004).

Unwilling and double-crossed greedy recruits (who perhaps expected a salary but did not receive one) account for almost half of the cases of table 8.1. Does this revive—at least in part—Collier's interpretation? Not necessarily. The problems surrounding the greed interpretation are sticky and appear at every level of the analysis. To see why, let us focus for a moment on a FARC member captured by the army who claims he was lured into the group because he thought he would increase his income. "My salary before enlisting was 8,000 pesos a day, and the guerrilla promised me that I would earn between 300 and 400,000 pesos a month. . . . In fact, that is why I joined." Suppose, reasonably enough, that this recruit wants to go on living, but he was captured after escaping a shooting in which the FARC suffered the worst casualties. In the simplest form, then, his overall utility is a multiplicative function of the utility of his economic gains (E) and the losses he incurs in risking his own life. By the concavity of the utility function over the domain of normal gains, the utility improvement he expected had an upper boundary: $E(300,000)/E(240,000)<300,000/240,000=5/4$ (or $5/3$ if the denominator of the left-hand side of the equation is 400,000 and not 300,000 pesos). This means that for him a very risky life is worth up to $4/5$ the value of a stable one.[29] In other words, a salary of 300,000 would be preferred to one of 8,000 pesos a day only if our subject is almost completely unaware of the enormous danger of losing his life by entering the guerrilla group. This preference is at odds with his survival instinct and with minimally sensible assumptions about what one could call "biological rationality."[30]

Perhaps the strange behavior—from the point of view of the *Homo economicus*—of FARC recruits can be explained by relaxing the assumption that fighters try to maximize a utility function. In particular, there seems to be room for a very simple application of the well-known reference-point effects (Kahneman and Tversky 2000; Bateman et al. 2000).[31] For the following explanation, it must be noted that the coca production cycle is punctuated by boom and bust cycles (caused by both economic and political factors), and in certain regions being a member of an armed group (perhaps any one) is status-boosting. Now, suppose agent A, a coca grower, assesses outcomes on two parameters only, status and income. A is considering joining the FARC. She starts from a reference point x (where x_1 is a certain level of status, and x_2 of income), and then the coca economy enters a crisis. If she chooses not to join the FARC, she will be transferred to point y, with the same social standing but less income (i.e., $y_1=x_1$, but $y_2<x_2$). Alternative z, joining the guerrillas, cuts her income to zero but increases her status (i.e., $z_1>x_1$ and $0=z_2<x_2$). Now, except in extreme cases, the income decrease is so steep that it cannot be offset by the status accretion; that is, in y, A's utility is higher than in z. But, according to reference point effects—which predict that decisions will be anchored on the reference, the status quo ante—A will not compare y and z, but x and y and x and z. Now, point y is strictly dominated by x, while z is not. Point y will be deleted by the domination criterion, and A will choose z even if income is more important than status to her.[32] Something similar can be said about incremented risk taking in the domain of losses, even if the agent exhibits the conventional risk-averse behavior in the domain of gains.[33]

In summary, it can be reasonably asserted that comparative qualitative studies have shown that recruitment cannot be reduced to coercion or greed and needs to take into account social motivations. Please note that the discussion about the possible existence of a reference-point effect had to introduce a social parameter. However, two problems remain. First, as Lichbach (2005) has noted, given the ubiquity of grievances, for Gurr the problematic is to explain why people *do not* rebel. Given the ubiquity of free-riding, Olson's problematic is to explain why people *do* rebel.[34] Social explanations—perhaps mediated by cognitive effects—can explain why joining makes sense, but not why a small but not negligible minority joins while the rest refrain.[35] This is a rather complicated and basically unsolved matter, which is beyond scope of this chapter. Second, it is not sufficient to identify motives in general. The next step is to pinpoint the peculiarities of the push factors of the main demographic categories that participate in war, and the interface between those factors and organizational characteristics. In particular, one would like to understand why child recruitment is much higher in the FARC than in the paramilitaries.

The Specifics of Children

Some specific child motivations have been described in depth—for example, in the context of African conflicts (Richards 1996; Skinner 1999). Conjectures made in those studies apply here as well. Children (especially poor ones) are more vulnerable than adults because their time horizons are short and their discount rates are higher.[36] They also have more reasons for escaping—(pre)adolescent rebellion against parental authority can prompt the decision of searching for illegal alternatives that always exist when there is war. In the case of girls, the decision may be much more strongly motivated, notably when sexual abuse (e.g., by the stepfather) is involved (Lara 2000, 66). These motives tend to go together. A small annoyance can trigger weighty decisions that do not take into account wins or losses in the (very) near future. In the midst of a fit of fury, family discipline or backwardness can appear so appalling that the only alternative is to leave. "I decided [to join the guerrilla] on the spur of the moment," said one child combatant (Human Rights Watch 2003c, 55). Hundreds of adolescents thus seek in the guerrilla groups and the paramilitaries an alternative to the miseries of daily family life. "My father was always fighting with my mother and with us, too. That's why I went off with the guerrillas, to get away from the fighting. It was mainly because I was fed up at home" (Human Rights Watch 2003c, 49). Apparently, this logic is frequent. FARC leaders find it necessary to warn recruits that their discipline is much more severe than that of a standard household, and that the guerrilla group is no solution to petty personal problems (Ferro and Uribe 2002). The traditional peasant society's weakening structures play a role here.

Benefits-oriented, hard-calculating children prefer the narcos and the paramilitaries to the FARC or the ELN.[37] These greed-presentists, who are unable to postpone gratification, are willing to pay very high costs (their life) tomorrow to have access to resources today. This type of youngster is a well-known character in the Colombian war, as well as in its literature and journalism (Salazar 1990, 1993). When no strong organizational structure harnesses the nihilistic tendencies that result from the combination of extremely high discount rates and the orientation toward immediate individual gratification, greed-presentists run amok. This is precisely what happened to the (leftist) urban militias in Medellín, an overwhelmingly teenage force whose members were guided by the motto "(there is) no future" (Salazar 1990, 1993; Jaramillo et al. 1998).[38] However, this type of fighter does not have a long, useful life. The Darwinist advantage of the FARC is its capacity (indeed, its need) to transform these motivations into warriorlike ones, which has a demonstration effect over new potential recruits.

As discussed, the FARC appears to foster wrong beliefs among some of its potential recruits with the hope of transforming them after they join. It may be the case that children are simply more gullible or are not able to calculate the negative aspects of engaging in an (insurgent) military career. Children may also be more exposed to framing effects. In the case of the paramilitaries, they promise salaries and they deliver, but still the recruit may hold wrong beliefs (for example, turning a blind eye to the worst aspects of the military life that awaits them). Additionally, minors are incorporated to the peripheral networks because the paramilitaries lack the Napoleonic drive of the guerrillas.

Human Rights Watch correctly asserts that in Colombia enlistment in the guerrillas is not forced. "The great majority of child recruits to the irregular forces decide to join voluntarily" (Human Rights Watch 2003c, 24). There are, however, two major sources of pressure on minors. First, the sheer asymmetry between the group and the child. Adults, after all, can choose to run away; children are much less mobile.[39] Second, peer pressure (especially strong when the peer is kin) goes hand in hand with a degree of territorial segmentation. Children tend to join the group that is available in the here and now (Brett and Specht 2005), but it is noteworthy that in the Colombian case there are long periods in which adversaries overlap territorially.

In many peasant societies, membership in an armed organization offers status and the possibility of upward social mobility. For children, this has an added meaning: joining the group is an explicit recognition of their status as adults. In their posterior recollections, many ex-combatants recognize that they learned not only how to obey but also how to command, an experience that their parents might never have had. More obliquely, life in a guerrilla group may provide extended training and education, an aspect that many combatants (particularly the young and the female) consider extremely valuable. An army-like structure can offer more of this than a loose federation of local dons.

Summary

Recruits have many motivations, including proximity, vengeance, fear, family conflicts, coveting local power, and visibility. It would be rather pedantic to assume those themes as inevitably nonpolitical; they can constitute the intersection between story and history, between personal trajectories and big processes. The key to understanding their potential political valence is that they are not activated until an organization does not come up with an ecumenical story that allows individuals to spell out their individual concerns in a universalistic idiom. But such concerns need not coincide with the organization's objective. To transform raw recruits into useful fighters, illegal armed groups promote preference transformations through ideology and/or socialization in key experiences. Each organization forms different types of fighters. Loyalty grows with length of service. Translated into rationalistic slang, this means that each fighter has two distinct utility functions.[40] The original motivations of the fighters are changed generally, and the reasons to join are quite different from the reasons to remain. The latter depends crucially on the type of organization. For the practical personnel engaged in reinsertion processes, it is important to recognize that the children recruited from group X will be very different than those from group Y.

Part IV

Empirical Assessments of Child Soldiers

CHAPTER 9

WAR, DISPLACEMENT, AND
THE RECRUITMENT OF CHILD SOLDIERS IN
THE DEMOCRATIC REPUBLIC OF CONGO

Sarah Kenyon Lischer

DISPLACEMENT IS ONE OF THE MOST COMMON PRODUCTS of violent conflict. When weighing the risks posed by civil war, many people decide that their best chance of safety lies elsewhere. Sometimes the chaos and destruction of war arrives so suddenly that families become separated—children flee from school, farmers leave their fields, mothers escape their homes. In other situations, soldiers force an evacuation at gunpoint and whole villages are exiled en masse. Displacement does not necessarily lead to safety, however. Refugees and internally displaced persons (IDPs) may become targets of attack or simply languish indefinitely in squalid, disease-ridden camps.[1] For the most vulnerable, especially children, the dangers of displacement may rival those of the conflict they hoped to escape.

The 1996 United Nations report on the "Impact of Armed Conflict on Children" determined that children separated from their families during conflict are one of the most at-risk categories of becoming child soldiers (Machel 1996). These "unaccompanied minors," as international organizations term them, include children orphaned by war or disease, as well as those separated from family in the chaos of conflict. Unaccompanied minors lack parental protection and generally live in a less supervised environment than other displaced children. The United Nations General Assembly has repeatedly recognized that displaced and unaccompanied minors are vulnerable to neglect, violence, forced military recruitment, and sexual assault.[2]

Even when children remain with their parents, forced displacement can disrupt family and social networks. In a refugee or IDP crisis, parents often lose customary sources of authority as they lack the ability to provide for their children. This can increase the difficulty of controlling adolescents and transmitting traditional values. Among refugee populations, children generally receive inadequate education and have little hope of permanent employment in the host state, even if they manage to complete secondary school. The educational prospects for IDP children is usually even grimmer, since conflict often leads to a complete breakdown of infrastructure. The combination of disruption and desperation increases displaced children's vulnerability to military recruitment.

The literature on child soldiers offers numerous explanations for the increasing use of children in war. P. W. Singer cites three main factors: social disruptions and failures of development caused by globalization and war; the proliferation of lightweight small arms; and the increase in economic motivations for civil war (Singer 2005, 38). These explanations can be applied to refugees and internally displaced people, even if the literature does not directly consider displacement. As discussed above, the experience of displacement often includes traumatic social disruption and drastically reduced economic opportunities.

Very little scholarship explicitly addresses the relationship between displacement and child soldier recruitment. The systematic study by Vera Achvarina and Simon Reich provides a valuable first step. They persuasively argue that "large numbers of children congregated together in easily identifiable locations, if left unprotected, make an easy target as recruits for belligerents" (Achvarina and Reich 2006a, 35). Achvarina and Reich assess competing explanations of child soldier rates of recruitment and suggest that refugee protection is an important, and generally overlooked, factor. My research builds on that finding and offers a deeper analysis of the conditions of displacement that increase the likelihood of the recruitment of child soldiers.

Causal Paths to Child Recruitment

There are two main patterns, or causal paths, through which displaced children are recruited as fighters. Children can become targets of recruitment when the displaced population is militarized or when the population lacks security (see figs. 9.1–9.3). My specification of the militarization and insecurity paths expands on the more general causal framework advanced by Achvarina and Reich.

FIG. 9.1. Militarization path

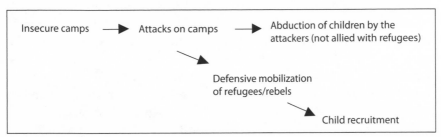

FIG. 9.2. Insecurity path

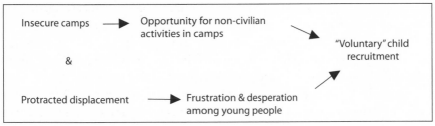

FIG. 9.3. Insecurity over time

International law mandates respect for the civilian and humanitarian character of refugee camps and prohibits refugee participation in military activity.[3] There is no comparable international legal framework concerning internally displaced persons. Thus, the phenomenon of militarization is harder to define and observe among internally displaced populations. The militarization explanation is generally more applicable to refugee situations, since cross-border camps provide increased opportunities for militants to train and regroup. The militarization of some refugee populations has led to cross-border raids by militias based in or near refugee camps, attacks on the refugee population by the sending state, and even international war.

The term "militarization" describes noncivilian attributes of refugee populated areas, including inflows of weapons, military training, and recruitment. Militarization also includes actions of refugees or exiles who engage in noncivilian activity outside the refugee camp, yet who depend on assistance from refugees or international organizations.[4] Militarization can occur due to the presence of soldiers or militant exiles (including war criminals) who live in or

near the refugee populated area and interact with the refugees. Refugees or exiles who store arms and train outside the camp, yet return to the camp for food,
medical assistance, and family visits, create a militarized refugee population.

The militarization explanation for recruitment of displaced children posits
that in such a generally mobilized population it will be easier for militants to
recruit children. Militarization implies that the refugee population lacks the
protection mandated by international law and has lost its civilian character. As
militants are able to operate freely, perhaps even with the support of the refugee population, children will become vulnerable to recruitment. During the
Sudanese civil war, the Sudanese People's Liberation Army (SPLA) rebels took
militarization to an extreme by creating a series of boys-only refugee camps on
the Ethiopian border. Separated from their families and surrounded by war,
the boys became a valuable fighting force for the rebels (Singer 2005, 24).

A similar pattern is likely among internally displaced populations, although
there is insufficient scholarship available to know with certainty. IDPs have
fled their homes, but not their countries. Therefore, international law presumes
that they are under the protection of their government. In reality, of course,
IDPs flee because their government cannot or will not protect them. The legal
and demographic distinctions between IDPs and recognized refugees likely
affects their patterns of militarization.

The militarization pattern of recruitment parallels the broader literature on
child soldiers that emphasizes life in a war zone as a high risk factor for recruitment. Singer describes children in a civil war environment as "surrounded by
violence," usually combined with a situation of extreme poverty (Singer 2005,
43). Rather than functioning as the safe haven intended by international law, a
militarized refugee camp approximates the conditions of a conflict zone.

The second explanation for child recruitment examines the physical security of the displaced population. This suggests that, regardless of the political
or military motivations of the inhabitants, poorly protected camps are vulnerable to raids in which the attackers abduct children for military purposes. Achvarina and Reich argue that "child soldiers will constitute a larger percentage of
belligerent forces where camps are relatively vulnerable to infiltration or raiding." (Achvarina and Reich 2006a, 12)

In addition to that straightforward mechanism for recruitment, attacks on
camps may also spur the refugees to mobilize defensively. In some instances,
opportunistic leaders convince refugees to mobilize by manipulating their
fear of attack. That may lead to further militarization and child recruitment by
fighters allied to the refugees. IDP populations are less likely to mobilize militarily because they are more vulnerable to government reprisals.

Living conditions and expectations about the future add a conditional factor to explanations of child soldier recruitment. My earlier study of refugee

militarization suggests that poor living conditions are an insufficient explanation for military activity (see Lischer 2005, chap. 2). In other words, militarization does not necessarily increase when living conditions, measured in terms of mortality rates, malnutrition rates, and levels of humanitarian assistance, decrease. However, examination of militant displaced groups does show that expectations about the future, such as the likelihood of resettlement abroad, imminent return home, or finding employment in the receiving state, affect the likelihood of militarization. Protracted displacement crises lead to reduced expectations for the future and thus a higher receptivity to military activity (Loescher and Milner 2005). Thus, one would expect that children are more easily recruited from long-term displaced populations who have few educational or employment opportunities.

For the purpose of clarity, I have diagrammed these paths as though they are mutually exclusive. It is certainly possible, however, that these paths interact with each other. In some instances, militarization can reduce the security of the camps by making them more likely targets for attack. Conversely, insecure camps increase refugees' vulnerability, making militarization an attractive option for opportunistic leaders.

Given these probable causal paths whereby displaced children are recruited into armed conflict, a logical follow-up question becomes, which causal path is more common? A major hindrance to charting the patterns of recruitment in camps is the dearth of reliable data. Systematic data on child recruitment does not exist for refugee populations, much less for internally displaced persons. The existing evidence on refugee militarization, however, suggests that insecurity and youth desperation play an important role in child soldier recruitment.

Conditions of Camp Insecurity

Regardless of their level of militarization, a poorly protected displaced population is more likely to suffer attacks and abduction of children. Camps and settlements for the displaced display a wide variation in their vulnerability to attacks. Among refugee populations, four main attributes determine camp vulnerability. These are the capability of the receiving state to provide security and maintain order; the porosity of international borders; the presence of international protection; and the security measures taken within the camp. The international aspects of these factors apply most directly to refugees, but issues of camp security also apply to IDP settlements.

Capability of the Receiving State

According to international law, the refugee-receiving state is responsible for maintaining the civilian and humanitarian nature of refugee camps.[5] This includes providing adequate policing to maintain law and order in and around the camps. A capable receiving state also has a functioning judicial system to handle any militants or criminals among the refugees. In IDP situations, international law assumes that the sovereign government can provide protection to its citizens. Thus, international forces generally breach a state's sovereignty only in cases of extreme human rights abuses or when invited in (e.g., as a peacekeeping force).

A weak, or failed, receiving state is unable to provide basic physical protection to its own citizens, much less to refugees. Most refugee camps are located in poor countries, often with a history of civil strife. Additionally, refugees generally reside in the geographic periphery of the receiving state. These peripheral regions are often the first areas to lose the protection of the central government. In Zaire during the Rwandan refugee influx of the mid-1990s, the eastern areas of the country had carved out virtual autonomy from the decaying central government. Political order collapsed and refugees (and local civilians) found themselves at the mercy of capricious, greedy local leaders and militias. The UN High Commissioner for Refugees (UNHCR) notes that the banditry rampant in remote areas in Ethiopia, Kenya, and Tanzania threatens locals and refugees alike (UNHCR 2006, 70).

In some instances, a capable receiving state may condone refugee militarization or even send government agents to recruit refugees for fighting. This may occur if the receiving state is allied with the refugees for ethnic or political reasons. Such an alliance formed between the Afghan refugees and their Pakistani hosts during the 1980s, leading to a high level of militarization and recruitment among the refugees. When the receiving state encourages military activity, the pattern of child soldier recruitment is likely to follow this type of militarization path (i.e., the presence of militants among refugees leads to child recruitment).

Porosity of Borders

Closely tied to the capability of the receiving state is the security of international borders. A weak receiving state cannot prevent illegal border crossings by rebels, state military forces, criminals, or smugglers. Refugee camps are usually sited near the border of their home state—for reasons of convenience and politics. When the receiving state is unable to protect the camp from hostile cross-border raids, recruitment becomes more likely.

In certain situations, the receiving state has the capability to police its border but chooses to allow military activity in the refugee camps. If the receiving state is allied with the sending state, it may allow hot pursuit raids across the border. Or the government of the receiving state may attempt to destabilize a rival neighbor by encouraging rebels to use the refugees as a recruitment pool. As discussed earlier, Sudanese rebels situated militarized refugee camps across the border in Ethiopia, where they trained thousands of boy fighters. When the regime in Addis Ababa changed, the new government proved hostile to the SPLA and forced closure of the camps (Singer 2005, 24).

International Protection

The presence of international protection forces, such as a UN peacekeeping mission, can ameliorate some of the problems posed by weak or hostile host areas. In 2003, the Economic Community of West African States Mission in Liberia (ECOMIL) deployed troops to the refugee and IDP camps around Monrovia. Commenting on the ECOMIL mission, UNHCR observed that "the rapid deployment of humanitarian and security personnel in and around the refugee-populated areas during the initial phase of a humanitarian emergency helped deter armed elements from infiltrating the population or targeting refugees" (UNHCR 2006, 77).

Missions such as ECOMIL are the exception, however. Most insecure camps do not benefit from an effective international protection force. Lack of funding and political will are the usual reasons why displaced populations do not receive international protection. In some cases, UN agencies and nongovernmental organizations (NGOs) hire private forces or provide funds to train local forces. Overall, these efforts have fallen short of preventing militarization and, in some situations, have worsened insecurity.

As a last resort, many humanitarian organizations attempt to protect displaced people by their presence in the camps. UNHCR and NGOs hope that their ability to witness any abuses and advocate on behalf of the victims will deter the more blatant offenses, such as abduction of children. This "protection by presence" usually breaks down in the face of life-threatening security situations. In 2006, riots in a camp for internally displaced persons in Darfur, Sudan, forced the evacuation of aid workers and journalists from the camp. The only security force consisted of a handful of unarmed African Union soldiers who barricaded themselves in their quarters in fear of their lives (Polgreen 2006). Such a dangerous and chaotic situation surely leaves children vulnerable to manipulation and recruitment, although the lack of witnesses makes it difficult to quantify the threat.

Camp Security Measures

Most observers agree that refugee camps "are unnatural, closed environments which can leave refugees vulnerable to manipulation and exploitation, with the danger increasing where such situations are prolonged" (UNHCR 2006, 85). Planning measures within the camp can either threaten or reinforce the security of children. This includes layout and organization that permits maximum supervision and protection of vulnerable groups like unaccompanied minors.[6]

Some observers note that allowing parents' input into camp organization and governance will help them maintain responsibility for their children. Similarly, extended educational and vocational opportunities can be viewed as a security measure if they dissuade adolescents from participating in military activity (UNHCR 2006, 87).

Threats to refugees and humanitarian workers have convinced UNHCR to attempt to "mainstream" security concerns into all of its programs. This effort includes a two-year work plan to incorporate eighty new recommendations on security, such as "strengthening policing in refugee camps and planning safer site locations, shelter, food and water" (UNHCR 2005, 9). Additional suggestions include implementing "comprehensive global birth registration, the prevention of family separation and where that is not possible, promotion of family reunification; and education for all (including girls and adolescents) even during conflicts and an explanation to children of their basic human rights" (Brett 2001, 19). Despite these goals and intentions, however, the vulnerability of refugee camps varies markedly, and they frequently fail to provide adequate protection for children.

The above discussion focuses on protection issues affecting formal refugee camps. Yet many displaced people, especially those displaced within their own countries, live in informal settlements or squatter camps, or they are dispersed among local residents. These IDPs generally lack even the minimal security measures provided in organized refugee camps. Internally displaced populations do not share the same international legal protection as refugees, in theory because they are still under the protection of their home state. In reality, the type of violence that causes their displacement—often government persecution—makes them even more vulnerable than refugees.

The conflict in the Darfur region of Sudan provides an example of the heightened vulnerability of IDPs. Since the war began in 2003, nearly two million people have been displaced from their homes. Nearly all the displaced are crowded into makeshift camps within Darfur. These camps have become targets for attack by the government-allied militias, as well as recruitment pools and staging grounds for various rebel groups. The United Nations reported eight aid workers killed in the month of July 2006 and increased levels of theft, including hijacking (United Nations 2006a).

Youth Desperation

High levels of physical insecurity combined with conditions of youth desperation increase the likelihood that displaced children will participate in military activity. Children interviewed by aid workers and human rights activists give varying reasons for their participation (in addition to physical coercion). The most common reasons cited include the lack of food and other basic necessities, pressure from adults to join, witnessing atrocities committed against family members or peers, the desire to alleviate their family's suffering, and the perception that there are no alternative options. There are six basic indicators by which I measure youth desperation.

The first is the length of time the person has been displaced. Quite often, displaced people become increasingly desperate as their crisis drags on. The initial enthusiasm of international donors quickly wears off and the displaced people feel forgotten. The length of the displacement crisis could also serve as a proxy for the length of the conflict. A longer war may increase the chance that combatants exhaust the supply of willing adult recruits and turn to children.

It is also important to look at the economic trends in the region of the state affected by the displacement. Often these areas are peripheral to the central government and receive fewer resources. The displaced population may experience economic discrimination based on ethnicity, religion, or other characteristics. Relying solely on state-level economic statistics could mask important regional variation. This measure should examine GNP per capita over time, employment statistics, and levels of humanitarian assistance. Declining economic status will affect children's well-being in terms of the availability of food, health-care, and other basic necessities. Young teenagers will realize that their families are suffering and their own future prospects are slim.

In the Liberian civil war, for example, both the government forces and the Liberians United for Reconciliation and Democracy (LURD) preyed on civilians, increasing the levels of desperation and vulnerability. Refugees from Liberia explained the seemingly wanton brutality that caused their flight: "[LURD rebels] burned the whole town. Everyone fled into the bushes ... Government troops were behind us. They came into the bush and took our clothes and materials" (Human Rights Watch 2002b, 8). Achvarina and Reich (2006a, 33) report that child soldiers constituted over half of the fighting forces in the Liberian conflict. Government soldiers routinely crossed the border to recruit young Liberian refugees as mercenaries. In one instance at Nicla camp in Ivory Coast, the recruiters, brandishing machine guns, signed up 150 young Liberians (including many teenagers) for the equivalent of seventeen dollars each. One new recruit explained, "We want money. Here we are nothing and we have nothing" (UNHCR 2003b, 18). In this situation it seems that a combination of camp vulnerability and poor living conditions enticed the recruits.

Depending on their status, refugees and internally displaced people receive varying levels of legal protection, making legal status a third indicator of youth desperation. Internationally recognized refugees have the greatest level of legal protection, at least in theory. Many internally displaced people, on the other hand, live as illegal squatters or have been sent to quasi–concentration camps by a vengeful government. It follows that children without legal protections are more vulnerable to both abduction and recruitment. One might expect that internally displaced children are more often recruited than refugee children, since refugees benefit from an international structure of laws and institutions meant to protect them.

The availability of education is an indicator that the UNHCR has recognized can function as a protection tool in two ways (UNHCR 2002, 4). First, when schools are secure, they allow children a safe place to gather. Second, providing IDPs with education gives them more choices about their future and hopefully reduces the allure of military recruitment.

Family status, as discussed earlier, is an important indicator as well. Separated and orphaned children are more at risk for recruitment into military forces than children living with their parents.

Traumatization is the sixth and final indicator of youth desperation. Many child soldiers interviewed during demobilization cite violent trauma as a catalyst for their recruitment. Such traumas include war-related violence as well as domestic violence (especially for girls). Child soldiers recall witnessing the murders or torture of family members and friends as turning points in their lives. This factor relates to the earlier discussion of the length of displacement and conflict duration. It stands to reason that children are more likely to suffer trauma in a longer conflict.

Child Soldiers in the Democratic Republic of Congo

A brutal civil war raged in the Democratic Republic of Congo (DRC) from 1998 to 2003. Pockets of conflict have continued to erupt following the peace agreement, particularly in the eastern provinces. The conflict has cost over four million lives and displaced millions more from their homes. The scholarly consensus is that greed, rather than grievance, sustains this war. All parties to the conflict pillage natural resources such as diamonds, gold, copper, and coltan. For the most part, the combatants aim to terrorize civilians, not to win them over to any particular ideology or political program. Some of the violence has an ethnic component, particularly the Hema-Lendu conflict in northeastern Congo, but that factor is deeply entwined with economic motivations (for more in-depth analysis, see Misser 2006).

Throughout the civil war, all sides conscripted children for use as soldiers, porters, and sex slaves. Early in the civil war, the government of President Laurent Kabila issued a call on national radio for youths between twelve and twenty to enlist and fight the rebels (Human Rights Watch 1999). Kabila's action followed the pattern he established as a rebel fighter in the first Congolese civil war (from 1996 to 1997) in which his Alliance of Democratic Forces for the Liberation of Congo-Zaire (ADFL) included at least ten thousand child soldiers (WCAC 2003, 24). Groups allied with Kabila's government, such as Rally for Congolese Democracy–Movement for Liberalisation (RCD-ML) and Mai-Mai militias, recruited children in large numbers. NGOs estimate that children under eighteen make up half of the Mai-Mai combatant forces (CSUCS 2004a). The RCD-Goma rebel factions focused on child recruitment when its ally Rwanda began withdrawing troops in 2002. According to Human Rights Watch (2001, 6), RCD-Goma relied on forced recruitment, abducting boys and young men from their homes, the market, schools, and on the way to church. By April 2003, the UN mission to Congo estimated that 20 percent of RCD-Goma's front line combatants were under eighteen.

In addition to the DRC government and rebel groups, foreign soldiers have also conscripted Congolese children. During the 1996–1997 civil war, Rwandan government troops aided Kabila's Congolese rebel forces. One Rwandan commander bragged about the army of children put in place by Kabila's forces: "it was an army made up of youngsters, obedient and disciplined, but who needed to be better supervised, better trained" (Human Rights Watch 2001, 10). The Mission of the United Nations Organisation in the Democratic Republic of the Congo (MONUC) estimates that 10,000 to 12,000 foreign fighters are still in eastern Congo (Refugees International 2005a). For example, the Rwandan rebel group Forces Democratique de Liberation du Rwanda (FDLR) faces difficulty in recruiting and retaining adults, so it has turned to children. Child soldiers can be frightened more easily by propaganda (for example, that all returning Hutus will be killed in Rwanda). Defection rates are lower for child soldiers, especially girls (Refugees International 2005a). There are also reports of children being abducted and sent to Uganda and Rwanda for training (BBC News 2001).

Reliable statistics on child soldiers in the DRC are difficult to obtain, but most observers agree that child recruitment is rampant. In 2002, the International Coalition to Stop the Use of Child Soldiers estimated that tens of thousands of child soldiers were active in DRC (WCAC 2003, 22). Aid workers and the United Nations suggest that at least 30 percent of the combatants are children under eighteen (Ngowi 2003; WCAC 2003, 23). UNICEF calculated that in 2005 there were 33,000 children associated with the fighting forces just in North Kivu Province (Refugees International 2005d).

The following pages explore the ways in which displacement and youth desperation interact and affect child participation in military activity in DRC. This analysis does not serve as a definitive test of causal paths. Such a test would require more comparative case studies and, if possible, a large-N statistical analysis of many cases over time. In addition, the DRC case study does not suggest that displacement is a necessary condition for child recruitment. The literature offers many examples of children who join military forces during conflict even if they are not displaced (e.g., Save the Children 2006a). The chapter in this volume by Achvarina and Reich more directly compares displacement to alternate explanations. My research does not evaluate those alternate explanations; rather, I specify the logic by which displacement might affect child recruitment.

Patterns of Displacement

The vast majority of people displaced by the Congo conflict remain within the DRC borders. At the height of the crisis in 2003, there were over three million internally displaced Congolese out of a total estimated population of 49 million. The United Nations estimated that 1.6 million people remained displaced as of June 2006. Of these, only around 250,000 were refugees in neighboring states (primarily Tanzania). Some IDPs fled to the bush, where they lacked food, medicine, and shelter. A 2005 Refugees International mission found IDP camps located on the outskirts of Kinshasa containing "displaced people from areas throughout the country who had been living in deplorable conditions for years" with virtually no humanitarian assistance (Refugees International 2005b). Another study found that some of the newly displaced people in Katanga province did not even have clothes to wear (Misser 2006, 14).

It is important to note that the national displacement statistics can be misleading, since there are wide variations among regions. Four provinces in the east—Orientale, North Kivu, South Kivu, and Katanga—account for over 90 percent of internal displacement. For example, Ituri district in Orientale Province has a population of four million, of which 500,000 have fled their homes since 1999 (Mwepu 2006). Refugees International estimates that 6,200 of the 15,000 combatants in Ituri are children (Refugees International 2005d).

In addition, the numbers reported as annual figures do not reflect the fluid-

TABLE 9.1   Displacement during the civil war

	1998	1999	2000	2001	2002	2003
Refugees from DRC in neighboring states (primarily in Tanzania, Republic of Congo, and Zambia)	158,833	255,950	371,713	392,146	421,362	453,465
Refugees from neighboring states in DRC (primarily from Angola and Sudan)	240,214	285,270	332,509	362,012	332,978	234,033
Internally displaced within DRC (primarily in the east)	131,000	Not enough data	Not enough data	2.0 million	2.2 million	About 3.0 million

Sources: IDMC 2006; UNHCR 2003a, 128–129; UNOCHA 1998, 2001, 2002a, 2.

ity of the displacement. People may be displaced multiple times within a year. Or they may be displaced and return home within the same year. Thus, population movements reflect the unpredictable ebb and flow of fighting in the region (IDMC 2006).

The patterns of displacement in DRC underline the importance of distinguishing between refugees and internally displaced persons when analyzing the role of displacement in child soldier recruitment. Refugee protection measures offer a misleading picture of the security situation. First of all, the internationally recognized refugees within the DRC are mostly from Angola and live primarily in regions that are distant from the conflict zones. In addition, the refugees generally do not reside in formal camp settlements. UNHCR indicates that only about 5,000 of 150,000 refugees lived in camps as of 2003. The majority live in informal settlements and rural areas, or they are dispersed among local populations (UNHCR 2003a, 128–129).

Refugees from the Congo currently live in Tanzania, Republic of Congo, Zambia, Burundi, and Rwanda. These refugees, especially the 150,000 in Tanzania, enjoy greater security and standards of living than those displaced within DRC. Congolese refugees in Tanzania are not highly militarized or politicized (unlike Burundian refugees in Tanzania). Based on those general facts, it seems reasonable to suggest that Congolese refugee children are less likely to participate in military activity than IDP children.

Low Levels of Protection

Inadequate protection, especially for displaced people, increases the likelihood of child recruitment. As discussed earlier, measures of protection include the capability of the state, porosity of borders, presence of international protection, and security measures within camps and IDP settlements. For the most part, eastern DRC is characterized by impotent state authority, completely porous borders, and ineffective security measures.

The central government is unable to provide political order in the war-affected eastern regions of DRC. One former soldier explains: "There has never been security in North Kivu . . . we live like we are in the Wild West where everyone makes his own law. The state is nonexistent in the province" (IRIN 2006a). Some regions are under the control of various militias or rebel groups who have little accountability or incentives to provide services to the population. MONUC reports that over 80 percent of attacks on civilians in North Kivu are perpetrated by the regular army (IRIN 2006a).

The presence of MONUC, with about 16,000 soldiers, has been unable to counteract the rampant insecurity. MONUC's mandate includes overseeing disarmament, demobilization, repatriation, resettlement, and reintegration. It is authorized under chapter 7 of the UN charter and is allowed to use force to protect civilians "under imminent threat of physical violence" (MONUC 2006). The continuing violence and high levels of displacement testify that civilians cannot put their trust in the protection offered by the international community.

Most of the internally displaced Congolese do not live in formal camps. Thus, the earlier discussion of security measures does not directly apply to eastern Congo. For the most part, both IDPs and local residents live in highly insecure situations. In 2002, the United Nations estimated that over 20 million Congolese were vulnerable due to "adverse effects of the conflict and chronic insecurity" (UNOCHA 2002a, 14). Thus, it is clear that the security problems of IDPs cannot be solved separately from the general security needs in the east.

There are two important additions to the general discussion of IDPs and they both affect children. Two particularly vulnerable groups in DRC are unaccompanied children and demobilized child soldiers. Aid organizations have found that unaccompanied children are targets of conscription and abduction. Human Rights Watch (1999) reported that rebel forces abducted children from local NGOs that worked with unaccompanied minors (see also Human Rights Watch 2004a). In 1998, the United Nations reported 4,600 "officially" unaccompanied children in DRC (UNOCHA 1998). That figure does not count street children or others who do not receive international assistance.

Another disturbing finding is that demobilized child soldiers are often re-recruited, sometimes from the very demobilization centers meant to prepare the children to return home. In one instance, Human Rights Watch reported that Laurent Kabila's ADFL rebel forces reenlisted about 100 demobilized children from a UNICEF-run transit center (Human Rights Watch 1999). In another example, the rebel group RCD-ML re-recruited "dozens" of children who had just been demobilized by the Mai-Mai militia (CSUCS 2004a). This phenomenon suggests that the poorly protected demobilization centers have become a tempting target of child recruitment. After all, the children gathered in the demobilization centers have already been trained and brutalized. They are separated from their families and generally lack even basic necessities for subsistence. Many child soldiers find that their families have disappeared or died during their absence, which increases the likelihood that they will be re-recruited.

High Levels of Desperation

A variety of economic and social factors increase children's vulnerability to so-called voluntary recruitment. Among displaced children, these factors are likely exacerbated by the breakdown of traditional structures of protection, such as the extended family. As discussed earlier, the factors that increase desperation include the length of time displaced, worsening economic trends, unstable legal status, lack of education, separation from parents, and traumatization.

The length of time that particular groups have been displaced is difficult to measure since it varies for different populations and regions of eastern Congo. Overall, the displacement crisis began with the influx of over a million Rwandan Hutu refugees and militants in 1994. This led to civil war from 1996 to 1997 which reignited in 1998 and ended (at least on paper) in 2003. Following the peace agreement the United Nations estimated that over 1.5 million people remained displaced, with their homes and livelihoods destroyed. Even as some groups return home, others are newly displaced when the fighting shifts to their towns and villages.

It is impossible to exaggerate the severity of the economic situation for the displaced residents of eastern DRC. Numerous NGOs report that the generalized poverty is manifested by acute food insecurity and a lack of water, sanitation, and health care. These problems are magnified during displacement when people lose access to their land and traditional coping systems. A 2002 United Nations map attempted to convey the scope of the problem by color-coding areas according to vulnerability. Vast swathes of eastern DRC are colored red, signifying the highest level of danger. As the map key explains: "these populations, continuously on the move, are considered as the most vulnerable in the DRC. The malnutrition rates registered in these areas are the highest in the country, sometimes beyond 50%. These populations are located in the most inaccessible areas of the country . . . rendering the delivery of assistance almost impossible" (UNOCHA 2002b, 43).

A Médecins Sans Frontières (MSF) study confirmed the dire situation described by the United Nations. MSF followed 16,000 displaced people who descended on the town of Dubie (population 10,000) in Katanga Province. Among the IDP population, the crude mortality rate was 4.3 deaths per 10,000 per day, which well exceeds the threshold for a humanitarian emergency (1 death per 10,000 per day) (Médecins Sans Frontières 2006, 3).

Many children interviewed by aid workers cite the suffering of their families as an impetus for recruitment. They hoped to protect their families by joining the rebels or to relieve their parents of having to provide for one extra mouth to feed. Watchlist on Children and Armed Conflict noted that "in the context of generalized poverty and breakdown of basic social services, unaccompanied children or orphans may be seeking protection, food and/or a place in society" (2003, 23).

The conflict and accompanying insecurity has wiped out any social services and made education beyond the reach of most families. UNHCR commented on the appalling state of social programs at the height of the conflict: "Government spending on children's programs is nearly non-existent. Primary school education is not compulsory, free, or universal" (UNHCR 2000, 26). Children, especially displaced or unaccompanied children, have little hope of using education as a means to a better future. Further disrupting the educational system, schools have become a target for forced recruitment by military forces. Many former child soldiers report being abducted at school or en route to and from school.

Former child soldiers who joined voluntarily often describe a traumatic event as the catalyst for their decision. Fourteen-year-old Patric Baraka explained, "I became a soldier two years ago after watching Lendus kill my parents and five siblings" (Ngowi 2003). Fifteen-year-old "Furaa" joined the military forces after her father beat her and tried to kill her with a machete (Save the Children 2006b). A teenage girl recounted how at age twelve she witnessed the rape and murder of her mother and sisters by RCD-Goma fighters. As she later explained to Amnesty International, "I was scared and I thought that if I joined the army, I would be protected. I wanted to defend myself" (Amnesty International 2003). Most of these children find, however, that further trauma and abuse awaits them in the military.

Summary

Currently, there is no comprehensive source of information about displacement, insecurity, and child recruitment. Obtaining numbers of refugees is difficult enough, much less describing the various levels of security affecting displaced populations and the detailed characteristics of camp organization. Even basic information, such as the percentage of children in the population, is not always available. For example, recent UNHCR figures present demographic data for only 11.7 million out of over 19.0 million persons of concern (see UNHCR 2004, tables 1 and 10). Gathering sufficient information will require a large-scale and detailed data collection effort.

The anecdotal evidence provided by aid workers and human rights reports is useful, but it does not offer a generalizable picture of child soldier recruitment. Further data is needed to attain a more systematic understanding of the relationship between displacement and child recruitment. It would also be beneficial to disaggregate data between refugees and internally displaced people, since each group receives different types of international protection.

The absence of a universal data set on child soldiers and displacement should not dampen policy efforts to stem recruitment, however. The reports from various crisis zones, in conjunction with the existing scholarly literature, indicate the need for better refugee protection policies and specific attention to unaccompanied minors. Evidence indicates that modifications in camp structure and management can increase security for the residents. Additionally, the literature on child soldiers and civil wars points to certain types of conflicts, for example "greed" wars, as being more prone to relying on children as fighters. With the constraint of limited resources, donors and aid agencies can concentrate their initial efforts on improving security for the most at-risk displaced children.

CHAPTER 10

DISAGGREGATING THE CAUSAL FACTORS UNIQUE TO CHILD SOLDIERING

The Case of Liberia

James B. Pugel

> Put the boys in, and may God forgive me for the order.
> —Confederate General J. C. Breckinridge, Battle of New Market, 15 May 1864

WITH A CONTEMPORARY INTERNATIONAL FOCUS ON THE ISSUE of employing child soldiers in inter- and intrastate conflicts, a new area of research for academics has opened to identify and quantify the causal factors attributable to the practice. While the practice of employing children in combat, both in direct actions and supporting logistical roles, is not new to the world stage, the increased usage and blatant disregard of moral and human rights have been so pervasive in recent years that numerous statutes and protocols have been set by international bodies in order to curb miscreant behaviors and bring some semblance of order to the chaotic nature of warfare.[1] International expectation may well be defined by a line that demarcates a child from an adult with respect to the attribute of age, but the researcher and analyst interested in determining the causal factors associated with child soldiering will find the line fraught with ambiguity and complication. The situation is further complicated by the plethora of nefariously enigmatic military leaders that accompany many of world's contemporary conflicts. The extreme variety of organizational and leadership styles advanced on the modern African landscape during the pursuit of power, glory, or resource attainment directly affects the conduct and environment within which the conflict is propagated. Through a rigorous investigation of a large-N data set of a sample of ex-combatants from Liberia, the relevance of factional disaggregation will become starkly apparent within the context of determining causal factors that are unique to the population of child soldiers.

Defining the Child Soldier

As Singer (2006) points out in his chapter, the phenomenon of child soldiering is not particularly new to the landscape of warfare. Confronting the issue and exacting punishment upon the heads of those who employ the practice within their respective fighting forces, however, is quite new. It was not until 1989 and the Convention on the Rights of a Child that a measurable attribute was offered to identify a child soldier—age fifteen. The UN Office of the Special Representative of the Secretary-General to Children and Armed Conflict currently cites thirty situations of concern around the world and estimates that over 250,000 children are currently serving as soldiers in conflict.[2] An increase in the propagation of child soldier employment across the African continent is quantified by Achvarina and Reich (2006) and allows great insight into the seriousness of the issue. World reaction to the "epidemic" has resulted in a further affirmation of the eradication of the phenomenon through the introduction of an optional protocol to the 1989 Convention which lifts the age to eighteen years. A step toward enabling enforcement was taken with the February 2005 Children and Armed Conflict Report of the Secretary-General when it framed a mechanism for monitoring and reporting on the gravest violations and their perpetrators (United Nations 2005b).

While eighteen years of age may be a fair delineation for adulthood in most Western societies, the threshold is looked upon by many societies and cultures in Africa, as well as South America, as inflated. In the chapter offered by Andvig and Gates (2006), the precision associated with the attribute of age as a competent variable from which to distinguish a child is challenged. The authors argue that "childhood is a social construct" and that the demarcation of the world's youth may be more properly identified within the context of their unique societies. Gutiérrez (2006a) reinforces this view in his chapter on the organization of minors in the conflict in Colombia. Citing Ferro and Uribe (2002), Gutiérrez remarks that the fifteen-year-old threshold for entrance into the very powerful guerrilla force Fuerzas Armadas Revolucionarias de Colombia (FARC) is justified as an "act of social inclusion which unequivocally shows the massive character of the cause."

The ambiguity that taints the international definition of a child soldier is also resident within the societal constructs that exist in Africa today. A universal feature of African social institutions is the concept of "age-grades" and "age-sets" (Khapoya 1998) that define a collection of a local communities' males by age groups. Khapoya notes that the cohorts subsequently proceed through "distinctive life stages" that pass them from infancy to elderhood. In Liberia, secret societies assist communities with the transition of these cohorts from boys and girls to men and women. The Poro and Sande societies represent the communities' male and female equities, respectively. One Liberian tribe, the Kpelle, has been known to initiate its members to young adulthood as early as seven years old (Erchak 1998). Once initiated into a society after undergoing all the tests of the rites of passage, the inductee is no longer regarded as a child and may pursue employment and marital opportunities as well as take on more significant communal responsibility. Defense of one's community is also an obligation of the society's members and is actually the primary objective of initiation training of communal cohorts in Liberia that fall outside the influence of the Poro and Sande.

A variety of theories have been put forth to explain some of the causal factors associated with the employment of child soldiers as well as postulations on rebel recruitment and allegiance. With regard to the general study of recruitment, Weinstein (2002) argues that how warring factions are organized, either around material incentives or through commonality of identity, affects the dynamics of the unit during conflict. Azam (2006) seeks to address the question of why warlords victimize their own civilians—an effort to model insurgent leaders for the determination of their propensity for violence. Gates (2002) offers a model of rebel organizations, based upon principle-agent analysis, that demonstrates the criticality of geography, ethnicity, and ideology in shaping recruitment.

In the examination of the causal factors associated with child soldier recruitment, many more theories have been derived in order to postulate predilections. The nature of a child's preconflict disposition is analyzed by numerous authors in this volume. Poverty and socioeconomic disruptions are examined by Achvarina and Reich (2006a), Becker (2006), and Singer (2006). The idea that one's unfortunate socioeconomic circumstance is causally related to child soldiering lies at the root of most of the anecdotal evidence in circulation today.

Recruiting techniques as well as the incentives utilized by warring factions are of primary concern when looking to uncover the linkages to the employment of child soldiers. Abduction and coercion are by far the most prevalent techniques cited by the popular media. Becker (2006) and Oluwaniyi (2003) examine methods of forced recruiting in Asia and Africa, respectively. The vulnerabilities that enable the recruitment are keenly addressed through Lischer's (2006) theory that vulnerability paths are key to understanding "voluntary," coerced recruitment, while Achvarina and Reich (2006a) examine the issues of human security involved with refugee and displaced person movements and settlements.

While many of the theories above infer causal relationships for the factors attributable to child soldiering, there has not yet been a study that examines the uniqueness of the suppositions in a quantitative approach. The failure to disaggregate the population of former fighters for analytical comparison has resulted in findings that, albeit valid for the category of children, are not necessarily unique to child combatants. As alluded to in the section on defining the child soldier, age can be a fairly subjective attribute. This subjectivity produces an ambiguity that makes it very difficult for researchers, analysts, nongovernmental organizations, and others to distinguish factors that are uniquely tied to the plight of the child soldier. Children are products of the general population and associated societal constructs and will exhibit many of the same vulnerabilities as the population they are derived from. Therefore, for example, it is possible that poverty and societal breakdowns, which garner much attention as a catalyst for conflict, affect adults as much as children (Kaplan 1994). With so many of the same contextual variables present within a given conflict or, for that matter, across conflicts, how does one discover variation?

Disaggregation is then posed as requisite to fully understanding the nuances of the causal factors associated with child soldiering, and the identification of an appropriate unit of analysis must be identified. Andvig and Gates (2006) postulate that the factors that "shape supply are largely invariant across conflicts" and that researchers should focus on the factors influencing the demand for the child soldiers. The theory advanced by the authors recognizes the impact of personal leadership styles, organizational structures, and a military group's resource endowment as factors possibly enabling high child/adult ratios within a fighting force. Gutiérrez (2006a, 2006b) provides an illustration of the uniqueness of warring parties within the context of the ongoing conflict in Colombia. The author contends that "organizations are a reference point" and that generalities regarding the causal factors of child soldiering attributable to the conflict (vice a particular faction within the conflict) have limited utility.

A Review of the Warring Factions

Fourteen years of civil war in Liberia saw a successive escalation of child participation. As a rebel leader on Christmas Eve 1989, Charles Taylor began his advance on President Samuel K. Doe's regime. Achvarina and Reich (2006a) suggest that Taylor carried with him a force comprised of almost 30 percent children by the time Liberia made it to an interim peace in 1997. A failed disarmament, demobilization, rehabilitation, and reintegration (DDRR) and the installation of warlord Taylor as president breathed renewed life into the conflict and plunged the country into anarchy again. The final stage of the conflict, from 1999 to 2003, Levitt (2005) labels the LURD (Liberians United for Reconciliation and Democracy) and MODEL (Movement for Democracy in Liberia) insurrections. By 2004, a joint needs assessment conducted by Liberia's transitional government, the World Bank, and the United Nations estimated there to be approximately 53,000 combatants—this time, almost 40 percent of them were children (World Bank 2004). All signatories (Taylor's government, LURD, and MODEL) to the Comprehensive Peace Agreement (CPA), which ended the conflict, were known to have children in their ranks. While each warring party operated generally within the confines of a nation-state slightly larger that the U.S. state of Ohio (111,369 sq km), each faction took on specific characteristics—driven in part by the goals of their respective organizations and the men at their helms.

Charles Taylor's troops were distributed throughout the depth and breadth of Liberia. The Liberian president had made his initial entrance in 1989 through the rural stretches of Nimba County. At the town of Butuo, across the border from Côte d'Ivoire, Charles Taylor's Libyan trained force of approximately 100 fighters began the march to Monrovia (Ellis 1999). During the seven years of conflict, Taylor especially recruited children to support his operational efforts. The most notorious of all was the Small Boys Unit (SBU). Many of these boys would obediently return to arms when Taylor called for support during the LURD and MODEL insurrections. The Armed Forces of Liberia (AFL) was a shell of an organization after two purges in seven years. The first was Doe's push to fill the ranks with ethnic Krahn, and the second was the result of a dismal disarmament process that failed to re-create a suitable national defense force. Taylor would now rely on his militias and a few specially trained paramilitary units to protect Liberian interests. When the two rebel organizations began to hem Taylor into the confines of Monrovia, the demand for child soldiers reportedly rose. By December 2004, the number of ex-combatants claiming government affiliation through registration with the National Committee on DDRR (NCDDRR) was 28,008, of which 2,886 were children (NCDDRR JIU 2006).

In April 1999, only two years after the end of the first round of violent conflict, insurgent activity erupted in the northern county of Lofa. The LURD, however, reportedly initiated the second major incursion of the new stage of the war in mid-2000 with the singular goal of ousting Charles Taylor. Journalist James Brabazon, who lived with the LURD during operations, stated that through his interviews that the rebel organization initiated the conflict with a group equal in size to the one Charles Taylor had on his Christmas Eve raid in 1989—approximately seventy fighters (Brabazon 2003). The largest and longest-acting antagonist of Charles Taylor the president, the LURD is said to have been formed in July 1999 in Sierra Leone as a result of dissatisfied Liberian exiles from the United Liberation Movement for Democracy (ULIMO)—a faction that competed against Taylor during the first stage of the war but had since disbanded. Brabazon (2003) and Levitt (2005) both note that the core members of the LURD came from the Krahn and Mandingo tribes and that many joiners were non-Liberians from bordering countries. Brabazon notes that during his stay with the LURD in the second half of 2002, the use of child soldiers in a combat capacity was discouraged, but employment of children as porters was commonplace. June and July 2003 saw heavy fighting, with the LURD putting Monrovia to siege, practically starving it. Discipline in the ranks was heavily dependent upon the unit commander. By December 2004, ex-combatants claiming LURD affiliation through registration with the NCDDRR was 34,285, of which 4,228 were children. This number of registered child soldiers is almost double the size of the MODEL and government forces (NCDDRR JIU 2006).

The MODEL insurgency came out of southeast Liberia and has been said to have run its operations from Grand Gedeh County. It is thought to be a breakaway faction from the LURD, whose membership was heavily dominated by the Krahn tribe (United Nations 2003a). Little has been published in the literature on this rebel organization that entered the fight in the final stages of the conflict. Entering the war in early 2003, news agencies reported that by 28 April, MODEL had attacked urban areas along the coast (Greenville) as well as Tappita, a major town deep in the interior county of Nimba (IRIN 2003c). The MODEL was reportedly supported from bases in Côte d'Ivoire and initially drew recruits from Liberian refugees. By December 2004, the number of ex-combatants claiming MODEL affiliation through registration with the NCDDRR was 13,156, of which 2,232 were children (NCDDRR JIU 2006).

Methodology

Against a backdrop of a nation emerging from civil war and a peaceful round of national democratic elections, a large-scale nationwide study was conducted. Fieldwork and data collection for this project occurred in February and March 2006—just over two and a half years from the signing of the CPA on 18 August 2003. The survey was conceived in order to provide an initial assessment of the progress made toward the objectives of national reconciliation, conflict prevention, and social and economic reintegration and the sustainable development made by the DDRR and the Community Based Recovery (CBR) interventions. A 185-question interview intake form collected respondent information that pertained to wartime factional recruitment and participation as well as postconflict socioeconomic expressions and status. A local Liberian nongovernmental organization, the African Network for the Prevention and Protec-

tion against Child Abuse and Neglect (ANPPCAN), was contracted by the
United Nations Development Program (UNDP) to take the interviews from
the respondents in private one-on-one environments, and the author served as
the project's principal investigator.

The study instituted a randomized, nationwide sampling approach in order to obtain a representative sample of ex-combatants by category of DDRR
program participation or nonparticipation and gender. Former combatants under the age of eighteen were excluded from this study for focus and logistical
reasons. Of note, however, is that approximately 108 of the 590 respondents
included in this survey would have been under the age of eighteen at the time
of the signing of the CPA in 2003. As of February 2005, the NCDDRR reported
that almost 11 percent of the disarmed combatants were children.

This chapter then disaggregates the sample population into two categories
that correspond to respondent ages at the time of the signing of the CPA. The
child soldier group consists of 108 cases that were between the ages of fifteen
and seventeen in 2003. Some of these former child combatants reported seeing
action as early as September 1990, but the majority of the respondents indicated that they joined the fighting between 2002 and 2003. The adult soldier
group contains 482 cases of ex-combatants who were over the age of eighteen
at the time of the signing of the CPA. Greater insight is provided through a second round of disaggregation into their associated factional affiliations. While
the original study separated the sample into groups that were present at various times throughout the entirety of the civil war, only the three major contemporary competitive factions will be addressed in this chapter. The LURD,
MODEL, and government forces and militias of Charles Taylor account for 388
of the respondents.

Findings

Disaggregation analysis of the Liberian ex-combatant data set is presented in a
staged, time-sequenced manner. The findings follow the sample from the onset
of hostilities through to an assessment of their efforts to reintegrate into their
communities two and a half years after the official close of hostilities. The findings discussed below are augmented with graphic representations of the data
for better understanding. In most instances, the findings are first discussed
within the context of the aggregate data set, separating only for child and adult
combatants, but then a second level of disaggregation is introduced to illuminate the variance that exists when contrasting the competing factions.

A number of questions sought to understand former combatant characteristics that have been identified through the literature as possible causal factors
of child soldiering. The findings of this section focus on the factors associated
with preconflict family structure and geographic locality.

Figure 10.1 demonstrates a lopsided urban locality characteristic when the sample of former combatants is disaggregated into child and adult components. The uniqueness of this finding is that it indicates a propensity for child soldiers to come from Monrovia at a rate of almost two to one when compared with their adult counterparts and is amplified by the LURD child soldier sample, which reports that over three-quarters of its ranks lived in the Liberian capital prior to hostilities. Charles Taylor's forces had their roots equally distributed across Liberia before the war, while MODEL fighters notably resided outside of the greater metropolitan capital.

Arguably, the primacy of family in the lives of Liberians holds the collective community together during times of strife. The absence of parental or guardian care in the lives of young children in conflict zones allows an acute vulnerability to surface when it comes to potential recruitment. Analysis of the prewar demographics that details the family structure that was in place before the war began provides little in the way of variation when disaggregated by faction. While all factions were similar with respect to the percentage of having both a mother and father present (57–63 percent), it appears that factional identity uniquely shaped the remaining 40 percent of each group. The LURD child soldiers reported that 20 percent of their rank had neither a father nor mother at the beginning of the conflict compared with only 6 percent in MODEL.

As discussed, the literature suggests that certain recruitment techniques and incentives are inexorably linked to the phenomenon of child soldiering. This section focuses on findings within the disaggregated sample that inform on how initial introductions were made by competing factions, the reasons for joining the three major contemporary former warring factions, and the incentives tendered to prospective members. The impact of forced migration and its associated vulnerabilities is also examined.

Again, disaggregation by age shows very little variance in the demographic profile, as shown in figure 10.2, which addresses how the ex-combatants were introduced to their former factions. When the disaggregation is placed within the context of their respective factions, some insightful information begins to emerge. It is apparent from the figures presented that each former faction had a distinctive approach with first encounters. LURD soldiers were the most prone to violent introductions by favoring village attacks and ambushes as a way to meet their potential recruits. Taylor's government forces and associated militias relied upon friend and family introductions to solicit new membership, while almost 50 percent of the future child soldiers of MODEL actively went looking for the faction to join them.

Figure 10.3 illustrates the various reasons that former combatants joined their factions. Key among the reasons is abduction. While abduction has been cited as a horrific atrocity that befalls children in conflict-torn lands, the find-

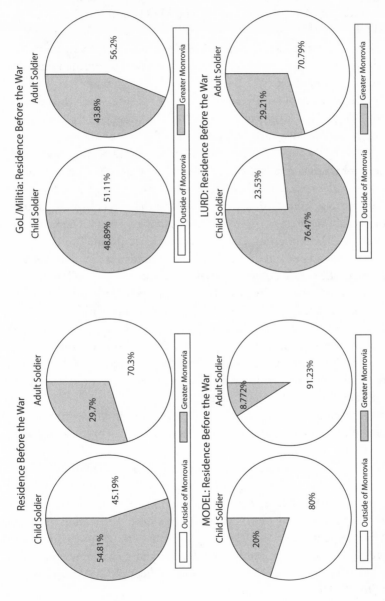

FIG. 10.1. Prewar residence dispositions

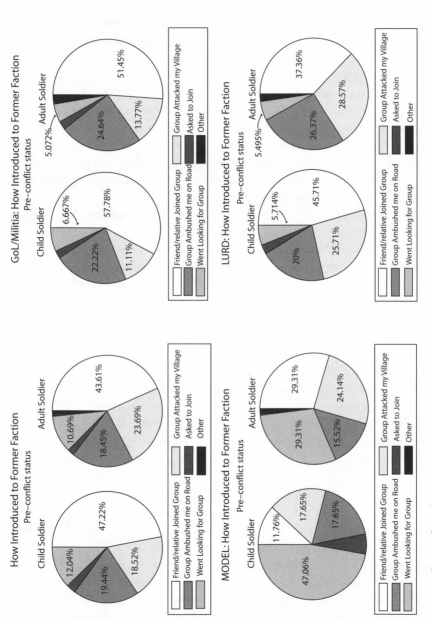

FIG. 10.2. Factional recruitment

ings of this study show that adults are equally at risk of being forced into military service. Alongside abduction lies a closely related catalyst for joining a faction: intimidation. In almost every disaggregation analysis, joining a faction because the recruit was scared accounted for at least 20 percent. Family protection was cited most often by the sample as the reason for joining, while child respondents affiliated with the LURD reported the highest rate of abduction.

Many incentives are offered to prospective members to encourage joining their cause. In the Liberian conflict, altruism was rarely pandered, as can be seen in figure 10.4. Fewer than a quarter of the competing factions focused on improving the situation in Liberia, but money and family protection were often offered as tangible enticements. Again, a simple separation of combatants by age shows little demographic variation until we disaggregate by faction. Almost 40 percent of the future MODEL child soldiers were offered family protection, which is more than double the offer given to the collective group of child soldiers (17 percent). The possibility of getting revenge was almost solely attributable to MODEL recruiters, and money was the major motivator for both the child and adult soldiers loyal to Charles Taylor. The children of all three groups demonstrated a different population profile for targeted recruitment.

When personnel are displaced from their home communities either as internally displaced persons (IDPs) or as refugees across their native borders, many personal security vulnerabilities surface. The analysis of the data failed to disentangle the issue of faction abduction and its relationship to displacement with regard to adults and children. At the surface, a simple disaggregation by age indicates that adults are actually more vulnerable to abduction while displaced than children are. Further separation shows that the three contemporary former factions prioritized recruiting among displaced persons differently with regard to abductions. The LURD accounted for the highest rate with almost 40 percent of their formerly displaced persons recruited through abduction, while MODEL's sample was only around 6 percent. While abduction of displaced peoples was found to be an issue of concern, its uniqueness to the plight of child combatants is yet to be determined.

A number of questions sought to understand former combatant characteristics as pertaining to their participation in particular factions. This section seeks to illuminate the attributes of the combatants within the organizations that they fought in. The findings include information on ranks and roles within the factions as well as a look at how often the combatants were injured.

An analysis of disaggregation shows that approximately 83 percent of both the child and adult soldiers served as frontline combat soldiers. Some corroboration of this fact may reside in the finding that indicates a near identical wounding rate among child (58 percent) and adult (52 percent) fighters. Again, though, the differences surface in the analysis of particular factions. While the

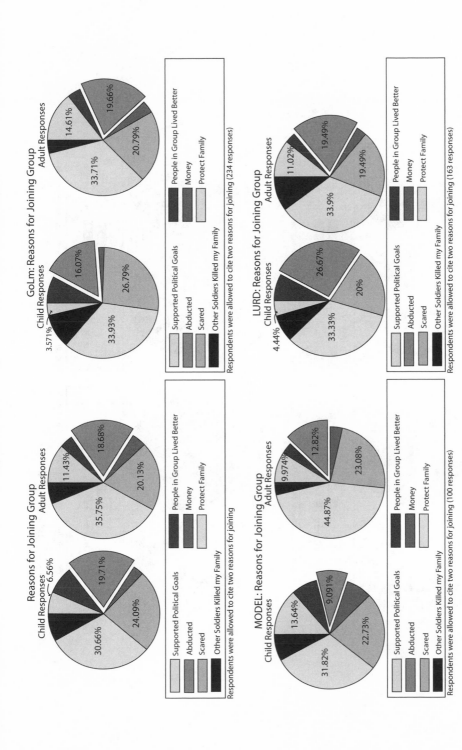

FIG. 10.3. Reasons for joining a group

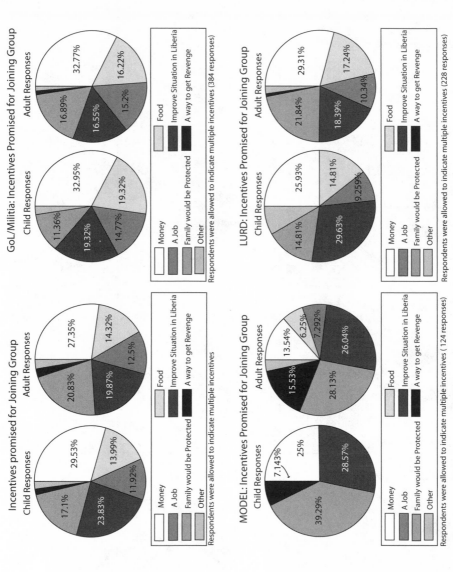

FIG. 10.4. Incentives for factional recruitment

government forces profile nearly mimicked the general demographic profile for factional roles, the LURD and MODEL had stark contrasts. While all (100 percent) seventeen child soldiers of MODEL indicated that they were combat soldiers, only twenty-four (69 percent) of the LURD soldiers reported themselves as combat troops. The remaining 30 percent, like their adult counterparts in the LURD, served in administrative or supporting roles.

A look at former combatant ranks held during the conflict provides an expected distribution. Over 98 percent of the child soldiers reported leaving their factions at or below the rank of captain (81 percent were privates or did not hold a rank). Conversely, 86 percent of the adults reported leaving their factions at or below the rank of captain, leaving 14 percent to hold the most senior military positions at the time of disarmament. Only 63 percent of the adults reported leaving their former factions as privates or members without rank.

While the challenges facing former combatants both young and old were daunting during the prewar and war years, a number of barriers stand in the way of reintegrating these citizens into their respective communities. Not only do the ex-combatants have to overcome the sometimes violent destruction of their family structures, they must also endeavor to reinsert themselves socially, economically, and politically into their respective communities.

The horrors of the civil war in Liberia did not leave many families untouched with respect to violence. If they did not experience the violent nature of war through the loss of a family member, they certainly knew someone close who did. While the majority of child soldiers affiliated with warring factions did not lose either parent (nearly 63 percent), almost 53 percent of the child soldiers who fought with the MODEL lost a parent, as demonstrated in figure 10.5. Fathers represented the biggest loss rate between parents during the war. MODEL children suffered a loss rate of 35 percent, while government forces and militia troops lost at a rate of 16 percent. Over 10 percent of MODEL's adult fighters lost both mother and father. Fewer than 2 percent of the child soldiers indicated losing both parents.

Preconflict home community resettlement in the postwar environment is addressed in figure 10.6. Reintegration is often termed a misnomer in postconflict research as some, if not majority, of ex-combatants will never really reintegrate into their home communities, but rather integrate into another (see Kingma 2002, 181–201). The decision to integrate may be made by the ex-combatant for a variety of reasons—better economic opportunities, home community completely destroyed, or simply as a mechanism to retain a modicum of anonymity after possibly participating in inexcusable wartime atrocities. In any event, the findings of this analysis show that child soldiers are more apt to return home (67 percent vs. 56 percent) in the aftermath. When examined through the factional filter, however, greater insight is available. The

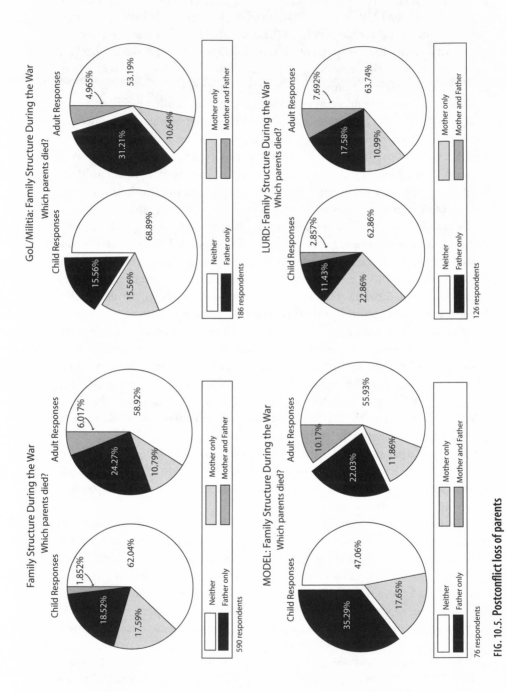

Family Structure During the War

Child Responses

- 1.852%
- 62.04%
- 18.52%
- 17.59%

Which parents died?

Adult Responses

- 6.017%
- 58.92%
- 24.27%
- 10.79%

Neither
Father only
Mother only
Mother and Father

590 respondents

GoL/Militia: Family Structure During the War

Child Responses

- 68.89%
- 15.56%
- 15.56%

Which parents died?

Adult Responses

- 4.965%
- 53.19%
- 31.21%
- 10.64%

Neither
Father only
Mother only
Mother and Father

186 respondents

MODEL: Family Structure During the War

Child Responses

- 47.06%
- 35.29%
- 17.65%

Which parents died?

Adult Responses

- 10.17%
- 55.93%
- 22.03%
- 11.86%

Neither
Father only
Mother only
Mother and Father

76 respondents

LURD: Family Structure During the War

Child Responses

- 2.857%
- 62.86%
- 11.43%
- 22.86%

Which parents died?

Adult Responses

- 7.692%
- 63.74%
- 17.58%
- 10.99%

Neither
Father only
Mother only
Mother and Father

126 respondents

FIG. 10.5. Postconflict loss of parents

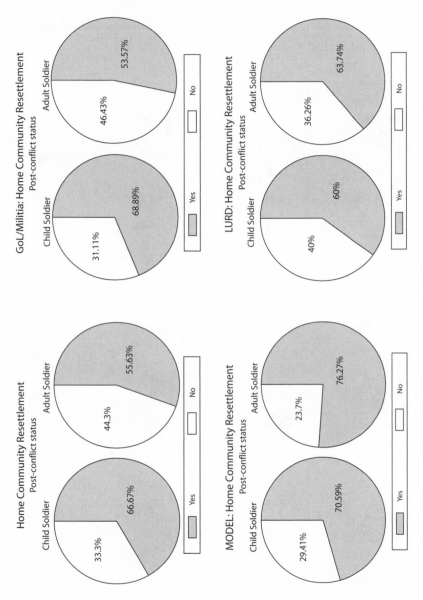

FIG. 10.6. Postconflict community resettlement

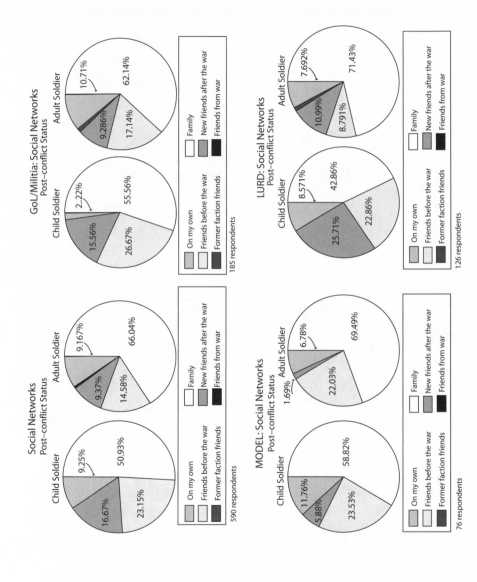

FIG. 10.7. **Postconflict social networks**

Liberian government/militia child soldiers returned home on average 15 percent more often than their adult comrades (69 percent vs. 54 percent). The LURD and MODEL exhibit similar return rates between categories, but the MODEL children returned at a much higher rate (71 percent vs. 60 percent).

Social reintegration is a major component of any international intervention program, and an understanding of the community dynamics and the degree of reintegration in this area is critical to ensuring that a program stays on track. With respect to social networks, figure 10.7 shows that the two groups tend to demonstrate a similar loner rate (9 percent), but the adults tend to spend more of their free time with family (66 percent vs. 51 percent).

As for the international intervention DDRR program in Liberia, children and adults exhibit a similar nonparticipatory rate of around 11 percent. The findings as to the stage of the DDRR program that the participants are currently in suggest that adults may have moved through the program slightly ahead of the former child soldiers, as the adults show a program completion rate at 16 percent (versus 10 percent) and an actively enrolled reintegration training participation rate of 27 percent versus 38 percent for the children.

The Merits of Disaggregation

A methodological approach that disaggregates by faction has surfaced many different types of variations to analyze. While this chapter reviews only one country case—Liberia—it unquestionably establishes a quantitative grounding in the method suggested for employment across other country cases. In most of the theory related to the phenomenon of child soldiering, simple disaggregation of child and adult former fighters yielded very little insight into the causal factors unique to youth employment with an armed faction. The sorting of the sample according to age and faction has given rise to two methods of comparison that provide much more tangible insight into the plight of the children in conflict. Comparisons surface variations between the adult and child members of particular factions (intrafactional) and also an extremely pronounced difference when only the children are compared as a group against the other formerly competing factions (interfactional). Through a combined approach in analysis, the causal factors unique to child soldiering can be uncovered.

With factional disaggregation complete, the findings amplify the nuances embedded in the sample previously separated only by age. In understanding that the aggregate sample of ex-combatants in Liberia consists of respondents from three very different organizations and commanders, it should be apparent that any statistical averaging would surely be imprecise. The findings presented in figure 10.1 illustrate the importance of this first method of comparisons. All three factions are unquestionably unique with regard to the variable of prewar locality disposition. The uniqueness of the factional disaggregation is overridden and hidden in the simple separation, as the LURD child soldiers' prewar dispositions were almost exactly opposite that of their adult comrades.

While intrafactional variations surface with disaggregation, the contrast is even more pronounced as one investigates the population of children across factions. As noted in the literature, the essence of a fighting unit is ultimately a reflection of its commander and the organizations' goals. The differences among the three factions under investigation have most certainly been identified in the findings presented, and each one paints a picture of child recruitment and participation that is unique. The variable on recruitment introductions in figure 10.3 provides an excellent example of contrast between groups of child combatants. The massive variance between an organization built on family/ friend recruitment (GoL), a propensity for violent introductions (LURD), and an attraction that draws the youth to them (MODEL) should be recognized as very much worth pursuing.

Characterizing the Warring Factions

Disaggregation by faction in this chapter seeks to characterize the fighting organizations in an effort to explain actions and identify linkages that may be attributable to the causal factors of child soldiering. Through an examination of variables that characterize Liberia's contemporary warring factions, the following section presents a summary of each faction as characterized in the findings that will serve to amplify the discussion of the chapter's most important findings on the phenomenon of child soldiering.[3] Take note of the extreme contrasts between groups as we begin to build a model from which to make our deductions.

The core of Charles Taylor's forces was the group of fighters that served the leader when the president was only warlord. The presence of Taylor's military force was resident not only within the capital but also throughout the hinterland. The findings on prewar dispositions note a ratio of Monrovian to non-Monrovian residents to be only slightly higher than the population's estimated national ratio. Approximately 40 percent of the ranks had lost either one or both parents before the conflict's onset. Recruitment into Taylor's forces appears to be quite familial, as over 50 percent of its members were introduced by their friends and family. Family protection and loyal support to Taylor's political ideals constituted the bulk of the reasons cited for joining; a method of coercion (abduction or scaring) was indicated in 41 percent of the responses. Pecuniary incentives were used as the primary means of recruitment by the subfactions under Taylor's control. Over 80 percent of Taylor's forces indicated that they were combat troops, with a fair distribution of combat support roles identified in the remaining 20 percent. The war impacted the family structures of the government forces and militias. Approximately 40 percent of the combatants lost a parent during the conflict. Only a handful of ex-combatants lost both their mother and father. The adult fighters of this group have been the least likely to return to their home communities. As of the time of the survey, 43 percent had not yet returned home.

The adult fighters of the LURD primarily resided outside the Greater Monrovian area. On average, 60 percent of the fighters had both parents alive before the conflict, but the youth of the faction had a 20 percent orphan rate, the highest percentage of the three organizations studied in this chapter. Violent introduction (54 percent) was the predominant method employed by the LURD in securing new recruits, and coercion (41 percent), through either abduction or scaring, was cited as the primary reason for joining the group. Pecuniary incentives—job, food, money—were cited the majority of the time as rewards promised for joining. Significant emphasis during the recruiting process was also placed upon ensuring family protection and touting the group's ideological goals. During operations the LURD maintained the lowest percentage of combat soldiers within their faction (71 percent). Dedicated camp workers made up over 15 percent of the fighting force. Similar to Taylor's forces, the LURD fighters had a little less than 40 percent impact on the family structure because of the war, losing one or both parents. At the time of the survey, almost 63 percent of the LURD combatants had returned to their home communities.

The MODEL prewar disposition identified only 11 percent of its members as residing in Monrovia. Just like the other two factions, approximately 60 percent of MODEL fighters had both parents living at the commencement of hostilities. The rebel faction had an attraction that induced over 32 percent of its members to actively seek them out and join. Violent introductions by the faction were made only 38 percent of the time for recruitment. Significantly, the fighters of this faction primarily joined to protect their families (42 percent), with coercion (35 percent) playing a smaller role than the other two competing forces. Nonpecuniary incentives topped the rewards scheme for joining the MODEL. Family protection was at 31 percent, while ideological goals and combined pecuniary incentives tied at 27 percent. The primary role during operations most cited by MODEL ex-combatants was as a combat soldier (93 percent). Very few of the respondents in the sample acknowledged a combat support role. The MODEL fighters' family structures were greatly affected by the war, the most of any other faction. Over 46 percent of MODEL's fighters lost one parent or both during the war. At the time of the survey, fully 75 percent of the MODEL fighters had returned to their home communities—the highest return rate of any faction.

Uncovering the Nuances

In employing the approaches to comparative disaggregation as outlined earlier, many factional nuances in the data have been amplified. Generally speaking, almost all of the variables investigated exhibited similar distributions when simply disaggregated by age. Stopping the analysis at this point informed us of unique variance associated with prewar locality dispositions and postconflict reintegration measures. The simple disaggregation did nothing, however, to inform us on the issue of factional recruitment and incentive techniques or the generalized child's participation in conflict. This section re-visits the findings presented earlier in this chapter as a function of conflict stage during the Liberian war (preconflict, conflict, postconflict). Analysis and discussion now focus on distinguishing the causal factors of child soldiering and are synthesized through the lens of the two approaches outlined earlier: the nuances resulting from intrafactional comparison and the variances observed across factions (interfactional).

While the aggregate of responses suggests that child soldiers were overwhelmingly recruited from the Greater Monrovian area, this finding holds true for only one of the factions—LURD. A generalized characterization that urban youth were the ones that predominately filled the ranks of the warring parties in Liberia would be a bit overstated. While the GoL and MODEL troops showed little variation at the intrafaction level, the LURD's makeup was weighted significantly by a population of Monrovian youth. As expected, the government forces indicated a distribution of recruits from across the country, and the MODEL's roots are characterized as coming from the hinterland. The LURD's preponderance of Monrovian children is also significantly greater when comparing youth populations across factions. The imbalance between child and adult preconflict dispositions in the LURD is possibly a result of the final push on the capital that the rebel organization conducted. The higher rate of children in the LURD from Monrovia is then consistent with the data that show very late entry into the war by most children. This finding highlights the vulnerability of children in a war zone with no other avenue of escape. As for family structures before the onset of hostilities, little variation is noted in an intrafaction comparison. Two minor findings do arise in comparisons across factions—the LURD had the highest child orphan rate entering the war at 20 percent, and nearly 30 percent of the MODEL soldiers were raised by only their mothers.

Simple disaggregation by age did not provide any variation at all in the variables pertaining to recruitment techniques. In examining the intrafactional child/adult differences of the variables concerned with recruitment, the MODEL shows an appreciable variance in introduction experiences, reasons for joining, and incentives; the LURD varied on incentives; while the population of child and adult fighters in Taylor's forces indicated a very similar generalization of the organization's recruitment efforts. MODEL's significant ability to attract new members was even stronger when it came to children. While adults went looking for the faction on average almost 30 percent of the time, children did so at a rate of over 47 percent. The adults in MODEL were more apt to cite "family protection" as a reason for joining (45 percent vs. 32 percent). MODEL child soldiers identified family protection as an incentive to join more often than their adult comrades (38 percent vs. 28 percent). An imbalance in pecuniary incentives within the LURD structure for children led to the recruiters' promising an improved situation in Liberia at a rate higher than that pitched to the adults (30 percent vs. 18 percent).

In the aggregate, child soldiers demonstrate a greater propensity for resettling in their home communities. This generalized parameter is in fact misleading when disaggregated by faction. In this case, only the soldiers who fought for the government reintegrate at a higher rate. Both rebel factions exhibit latency in hometown youth reintegration with respect to their adult counterparts. Social network disaggregation shows that the former child soldiers tend to be a bit more independent in their free time as opposed to the adult ex-combatants, who reserve their nonworking time for family. In analyzing postconflict family structures, on average 38 percent of the child soldiers lost a parent during the war. Interestingly, fewer than 2 percent actually lost both parents. Of the 108 respondents who were child soldiers during the conflict, only those that participated with the LURD indicated a catastrophic loss of the family structure. The government forces and MODEL soldiers survived with at least one parent. Intrafaction comparisons show that the parents of Taylor's child soldiers survived the war exceptionally better than their adult comrades and also at a higher rate when compared across factions. MODEL children exhibited vulnerability in the area of postconflict family structures, as their population suffered parental loss at a rate higher than both the adults in their faction and members of the other competing factions.

Understanding the Impact and Relevancy

As demonstrated in the analysis and discussion of the contemporary former warring factions of Liberia, identifying unique causal factors of child soldiering is quite an onerous and complex task. In the end, it is quite difficult to distinguish singularly unique casual factors within the context of a generalized country-oriented study that only distinguishes adults and children within the population of former fighters. This fact was demonstrated in the previous section, where the aggregate data did not surface many variances between adults and children—most of those variances that were identified were shown to be misleading when we disaggregated factional representation. With a limited amount of international donor support to dedicate toward eradicating the phenomenon of child soldiering, the precision of our policy recommendations must be tight and based upon evidenced-based research. A failure to identify and analyze the appropriate unit of analysis in conflicts involving children has a very real possibility of wasting precious resources on inefficient program schemes and preventative measures that never really target the intended audience, children in conflict.

Disaggregating the population of former combatants by age and factional affiliation has been shown to yield the richest possible variance for the analyst and researcher during the exploitation and search for identifying causal factors unique to child soldiering. Analysis of the sample of child soldiers from across the former warring factions produced very complex insights into the recruitment methodologies implemented by the diverse set of competing organizational leaders. Characterizing former warring factions as functions of the variables relevant to the causes and consequences of child soldiering is crucial to disentangling the nuances that point toward causality. The recruitment modalities implemented by the competing military factions and the unique ways that each prosecuted the war during operations reinforces the point that unit of analysis in research needs to reside as a minimum at the faction level. Any higher level of disaggregation would completely neutralize the disturbing anomalies and nuances that the international community is keen to target.

A vision for continued research in this field would involve the modeling and characterization of military factions as a function of their recruitment modalities and operational patterns.[4] Expectation is that production of these models will produce a finite number of characterizations that begin to highlight similarities across cases. The motives of men in war are not that divergent across the globe, and once a set of inclusive models is formulated, the community will be armed with a predictive capability that should enable precision of policy and efficiency in implementation. As demonstrated through the numerous dimensions of life as a potential, current, and former combatant during the Liberian civil war, inclusive contextual disaggregation analysis in the determination of causal factors unique to child soldiering has been shown essential to proper understanding. Through detailed discussions of findings that separated the child from adult fighter on issues of recruitment, participation, and incentive schemes, only a further disaggregation by faction illuminated the unique variances. In many instances, the issues previously touted as singular to the phenomenon of child soldiering were shown to be just as pervasive in the sample of adult combatants. More systematic research in this area is required in order to properly and efficiently channel the valuable resources meant to target former child soldiers.

CHAPTER 11

GIRLS IN ARMED FORCES AND GROUPS IN ANGOLA

Implications for Ethical Research and Reintegration

Michael G. Wessells

ONE OF THE MOST SIGNIFICANT VIOLATIONS OF HUMAN RIGHTS is the recruitment of children, defined under international law as people under eighteen years of age, into armed forces such as national armies or armed groups such as the opposition groups that fight government forces in more than twenty countries (CSUCS 2004a, 13). This violation of children's rights takes an enormous toll on children and societies. Although the physical damage to children garners the most attention, extensive harm arises also from the interaction of physical, psychological, social, and spiritual factors (Wessells 2006, 126–153; Williamson and Robinson 2006). This damage to children weakens an important source of social capital, particularly because children in war-torn societies are half the population. Also, child recruitment produces damage at the societal level, enabling continuing war. In some societies, children comprise a significant percentage of the fighting forces, and commanders are able to continue fighting by recruiting children. Often, societies suffer damage through intergenerational fighting, as the socialization of children into fighting and systems of social division and hatred sets the stage for ongoing cycles of violence. In this respect, child recruitment is not only a human rights issue but also an issue of peace and human development.

Until relatively recently, the study of child soldiers was, in effect, the study of boy soldiers because girls who had been recruited by armed forces and groups were either invisible or marginalized (Mazurana et al. 2002; McKay and Mazurana 2004, 17–20). The emphasis on boys probably reflected the patriarchal values that pervade most societies and that systematically privilege males over females (Mazurana et al. 2002, 98–101). Also, the concern with boys reflected a concern over building security in the postconflict environment, where important tasks are to stand down opposing armies, reform the security sector, and enable former combatants to integrate into civilian life. This security lens, with its emphasis on former combatants, relegated to the margins the girls who had not been fighters but had filled roles such as servants, porters, cooks, and concubines. Regarded as "camp followers," girls were typically left out of the programs of disarmament, demobilization, and reintegration (DDR) that boys and men participated in (Wessells 2006, 154–180).

Today, a new generation of research is bringing girl soldiers out of the margins, shattering the view of girls as passive followers and challenging girls' exclusion from DDR processes. Although hard figures are difficult to come by in war zones, some studies have estimated that as many as 40 percent of the fighters in contemporary intrastate wars are girls (Machel 2001, 17; Save the Children 2005, 1), and in particular areas, they comprise as much as half the armed group (Human Rights Watch 2003c, 53). In addition, an expanding array of data indicates that girls serve in a wide variety of roles, including combatants, and are actors who make choices and exhibit significant agency (Brett and Specht 2004, 85–104; Wessells 2006, 85–106; West 2004). In fact, I have known girls in Sierra Leone who had served not only as fighters but also as commanders who prided themselves on their toughness. And in Sri Lanka, girls are often selected for the task of conducting suicide bombings since they are more likely than boys to successfully slip through security checkpoints (Pape 2005, 139–146). These data caution against the marginalization of girls, make the prevention of girls' recruitment a high priority in situations of armed conflict (UNICEF 2007, 12; Wessells 2006, 165–180), and indicate the need to extend to girls DDR benefits that are equivalent to those boys enjoy.

However, research on girl soldiers is still in its infancy. There is a paucity of data on the prevalence of girl soldiering and on fundamental questions such as why girls are recruited and how recruited girls differ from girls who are not recruited. Also, relatively little is known about how to support girls' reintegration in situations where the levels of stigmatization are very high. At this early stage of research, it is useful to consider different country cases in an effort to move beyond monolithic images of girl soldiers and to identify even in a preliminary manner the different patterns of girls' recruitment and use. At the same time, it is crucial to analyze the complex ethical issues that attend research on girl soldiers.

This chapter examines the case of Angola, which has received relatively little attention. The Angolan case is particularly interesting because it reveals that girls' recruitment is neither incidental nor driven by convenience, but owes to commanders' desire to exploit girls as resources in ways tailored to the local context and are aimed to procure the resources needed to fight in an effective manner. Further, the Angolan case underscores the issue of girls' stigmatization and its implications for reintegration efforts. Typically, DDR supports are provided in an open manner. This approach, however, could increase the risks to formerly recruited girls, who are already severely stigmatized and who wish not to be identified as formerly recruited. The international humanitarian community needs to learn how to support girls' reintegration in quieter, contextually appropriate ways that likely consist of nonformal supports rather than formal, publicly announced supports. A high priority is to learn from girls how they have been affected, what their current situation is, and what supports them, but to do so without increasing the girls' stigmatization. Although few roadmaps exist on how to do this, the Angolan case offers a useful model.

The methodology of the research reported here is deliberately qualitative, inductive, and designed to capitalize on the richness of narrative data and a highly supportive interview process. The qualitative approach is appropriate because it enables the probing of the girls' own understandings of their war experiences and what has helped them or not helped them afterward. By giving girls the opportunity to tell their stories, the research helps to give them a voice and to end their invisibility. By eliciting the girls' own understandings and then inductively forming categories that embody key elements of their experience, this methodology avoids the common error of using adult defined categories and descriptors of the girls' experience, which are then imposed on girls in structured or semistructured interviews. Since girls' understandings of their situation often differs from that of adults, an essential first step was to listen carefully to the girls and work inductively in categorizing their experiences.

Although the qualitative approach has many benefits in its own right, the participatory approach taken here also provides a foundation for more quantitatively oriented research. The latter approach would have been premature in the context in which this research was conducted since it would have entailed identifying large numbers of girls who had been in armed groups. The infeasibility and inappropriateness of identifying large numbers of formerly recruited girls made it difficult to use quantitative methods for deriving accurate estimates of how many girls had been recruited or had experienced particular stressors and supports.

A key feature of the research methodology was its attention to the humanitarian imperative "do no harm," which is often violated by well-intentioned researchers and practitioners. In studies involving interview methodology, it is not uncommon for researchers to ask questions that trigger powerful memories and feelings. Without careful forethought about how to support girls and avoid harm, there is a risk that the interview process may leave the girls in a state of heightened vulnerability. Also, the emphasis on narrative data reduces the risks that the girls would feel objectified by being asked large numbers of structured questions, thereby weakening their sense of dignity and agency at a moment when they needed support. For these reasons, the research focuses on narrative methodology that brings girls' own views to center stage while recognizing the limits of self-reporting. The study reported below offers a potential model of how to address these ethical complexities.

The Nature of the Conflict

The recent Angolan wars, although they were punctuated with intermittent phases of relative stability, lasted forty years and had a profound impact on civilian populations, including children (Christian Children's Fund/Angola 2002, 19–52). One significant impact was the recruitment of children by the Angolan army and even more by the opposition group, UNITA (the National Union for the Total Independence of Angola). In the interlude in the fighting ushered in by the Lusaka Peace Accords in 1994, there was a DDR process in which approximately nine thousand boys were registered. However, there were no reports of girls' recruitment and accordingly no inclusion of girls in the children's DDR process overseen by UNICEF. In fact, when the author repeatedly queried child protection agencies at various levels, we were told that there were no girl soldiers. When the fighting re-erupted in 1998, the same view persisted that girls were not being recruited. Fortunately, the fighting ended with the signing of the Luena Ceasefire in April 2002. In keeping with a wider, if worrying, tendency of many reintegration processes to exclude children, children were left out of the national DDR process, which served people twenty years of age or older and was designed mainly as part of a security sector reform effort.

Despite children's exclusion from the DDR process, there had been increasingly frequent reports that girls had in fact been recruited during the conflict. Still, an enormous information gap existed regarding the scale and nature of the problem. This information gap owed mainly to the profound stigma associated with having been recruited or used by armed groups. So great was the stigma that most girls sought to exit armed groups and go to self-selected destinations on their own, without public attention. A high priority was to collect information in a sensitive, ethical manner since without accurate information, there were few clues about the girls' situation and what kinds of reintegration supports might assist the girls.

To fill the information gap, a mostly Angolan team from Christian Children's Fund (CCF), led by Vivi Stavrou, organized the first systematic research on girl's recruitment in Angola. Conducted November 2003 to July 2004, its purpose was to learn about the pattern of girls' recruitment and the experiences and reintegration needs of forcibly recruited girls. The girls themselves preferred the term "forcibly involved girls" over the term "former girl soldiers," which might have added to their stigmatization by suggesting that their participation had been voluntary.

Methodology and Ethical Considerations

The methodology consisted of focused, semistructured, individual interviews with forty participants from Luanda, the capital city, or Huambo Province.[1] Luanda was included because it offered ease of access to girls who had migrated from many different provinces. Huambo Province was included because it offered a means of working in a rural setting, was reportedly a place from which many girls had been abducted, and also included many girls displaced from other provinces. The age of the young women interviewed ranged from thirteen to thirty-four years with a median age of twenty-one years. Although many of the participants were over the age of eighteen years at the time of the interview, all were under eighteen for at least part of the time they spent inside an armed group. The purpose of interviewing young women of a relatively wide age range was to obtain a picture of girls' recruitment in different phases of the war.

The individual interviews included three sections: life before the war and the abduction, the girl's experience with the armed group, and life after the exit from the armed group, including her current living situation, her future plans, and what she needed to implement her plans. A pilot study had indicated that individual interviews conducted in one setting of three to four hours yielded insufficient depth of information. Accordingly, a decision was taken to extend each interview to two days, with a total interview length of three to six hours. To match the participant's native language, the interviews were conducted in Portuguese, Umbundu, or Tchokwe.

Because of the sensitivity of the girls' situation, the researchers had more than the usual concerns about respecting confidentiality and obtaining informed consent. In some respects, these traditional concerns were only the tip of the iceberg of ethical issues since even approaching and talking with girls could have put them at risk. An essential first step was to develop a culturally appropriate, ethically sensitive means of identifying, selecting, and engaging with the girls. Random selection was inappropriate in the Angolan context.

To manage this issue, the research team decided to use a combination of a preselection process and snowball sampling. The preselection process involved talking with respected local elders, including the *soba* or traditional chief and women elders, explaining that the aim of the study was to learn from the girls in order to be in a better position to support them and asking whether and how they could be approached in a quiet manner. This process banked on the respected position of elders, who often are effective community networkers and key sources of information pertaining to girls' well-being. Most elders agreed that the study was important to conduct and said they felt solidarity with the researchers, whose goal was not to publish papers but to guide effective reintegration supports for the girls. Rapport was also established by talking first about how the war had affected everyone, as local people had a communal understanding of their suffering. This recognition of the communal nature of the suffering made it appropriate to then explore the experiences and situation of a particular subgroup.

The elders also indicated that they knew formerly abducted girls and said that some were doing relatively well and might be in a position to talk. This process, which relied on the elders' knowledge about who was in relatively good shape, was useful simultaneously as a preselection mechanism and a means of enabling access to young people. Most important, this process is believed to have led the researchers only to people who were in a position to talk, reducing the prospects of inadvertently harming people by discussing difficult topics before the participants were ready. As the discussions with the preselected girls occurred, the girls offered that they knew other girls in the local area who might be in a position to talk. Following this snowball sampling process, the researchers identified other prospective participants in the study.

To reduce the potential for the interviews to leave the girls feeling vulnerable, the researchers avoided asking aggressive questions such as, "What was the worst thing for you?" or probing topics that clearly made the participants feel uncomfortable. Also, they explained carefully as part of obtaining informed consent that it was perfectly acceptable not to answer any question or to stop discussing a particular topic for any reason or at any time. Furthermore, in the space where interviews were conducted, there was a trained social worker present who was ready to provide psychosocial support if needed. Recognizing that traumatic memories and feelings of being overwhelmed might occur one or several days afterward, the social worker made a check-in visit with each participant the day after the interview.

The issue of informed consent was tricky because in a situation of severe poverty and deprivation, there is a natural tendency for local people to think that outsiders who work for a nongovernmental organization (NGO) have many resources and will provide help if they are treated well. Also, local norms of hospitality augur strongly in favor of meeting and talking with people who have demonstrated respect and followed the cultural script of first meeting and obtaining the *soba*'s support. Speaking in the local language of the participant, the interviewers explained their purpose, outlined how confidentiality would be protected, reiterated that the participant was free not to talk or to not answer a particular question, and took care not to make promises or imply that more aid would be forthcoming. Each participant signed an informed consent form that had been read aloud for those who were not literate. Most of the girls, particularly those in Huambo, were clearly eager to spend hours discussing their experience, current situation, and hopes.

To protect the girls' confidentiality, the interviewers and social workers were trained on the importance of confidentiality and how to protect it. Interviews were conducted not in the girls' homes but in the private offices of local NGOs or other spaces that afforded privacy, and CCF provided transportation to the interview sites. The interviews were tape recorded, but no personal identifying information was on either the tapes or the field notes for an interview, and the individual codes were locked in a secure place.

In addition to the interviews with individual girls who had been forcibly recruited, the study included key informant interviews with elders, traditional healers, church workers, government officials, health workers, military personnel, and other people who were knowledgeable about war-affected girls, including forcibly recruited girls. Also, focus group discussions were conducted with three groups: female relatives of forcibly recruited girls, teenage girls, and teenage boys. The latter two groups were interviewed partly in order to obtain information about how other young people viewed the forcibly recruited girls and also to enlarge the network that could be used to identify other girls to be interviewed. Both the key informant interviews and the focus group discussions were instrumental in obtaining a community perspective on the situation of the forcibly recruited girls. This community perspective was of central importance since the local people conceptualized the war and the reintegration process as communal rather than individual in nature.

Analysis of the narrative data entailed the reading and rereading of the interviews by multiple team members with an eye toward identifying emergent, common categories and themes. These inductively derived categories were used to code transcripts and prepare summary tables of narrative passages that illustrated particular themes. Through this process, an effort was made to identify representative passages rather than to select the most sensational or gripping narratives (Stavrou 2005, 23–24).

Key Findings

All the participants had been forcibly recruited and knew of no girls who had decided on their own to join armed groups. The median age at which the girls had been captured was twelve years. The recruitment of girls occurred in numerous Angolan provinces and mainly by UNITA but also by the Angolan army. Although half the participants came from Huambo Province, others came from diverse regions: Bie (5), Benguela (4), Lunda Norte (3), Uige (2), Kuando Kubango (2), Malange (1), Kwanza Norte (1), Kwanza Sul (1). Of the forty participants, thirty-one had been abducted by UNITA, whereas nine had been captured by the Angolan army. Five participants had experienced multiple abductions by both the Angolan army and UNITA. The number of years spent inside an armed group ranged from two to eighteen years. Eighty percent of the young women had children, yet most were either not married or had been abandoned by their war husbands (Stavrou 2005, 25–27).

Most of the girls offered relatively little information about their lives before their abduction. In part this may have reflected their young age at their time of recruitment and the fact that because villages were often attacked or under imminent threat of attack, families moved frequently in search of safety. Also, the captors sought to suppress the girls' memories apparently as part of a strategy of promoting a break with their previous lives and of preventing escape. As one girl said: "It is like this: there, when you are speaking, sometimes they hear what you are saying about your past, how you lived, then they say that you are preparing to escape and they control you all the time. We knew because when you talk about the past they start alert listening: these girls have a program to escape. We say that they don't like when we talk about the past" (EM 2, Luanda). To help break the girls' civilian identity, UNITA often called each girl by a particular number rather than by her name. EM 2 is one such girl.

Typically, girls were abducted during and soon after raids on villages. As resources became increasingly scarce during the war, armed groups often attacked villages to obtain food and other supplies. The abduction of young children appeared to be part of a deliberate strategy of building the labor pool that the military needed, and commanders apparently preferred young people because of their compliance. Often, old people were left behind and men were killed, whereas the children were taken. Girls appeared to be preferred because of their ability to carry heavy loads long distances without making the noise that mechanized vehicles would have made, thereby reducing the chances of being detected by the enemy. To increase their control over the children, the armed groups typically separated children from their siblings and caretakers. "On that day they separated us from our mothers—the mothers going back and we going forward. We were not allowed to look back. It was just that, to separate and to cry. The abducted girls were together for a day; there were five of us. The second day they started separating us, each one allocated to their chiefs that they called elders. Every one of us was given to a different house" (EM 4, Luanda). Similarly, boys described UNITA's preference for the young: "'All you old people can stay. We'll only take the young.' And so they took me and my three children, my teenage sister, another brother of mine, and another; in all, seven people from my house. Just like that and off. If your sister says, 'I don't go,' she dies right there or they make her suffer" (boys' focus group, Huambo).

UNITA, which was a tightly knit political structure as well as an armed group, recruited girls not only during attacks on villages but also by forcing them to join the JURA (Juventud UNITA Revolucionarias de Angola), a youth political organization that morphed during the war into a collective workforce consisting mostly of twelve- to sixteen-year-olds. One girl described how families were forced to give their children to the JURA: "They had held a public meeting to say that all those parents who had a child above nine years old, except those that were married, they could not now be with them because they had to come too, had to join with all the JURA, to help with the movement of troops. So there they became conscious that that was how it was. We have to let go of our children to help the troops" (EM 14, Huambo).

Inside the JURA, girls received political indoctrination, and some rose to command positions in which they directed the activities of other girls in the JURA. Numerous other participants told how younger children were given over not to the JURA but to the children's organization Alvorada (Dawn), which allocated them to work in the houses of important people doing their housework. Men were prepared for the front lines as soldiers, whereas most girls were not.

The girls who had been abducted by UNITA soldiers, whose families usually stayed nearby unless attack was imminent, were allocated to UNITA leaders. In a typical UNITA camp, there were ten or more houses occupied by individual leaders, who each had three or four abducted girls. According to one girl, "thirty-six lived in the houses of the elders. Everyone had three girls to work in their house, and then the others were living in a room together, their job was just to transport the material. So when they go to attack and they find material, their job was to carry the material, to take it from there to another place to keep it there. Material, munitions, mines, bombs and sometimes guns were found and carried by the JURA. The JURA did not go with the combatants" (EM 1, Luanda).

Apparently, the recruitment of girls occurred on a large scale, for there were many UNITA camps at any point in time. Rather than an incidental phenomenon, girls' recruitment was part of a deliberate, systematic strategy of exploiting girls for their labor and also for sex, as explained below.

Whether girls were forced to join through the JURA or were abducted during raids on villages, they endured long marches and severe deprivations. Constantly under threat of attack by the government army, UNITA moved continuously, killing people who were too slow and also young children who risked making noise and giving away their location. Two women, one of whom was a key informant, described their suffering.

Suffering is lack of clothes, lack of salt, to sleep in the leaves without clothes under the rain, sleep seated near to the fire because of the cold, blemishes on the skin due to the dry skin. I hate my memories of the rain showers and the walking. My children were so young and shouldn't have been walking like that, but had to walk because you can't do otherwise, and on the back you have another one. Life was just walking from one place to another, by day and by night. At first you were crying, but then you had no more tears left. (Key Informant 5, Huambo)

Whoever is too slow they shoot; suffocated the slow children not to waste bullets. We had to carry too heavy loads, 30 kg each or even more. We slept every three nights, with the children on the back, in the bush under the trees. (EM 19, Luanda)

Because of the extensive carrying of heavy loads, most of the girls interviewed had a bald spot on top of their heads. Among their many health problems were malaria, anemia, exhaustion, malnutrition, TB, and sexually transmitted diseases. One of their greatest sources of distress was their inability to participate in education, which created an enduring gulf between themselves and their peers who had not been recruited.

In view of the girls' suffering, it is not unsurprising that some attempted to escape. However, severe punishment or death was usually the penalty for captured escapees. "There in the base where I was they caught a girl who had left a one-year-old baby behind when she tried to escape. They went after her and caught her and killed her when they brought her back. Everybody had to assist. They put a red band across her eyes and then they killed her. They did it to make the other afraid so that they would not try to escape" (EM 1, Luanda).

UNITA also exploited girls sexually in a variety of ways. The girls reported that rape was common wherever there were large numbers of troops present. In some cases, soldiers from other battalions attacked and raped girls as they worked in the fields or were collecting food or water. Inside the JURA, rape was reportedly frequent. "It seems that was their law. In their village they would see a girl and say that she was ripe to go into the JURA. They saw her age, saw she was getting big and it was time to go. Once there she simply had to be raped . . . yes my sister was raped, by the other old men as well. Anyone living at the base can be raped by other men" (EM 14, Luanda).

In addition, girls were often forced to dance all night, presumably to rouse the troops and keep them awake and capable of responding to attacks. As the girls danced into the early hours of the morning, older men pulled them into the shadows and raped them. The fact that the rapists included elder men, who were normally expected to protect young people, was particularly upsetting to the girls. Perhaps the most common form of sexual exploitation was the widespread practice of assigning girls to particular commanders, chiefs, or elders, often according to their rank. "The elder that liked me was the big chief [the commander of the military camp]. They were three; the big chief, his assistant, and a chief from another department; they used to complicate my life [*she let her head fall and started rubbing her hands on her skirt. She smiled*]. They forced me to sleep with them, each elder when they called me to sleep with them, if I didn't accept they sent the guards to beat me" (EM 1, Luanda). A common protective strategy for the girls was to "marry" or associate with a particular older man. This strategy had its price, since often the girls had to forgo desired relationships with younger men. Also, the "husbands" frequently abandoned them.

Yes this happened to me. If you do not accept they put a bullet in their pistol and point it at you. . . . In the bush you cannot complain. If you complain, they will kill you. . . . When you are out with the troops, if you say that you are tired and want to sleep they call you and kill you straight away. So one older man said that it is better to stay with me [marry me] and this was the father of this child. But in the end he was only lying, so last year I left him, in the month of January. He already had three wives in the village. . . . I thought that if I had a husband it would possibly be better. Even though I was only a child I would put up with that suffering. But actually he had his own wives. (EM 2, Huambo)

Through such unions, many girls became pregnant, and if their husbands left, the children were often among the most vulnerable.

Fortunately, there were also some positive aspects of life inside the armed groups. One of the most important was friendship and solidarity, which was an important basis for the girls' resilience.

Many [*smile*] my friends were really good. There, all of us abducted girls lived as sisters, yes . . . we used to tell our stories: Oh! When we will find our families . . . so and so. (EM 2, Luanda)

I had many friends. We ate together and did our hair together and even chose to go to the front together. (EM 14, Huambo)

Such friendships appear to have been tolerated so long as they did not threaten to encourage the girls to escape or to rekindle their civilian identities.

Following their time in the armed group, only one of the girls was recognized as a soldier and given a one-time demobilization payment as part of an official DDR process. Apparently, their noncombatant labor had conferred little military status, and many girls were considered too young to be regarded as soldiers. Also, the DDR planners targeted benefits for men on the assumption that the benefits would trickle down to dependent girls. Most girls, however, went with their bush husbands or the elder's family they lived with to military gathering areas. Recognizing that they would be severely stigmatized, most girls sought to enter villages quietly and on their own, although they in some cases chose not to return to their places of origin. As one girl put it, "My heart does not accept to go back to my village. I'll just stay here. Maybe I'll find a field, or a *naca* [field on the river's edge], and then I can sustain myself. When I have nothing, then I peel a potato and make porridge. That's what I give to my child to eat" (EM 2, Huambo). This girl's testimony shows clearly the problems inherent in the term "reintegration," which is often interpreted as meaning going back to one's village of origin and to a life that existed before. Following the Angolan wars, many girls chose to go to new environments where no one knew them or where they had better hopes for earning a living. Also, some children were born into UNITA families and grew up inside the armed group or its satellite families. For them, too, the challenge was one of integrating into a civilian social system about which they knew very little.

Chief among the reintegration challenges that the girls faced was discrimination. This included relatively indirect elements such as not being included in the welcoming and reintegration rituals that men received or being unable to matriculate in schools due to a lack of identity documents or appropriate clothing and shoes. It also included negative comments about people who come from the bush, the differences in the habits of people from the bush, their illnesses, and their links to the damage caused by the war. As one participant in a girls' focus group discussion said, "Few people in Luanda know who they are or what their experiences have been. This is because they say nothing, because there are people who are abusive about people who came out of the bush" (girls' focus group, Luanda). Also, the girls lacked access to basic services such as health care due to a lack of income. Unemployment was a major problem, although girls in rural areas engaged in agriculture and those in peri-urban areas engaged in petty trading. The desire for money led some girls to seek better options in Luanda.

The suffering once we arrived in Huambo was too great. What with being pregnant, and with small children and other children, it was too much. I couldn't work. And furthermore, where we were in Bom Pastor, a person working might not earn any more than 300 KZ a month. I could see nothing for myself, no advancement, so I thought I might go to Luanda. I had a friend who was in Luanda, and she told me that in Luanda you could do business. Those little business deals would earn you money, and your children would eat. (EM 14, Luanda)

The girls, however, gave mixed reports regarding how much help they received in Luanda when they or their children became ill.

Psychosocial distress was also a challenge for many girls after they left the armed group. As one key informant said,

The girls lived for so long with the idea that they would be beaten for everything that they cannot get rid of this fear. They have difficulties of adaptation as would anybody adapting in another society—like a fish out of the water. They do not sleep properly because they are used to being woken up at all hours. They feel that what they want to say is not going to be accepted by other people, so they do not speak much when they are with people of their own age. They are frightened when they hear a loud noise, having seen so much shooting in their lives. . . . I think that people coming from the war need to be assisted to insert themselves in society. It is necessary to take the idea out of their heads that they will be spoken of badly. (Key Informant 2, Luanda)

To help themselves feel better, the girls often turn for support to women relatives and friends. "What has helped is talking with my mother, my sisters and my aunt," one said (EM 1, Luanda). Another explained, "Now I visit my girlfriends, we talk and I feel well" (EM 11, Huambo). Buoyed by this support, the girls dreamed of better times ahead. Foremost among their hopes were to study and become literate, to start their business and be successful in buying and selling, to obtain vocational training, and to improve their children's lives. Like many formerly recruited children, the girls also said they wanted not to be different but to be like other girls or young women.

Comparative Perspective

It is valuable to consider these findings in comparative perspective, discerning both their similarities with data from other situations in which girls have been recruited and the unique aspects of the Angolan situation. Five similarities are prominent. First, the recruitment of girls is not incidental or something that occurs on a small scale but is systematic and widespread. This observation fits with the increasing reports that girls worldwide are a significant part of most armed forces (McKay and Mazurana 2004, 21–26; Save the Children 2005, 1; Wessells 2006, 85–106). There are no precise quantitative estimates of how many Angolan girls had been recruited, but based on the triangulated reports obtained in this study, it seems likely that they numbered in the thousands.

Second, the Angolan data support the view that abduction is one of the primary means of girls' recruitment. Girls' abduction into armed groups is visible in many regions, including in countries such as DRC, Liberia, Sierra Leone, and Sri Lanka (McKay and Mazurana 2004, 105–108; Wessells 2006, 85–106). Third, the Angolan case adds to an already expansive array of exemplars showing that most armed groups sexually exploit girls. Although some armed groups such as those in the Philippines and Sri Lanka strictly prohibit the sexual abuse of girls (Keairns 2002), a conspicuous feature of the global pattern is that most armed groups sexually exploit girls, and some exploit boys as well. Fourth, the recruitment of Angolan girls as a means of exploiting their labor fits the global picture in which girls often serve as domestic servants, porters, and laborers (Wessells 2006, 85–106). Fifth, the stigmatization faced by the Angolan girls who had been abducted reflects a wider pattern wherein formerly recruited girls are stigmatized (McKay and Mazurana 2004, 165–180).

The case of Angola also departs from the global pattern in numerous respects. The most unusual feature is the very high levels of stigmatization of formerly abducted girls and their associated attempts to remain invisible when they exited armed groups and entered civilian society. In the author's experience in over fifteen conflict-torn countries, it is exceptional to have a situation of widespread recruitment of girls occur with a complete lack of awareness among highly concerned and vigilant child protection actors. This total invisibility of girl soldiers probably does not result from the recruiters' suppression of information alone. More likely, it owes to the girls' efforts to conceal their experiences and situation due to fear of unusually strong stigmatization. An important question that warrants additional research is why the girls' level of actual or perceived stigmatization was so great as to enable this unusual level of invisibility of the formerly abducted girls.

Additionally, the roles played by the recruited Angolan girls were unusual, such as the low percentage of girls who were combatants. This observation is unlikely to be an artifact of the selective sampling of the girls since boys and key informants from many areas agreed that girls were not in combat roles. Most likely, commanders valued Angolan girls for their labor capacity and sexuality more than for their fighting ability. This situation is unusual because in conflicts as diverse as those in Sierra Leone, Liberia, Colombia, and Sri Lanka, girls have served regularly in combat roles (Wessells 2006, 85–106).

Also somewhat unusual was the highly singular mode of girls' recruitment. Virtually all the participants in this study were forcibly recruited in one manner—abduction—and they said that this was the only means through which other girls were recruited. Although abduction is a key means of recruitment in African countries, it is often mixed with forms of recruitment in which girls decide to enter armed groups. In the armed conflicts in Mozambique and Ethiopia, some girls were abducted into armed groups, whereas other girls decided to join armed groups to liberate their society from oppressive regimes or to achieve greater equality with men (Veale 2004; West 2004). This mixed pattern of recruitment is also visible in countries such as Nepal (Human Rights Watch 2007a, 23–25) and Sri Lanka. As Jo Becker points out in her chapter in this volume, the Liberation Tigers of Tamil Eelam (LTTE) often recruits girls forcibly in Sri Lanka. Yet other girls apparently join the LTTE because they succumb to the political propaganda and believe that they are fighting to help liberate Tamil people from oppression.

The reliance on forced recruitment may have reflected the relatively low levels of support for UNITA by civilian populations outside UNITA's immediate sphere of control. Not uncommonly, people living in areas ripe for attack by UNITA were also subject to attacks by the Angolan army. To survive in such an area, people often learn to avoid taking sides because allegiance with one side may invite attack by the other side. It remains for future research to determine whether it was this factor, weak propaganda methods, or other factors that made forced recruitment the sole means available to UNITA for recruiting girls.

Overall, this research helps to point out that methods of recruitment are highly contextual and varied. It is too simplistic to talk about girls' recruitment as if it occurred in the same manner in all situations. Methods of recruitment vary according to cultural norms, armed groups' situation and objectives, and levels of civilian support for the fighting. Ultimately, universalized images of "girls' recruitment" are as questionable as are universalized images of "the girl soldier."

Implications for Research, Practice, and Policy

The Angolan case presented above highlights the importance of ethical sensitivity in conducting research with formerly recruited girls and in organizing reintegration programs to support them. Often researchers assume that formerly recruited boys and girls are in similar situations and apply the same research approach to both. This is ill-advised because girls experience a fundamentally greater degree of stigmatization than boys, and they face other gendered risks such as those associated with pregnancy. For these reasons, the methods that are appropriate in working with boys may harm girls. Sensitive research should be tailored specifically to girls and be cautious about using methods such as predetermined random sampling or interviews that could prematurely end the girls' anonymity. Stigmatization is a sufficiently widespread problem to warrant considerable caution in the design and conduct of research on formerly recruited girls. Indeed, it is beneficial to attend to the girls' well-being before, during, and after the interviews. Although ethical supports in research need to be tailored to fit the local context and may not need to be as stringent as those developed in Angola, researchers should aim to err on the side of caution.

The ethical sensitivity of research activities is also an issue because the presence of researchers often raises expectations in unrealistic, unintended ways. In situations of severe poverty and deprivation, it is natural for war-affected people, including girls, to expect that outsiders who come and ask questions will provide much needed money and material supports. This creates an unspoken gap in expectations. On one hand, the researchers expect only to collect scientific information and make no promises about future support. On the other hand, the participants may experience raised expectations about future supports. Long delays in the provision of support or the lack of follow-up support inevitably creates frustration and feelings of exploitation and abandonment, which only add to the suffering of the girls and their communities. To address this problem, researchers should work to manage local peoples' expectations and, more important, to connect their research with practical action and steps that will assist formerly recruited girls. One way to achieve this is by partnering with an international NGO or other agency that seeks to support girls' reintegration.

The findings outlined above also have significant implications for practice, which also encounters significant ethics issues, including those related to stigmatization. The following are key steps toward supporting formerly abducted girls in an ethically appropriate manner: design and conduct assessments in ways that minimize stigmatization and protect the girls' anonymity to the extent that they desire to remain unseen; tailor programs to address girls' specific needs, avoiding the tendency to create a single set of reintegration supports for formerly recruited girls and boys; use a participatory approach that strengthens girls' sense of agency and enables them to define which supports are most useful and the appropriate implementation schedule; develop integrated programs that support not only formerly abducted girls but also other at-risk children; avoid the reverse stigmatization that can result from supporting only formerly recruited girls, who may be better off than other vulnerable children in the community; work through local networks to build community supports that will decrease the stigma the girls encounter and encourage collective acceptance of the girls; take a holistic approach, recognizing that the girls need support in areas such as health, education, livelihoods, and psychosocial support; and make the work flexible and long term so that it adjusts to the girls' changing circumstances.

At a policy level, too, there are specific steps that ought to be taken to support formerly abducted girls in a more effective manner. DDR processes should take into account the distinctive, gendered needs of girls. It is also important to recognize the diversity of the girls' age, experiences, and current situation, and to avoid a one-size-fits-all approach to DDR. Organize nonformal reintegration supports for girls, since they often prefer these and are frequently denied access to formal DDR programs. Conduct national campaigns using media such as radio to reduce the stigmatization of formerly recruited girls. And provide flexible, long-term funding to support girls' reintegration.

A significant challenge is to interweave research, practice, and policy in constructive ways that increase girls' protection and prevent their recruitment and re-recruitment by armed forces and groups. A particularly urgent need is for applied research—including participatory action—on the impact of different program approaches. This research could help to guide future supports for girls and provide the empirical foundation needed to construct policies that protect girls' rights and well-being. This chapter will have succeeded if it spurs even a few researchers to accept the challenge.

Part V

Policies to Stop the Recruitment of Child Soldiers

CHAPTER 12

NATIONAL POLICIES TO PREVENT THE RECRUITMENT OF CHILD SOLDIERS

Emily Vargas-Barón

> Armed conflict—increasingly involving child soldiers—and internal displacement call for urgent interventions offering basic education services and medical and psychological care.
> —Nicholas Burnett, *EFA Global Monitoring Report*

CHILD SOLDIERS LIVE IN A GRIM WORLD OF VIOLENCE AND deprivation that largely exists outside of international and national laws. Because the actions required to prevent child soldier recruitment are diverse, prevention policies should include a variety of intersectoral and integrated approaches, especially for education and training, in the broadest and most flexible sense.[1]

The recruitment of child soldiers has been condemned by the international community through the adoption of several international conventions, protocols, and UN resolutions for human rights, fundamental freedoms, and international security, including those for educational and children's rights. Of special note is the groundbreaking Optional Protocol to the Convention on the Rights of the Child, which deals specifically with child soldiers (ICC 2002). When the Rome Statute of the International Criminal Court entered into force, the basis for criminalizing the recruitment of child soldiers was established.

In addition, there are several other international declarations and agreements that lack the force of law but nonetheless have a certain normative power. A number of regional agreements to end the recruitment of child soldiers have also been adopted (Singer 2004, 569). Several international and regional legal and organizational structures have been developed to enforce these instruments. The UNs child protection activities, led by the Office of the Special Representative of the Secretary-General for Children and Armed Conflict, is particularly notable in this regard, and it has made significant progress in recent years (Chikuhwa, this volume).

As noted by Achvarina and Reich (2006a), international norms precluding the recruitment of child soldiers still do not restrain many irregular armed groups and some national militaries of countries with community wars. Many of these international instruments and procedures are not honored in fragile states and countries that are experiencing violent conflicts. Consequently, it is important to consider options for developing national-level policy and program initiatives tied to the implementation and enforcement of international conventions, laws, and protocols. This path for building national policies, standards, guidelines, and regulations will be admittedly difficult, but as stated in the CRS, it is essential that nation-states take leadership in protecting their children, especially the most vulnerable ones.

Although many international specialists have argued that policies and plans for socioeconomic development cannot be drafted and implemented during conflicts, examples of outstanding policy formulation and program development during conflicts do exist within the education sector, as in El Salvador and Colombia (Vargas-Barón and Bernal Alarcón 2005). In Colombia, integrated approaches have been used, including education, health, nutrition, sanitation, and protection for children (Vargas-Barón and Bernal Alarcón 2005). During the conflict in the Democratic Republic of Congo in 2000, a participatory process was undertaken to develop a policy for demobilizing and reintegrating child soldiers (Aborsangaya 2000). Although not all policy implementation measures could be pursued at the time, Aborsangaya reports that this policy planning process was successful. Stakeholder consultations were undertaken in various areas of the country, and the government formally adopted the policy. Thus, in addition to manifest need, there is precedent for proposing that, to the extent possible, national policies and policy guidelines in line with international conventions and mandates can be pursued before and during conflicts.

Governments usually lead and dominate policy development at the national level, but increasingly nations with enlightened leaders include civil society and private sector institutions in policy planning processes. However, in fragile states and nations plagued by violent conflicts, government leaders often lack the will or may have limited knowledge or power to conduct participatory processes for policy planning. Because of this, they may resort to quick forms of centralized policy planning conducted by small teams buried in ministerial offices. Almost without exception, the central control of policy planning for social policies is ineffectual, and such policies are rarely well implemented or evaluated. This is especially true of centrally planned social policies developed during and soon after violent conflicts (Vargas-Barón and Bernal Alarcón 2005).[2]

Achvarina argues that when the leaders of certain nations have not been democratically elected and they have been openly condemned by the international community, then armed opposition groups within their borders may be more open to following international norms regarding the nonrecruitment of child soldiers as they attempt to gain greater international legitimacy (Achvarina 2007). If true, this would appear to argue in favor of efforts to open the way for policy dialogue with such groups. However, in situations rife with banditry, kidnapping, and illicit trades, it is doubtful that guerrillas, paramilitaries, and other irregular groups would be interested in discussing, adopting, or following any of these international norms.[3] The policy options presented in this chapter are mainly focused on working with existing governments and institutions of civil society, fragile though they may be. As possible, armed opposition groups should be included in policy dialogue. At a minimum, policy approaches for ending the recruitment of children into conflicts and releasing child soldiers should be thoroughly and repeatedly discussed during Track Two negotiations, as well as formal negotiations for cease-fires and peace agreements.

Child soldiers are recruited from settings with preexisting fragile institutional realities. Before conflicts begin, many education and health systems are deficient in terms of coverage, structure, financing, contents, methods, and quality. This situation is largely due to weak organizational structures, poor or mediocre governance, limited human resource capacity and quality, limited investment in social services, and the lack of accountability systems. Corruption and a lack of transparency further complicate the situation, causing a widespread sense of hopelessness on the part of citizens. Once conflict erupts in a nation, entire education and health systems can fail, as in Liberia and the Central African Republic (Dolo 2007). In most nations with violence, many schools are destroyed or damaged and teachers may be targeted and persecuted (West 1997). As a consequence, educational planners remaining in a country with violent conflicts usually feel shell-shocked by these events as well as by the trauma of losing relatives, their homes, and even their communities. In spite of these situations, the bases for participation in policy formulation can be established if timely international support is given in appropriate ways to committed national leaders and planners (Guzmán 2005).

In the author's experience, committed planners for social development are always found in nations enduring violent conflicts. Valiant people continue to work in spite of chaotic situations and what they perceive to be overwhelming odds or failure. These devoted civil servants should be identified, reinforced, and supported. They usually require outside technical and financial support that can help them keep a steady course and bring them new ideas regarding alternative planning approaches. They need personal support from specialists who can help them continue to work creatively, and most especially when they are dealing with traumatic situations.

Activities for national policy formulation before or during conflicts are always fraught with difficulties and high political tensions, often including social, economic, interethnic, or religious strife. However, policy development should not be abandoned as a goal. It is essential that formal and informal policy guidelines or regulations for social development and child protection be developed in a participatory manner even though they may not yet be fully ratified. In situations of tension, draft policies that represent a broad consensus are often followed as though they had the force of law. Later they can be ratified. Such social policies could include those that would help prevent the recruitment of child soldiers. They could also serve to give program personnel, communities, and parents hope and a way to structure their actions.

In all forms of educational, health, and other social policies and guidelines developed in conflict situations, gender dimensions are important, especially but not solely with respect to girls. Gender considerations are of key importance in the shadowy world of child soldier recruitment because usually boys and girls are expected to play very different roles in irregular combat groups, and they are treated very differently. Similarly, a gender lens should be applied to policy planning to ensure both boys and girls are protected from recruitment into armed bands. Indeed, relatively little attention has been given to the prevention of the abduction and recruitment of girl child soldiers (Carpenter 2007; Verhey 2001).

Gender differentiation begins before birth because parents and the extended family project their cultural and family values on the expected child. From birth onward, girls from all cultures are treated very differently from boys, and these cultural expectations also ultimately affect child soldier recruitment and treatment. For these and many other reasons, it is essential to develop prevention policies that will have a gender dimension with respect to the differing status, roles, and needs of boys and girls.

This chapter presents an overview of various possible policy options for preventing the recruitment of child soldiers before and during conflicts. It does not deal with policies for the demobilization and reintegration of child soldiers, except for a few considerations regarding the prevention of recidivism. Although several of the policy options presented below would be helpful for all young children and youth affected by war, this discussion will focus mainly on preventing the recruitment of child soldiers.

Policy options for preventing child soldier recruitment exist at two main points in conflict situations: precursor situations and during conflicts. Many conflicts lack a declared cease-fire or a specific date for a national peace accord, as was the case in El Salvador and more recently in Nepal. In most countries affected by violence, conflicts drag on for years, often moving from region to region, as in Senegal's Casamance region and Colombia, with children recruited by various types of combatants in different places and at various points in the struggle. At any time before or during a violent conflict, children may be enticed or abducted into groups such as guerrillas, paramilitaries, mercenaries, bandits, kidnappers, suicide murderers, illicit traders, or regular military troops. However, child soldier recruitment becomes possible more as a result of antecedent security and social conditions that negatively affect children, families, and communities than because of the specific recruitment efforts of violent groups. To prevent child soldier recruitment, nations must address those antecedent security and social conditions.

Precursor Situations

Many leaders of humanitarian assistance programs decry the recruitment of children into war, yet they rarely analyze the previous status of such children. From a review of gray literature, studies on child soldiers, and direct observation in several nations, it is clear that the great majority of child soldiers have been born into families living in poverty, both in urban and especially rural areas. Many of them come from a variety of types of broken homes or single-parent households. Often, their parents or teachers have abused them physically, sexually, or emotionally. Child abuse is highly correlated with wife abuse, and usually these children have seen their mothers abused by their partners. Domestic violence always increases during times of community violence, and both are usually also correlated with severe poverty. It appears that most future child soldiers were directly affected by the conflict into which they were later recruited (Dolo 2007, 52–58).

In addition to having been previously impacted by domestic and community violence, as observed by the author, child soldiers often exhibit high indices of malnutrition, chronic illness, and moderate to severe delays in their cognitive, socio-emotional, and physical development. Essentially, most of them have been subjected to severe deprivation, and they lack services for social and juridical protection that are called for in the Convention on the Rights of the Child.

As a result of poverty, domestic and community violence, and a lack of basic health, nutrition, education, sanitation, and especially protective services for parents and young children, some children run away from home in order to join armed groups that they perceive to be safer and more supportive than their family and community environments (Aborsangaya 2000).[4] Promises of a better life and an income often entice such children into becoming child soldiers. However, if parents were to improve their economic status, learn skills to nurture and develop their children better, as well as gain access to basic health, nutrition, education, and protective services, it is doubtful that armed groups could talk children into running away from home or entice parents into selling their children to such groups. Well-supported parents would be better able to protect their children and maintain their affection as well as prepare them to resist the offers of armed groups. Of course, the forceful armed abduction of children will nullify all such efforts if adequate security systems for communities, schools, and homes are not in place.

Many children who are conscripted into armed groups have never attended primary school. Others who were able to enroll in a school repeated grades and/or dropped out at an early age. These child soldiers lack basic literacy, workforce skills, and a sense of attachment to their communities and nations, making them highly susceptible to being recruited into armed groups. Essentially, the school systems in many fragile nations are failing the children and failing their communities.

In addition, as noted in the 2007 EFA Global Monitoring Report: "New forms of war, practiced by armies and warlords alike, target children and youth, seeking to turn them into soldiers. As more young people are drawn into long-term conflicts, education offers an increasingly effective way to reduce tensions, and promote tolerance and other values conducive to peace" (Burnett 2007, 74).

The lack of good quality and culturally and linguistically appropriate education services has been shown to cause or exacerbate many conflicts (Vargas-Barón and Bernal Alarcón 2005). For example, one of the main causes of the revolts of Albanian Kosovars in Kosovo and of the Kurds in four nations was their inability to secure culturally appropriate education for their children. All in all, in nations moving toward conflict, school systems that are failing and culturally inappropriate, poor in quality, and do not protect children are major factors in exposing children to the danger of recruitment into armed groups.

In addition to poor quality, the schools in some nations serve as centers for indoctrination for purposes of future recruitment into armed struggles. Ideological takeovers have included the control of education and communications, as well as the military and finance, because the role of education in forming future cadres has been considered essential for quashing unacceptable cultural traditions, achieving long-term social control, and conducting advanced social mobilization. More recently, attention has been drawn to various types of religious combatants in several nations that have been using schools to try to control youthful minds and prepare the next generation of young fighters for their cause.

Poverty-stricken rural and urban communities in fragile nations usually lack access to comprehensive and integrated services, including primary health care services for children and mothers; nutrition education, supplementation, and rehabilitation; parenting education and early childhood intervention or preschools; home, community, and water sanitation; juridical protection and protective services; workforce training programs; and basic community security services.[5] Instead, these poor communities may have only a few inadequate and poorly articulated sectoral services, such as a health post without medicines or a small school without a trained teacher and textbooks. Many parents are unable to meet their children's basic needs for survival and development. Such parents may believe that armed groups represent the only way for their children to receive the food, clothing, and lodging they need, and as a result, some of them have not opposed their children's entry into groups.

Some countries have suffered from cyclical violence, such as Colombia and certain indigenous regions of Mexico. Due to a lack of services for trauma healing, reconciliation and conflict resolution, families, communities, and political groups have embarked on vendettas and thrust children into a culture of violence and reprisal. Whole generations have grown up without knowledge of any way of life except war and vengeance. These children are essentially conscripted from birth into armed bands and their fate is sealed. This is one of the main reasons for the existence of the more than fourteen thousand child soldiers currently found in Colombia (CSUCS 2004a, 113). Some of Colombia's most notorious and cruel guerrilla fighters began as young child soldiers. Trauma healing, conflict resolution, and, above all, individual, familial, and community reconciliation are essential measures for inhibiting the intergenerational conscription of children into armed groups.

Children and youth are becoming increasingly aware of profound inequities and injustices in their societies. Access to mass media and the Internet enable them to become aware of how others live. Perceived inequities cause depression and fan the insecurities of the young. These inequities often light the wick of anarchy and attract the young to lawless movements that give them hope. It is notable that many young people designated as international terrorists were born into middle-income homes where they first became aware of socioeconomic inequalities. Indeed, some relatively well-educated yet radicalized parents encourage their children to become engaged in intergenerational battles in order to achieve their vision of better futures, in economic, cultural, or religious terms. These revitalization movements usually seek to resurrect idealized past cultural glories, and they can serve as frameworks for attracting children to radical activities.

To prevent the recruitment of child soldiers, bold new policy initiatives are needed at the national level to complement international agreements and conventions that are aimed at ending the use of children as armed combatants. However, relatively few national policies and policy guidelines have been adopted to prevent the recruitment of child soldiers (Achvarina and Reich 2006a, 130). Until a body of national policy instruments and databases is developed along with baseline information on child soldier recruitment in specific countries, it will be impossible to know if such policies could be effective in reducing or ending recruitment (Lischer, this volume).

Preventing Child Recruitment before Conflicts

In fragile states that appear to be moving toward violence, it is critically important to create, implement, and evaluate national policy frameworks and plans for social protection, education, health, and nutrition that are focused on the prevention of the recruitment of child soldiers. Usually, many signs of potential unrest can be discerned in such nations. For many years, some development specialists that work with fragile states have called for policies such as the ones that are outlined below. However, they have not been successful in developing social protection and development policies because most bilateral donor agencies have placed priority on supporting stable sustainable development nations. Also, investments in social protection and development have been viewed as developmental approaches rather than as violence prevention initiatives. The UN system, and especially UNICEF, has been much more open to considering such investments.

Given the escalation of guerrilla movements, community wars, the worldwide reach of terrorism, and the increasing conscription of children as armed combatants, it is imperative that past approaches be reconsidered. The neglect of human rights and development agendas in fragile states must be reassessed. The promotion of the preparation of new national policies for social protection and development should be undertaken to ameliorate detrimental socioeconomic situations that can enable—and even promote—the recruitment of child soldiers.

Several types of policy initiatives could be undertaken rapidly in many fragile states at national and subnational levels, with technical support from UN, multilateral, and bilateral international agencies:

Integrated Parent Education and Support Systems

It is impossible to eliminate high levels of severe poverty rapidly. However, certain focused interventions are particularly effective in improving the standard of living of impoverished home and community settings that can become the seedbed for child soldiers and other belligerents.

In particular, policies for developing integrated early childhood development, parent support, and social and juridical protection programs can be instituted quite rapidly to strengthen families and improve parenting behaviors in relatively short periods of time (Burnett 2007). Child development, safety, and protection, as well as parenting skills, can be improved without fully eliminating poverty, although, of course, it is very helpful to improve families' standards of living as well. Essential social services for education and health should also be given priority, especially in regions of fragile states with failing education systems and high levels of child mortality, famine, and chronic diseases. Special attention should be given to the parents of vulnerable children who lack basic services and exhibit ill health, malnutrition, developmental delays, and signs of abuse. These children require early childhood intervention services and enriched education activities in order to help them develop well, be ready for school, achieve well in school, and ultimately have the knowledge, attitudes, and skills that will enable them to avoid falling prey to the enticements of armed groups offering a better life.

Guidance is available for preparing integrated national policies for early childhood development as an essential first step for nations to develop comprehensive early childhood and parenting programs that will include components for education, health, nutrition, social and juridical protection, and sanitation (Vargas-Barón 2005–2006). To assist with this process, international standards for parenting programs focusing on vulnerable children have been advanced (Vargas-Barón 2007).

Integrated Basic Community Services

In conjunction with integrated early childhood and parent education and support services, comprehensive community systems are required for ensuring the provision of protective services, community security, basic health care and education, nutrition education and supplementation, literacy training, sanitation, workforce skills training, and agricultural development. The era of high-cost, specialized sectoral services is waning, and integrated, comprehensive, lower-cost, and well-coordinated services are increasingly being developed. For this to occur, each fragile nation should undertake a multisectoral policy planning process that will give priority to those geographical regions with a high prevalence of underserved families living in poverty. This can often be accomplished during the planning processes for the preparation of poverty reduction strategy papers (PRSP) and National Development Plans. For PRSP and other multisectoral policies to be translated effectively into operational plans of action and programs, comprehensive situation analyses, mapping, and simulation exercises will be required.

Comprehensive Education Reform

A national policy for education reform should be developed to improve fragile and failing education systems, with priority attention given to regions where children could potentially be conscripted into armed groups. Both formal education and nonformal education systems should be addressed through the development of partnerships among institutions of the public and private sectors and civil society. To the extent possible, leaders of indoctrination movements in formal and nonformal education settings should be identified and restrained, if not removed, from guiding children's learning. Curricula, materials, methods, and teacher training systems should be revised and changed as rapidly as possible to improve educational quality and avoid contents promoting the use of armed force. As specified in the 1960 UNESCO Convention Against Discrimination in Education and the Salamanca Statement and Framework for Action on Special Needs Education of 1994, priority attention should be given to safeguarding the educational rights of all ethnic and language groups, as well as to providing enriched learning opportunities for children with developmental delays and disabilities.

As noted above, nations where the educational rights of populations have been abrogated tend to engender community wars. Parent education provided through early childhood programs and schools should include components on how parents can teach their children to resist the lure of armed groups and on ways for them to build community solidarity to confront and reject the incursions of such groups (Ospina Serna and Alvarado Salgado 2001). This type of community resistance in regions of Colombia helped to deter and stop the advance of armed groups that wanted to take control of many rural towns in the region of Boyacá.[6]

Integrated Educational, Trauma Healing, and Protective Services

For children buffeted by domestic, community, or intergenerational violence prior to the outbreak of open warfare, services that integrate educational, trauma healing, and protective activities are required—but they are seldom available. In education policies of fragile nations, the training of teachers and community facilitators in methods for conflict resolution, trauma healing, and reconciliation should be given top priority, along with other curricular contents. Trauma healing services may be provided during or after conflicts but seldom before major conflicts begin. Yet children affected by domestic and community violence are often traumatized. When such services are offered, they are usually short term. They are rarely integrated into long-term education and protective services. Policies for trauma healing can and should be included in policies and plans for education and protective services in fragile nations. Protective services policies should establish long-term, community-based trauma healing programs with a special focus on the prevention of the conscription of children into armed conflict. Protective social services should be available for communities, schools, and families with children at high risk of being forced or enticed into armed groups. New programs for National Trauma Centers for Children Affected by Conflicts, including child soldiers, could be developed along the lines of the many national and international Centers for the Victims of Torture.[7]

Security Systems and Networks

Policies dealing with governance, community policing, justice systems, and camps for internally displaced persons (IDPs) or refugees should include provisions for ensuring greater security, with a special focus on preventing the conscription of child soldiers. Achvarina and Reich (2006a, 138, 148) posit that the protection of children and youth in refugee camps in Africa explains the lower incidence of child soldiers in certain African countries, such as Senegal, Angola, Mali, Lesotho, and Niger. Systems for training teachers, community leaders, and organizations in primary security and reciprocal neighborhood protection methods should be developed and supported, and police systems need to be reinforced to support community and neighborhood security efforts.

Above all, emphasis should be given to using and protecting schools and refugee or IDP camps as "safe spaces" or "child friendly spaces" for children, teachers, and parents (McClure and Retamal 2007).[8] Building linkages between community and camp security structures and networks in many places would enable shared learning and the reinforcement of primary security measures.

Preconflict Childhood

Research is urgently required on the early childhoods of child soldiers during preconflict periods. Both quantitative and qualitative studies should be undertaken. These studies should include child health; nutritional and developmental status; parenting behaviors; service access and use; exposure to traumatic domestic, community, or intergenerational violence; preschool experiences (if any); and children's school histories and achievement. Research should also be undertaken regarding the types, contents, and methods of informal and nonformal education received (or not received) by children before becoming child soldiers, as well as during conflicts. These data should be studied in relation to prevailing types of child soldier recruitment and the degree of security provided children in communities, IDP and refugee camps, schools, and play areas.

Study results should be used to tailor national policies to fit the sociocultural and economic realities of children affected by war, with a special focus on those who are enticed or abducted into armed groups.

In addition, case studies should be conducted on integrated early childhood development programs and their results in violence zones where children have been conscripted into armed groups with the intention of discovering whether or not such programs are successful in curtailing conflict and conscription. For example, a case study on a preschool program in camps for IDPs in Ambon, Indonesia, describes a compelling approach that reduced violence and intolerance in children and at familial, community, and interreligious group levels (Tualeka et al. 2005).

Once policies are in place for preventing the recruitment of child soldiers in precursor situations, policy evaluations should be undertaken to assess their effectiveness and revise the strategies and programs used in order to improve their impacts.

Preventing Child Recruitment during Conflicts

During conflicts, many nations cease to provide basic health, nutrition, education, sanitation, protection, and economic development services in violence zones. In addition, some countries with conflicts have always had an inadequate infrastructure of social and economic services.

Disease, malnutrition, out-of-school children and youth, and heaps of garbage abound in violence zones the world over. However, it has been demonstrated that impressive programs for social and protective services can be developed and maintained, even in situations filled with chaos (Vargas-Barón and Bernal Alarcón 2005). Nonetheless, some places are too dangerous for any service provision, apart from highly protected humanitarian assistance teams.

Many techniques for the maintenance of program services during conflict have been developed in countries such as Algeria, Bosnia and Herzegovina, Colombia, Eritrea, and Senegal. Virtual learning centers, community outreach programs, early childhood and parenting services, and many other types of programs have functioned successfully during conflicts, and they have helped not only resident populations but also IDPs, street children, orphans, and refugees from other nations (Vargas-Barón and Bernal Alarcón 2005).

Local, regional, or national governments sometimes conduct these programs; however, usually they are run by organizations of civil society, including national and international nongovernmental organizations (NGOs), community development organizations, universities, institutes, and faith-based organizations (Chickering et al. 2006). Partnerships between civil society and government are critically important in such settings. Maintaining a nation's infrastructure of civil society institutions will help ensure the provision of services that can help to prevent the recruitment of children into armed conflict. During conflicts, national civil society organizations should be strengthened and united, as possible, with governmental policy planning efforts to assist all children who are negatively affected by conflicts and trauma.

During conflicts, educational programs and especially schools and preschools can serve as safe places, often providing the only secure environments for children. Many writers have noted this attribute of the school as a safe place (Aguilar and Retamal 1998; Machel 1996). However, schools are not always safe places. When child soldiers are abducted or recruited from their schools or homes, usually national, regional, and local governments take little note of their disappearance. Often they do not put protective services and police security groups into place to guard the children. National database systems for recording the recruitment and disappearance of children rarely exist. Those few database systems that have been developed by international agencies for use in conflict situations, such as the databases of the International Organization for Migration, usually lack variables or indicators dealing with the recruitment and status of child soldiers as well as other variables that would be useful in designing action plans. Databases for the prevention of child soldier recruitment should help nations design policies and program services for finding conscripted and abducted children, mounting efforts to rescue them, ensuring accountability, and evaluating service provision.

Systems should be developed for protecting places where armed groups capture children, such as schools, homes, community play areas, and IDP and refugee camps. Although they are of prime importance, programs for child security are rarely available in violence zones. Rather, priority is given to protecting police stations, businesses, and public buildings rather than young children. During conflicts, outreach services are required to train communities about how to protect their children.

In some circumstances, abducted or runaway children could be quickly rescued, and some may be able to be enticed out of the armed groups they have joined. However, few systems for the rapid demobilization of child soldiers have been developed during conflicts. Communications media to encourage defections have targeted adults, and they have rarely been used to encourage child soldiers to flee their captors. Perhaps leaders of demilitarization efforts believe that children are so affected by the Stockholm syndrome that they will not dare to escape.

Demobilization programs during conflicts represent opportunities for encouraging young child soldiers to defect. It is important that demobilization programs for child soldiers provide enriched and accelerated educational contents, conflict resolution, trauma healing, and reconciliation with family and friends, as well as with former enemies. However, indoctrination can occur during training programs for ex–child soldiers, and vigilance is required to ensure a balanced curriculum is provided, including academic subjects, skills training, and citizenship education in order to prevent cyclical violence. Special attention should be given to the different needs of former girl and boy fighters.

As adult men and women leave armed groups, they are usually given some form of training and support program for reinsertion into society. However, the young children of ex-combatants, who have been heavily impacted by community and often domestic violence, are rarely given services. Many of the children of ex-guerrillas and others have served as child soldiers although they are not labeled as such. If they do not receive appropriate education, trauma healing, conflict resolution, and reconciliation services, they may return to the conflict as full-fledged child soldiers.

To prevent a return to fighting, the children of ex-combatants require comprehensive and accelerated education and training services similar to those given to ex–child soldiers. If they are very young, programs that are appropriate to their levels of development should be provided. They may require special security because sometimes they are hunted down as renegades. The children of ex-combatants have usually suffered from major trauma, and although some may appear to be resilient, the negative impact of their experiences will rise to the surface at many points during ensuing years. It is critically important that these children receive long-term trauma healing services, skills in conflict resolution, and, to the extent possible, acceptance within their families and local society. Often these children are rejected by the local populace, who fears them and does not want their children studying and playing with them. Community education is required to prepare communities to accept ex–child soldiers as well as the children of ex-combatants.

As noted before, many international specialists continue to believe that during conflicts it is close to impossible to develop policies or guidelines to deal with human rights, social protection, and development issues. However, experience has shown that in many conflict situations, formal or informal policies could be developed that would provide guidance for warring parties in some places or phases of a conflict. Because each phase of a conflict can present different types of problems and opportunities for planning and implementing policies, guidelines, and services, it is important to assess each country situation carefully.

During conflicts, special attention should be given to interinstitutional coordination in all aspects of policy development and application. Coordination between NGOs and governments is often neglected during conflicts. In some cases, such coordination is rejected as an option. The competition for contracts from international organizations has exacerbated this situation both during and after conflicts. To develop and implement effective policies and policy guidelines, coordination systems including both government and national NGOs are essential.

Since most child soldiers are recruited after conflicts have begun, to the extent possible during conflicts, effective national and local level policies or policy guidelines should be developed in the areas listed below.

Maintaining and Developing Essential Basic Services

To prevent the recruitment of children during conflicts, it is essential to maintain basic protective and social services to the extent possible as frameworks for action and deterrents to armed groups seeking to entice or force children into their webs. Existing national development policies that mandate protective and social services should be maintained and improved to the extent possible. Emphasis should be given to helping social sectors work together to conduct integrated and culturally appropriate services, especially for health, nutrition, education, sanitation, social and juridical protection, workforce skills, and community security. Special attention should be given to maintaining institutions of civil society as a bridge to postconflict national development (Chickering et al. 2006).

To forestall the recruitment of child soldiers, priority should be given to establishing or expanding community and family-based education and support services, especially in locations with many IDP or refugee families (McClure and Retamal 2007). Over time, prolonged displacement and suffering in camps with few, inadequate, or no services for education, health, training, and employment can lead traumatized children and youth to seek a way out. When they feel this way, they can be easily enticed into armed groups.

To achieve this true safety net of basic services, it will be essential to forge partnerships with national NGOs and other institutions of civil society. This can be complicated when some of these institutions pertain to the opposition, but new groups usually appear to meet core service needs in conflict situations.

Monitoring, Tracking, Preventing, and Rescuing Child Soldiers

In addition to international statistical databases on child soldiers, national and subnational policy guidelines and plans should be established for developing, coordinating, and maintaining systems to monitor the recruitment and status of child soldiers. On the basis of data gathered, plans should be prepared to protect children and prevent the further recruitment of children in affected regions.

Recruiters of child soldiers, their methods, and results should be found and monitored, with an eye not only to understanding their modus operandi but also to capturing and branding them as legal transgressors, convicting them in a court of law, seizing their bank accounts and other resources, and thereby ending their impunity and preventing the continuation of their recruitment practices (Singer 2004). Over time, these measures should result in setting examples for other recruiters who think they may be able to operate with impunity.

Policies should also call for situation analyses and the development of databases that would help security teams find, rescue, and reintegrate child soldiers into society as well as prevent further recruitment and recidivism.

Preparing for Education Policy Reform

Experience has shown that nations with failing education systems rarely reform them thoroughly until a catastrophe hits in the form of a conflict, such as in Sierra Leone and El Salvador, or a natural disaster, as was the case in Nicaragua and Honduras. In countries with conflicts, major education policy reforms with new objectives, strategies, and programs are required in order to improve quality, equity, and coverage; help restore normalcy; and ensure young children will be productively engaged in school, well protected, and not easily conscripted into armed groups (Vargas-Barón and Bernal Alarcón 2005).

In addition, research has revealed that education reforms can and should be begun during a conflict. For example, El Salvador began its successful and highly participatory educational reform well before its war ended in 1992 (Guzmán 2005). As soon as peace accords were signed, the nation was ready to accelerate its highly participatory educational reform process.

Research has demonstrated that nations have a window of opportunity of approximately eighteen to twenty-four months after a conflict ends to reform its education systems (Vargas-Barón and McClure 1998). If reform is delayed beyond twenty-four months, countries tend to return to old, counterproductive approaches and procedures, and it then requires many years for reform to be undertaken. In the meantime, social problems linked to education will grow and fester, often leading to yet more social problems, as was the case in Lao PDR and Vietnam, which waited over a generation to begin their educational reforms (Lachanthaboun et al. 2005; Thomas 2005).

Establishing Community Security

Nations should develop policies for establishing community security plans that will help them protect children in their schools, homes, and community play areas—wherever they tend to be captured by armed bands. The policy for community security should prioritize support for communities in or near violence zones. In addition, training should be given to parents, teachers, coaches, and others on how to protect children and help them protect themselves should they come under attack when adults are not present.

Using the Media to Prevent Recruitment

A social communications policy or guidelines should be developed in each country experiencing the recruitment of child soldiers to encourage all citizens to help efforts to resist and stop recruitment. A public information campaign that presents key elements of the Optional Protocol to the Convention on the Rights of the Child and international decisions of the International Criminal Court should be combined with information on implementing legislation and social protection and development policies in each nation.[9] This type of activity could be initiated during the precursor phase, but it is hard to attract media attention to this matter until actual recruitment of child soldiers occurs within a nation. Public information campaigns are essential in nations once violence has begun.

Some nations, such as Colombia, have made extensive use of media messages (especially radio), pamphlets, and items such as matchbooks to encourage adult guerrillas and paramilitaries to leave armed brigades. This approach has been very effective. Media usage has been instrumental in demobilization in Colombia, where over 32,000 paramilitaries and a large number of guerrillas defected during 2005–2006. The use of radio and visual print media could be considered for reaching child soldiers, many of whom are likely to be illiterate. If children and youth can be enticed into leaving soon after they enter armed groups, then this late prevention work would help to keep them from becoming further radicalized and traumatized. Given children's fears, in some situations it may be necessary to place individuals behind the lines to contact child soldiers, convince them to leave, and help them reach safety.

Media campaigns could also be used to help prepare the civilian population regarding ways to receive former child soldiers in a positive manner rather than reject them, as often happens.

Demobilizing Child Soldiers

Demobilized child soldiers always require comprehensive programs with psychosocial rehabilitation, learning, and support for reintegration into their families and society. If these programs are successful, then recidivism will be low. If they are not effective, then child soldiers tend to return to their former group or enter other rebel groups, bandit groups, mercenary bands, youth gangs, or networks running illicit trades. Once they become dedicated to a life of violence and criminality, it is very difficult to convince them to return to civilian life or enter rehabilitation programs.

Significant attention has been given to developing policies and plans for demobilizing and reintegrating child soldiers (e.g., Verhey 2001). However, little attention has been paid to including components for the prevention of the rerecruitment of child soldiers. These policies should give priority to improving services for rapid demobilization and reintegration. Attention should be given to ensuring these services are comprehensive, culturally appropriate, and attentive to the needs of former child soldiers.

Reintegrating the Children of Ex-combatants

As noted in the introduction to this section, some child soldiers are the children of adult combatants. The children of guerrillas and other fighters who are not yet engaged in violence are at very high risk of becoming child soldiers. However, when these children's mothers or fathers demobilize, the children usually are overlooked. They are the most forgotten children in war and the ones that national programs for demobilization are least likely to serve. Their parents are usually deeply depressed, worried, and disoriented, and this situation has an additional negative impact on children. Carpenter discusses the need to address the special requirements of child soldiers who are young mothers with children born in violent situations. Carpenter also notes the various types of interventions such children and their parents should receive (Carpenter 2007).

Each nation with community wars and child soldiers should give priority to developing policy guidelines, plans, and programs for the reintegration of the children of ex-combatants, emphasizing long-term trauma healing, conflict resolution, reconciliation, academic study, workforce skills, preparation for citizenship, and participation in democratic governance processes (Universidad de Ibagué and Universidad del Rosario 2006).

Providing Long-Term Support

Many nations have looked for quick fixes to the child soldier problem. However, long-term follow-up and continued support services are required to ensure former child soldiers and the children of ex-combatants will be well integrated into society, receive nurturing care from their own or new families, continue their education and training, receive trauma-healing services as needed, and be given security, especially from those who may wish to harm them. Also, the families and schools who receive them may need protection and monitoring to prevent the possible occurrence of indoctrination as well as continued support services. Workforce training systems will be required to ensure former child soldiers receive training and become gainfully employed or develop small businesses (Guzmán de Luna 2005).

Assessing Policies for Demobilized Child Soldiers

It is essential that rapid mapping exercises and assessments be undertaken regarding the provision and quality of basic and integrated services given during conflicts. Special attention should be given to evaluating the impact of services on the prevention of the recruitment of child soldiers, and to identifying high-risk populations.

Data gleaned through the development of systems for monitoring the recruitment and status of child soldiers should be analyzed carefully, with the goal of helping nations prevent further recruitment and of building protective policies that will become increasingly effective over time. Situation analyses on child soldier recruitment will be essential, as well as studies on short- and long-term policy results.

Studies on the short- and long-term results of programs for demobilized child soldiers are urgently needed, with a special focus on the reasons for recidivism. In addition to assessing the reasons why some child soldiers return to conflicts, become bandits, join youth gangs, work in illicit trades, or become international mercenaries, it will also be important to identify why and how some of them are able to reintegrate well. Ultimately, a combination of ethnographic research, comparative case studies, statistical analyses, and evaluation research projects will be needed to inform future policy planning activities to prevent the recruitment of child soldiers.

Summary

A wide array of studies, policies, plans, and programs will be required to prevent armed groups from abducting children and to keep children from voluntarily joining armed groups. Several policies working in tandem will be required in each national setting.

Integrated policies and programs for child development and protection, parent education and support, and child and family security are essential for preventing situations that can result in vulnerable children becoming attracted to and conscripted or abducted into the ranks of child soldiers. These policies and programs can also help to stop cyclical violence, reduce poverty, avoid child abandonment, and overcome the lack of services that help to generate conflicts. Additionally, youth policies and programs can provide educational opportunities, skills, and citizenship training through formal, nonformal, or informal learning activities. If they are well structured and nondoctrinaire, such programs will help stop child soldier recruitment and recidivism as well as end the cycle of violence. It is also important for protective and security services to be given high priority and instituted in communities, neighborhoods, schools, play areas, and camps for IDPs and refugees.

Ultimately, given that over seventy million children lack access to basic education, and yet more children live in severe poverty, it is surprising that there are not many more child soldiers in the world. To prevent an increase in the number of children whose only recourse is violence, it is essential that protective and social policies be developed and implemented that will give vulnerable children a fair start in life.

CHAPTER 13

WISE INVESTMENTS IN FUTURE NEIGHBORS

Recruitment Deterrence, Human Agency, and Education

Maureen W. McClure and Gonzalo Retamal

> The child is usually defeated by the superior strength of the adult, but the defeat does not remain without consequences; it would seem to activate a tendency to overcome defeat by doing actively what one was forced to endure passively: to rule when one had to obey; to beat when one was beaten; in short, to do what one was forced to suffer, or to do what one was forbidden to do.
> —Erich Fromm, *The Anatomy of Human Destructiveness*

HUMAN SECURITY IS EMERGING AS A SOPHISTICATED and compelling strategy to address the extreme problems of children in contemporary wars. The child soldier is increasingly seen as an icon of new wars—transformed from a young person into a weapon (Kaldor 1999). Whether as members of local militias or as suicide bombers, child soldiers are children growing up among failed adults in failed communities. Some not only fail to learn to read or write, they also fail to learn the humanity they need to be successful neighbors and parents.

Turning children into weapons is an act of generational destruction.[1] Failed adults are more likely to make failed neighbors and failed parents. The cycle can continue for generations. Thus the real costs of war cannot be tallied for years, for decades, for generations.

Child soldiers reveal the genocidal aspects of contemporary wars. Child soldiers are, explicitly or tacitly, direct attacks on the generational transitions of communities. The cruelty of new wars reveals major gaps in educational policy frameworks currently in use by the international community. Education policy today focuses thinking about education as a civil rights problem. This leads to concerns for access to the provision of institutional services. Developed during the post–World War II period, education was constructed as a neutral, technical process complete with generic experts who taught and generic students who learned. Their classrooms were ordered around literacy and numeracy. Little attention was paid to security issues and their consequences, either short or long term.

This approach to development, while admirable, is insufficiently compelling to drive today's strategic operations in the brutal, even genocidal face of cultural identity wars and their aftermath. Under these conditions, when civil societies are threatened to their generational core, traditional classrooms and curriculum are no longer sufficient. The problem is no longer one of civil rights. It has become a much larger problem of generational survival.

This chapter suggests that the emerging human security frameworks, while still mired globally in failing narratives, may offer the best direction for future work. Emerging human security narratives focus on the protection of local populations, especially children. They require defense against the forced recruitment of child soldiers. These new narratives center on the protection of generational agency. They mobilize local and external communities to actively secure safe places for children to grow and develop as normally as possible.

Against the allure of muscular and violent warriors stands a small group of internationals working side by side with caring local parents and neighbors desperate to defend their children. Together they have constructed an emerging strategy of local community protection that places at its center the protection of children's agency in the face of those who seek its annihilation (UNICEF 2004).[2] This chapter examines the problems of research and data collection under these conditions, turning to fugitive literature and strategic desk reviews. It briefly surveys general, large-scale responses to recruitment deterrence in Bosnia, Albania, Ingushetia, Sierra Leone, Colombia, and Panama. It concludes that while causal claims may not be advisable, scholars can at least begin to map the strategic intent of the institutions involved. Beyond that, more work is needed to map the political and cultural economies that either threaten or defend children.

Most contemporary work in the area of education and child soldiers has been based either on child rights advocacy (getting governments and their oppositions to refrain from the use of child soldiers) or on programs for the rehabilitation of child soldiers in the demobilization process.

The research literature in the area of institutional responses to the complex emergencies that include child soldiers, while still small, has grown exponentially over the past decade.[3] Today there is a very large and growing body of program assessment, planning, and other technical documents that are helping to inform internal institutional policy as donors lurch from one catastrophe to the next. Some of these materials are used to drive advocacy and marketing. Others are used to drive field operations.

These latter documents can help scholars understand how institutions frame their responses to conditions on the ground. Some materials can be quite helpful in understanding how problems are framed and how narratives are constructed to drive strategy. International education scholars also map both highly complex political economies and their culturally diverse interpretations. Prior to the extensive use of pdf files, locally generated reports were rarely distributed beyond a few internal and local copies.[4] The headquarters of both bilateral and multilateral agencies rarely collected and archived field-generated documents.[5] As the Internet became more accessible, field-generated reports began to provide strategists with access to the timbre of ongoing operations. They often translated truth to power by describing high-action environments to lower-action environments in distant headquarters. This high-low context division was especially visible in international relief agencies torn between successful action on the ground and donor compliance at headquarters (Beer 1997–2003).

Large international agencies and nongovernmental organizations (NGOs) working in education, such as UNICEF and Save the Children, eventually began developing searchable online databases and making more extensive use of institutional desk reviews. These reviews distilled the deluge of documents into lumps of lessons learned or emerging themes, such as a special focus on girl soldiers (UNIFEM 2004). These reviews often were integrated into the institutional planning process.

Unfortunately, fugitive literature can rarely answer causal research questions about the impact highly specified activities had on highly specified groups of children. There are two principal reasons for this structural messiness. First, protective strategy requires rapid large-scale coverage of populations through highly leveraged integrated services. Second, rapid large-scale coverage is intentionally inclusive. Grounded in human rights, relief operations throw wide safety nets to ensure the highest survival rates. Programmatic boundaries are blurred by design. The best scholars can do is shed light on a few interwoven threads in a much larger cloth.

What the fugitive literature CAN address is how scarce institutional resources were allocated. It can help us map the strategic terrain and provide glimpses into the complex political economies out of which deterrence policy can emerge. Measures of success need to be framed in terms of institutional investment. Did things work well enough that the investment strategy was used again in other settings and/or under different conditions? Fugitive literature helps form institutional perceptions. These can help reveal the organizational stories that both drive and limit operations. The fugitive literature never lets us forget that institutions are rough beasts from the past slouching toward the present to be born.

Thus recruitment deterrence policy today is most likely to be based on successful historical institutional responses. For example, UNHCR's policies framed recruitment deterrence as a problem of local communities. They focused on security through demobilization and reintegration into civil communities. UNICEF framed its emergency policies with a strategic narrative of child protection. This drove strategy toward the creation of safe spaces for learning for children and their caregivers. The World Bank and UNESCO framed recruitment problems in terms of access to social sector services, which drove strategy toward institutional capacity building and back-to-school campaigns.

Beginning almost two decades ago, a small number of education and humanitarian policy researchers and strategists began collecting gray or fugitive literature (Honduras, Afghanistan, the Horn of Africa).[6] In the early days, the emphasis was on collecting documents and materials that had been created in the field, especially education packages and kits designed to help people reduce major threats to their survival. These materials covered topics such as avoiding cholera and land mines. They also included trauma identification in children, with simple activities for parents and teachers. Later, UNHCR led the introduction of peace education into the postconflict reintegration processes, particularly in Africa (UNHCR 2002).

For example, early work on child soldiers by Neil Boothby in Mozambique generated program narratives that drove successful demobilization strategy toward greater attention to adolescent development, trauma healing, and local community safety (Arnston and Boothby 2002; Boothby 1992). His work was widely distributed through UNHCR and other venues and led to the development of more complex child soldier–centered program tools over time.

In the mid-1990s the Global Information Networks in Education (GINIE) project was designed by USAID, UNESCO, and UNICEF to work with the Ministry of Education in Bosnia and Herzegovina after the war. Its purpose was to create virtual spaces where high-quality knowledge and expertise could be rapidly captured, analyzed, and widely shared. Early listservs populated by globally based practitioners, researchers, and headquarters staff created for the first time both a professional and institutional living memory that remained continuously alert and helpful as crises broke out.

The project first focused on the collection of supplemental educational materials: mine awareness, cholera prevention, HIV/AIDS, education for peace, etc. These materials were tested and produced in the different emergency settings. They were made publicly available and ready for adaptation into the next crisis. From its inception, youth policy and recruitment deterrence were local concerns. For example, in Bosnia and Herzegovina after-school sports clubs were seen as fertile grounds for recruitment of youth into the black markets run by ethno-paramilitary groups. There were some local discussions, particularly in Travnik, about the need to break with tradition and integrate long-standing independent sports clubs for youth into secondary school after-school activities as a means of recruitment deterrence.[7]

Other novel deterrents were after-school Internet clubs organized to promote civil society. UNESCO's Associated Schools Project (ASP) in Germany helped organize youth groups to create online magazines (see Bender 1999). The most famous youth project was Radio Zid, a youth-operated radio station founded in Sarajevo during the war. The station's civic engagement messages greatly boosted morale for the city's adults. The listening audience was estimated to be over 80 percent of households.

After Rwanda and Bosnia, humanitarian education workers soon realized that the brutality of the new wars meant that many children and youth were repeatedly exposed to violent trauma. Early supplemental programs for trauma healing met with limited success, especially with young people who had been exposed to both intense and repeated trauma. Traditional pedagogy often failed and new methods were needed. Many children could not sit still, could not concentrate, and could not control their emotional responses. Teachers were sometimes put at risk by children who had lost control of their anger.

The very high risks to children's survival during and after new wars meant that educational training and materials had to be quickly grasped and easily understood. Educational programs and materials were created not only in local languages, but also embedded in local cultural sense-making. Alas, the nuanced responses to success in local conditions often proved to be problematic to headquarters staff embedded in corporate cultures of consistency.

For example, one of the authors visiting UNHCR headquarters overheard a program manager speaking on the phone to someone in accounting. The gist of the conversation went something like this, "Yes, I am afraid so. There really was a goat in the program budget. Yes, there had to be a goat in the budget. A former child soldier needed to offer a sacrificial goat in a peace and reconciliation ceremony of reacceptance into his community. Gosh, I really wish I could help you, but I can't. The goat stays."

Over time, internationals learned that deterrence strategy appeared to work when rooted in local communities highly engaged in their children's security. Thus, where possible, child soldiers were treated inclusively. They were separated from others in the local community only when their specific conditions warranted it, and then as briefly as possible. Repeated assessments and evaluations have supported this view. It has become an increasingly standard response in many UN-based operations.

As a result, refugee camps were increasingly designed around protective spaces for children. Activities and services for the young were located in the safest areas with the most visibility. For example, sometimes they were located near the water supply. Camp traffic ebbed and flowed past children and youth at play. There was safety in numbers. The scene offered chronically depressed adults a visible, tangible symbol for a brighter possible future.

The following section primarily focuses on large-scale responses to the problems of recruitment deterrence. Many small-scale success stories exist elsewhere. This chapter intends to inform rapid large-scale education responses in emergencies and their aftermath. It therefore draws on internal documentation primarily of frontline operations conducted by large-scale organizations, specifically UNICEF and its international and local partner NGOs.

The largest international agency with the most experience, UNICEF, consistently invested in recruitment deterrence through locally designed safe places where children could be isolated from predators and through the engagement of youth in building meaningful civil identities. Youth activities included volunteering to protect younger children by helping them participate in trauma healing activities.

There are several reasons for a focus on UNICEF. First, UNICEF is the designated UN agency for children's rights and welfare. No bilateral agency or NGO is adequately organized to manage large-scale, security-based relief efforts for children. UNICEF's strategy is focused on child security through the protection of individual human agency—the relationship between child and caregiver. UNICEF is structured internally to deliver integrated services to children in extreme conditions. It necessarily has a long history of work with security officials. Its strong structural core, which was built on integrated services and decentralized country-based operations, made it uniquely qualified to generate coherent and compelling strategy in the service of child soldiers.[8]

Second, UNICEF is the only large relief agency with long-term in-country offices. The country staff is a mix of locals and internationals. They are on the ground closely connected to local communities before, during, and after conflict. They know both the people and the terrain. They are better able than others to tailor lower cost, higher impact solutions because they have the social capital others lack. UNHCR and other relief agencies and most NGOs cannot generate the high levels of social capital that UNICEF's continuing ground level operations can.

Third, UNICEF is a founding member of the Inter-Agency Standing Committee (IASC), the primary international mechanism for interagency coordination of humanitarian assistance. It is a unique forum involving the key UN and non-UN humanitarian partners.[9] Under the leadership of the Emergency Relief Coordinator, the IASC develops humanitarian policies, agrees on a clear division of responsibility for the various aspects of humanitarian assistance, identifies and addresses gaps in response, and advocates for effective application of humanitarian principles. Together with Executive Committee for Humanitarian Affairs (ECHA), the IASC forms the key strategic coordination mechanism among major humanitarian actors.[10]

Within this context, UNICEF plays the leading agency role in the area both of childhood and youth protection in complex emergencies. Its presence and field coordination is well defined and is based on a clear-cut set of policy and strategic concerns that are legitimized at the level of the IASC. Mission-based concerns for children and youth's well-being have been translated by UNICEF into an increasingly coherent strategy that focuses on childhood protection through the construction of safe environments for generational development and learning.

According to UNICEF policy, integrated services for children must be a core element from the start of an emergency response. UNICEF is joined in this strategy by NGOs such as Save the Children and the International Rescue Committee (IRC). These spaces integrate fundamental services in security, health, education, and psychosocial development into a single protective environment that is both family focused and community based. Where possible, child soldiers are reintegrated into their communities through trauma healing programs for the community. Where this is not possible, a series of alternative, individualized options are available, such as the formation of veterans or other peer associations.

The power of UNICEF's protection strategy is in its mobilization capacities. It uses flexible tactics built on compelling narratives of child protection. For example, the Return to Happiness programs designed to help children and adolescents return to a civil life in Mozambique were agilely translated into protective environment programs in Colombia. Programs that were successful in war zones have been adapted to protect youth from criminal gangs that emerge after natural disasters. Bottom line: these programs work. Or at least a lot of local communities and international agencies and donors think they do.

Top Priority in New Wars: Protection of Human Agency

UNICEF's security-based strategy relies on both integrated and inclusive services. Child-friendly service areas create developmentally protective environments within camps and local communities. Local adults are encouraged to actively participate in child protection—for example, helping to walk children to and from school areas safely. Once inside, the classroom not only becomes a place for physical safety but also for emotional safety and healing. Teachers are drawn from local communities where possible and trained in recognizing and managing emotional trauma, building on successful and appropriate local practices.

Child soldiers in particular have often been deeply traumatized by the absence of protection from responsible, caring adults who can actually protect them. The normal relationships of generational trust may have been so shattered that learning or relearning trust is a major challenge. UNICEF's developmental approach is mindful that adolescents need peers. Ex-combatant adolescents who see themselves as adults are likely to want access to adult education, as in Liberia and Sierra Leone. Others may need access to developmentally related peers, as in Ingushetia.

Albania

One of the important lessons of the Bosnian conflict was the importance of peers in the protection of youth. These lessons were remembered in Albania and later in Kosovo and Ingushetia. Most powerful were activities that helped adolescents actively participate in the defense of civil society.

In February 1999, negotiations between Yugoslav and Kosovo Liberation Army (KLA) representatives in Rambouillet broke down. Organisation for Security and Cooperation in Europe (OSCE) withdrew its mission. On 24 March, NATO launched air strikes. Within seventy-two hours, thousands of Kosovar Albanians, many expelled from their homes, were forced to flee. Between April and May, one million people—about half of the population—took refuge in countries close to Kosovo (UNICEF 2001). Albania alone received approximately 450,000 escaping Kosovo refugees. While many children volunteered to join, "not all recruitment by the KLA, however, was voluntary. Reports indicated some press-ganging, notably among the refugee population. KLA denied the allegations of forced recruitment of children in general although a KLA spokesperson admitted that there might have been some isolated cases of forced recruitment. To guard against such possibilities, UNICEF in close collaboration with the Albanian government, UNHCR, WHO, and other partners or actors, developed the Child-Protection system known as Child-friendly Spaces Initiative within refugee camps one of the specific aims of which was to lower the risk of sexual exploitation/trafficking" (Deng Deng 2001, sec. 2.7.1).

These spaces were special tented areas located in the heart of the camps and dedicated to meeting the needs of women, children, and young people. The child-friendly spaces concept balanced a complex range of relationships across physical and emotional security, social and cognitive development, health and nutritional status. This integrated and inclusive development-oriented approach to child protection provided both a concrete focus and an agile strategy for assessment and operational planning.

The package also included flexible spaces, supplies, and training activities with clearly set and highly visible boundaries. Minimum standards were established to ensure that sufficient space and equipment was provided for each service. Nondiscriminatory protection and access for all to the space and its services were guaranteed.

The holistic approach of the Convention [Rights of the Child, 1989] emphasizes the importance of promoting a multi-disciplinary and cross-sectoral perspective when consideration is given to policies, programs or actions in favour of children. The aim is to focus on the whole child and to promote the effective realization of all his or her rights. It is essential, therefore, to foster an increasing synergy amongst the various sectors which are relevant to the child's life, and prevent fragmented interventions. With a cross-sectoral and inclusive perspective, the value of each specialized sectoral component will be taken into consideration, but a common context will be promoted where complementarity and interrelationship will prevail. (Pais 1999, 9)

This inclusive strategy rested on networks of adults and peers who actively provided mobile webs of security for children and youth. The reliance on relationship networks allowed successful deterrence programs and policies to be created across refugee camps as well as dispersed communities.[11]

The refugees did not stay as long as expected. Within six weeks of the Yugoslav army withdrawal agreement, most refugees had returned home; by August 6, only about 6,667 refugees remained behind in Albania. UNICEF and UNESCO followed young refugees back to Kosovo, helping with reconstruction. Their emphasis on youth participation in reconstruction through peer-based activities remained a strong current throughout the next few years. A large youth initiative targeted teenagers with opportunities to participate in the rebuilding of civil society through supervised sports clubs, structured Internet café activities, and large, innovative rock concerts with civil society messages. The Balkans Sunflower project was formed in 1999 to build on peer volunteer associations with global neighbors. It is still operating.[12]

The child-friendly spaces experience was considered so successful that it has since been not only applied to a number of countries affected by war but also extended into regions affected by natural disasters. These countries and regions include Turkey, El Salvador, India, Angola, Afghanistan, Colombia, East Timor, North Caucasus, and currently South Asia, the Caribbean, and Central America (UNICEF 1999). When civil societies collapse, whether due to conflict or natural disasters, children are at risk for recruitment into predatory economies.

Ingushetia

Ingushetia, or "Galgaachia" in the native tongue, is the smallest constituent republic in the Russian Federation. It is located in the Northern Caucasus. The Ingush and their eastern neighbors, the Chechen, are distinct ethnic groups with distinct languages, histories, and political identities, but they are so closely related and so similar that it is convenient to describe them together (Otunnu 2003). Present-day Chechnya and Ingushetia correspond roughly to the traditional territory where, until recent decades, almost all Chechen and Ingush have lived. This complex human geography is the consequence of events of recent decades: mass deportation of both groups to Central Asia from 1944 to 1956.

In late October 1992, tens of thousands of Ingush were forced from their homes in the Prigorodni District of North Ossetia. This refugee crisis became a major problem for the beleaguered government of Ingushetia, already faced with soaring unemployment (as high as 50 percent), a worsening ecological crisis, a high concentration of Russian troops stationed there because of the war in neighboring Chechnya, and a flood of Chechen refugees from that conflict.

Chechen families and their children had not yet recovered from the 1995–1996 civil wars when they were again uprooted from their homes in late August 1999. The bordering Republic of Ingushetia absorbed nearly 200,000 internally displaced persons (IDPs) from Chechnya. There were almost as many IDPs as Ingushetians. These proportions were phenomenal; the peak figures for Kosovar and East Timorese refugees were about 15 percent. Prior to the IDP influx, Ingushetia was already one of the poorest and most densely populated republics of the Russian Federation (Nichols 2000). Over 45 percent of the displaced were below eighteen years of age (UNOCHA 1999).

In Ingushetia in the displaced camps, there were widespread reports of the use of child soldiers on all sides. Insurgents were believed to have especially targeted both IDP camps and dispersed communities. Deterrence was critical. UNICEF/IRC's Children Affected by Armed Conflict Unit, in collaboration with a researcher from the Harvard School of Public Health, embarked on a longitudinal study of the impact of the program on Chechen adolescents involved in community work and educational activities with families and children (Broughton 2003).

Initial findings indicated that Chechen youth saw the education program as helping by returning young people to their studies as well as giving children a safe and reliable place to go and an emotional space to turn their thoughts toward more age-appropriate concerns. Not only did teens feel that young people needed a place to forget about the war, they also needed a place to be understood. The education program was seen as providing a place for children to connect to others, gain social support, and offer hope for a better future. Many adolescents spoke about the opportunity to study in any form as a means of improving the potential for peace and success within their generation and for the region as a whole. The teens spoke generally about their desire to overcome the ravages of war and have future opportunities to be productive and successful (Stichick et al. 2002).

Sierra Leone

In Rwanda, UNICEF and its partners' massive response to children and teachers helped to mobilize communities emerging from genocide. This worked because it helped communities to reframe their damaged self-images around healthy protective activities that focused not on often failed, abstract ideologies, but on a concrete, visible future. The children in their midst. What worked were inclusive strategies for local community healing and rebuilding. What did not work was trauma healing using individual clinical approaches.

Integrated services and support networks better reshaped emergency aftermath. For most internationals, emergencies were events to be contained, controlled, and escaped. For many experiencing emergencies at home, however, escape was not an option. The event never ended. Its consequences persisted for the rest of their lives and into the next generation. Children were not the same after armed conflict in Sierra Leone. A return to traditional schooling was not an option.

Lessons learned in Rwanda and elsewhere later helped to systematize an integrated response in Sierra Leone. The Sierra Leone Ministry of Education (MOYES), UNESCO Institute for Education (UIE), and Plan International created new interventions.[13] For the first time, a Rapid (response) Education (RapidEd) curriculum included pre- and post-program assessments to evaluate the impact of cognitive and expressive activities on profoundly traumatized children and child soldiers who were exposed to war-related violence in displaced camps in and around Freetown (UNESCO Institute for Education/ Plan International 2000).[14]

Complex programs in Sierra Leone paid particular attention not only to the cognitive and psychosocial sides of education, but also to its developmental aspects. Strong peer interaction contributed to a return to normalcy—so did the acceptance of ex-combatants into a community of strong, protective adults.

A primary focus for education for child soldiers was to unlearn the violence that had become their identity. Ex-combatants needed to relearn how to protect themselves and others from their own violent impulses. This reclaiming of self became part of the core of a community-based security, healing, and deterrence strategy. As reported: "This study demonstrates that providing an opportunity for war affected children to express their bad memories and painful feelings to trained adults in a safe environment like the RapidEd schools, can reduce the prevalence of traumatic symptoms while restoring a sense of hopefulness about the future. Finally, it is important to keep in mind that the inclusion of a psychosocial trauma healing intervention within the RapidEd literacy and numeracy education curriculum is an innovative and pioneering effort" (Gupta 2000).[15] Less sophisticated back-to-school campaigns and other rapid educational responses did not confront the multigenerational transmission of traumatic reenactment. In the past, many demobilized child soldiers received minimal literacy and skills training without trauma healing and, where possible, community reintegration.

In genocidal wars that was no longer an adequate response. Ex-combatants sometimes were not only traumatized but also a very real danger to themselves and to their loved ones. Breaking the cycle of abuse of children (especially child soldiers) meant that education needed not only to help improve cognitive skills but also to prevent recycling anger and human destructiveness within and across generations (Gupta 2000, 57–59).

It is stunning that this simple understanding has been so lost in the stampede to get child soldiers back to school, into the marketplace, or signed up for fund-raising activities. Breaking the cycles of abuse within and across generations requires adolescents, adults, neighbors, and parents to accept long-term responsibility for each other. Civil society associations, so popular in some countries, have helped ex-combatants through social crises for many generations. Examples include veterans groups, religious communities, and political advocacy and self-help groups. Relatively little is known about their benefits to adolescent veterans.

Colombia

The current heroics of humanitarian intervention treat emergencies as events to be managed by international actors. Contemporary donor funding supports this view. The contemporary culture of philanthropy in humanitarian circles is heavily biased toward the dominance of international agencies and NGOs. It does not and cannot address the central objective of civil societies: learning how to inherit, improve, and pass on knowledge, expertise, and humanity to the next generation. In strong contrast, the Colombian experience of child protection environments was designed, managed, and implemented by local actors. UNICEF's local defensive and preventive strategies were cheaper and substantially more effective and sustainable than international programs elsewhere.

A forty-year insurgent campaign to overthrow the Colombian government escalated during the 1990s. An anti-insurgent army of paramilitaries grew to be several thousand strong in recent years, challenging the insurgents for control of territory and illicit industries such as the drug trade and the government's ability to control oil pipelines in rural areas.

The two main guerrilla groups still active, the Ejército de Liberación Nacional (ELN) and the Fuerzas Armadas Revolucionarias de Colombia (FARC), began operating in the mid-1960s. More than 40,000 people, most of them civilians, have been killed in Colombia as a result of the armed conflict since 1990 alone. More than 1.5 million displaced persons are registered with the Colombian government, but NGOs estimate that the real figure is more than double this. Official sources claim that 74 percent of the internally displaced are women and children. The vast majority of those displaced are dispersed rather than living in organized camps, and many seek anonymity in the country's big cities.[16] It has been estimated that only one in eight internally displaced pupils have returned to school after having been displaced. Displaced girls are more vulnerable to sexual exploitation and pregnancy than other teenagers. Displacement has often been an end in itself rather than just a by-product of Colombia's conflict.[17]

In some areas, there were chronic reports of internally displaced young men being forcibly recruited into irregular armed groups. In the cities, large sections of the population were increasingly being drawn into gang warfare, which replicated war allegiances and divisions at the national level, bringing with it intra-urban displacements. Families were displaced two, even three times (UNHCR 2006).

An IDP survey at the time reported that 94 percent of households were displaced as a result of direct threats to their lives, while 40 percent resorted to this solution out of a more general fear. Prior to displacement, the vast majority (75 percent) worked in agrarian activities. After, more than one half (59 percent) worked primarily in the service sector, mostly in stores or as street vendors (UNCT 2003; OCHA 2003).[18] Some of these displaced persons were teachers.

In Colombia, teachers in the government school system were often directly targeted by armed groups aiming at destroying communities. Clearly, teachers—and schools—were not perceived as neutral actors. Many of them held public positions in their communities, often as the sole government representative. At the time, the IDP 2003 Colombia Report stated that "2,900 teachers were forcibly displaced and 82 teachers and school employees were killed during 2002, twice as much than during 2001" (UNCT 2003; OCHA 2003). Furthermore, "around 290,000 children—equivalent to 3.6 percent of the public education system's primary school students—had to leave school temporarily or permanently due to the forced displacement of [those] 2,900 teachers. Threats forced many teachers to request transfers to other schools. . . . As a result, according to information available to the Commission, there is a lack of teaching personnel in some especially violent areas due to the displacement of teachers who were working in those areas" (IACHR 2000, 79).

Return to Happiness

UNICEF's emergency strategy was integrated into ongoing and locally designed children-friendly programs. The reports from the field stressed the unequivocal commitment of members of local communities to help children. In addition, the successful experiences of Colombia's ongoing high-quality rural education program, the Escuela Nueva, provided a solid strategic base for rural emergency responses.[19] Escuela Nueva provided the local know-how for rapid and adequate responses for IDP children and their communities.[20]

Escuela Nueva differed from traditional schools in the following ways: it was multigrade; it featured flexible and not automatic promotion; special instructional materials were used, such as self-instructional textbooks; the curriculum was rural oriented; specially trained teachers were required; mastery learning or peer instruction was supported; study corners and small libraries were established; and teachers, students, and the community all became active participants in the school. Students learned democratic behavior by participating in student government. Most important, community responsibility was learned because older students tutored younger students (Schugurensky forthcoming). UNICEF Colombia decided to reinforce the Escuela Nueva model with a strategy of education for peace, social mobilization, and the psychosocial recovery of war-affected children and adolescents.

The Return to Happiness Program was designed to provide urgent mass psychosocial support to children affected by violence. Its core concept was rebuilding lost generational trust in communities where it had been ravaged. The program encouraged families and community members to actively participate in the recovery process. Parents, teachers, church volunteers, health workers, and community leaders assisted the program as supervisors or trainers, also serving as leaders of self-help groups within the community.

Adolescent volunteers from the community, supervised by teachers, became the agents of psychosocial recovery. They were the key to the program. Young volunteers were trained in play therapy and taught how to encourage the trust and hope of younger children through games, art, puppetry, song, and storytelling. A "knapsack of dreams" contained materials handmade by members of the community, including rag dolls, puppets, wooden toys, books, and songs.

The Return to Happiness program brought help to children in their own communities. It broke with the Western clinical model of psychosocial therapy by offering a community-based participatory approach. The child-to-child relationship, which was the foundation of the Return to Happiness program, helped rebuild the children's trust through play. Through their work as play therapists, the adolescent volunteers came to serve as role models in their communities. They created a link between families, schools, and communities, forming a network of reconstructive peace-building. The simplicity of the program was its cornerstone: children's right to play.[21]

From the start, adolescents proved ideal role models for younger children. They consoled and supported each other. "Six of every ten refugees are children. Many of these refugee-children don't go to school. . . . There are at least 6,000 child soldiers in the country, divided between the various armies and troops. Every sixth child soldier has killed someone, and six of ten have seen others kill" (World's Children's Prize for the Rights of the Child 2008). One volunteer, age seventeen, described his efforts to create a sense of normalcy in the lives of younger children, some of whom had seen terrible things. He explained that if the children had experienced something very bad, like watching their father be tortured and killed, then it is very difficult for them to explain what happened. The story comes out in pieces and may take weeks to tell.

The play sessions not only created open communication and trust in the relationship between adolescents and younger children, but also built self-esteem among the adolescent volunteers. Consoling younger children and helping them overcome their distress taught coping skills to the young volunteers and helped them strongly identify with a civil society. Many of these adolescents became internationally famous for their organization of the Children's Movement for Peace, the largest mobilization of children of its kind.[22]

The Return to Happiness program demonstrated its success through improved relationships between teachers and children, and among the children themselves. The strategy again was to strengthen local communities by strengthening support for children and youth through physical protection and opportunities to build a strong civil identity. This approach was preferred to programs that directly targeted child soldiers exclusively. Targeted programs for child soldiers were developed as needed when they required extra help reintegrating into their communities or moving away from them.

Child-Friendly Spaces in Panama for Colombian Refugees

In the northwest of Colombia, refugees fled across the border into Panama, taking refuge in the border province of El Darien.[23] Although humanitarian agencies had access to the refugee communities, there was a high risk of attack and forced conscription. In January 2003, attacks were carried out by paramilitary groups, resulting in the death of several indigenous community leaders. The vulnerability of the refugee communities in El Darien left children exposed to fear and violence.

Child protective spaces were integrated into the displaced communities of El Darien. As designated areas in displacement camps and communities, these spaces were set aside as safe havens. They provided a location for the safe delivery of integrated services, such as infant feeding, nutritional support, hygiene, water, and sanitation services, early childhood care, education, recreation, and psychosocial support. Children's protective spaces were informally constructed or simply set up outdoors and marked with yellow tape.

Located close to the heart of the community, the child-friendly spaces in El Darien were seen as a kind of interior space, with local and international workers literally using their own human bodies as a shield. After only six months, more than 500 young people were trained as play therapists in the Return to Happiness program. Although the risk of violence in the refugee communities of El Darien continued, the program contributed to a sense of security and brought new life to the children. On one occasion, when the community was threatened by an armed group, a priest prepared a letter about the situation and the children signed the letter, stating their neutrality.[24]

How then can civil societies deter forced recruitment and re-recruitment of children in the face of the sociopathic cultures of impunity found in contemporary wars? UNICEF over and over again invested in the protection of communities' human agency through a strategy of child protection. At the core of this strategy is a strengthening of generational identity. It is important to note, because this tacitly assumes that it has been weakened and thus needs to be strengthened. This implies a catastrophic collapse of the civil societies necessary for generational transition. It further implies that the re-establishment of relationships of generational trust require the active agency of all possible adults working directly with child soldiers whose generational trust has been shattered. They need networks of relationships that can act as webs of support. This is even more difficult than it looks.

One of the most important heuristics that international humanitarian education workers tell each other is that, after wars, the local adults rush to return to the life they had before the war. This inevitably leads to a catastrophic failure in youth policy. In their rush to rebuild the world the way it was for them before the war, adults failed to recognize that their children are too altered to be able to return to it. Srebren Dizdar, the permanent secretary for education in Bosnia after the war, repeatedly warned his countrymen and the international donors who were listening carefully, to, above all else, avoid the backward rush to the future (McClure and Retamal 2007). So it is not that difficult, with all the best intentions, to rebuild community education services that are instantly obsolete, perhaps even harmful.

UNICEF's child protection strategy focuses on three human agency–based responses to new war tactics. The first response is community engagement and mobilized communities. In attacks on civilian populations, local adults participate in the construction of safe public spaces and work with local and external security forces to physically prevent recruiter access. The second response is generational identity. Against nihilist appeals to cultural identity through ethnicity, ideology, and brute force, adolescents are mobilized to actively participate in the construction of a civil identity by defending younger children against the trauma they have faced. This is a shift away from war fatigue and fatalism toward active planning for and construction of less violence-prone futures. The third response is civil economy networks. Webs of support are created by responsible and caring adults locally and internationally (including diaspora), with security hubs or islands of civility that support education for the future teachers and volunteers who support, teach, and mentor children, offering viable alternatives to predator economies.[25]

These new security-based, agency-centered narratives drive strategy toward local community policing. Many caveats need to be included. For example, when wide safety nets are thrown around populations, predators can not only be permitted into camps, they may begin to control them. Adults participate in the construction of public safe places for children through their own resources or by allying with others. This suggests that the problems of child soldier deterrence may be better solved through communities' active protection of their young. When this is not possible, peer networks become critical.

This chapter can only address a very small piece of a very complex problem. There are times when communities cannot come together to defend either themselves or their children. They may lack the local security partners they need to create safe places for children to play. The mapping solidly supports Reich and Achvarina's (2006a) findings that camp placement can be a problem. The need to isolate children and youth from predatory recruiters either in camps or in dispersed communities is a chronic problem in many countries. Thus child and youth protection activities such as UNICEF's integrated and inclusive services are critical components to recruitment deterrence.

Next Steps

There is, of course, much work to be done. UNICEF's approach has been widely used and accepted, but UNICEF will be the first to acknowledge that there are times when communities are too weak to bear the burdens of responsible parents and neighbors. Child abuse rates climb dramatically in extreme crises when generation survival may be a life and death choice.

It is quite clear that UNICEF and its partners' responses to new wars have, at least in education, focused squarely on the protection of children's human agency through the mobilization of community adults' agency. This child protection narrative offers a concrete and compelling story to drive action toward community engagement in generational protection activities in alliance with local security forces. This clear appeal to generational identity also helps inoculate civil societies against the ethnic gangster identities of violent exclusion and impunity that can drive the young into new wars. As Martin Shaw has said so artfully: "The new warfare . . . is above all a political rather than a military challenge. It is about the breakdown of legitimacy, and we need a new . . . politics to reconstruct this in the zones of war . . . here is a set of principles and a positive political vision, tied to the rule of law. Cosmopolitans are to be found within the local communities at the heart of the violence—particularly in 'islands of civility' where identity politics has not taken full hold. . . . Genuine cosmopolitanism does not mean negotiating truces between warring ethno-nationalists but building up pluralist democratic politics" (Shaw 2000, 172–173).

Today most international responses to recruitment focus on direct program services. The problem of child soldiers is not an engineering problem to be fixed by technically competent people from Western cultures. It cannot be fixed by building more schools or offering more workshops, short-term training programs, educational quality standards, or individual therapy. Nor is it a problem of access. Neither government nor market schools nor quality teacher training are likely to loom as important as first strengthening local alliances of parents and neighbors. Quite simply, local communities are more likely to create local social capital than internationals who parachute in with cameras blazing. The ongoing need to strengthen social and cultural capital formation has been badly neglected in the education literature.

After child soldiers have witnessed the collapse of their lives within civil societies, many must begin again at the very beginning—to reestablish contact, first within and then across the generational divide. When even this is too painful, they can return to some small experience of happiness by protecting younger children. Ex-combatants suffer deeply because of two massive social failures. The first failure was by capacity—adults who wanted to protect children but could not. The second failure was by malevolence—adults on the inside or outside who benefited from the children's misery or from a larger silence. The first is a technical failure of human security. The second is a moral failing of human agency. Deterrence policies must face both squarely.

The developmental needs of adolescent combatants during generational transitions, however, remain sadly overlooked in the policy literature either for human security or for education. The child soldier problems in new wars are ones of personal safety, cultural identity, community acceptance, and access to a civil economy. Youth remain accustomed to abandonment. They need genuine protection from adults claiming the moral high ground of civil society.

Human security as the generational protection of human agency is a relatively new perspective based on fifteen years of field work by education professionals working in large-scale, complex emergencies internationally. This

generational protection narrative has been chosen repeatedly over older strategic narratives built on mid-century political ideologies based on civil rights and
economic ideologies of neoliberalism. Brutal new wars need compelling new
strategy with visible moral roots in human rights protection (Becker 2004a,
2004b, 2006). New wars are not about contests for public or private control of
state apparatus. They have instead shifted the front lines of civilization to the
next generation.

New wars are new games with new rules, or lack thereof. Scholars need to
pay much closer attention to how institutions allocate resources to support
recruitment deterrence both locally and externally. There is a growing policy dilemma. On one hand, the lessons from the field say over and over again
that services integrated at the community level work better than most other
options. On the other hand, no multilateral or bilateral agency in addition to
UNICEF is organized to deliver integrated services for children and youth in
partnership with local policing and broader regional security.

The current stream of donor resources is channeled through sector-based
institutions that have more structural incentives to compete than to cooperate. The challenges created by this bifurcation grow daily and need much more
attention. Only by more closely mapping the political economy and cultural
identity networks that threaten, as well as feed, house, and protect, children
can we hope to make wiser investments in our future neighbors.

CHAPTER 14

ENDING THE SCOURGE OF CHILD SOLDIERING

An Indirect Approach

Andrew Mack

> Despite near-universal condemnation of child soldiering, and a solid legal and
> policy framework, lack of political will is an obstacle to achieving concrete
> improvements and effective child protection on the ground.
> —*Coalition to Stop the Use of Child Soldiers, Child Soldiers Global Report 2004*

PETER SINGER, THE MOST-CITED CONTEMPORARY ANALYST writing on
child soldiers, has claimed that the practice of child soldiering has dramatically
increased because the global norm against the use of children in war—what he
calls "the single greatest taboo of all"—has dramatically eroded. In "the chaos
and callousness of modern-day warfare," he argues, this norm "has seemingly
broken down" (Singer 2006, 4).

Although accessing good data in this field is a major challenge, what evidence we do have suggests that the claim that child soldiering has increased
because a taboo against the use of children in war has broken down is quite
untrue. In fact, the norm proscribing the use of child soldiers is almost certainly stronger today than it has ever been. The evidence for this is compelling—from the creation of new legal instruments, commitments from regional
organizations,[1] information campaigns by UN agencies like UNICEF, and
well-organized, well-coordinated, and politically astute advocacy campaigns
by transnational NGOs.

Further evidence of normative change comes from the recent actions of
the UN Security Council, which has been increasingly engaged in addressing
the child soldier issue. As the Coalition Against the Use of Child Soldiers re-

ported in January 2008, Security Council action has included the following: the adoption of six resolutions on children and armed conflict (1261, 1314, 1379, 1460, 1539, and 1612); requests to the secretary-general for regular lists of parties to armed conflict that recruit and use children as soldiers in violation of international law; the initiation of dialogue with parties to armed conflict regarding violations; the establishment of a monitoring and reporting system to document violations against children; and the creation of a working group on children and armed conflict. The problem is that the norm, now well-entrenched in the international community, has had little impact where it is needed most—in changing the behavior of those who exploit children by employing them in the armed forces of rebel groups or government forces.

The international community condemns child soldiering, legislates against it, engages with governments to stop it. But there is little evidence that any of this activity has had more than a marginal impact. So rather than an erosion of the taboo on using child soldiers causing an increase in recruitment, the widespread use of child soldiers has revealed that, where it mattered, the taboo never existed in the first place. So why have norms and legal instruments created at the international level had little or no impact on the employment of children in the armed forces of governments and nonstate armed groups? As is the case with human rights legal instruments, there is a big difference between signing and ratifying agreements and enforcing them effectively. The international community is much better at the former than the latter.

Take case of the Optional Protocol to the Convention on the Rights of the Child on the Involvement of Children in Armed Conflict, which entered into force in February 2002. Enforcement of the protocol is complicated by the fact that the UN's Committee on the Rights of the Child, the body charged with monitoring abuses that fall under the purview of the Protocol, has no power to apprehend or punish violators and only reviews cases once every five years. The UN Security Council does have the mandate to act and, as noted earlier, has been increasingly active on the issue of child soldiers. But as the Coalition to Stop the Use of Child Soldiers noted in its January 2008 report: "Despite its stated intention to apply targeted measures against perpetrators that refuse to end their use of child soldiers, the Security Council has been timid about taking such action. As a result, perpetrators may conclude that they will face no significant penalties for recruiting or using child soldiers or committing other grave violations." "Timid" is a generous interpretation of the council's inaction in this area. The UN has various levers that could in principle be used to pressure governments to stop using child soldiers. None is unproblematic, however, and none has been used to any measurable effect.

The council has imposed travel bans on a small number of individuals. But travel bans are perhaps the weakest form of international sanctions, and there is little evidence that the bans that have been implemented have had any effect. Aid conditionality is potentially a much more powerful lever for change simply because its effects are so much greater than other forms of sanction, though it is obviously not a strategy that can be used against rebels who are not aid recipients.

Unsurprisingly, the council has focused overwhelmingly on nonstate actors. The UN is an institution whose members are states, and, particularly in the developing world, there is great sensitivity to anything that smacks of interference in the internal affairs of member states. Donor states and the international financial institutions do not confront the political constraints that hamper efforts to impose sanctions at the UN. But a major difficulty with aid conditionality, apart from the intense resentment it generates among recipient countries, is that it is rarely effective in changing state behavior. The World Bank and the International Monetary Fund have repeatedly sought to condition aid in order to pressure governments to change their social, fiscal, and even defense policies. But while conditionality strategies, like sanctions regimes, occasionally succeed, they have a very poor track record overall.[2]

The real problem with legal instruments, norms, and advocacy campaigns that seek to stop child soldiering is that they make little impact on the incentive structures that make children the soldiers of choice for so many governments and rebel groups. Take the case of rebels first. If employing child soldiers increases the probability of victory—or even if it only reduces the prospects for defeat—then rebel groups will do so, notwithstanding the fact that child soldiering is a gross breach of international law. They can do so because the norms and international legal instruments created in the North have little traction in the global South.

In the amoral calculus of military strategy, employing child soldiers makes sense for all the reasons noted in the literature. They are cheap, available, simple to recruit or abduct, malleable, and—in poor country wars—make capable soldiers—in combat or noncombat roles. The costs of employing child soldiers are minimal. The only sanctions that have ever been applied are minimal in their impact and thus easily ignored. Prosecution of former rebel leaders for employing child soldiers is rare—impunity remains the rule. If the rebels win, there is little chance they will be indicted for using child soldiers, and none that they will be extradited.

If rebels who use child soldiers are defeated, there is a greater chance that they will face prosecution. Indeed, indictments have already been brought against individual rebel leaders by the International Criminal Court (ICC) and the Special Court in Sierra Leone for, among other things, employing child soldiers. (No charges have been brought against members of any serving governments, though former Liberian leader Charles Taylor has been indicted by the Special Court in Sierra Leone and is being tried in the Hague.) In principle, the prospect of arrest and long prison sentences should serve as a deterrent to the recruitment of child soldiers in the future. But with respect to rebel leaders who are already employing child soldiers, the threat of criminal indictment provides a perverse incentive for rebels to continue to rely on child soldiers. Giving them up would reduce the rebels' military capacity and increase the probability that they would lose, but the prospect of prosecution would remain unchanged.

Such situations can create classic peace-versus-justice dilemmas of the type that have made securing an end to the Lord's Resistance Army's (LRA) terror campaign in Uganda so difficult to achieve. If rebels know that in the event of a peace agreement they will be prosecuted for employing child soldiers and will likely have to endure long prison sentences, they will have few incentives to stop fighting.

Government leaders have the same strategic interest in using child soldiers as rebel groups—but even fewer reasons to be concerned about the possibility of arrest and imprisonment for their gross breaches of international law. Not one of the governments known to be using child soldiers has been sanctioned by the Security Council. The somewhat depressing reality is that both governments and armed groups that employ child soldiers have found that—thus far at least—they can get away with doing so without any real penalty. And without penalties there can be no deterrence.

None of this means that the advocacy efforts pursued by NGOs and a small number of northern states to build a normative regime against the practice of child soldiering are futile. On the contrary, they play a critically important role in creating the changes that are necessary if the culture of impunity that currently shelters those who employ child soldiers is to be broken down. The key claim made here is that the prospects of the top-down normative approach to stopping child soldiering from making much difference in the short term are not great—in large part because they do not address the strategic incentives that make the employment of child soldiers in poor country wars so pervasive.

But there is another approach, which already has an excellent track record, to attacking the problem. It, however, has been almost completely ignored by both governments and NGOs advocating for change on this issue. Rather than trying to stop children from being used in wars, it makes far more sense to try to stop the wars themselves. Over the past decade and a half, more than three-quarters of the conflicts that employed large numbers of child soldiers have come to an end. Not all child fighters have been demobilized, but most have.

None of the children who ceased to be soldiers did so because of the actions of the Security Council, UNICEF, the ICC, the ad hoc tribunals, or the efforts of the Coalition Against Child Soldiers. Trying to address the child soldiers issue directly is, as argued above, fraught with huge difficulty, and an indirect approach may make more sense. The international community has become increasingly adept at helping to end wars (peacemaking in UN-speak) and preventing them from restarting again (postconflict peace building). This suggests that the indirect approach to stopping child soldiering—by stopping the wars that create the demand in the first place—should be taken more seriously.

Since the end of the cold war, there have been extraordinary changes in the way wars start and end—changes that have profound implications for human security. In the 1990s, three times more conflicts ended in negotiated settlements than in any previous decade. This pattern is even more pronounced in the new millennium. The sharp increase in the number of negotiated settlements reflects the sharp increase in peacemaking—the practice of seeking to end wars via negotiation rather than on the battlefield. In the past, a major downside of negotiated settlements had been that they were highly unstable— that is, likely to relapse into war again. This long-established pattern appears to have changed in the new millennium. Negotiated settlements seem to be far more stable than was the case previously. There were seventeen negotiated settlements between 2000 and 2005, and only two relapsed back into war. Over the equivalent period in the 1990s, almost 90 percent of negotiated settlements failed. This change has come about primarily because negotiated settlements are now far more likely be supported by the international community.

The past decade and a half has seen a veritable explosion of international activism directed toward stopping wars and preventing them from restarting. It is this activism, rather than conflict prevention, that has driven the 40 percent decline in the number of armed conflicts since the end of the cold war. The decline in the most deadly armed conflicts (those that incur one thousand or more battle deaths a year) has been even greater—around 70 percent. It is these latter conflicts that employed the lion's share of children under arms.

Whether or not the positive changes of the past decade can be sustained is a complex and difficult question—and one far beyond the scope of this short essay. There are certainly no grounds for complacency, but experience of a decade and a half of international activism has demonstrated that third-party mediation really can help end wars—and help prevent them from starting again. If the current level of commitment to peacemaking and peacebuilding can be sustained or—preferably—increased, then more wars can be brought to an end. Ending wars is the soundest way of ensuring that children can surrender their arms and embrace the opportunity to live normal lives.

CONCLUSION

Children and Human Security

Scott Gates and Simon Reich

CHILDREN HAVE ALWAYS BEEN PART OF WAR, YET THEY constitute an understudied dimension of human security. In this regard, our volume contributes to the shift in focus away from traditional notions of national defense toward what former UN Secretary-General Kofi Annan described as "the protection of communities and individuals from internal violence" (Human Security Center 2005). Focusing on children in armed conflict clearly enlightens us about an important aspect of human security. Given the inherent vulnerability of children, such attention is warranted.

The definition of human security is vigorously debated; there is no consensus. The narrow definition, to which this volume conforms, is reflected in the Kofi Annan quote above; the focus is on the consequences of war for individuals and communities (sometimes referred to as "freedom from fear"). Advocates of a broader interpretation of human security often include hunger, natural disasters, crime, and disease. Wars, of course, can cause these problems or make them worse. Indeed, as Lacina and Gleditsch (2005) demonstrate, the indirect costs of war far exceed the direct costs. Direct battle-related casualties contributed to less than 10 percent of the war deaths in six wars in sub-Saharan Africa. In the Democratic Republic of the Congo civil war, 1998–2001, for example, 2.5

million people died, but only 145,000 of them were battle deaths. Nonetheless, there is an analytical difference between examining the indirect effects of war and assessing all factors that threaten the well-being of individuals. We side with the former group, and the chapters in this volume analyze how war affects children during the fighting and in its aftermath. Most interstate conflict does not involve uniformed armies facing off in a battle space, disassociated from broader noncombatant civilian populations. As Kalyvas (2006), Weinstein (2007), and Azam (2002) have demonstrated (despite critically different conclusions about the logic of violence and conflict), belligerents in a civil conflict intentionally target noncombatants for strategic purposes. Violence serves as the means of achieving these ends. Children, like noncombatants in general, are recruited (forcibly and voluntarily), displaced, and killed; they play all too large a role in civil conflict. As evident in most of the chapters of this volume, many rebel and militia groups target children in particular. Examples examined here include the LRA in northern Uganda, the RUF in Sierra Leone, the Maoists in Nepal, the Tamil Tigers in Sri Lanka, FARC in Colombia, UNITA in Angola, and nearly all the groups fighting in Burma/Myanmar, Liberia, and the Democratic Republic of the Congo. The policy shift from national security to human security and its incumbent shift from the national interest to individual welfare would seem to reflect an academic debate in which the ascendance of neo-Realism is eclipsed by the rise of a form of neoliberalism. Yet, the notion of human security did not originate in academia. As Friman and Reich (2008, 136–154) observe, "Interestingly, the concept of human security is a rarity; it originates from the policy community, perhaps explaining its relative lack of theoretical and analytic precision. Attempts by academics to wrestle with the concept over the course of the last decade have produced uneven results and contrasting conclusions about the substance of and appropriate tools employed in studying issues from a human security perspective."[1] *Security Dialogue*, for example, ran a special forum on human security with a wide variety of views on the concept, and no clear consensus was reached.

Yet, despite the lack of intellectual coherence and theoretical consistency, the shift in focus to individuals away from nations is also reflected in a contemporaneous shift from international law to criminal laws. States are held accountable by international law. In contrast, under international criminal law, individuals are deemed culpable for their deeds and wrongdoings. Thus, as with the shift from the national interest evident in traditional notions of security to a focus on the individual as seen through the lens of human security, we see a parallel shift in the criminalization of the conventions of war shifting from the state to the individual.

Focusing on human security also requires broadening our perspective and examining factors typically not associated with other formulations of the concept of security, especially national security. One such factor is intergenerational violence and the breakdown of the rule of law in the absence of effective governance. Paul Richards, writing on Sierra Leone and Liberia, describes how chiefs control property; there is no private ownership. As a result of a youth bulge, many young adults found their ambitions stifled. Land ownership was too concentrated; there was no land for these youth, so they went to diamond mining areas and urban centers in search of money, often becoming susceptible to military recruitment.[2] In this way we can see how issues of guaranteeing property rights can relate to the incidence rate of child soldiering.

New Trends

The most prevalent form of conflict is civil war, and most civil wars are classified as small wars, or as Clausewitz called them, *kleinkrieg*. The signature tactic of a small war is guerrilla warfare.[3] Such unconventional warfare involves small groups of combatants that employ mobile and surprise tactics, such as ambushes, raids, and sabotage in an effort to cripple the state, particularly the military capacity of the state. Children can serve a valuable role in this kind of fighting—indeed, much better than they can in conventional warfare. In fact, we do not see much evidence of the use of child soldiers in interstate conflict, which is reflected in the general lack of child soldiers in national armies. Child soldiers for the most part are limited to nonstate militias and rebels groups engaged in intrastate conflict. The global spread of cheap sophisticated handheld weapons (primarily the AK-47) can be explained to a large extent by the demand for such a weapon perfectly suited to guerrilla warfare.

Another important trend is that the number of civil conflicts in the world peaked in the early 1990s and has since been declining.[4] The main reason is that the number of wars ending began to exceed the number starting for the first time since the early 1970s. The cold war fueled a large share of these conflicts as the U.S. and Soviet Union fought proxy wars. With the end of the cold war came the end of large-scale financing of surrogate wars. Some groups, such as UNITA, although no longer financed by the CIA and South Africa, reengaged in conflict financed by natural resources looted from local populations (in UNITA's case, diamonds). Groups no longer able to finance their conflicts pursued peace negotiations, were defeated militarily, or started recruiting or abducting relatively cheap child soldiers. Even groups able to finance their armed struggle with money from drugs, diamonds, racketeering, and/or smuggling began to rely more and more on children to fight. Examples include UNITA in Angola, the LTTE in Sri Lanka, and the FARC in Colombia. This produced some of the worst abusers of children among all rebel groups. Indeed, wars of long duration and countries exhibiting patterns of intermittent war are much more likely to involve the use of child soldiers.

The trend in the number of civil wars since 2000 has been one of slight shifts in the aggregate numbers from year to year, which makes it seem as if the number of wars is stable, but the list of wars changes dramatically from year to year. For example, while ten conflicts active in 2004 were no longer ongoing in 2005, nine conflicts that had not been active in 2004 restarted. Many of these wars do not formally end through victory or negotiated settlement; they are low-intensity conflicts that slip below the twenty-five battle casualty threshold only to rise above a few years later. It is in these types of environments that we are most likely to encounter the use of child soldiers.

Low per capita GDP is one of the most significant factors associated with civil war and armed civil conflict (Hegre and Sambanis 2006). Indeed, most guerrilla wars are fought in low-income countries. In recent years, three prominent articles explaining the onset of civil war have used this indicator to produce vastly different theoretical explanations. Collier and Hoeffler's (2004) theory features the lack of economic opportunity in low-income countries, which makes it easier for a political entrepreneur to raise an army against the state. Hegre, Ellingsen, Gleditsch, and Gates (2001), in an article in the *American Political Science Review,* focus on political and economic modernization, using this indicator to denote underdevelopment. Fearon and Laitin (2003), in another article appearing in the same venue, use per capita GDP as an indicator of state capacity, whereby weak states are hypothesized to be more likely to experience civil war. While no consensus has emerged to explain the finding, we do know empirically that low GDP countries are more likely to experience civil war. This result holds across data sets and across statistical estimation techniques.

Empirical evidence further suggests that those countries that have experienced civil war are much more likely to experience it again and that poor countries that have experienced civil war are the most likely to repeatedly experience intrastate armed conflict. Economic evidence, furthermore, indicates that those countries that experience civil war experience very low (if not negative) economic growth rates. The poorer that country, the more devastating the economic costs of war. Poor countries that become embroiled in war remain poor and are hence more likely to become embroiled in war again. Collier and his coauthors, in a World Bank publication, refer to this as the conflict trap (Collier et al. 2003).

Conflict and poverty work together in a vicious cycle. Richer countries such as Northern Ireland can escape the cycle, but most poor countries cannot, whether due to a lack of economic opportunities, a lack of development, or a lack of state capacity. This would seem to indicate that the pool of countries in war will get poorer and poorer over time.

Concomitant with this pattern of conflict, the number of displaced persons gets larger and more vulnerable as the burden shifts to an international community unable to cope with the downward spiral of poverty and war, war and poverty. We see a proliferation of regional refugees. Accordingly, as seen in the chapters by Achvarina and Reich and by Lischer, refugee camps are prime grounds for recruitment and abduction of child soldiers.

Another consequence of this spread of refugees is that conflicts become harder to contain as they become regionalized. The wars in Iraq and the DRC (Africa's world war) serve as examples.[5] Moreover, as Hegre and Sambanis (2006) have concluded, unstable undemocratic neighborhoods increase the risk of civil war. Kristian Gleditsch (2007) clearly demonstrates the importance of transnational dimensions of civil war; we simply can no longer view them as isolated events. This makes the job of the international peacebuilding community all the more difficult.

This discussion of conflict trends thus leads us to some implications for trends in the incidence of child soldiers. Given that it is nonstate armed groups that recruit children, we should mostly expect to see child soldiers in wartime. They are not a peacetime phenomenon. So we should expect to see the number of children involved in conflict to shift with trends in global conflict. Indeed, with the end of conflict in Liberia, Sierra Leone, and Angola (countries where there was an extensive use of child soldiers), the number of child soldiers should have fallen. This prediction, however, stands in stark contrast to many sources in the NGO and child soldier advocacy community. Diverse sources claim that there are some 300,000 child soldiers in the world today, and that this figure has been relatively constant for many years. This figure is now clearly outdated given the cessation of hostilities in so many cases, with a more realistic one being in the 200,000–250,000 range. Nonetheless, the proportion of wars being fought with child soldiers is likely to rise in the foreseeable future as countries slip back into war. Falling per capita GDP, recurring conflict, and the spillover effects of transnational civil conflict are all associated with a higher prevalence in the use of child soldiers. So, despite the decline in the total number of ongoing civil conflicts in the world, the proportion of wars involving children fighting in armed groups is likely to increase. We are unsure whether the absolute numbers of child soldiers will increase or remain constant. Given the relatively low number of civil conflicts being fought today, it is unlikely to increase dramatically unless the proportion of children employed in conflict increases. Countries experiencing incidences of repeated war or conflicts of a long duration tend to employ more child soldiers than countries experiencing short intense wars. If the proportion of wars reflects this pattern, then we should expect to see the total number of children in war rise.

Prescriptions

So where does that leave us? Current strategies rely on three components: deterrence, naming and shaming, and criminalization of the recruitment of child soldiers. These are generally employed by an assortment of NGOs and the United Nations. Proponents claim that all three have made great headway in convincing states, rebels, and militias not to use children in their armed forces. But the evidence suggests that they have limited beneficial effects. As discussed earlier, rebels have proven to be largely impervious to threats or the notion of shaming, while the activities of criminal courts are so remote from most conflicts that deterrence is ineffective in the absence of the real threat of the overwhelming use of force.

Another commonly stressed prescription focuses on ending the poverty that fosters child soldiering. But the evidence of this volume suggests that the linkage between poverty and child soldiering is indirect and the time span for generating such a change impractical. The international aid community has been addressing the problems of development and poverty for over fifty years with debatable success. International peace building efforts may have played a role in reducing the number of conflicts in the post–cold war era, but these successes are limited.[6] Indeed, if the alleviation of poverty is key to decreasing the use of child soldiers, then the prospects are dim because data suggest that the poor are getting poorer. Likewise, global trends in terms of conflict are equally depressing, indicating that the proportion of wars being fought with children is likely to increase and the total number of child soldiers could again rise.

So what should the international community do? Prescriptions are hard to formulate—and harder still to implement—for both political and logistical reasons. One relatively doable policy prescription would be to implement measures to enhance the security of IDP and refugee camps. In contrast to poverty eradication policies, such securitization of refugee camps is something that the international community could do with unambiguous benefit to children.

Education is another policy arena with great potential. In the context of child soldiers, education policy is usually limited to how it relates to disarmament, demobilization, rehabilitation, and reintegration. But education may have a preventative component: it can also work to reduce the incidence of child soldiering before conflict even breaks out. Investment in education in the broadest sense, including the physical protection of schools, can foster what McClure and Retamal refer to as child-friendly spaces. Given the developmental aspects of childhood, education must remain a key policy avenue toward remedying this problem.

The greater globalization and utility of guns, as Singer points out, presents a singular problem. The portability, plentitude, and durability of weapons add a new dimension because children can now use them. Questions remain as to whether this is really the heart of the problem (given that so many child soldiers do not, in fact, engage in combat or, if they do so, do not actually use guns). But one means to address this problem is the new focus on ammunition control. Bullets are always in demand, but their source of production (often unlike guns) can be more easily traced. A greater regulation of their flow, with sanctions attached to those supplying conflicts with high levels of child soldiers, offers the possibility of a denial of supply coupled with the use of an effective deterrent.

Another policy prescription might be to enhance the reach of international legal bodies such as the International Criminal Court. UN Resolution 1612 attempts to build on prior protocols by defining the use of child soldiers as a war crime and creating a working group that monitors and reports to the United Nations General Assembly.[7] The increase in apparatus, albeit incrementally, adds to the organizational capacity of the United Nations to identify those transgressing the law and effectively prosecute them. To be effective, however, this strategy would require great power engagement. Small states are fearful of joining multilateral interventions and so do not support initiatives that might entail such activity. Great powers have to facilitate such actions because they can either offer alternative incentives in exchange for the support of smaller states or they can simply overrule them.

Why should the United States take a lead in this area? First, geostrategic interests constitute a good share of U.S. foreign policy, and such policies have typically transcended partisanship across U.S. administrations. As discussed in the introduction to this volume, states-at-risk prove to be breeding grounds for terrorism, and child soldiers often grow up to be criminals who destabilize their societies or are involved in the drug trade, damaging Western societies as well as their own. Second, isolation may appeal to many Americans in the aftermath of U.S. action in Iraq. In general, however, the United States should seek to avoid the narrow realist version of withdrawal. A retreat on issues such as child soldiering does not help U.S. interests nor does it address the need to work collaboratively. There are current precedents for such policy activism. The United States has taken a leading role in combating human trafficking, using the State Department's annual Trafficking in Persons (TIPS) report as the basis to identify and coerce offending states who do not address their trafficking problems. Likewise, as some NGOs have suggested, the United States could use the issue of the supply of military aid, as well as trade and financial sanctions, to get states to reduce their use of children or to get them to negotiate more earnestly with rebel forces on the issue. In the absence of such activism designed to address the issue of child soldiering, the humanitarian and geostrategic problems (intergenerational violence, criminality, insurgency, and terrorism) that appear endemic to many states-at-risk outlined in the introduction, and reinforced by many of the chapters in this volume, are most likely to grow.

NOTES

Introduction

1. We do not differentiate between cooks, drivers, and those who carry weapons.

2. See *Convention on the Rights of the Child*, adopted and opened for signature, ratification, and accession by the United Nations General Assembly resolution 44/25 of 20 November 1989, entry into force 2 September 1990, in accordance with Article 49.

3. The most important international documents related to recruitment of children in armed conflicts are the following: Protocol I Additional to the Geneva Conventions of August 12, 1949, and Relating to the Protection of Victims of International Armed Conflicts (Additional Protocol I or API, Geneva, June 8, 1977), especially Article 77(2) (relating to international armed conflicts); Protocol II Additional to the Geneva Conventions of August 12, 1949, and Relating to the Protection of Victims of Non-International Armed Conflicts (Additional Protocol II or APII, Geneva, June 8, 1977), especially Article 4(3)c (relating to non-international armed conflicts); Convention on the Rights of the Child (CRC), Article 38; Rome Statute for an International Criminal Court (ICC), 17 July 1998, 2187 U.N.T.S. 90, entered into force 1 July 2002, Article 8 (on War Crimes), section 2b (xxvi); Article 4(1) and (2) of the Optional Protocol to the Convention on the Rights of the Child on the Involvement of Children in Armed Conflict (OP-CRC-CAC), 25 May 2000, entered into force 12 February 2002, in accordance with Article 10 (1); and the *African Charter on the Rights and Welfare of the Child (ACRWC)*, OAU Doc. CAB/LEG/24.9/49 (1990), entered into force 29 November 1999.

4. See Jo Becker's chapter in this volume. Her information comes from Human Rights Watch (2002).

5. Among the signatories were Burundi, Chad, Colombia, Ivory Coast, the Democratic Republic of Congo, Nepal, Somalia, Sudan, Sri Lanka, and Uganda, which are on a UN blacklist of countries that recruit child soldiers.

6. This is not to say that governments do not recruit children. They do, but just not to the same extent as nongovernmental groups. More important, few if any governments recruit young adolescents (twelve or thirteen years old), while rebel and militia groups do.

7. Thomas Lubanga Dyilo is the president of the Union des Patriotes Congolais

(UPC) and was the commander in chief of its former military wing, the Forces Patriotiques pour la Libération du Congo (FPLC).

8. Nora Boustany, *Washington Post*, 3 July 2008, http://www.washingtonpost.com/wpdyn/content/article/2008/07/02/AR2008070202893.html.

9. Uganda is described in the literature as "a war fought by children on children," where "minors make up almost 90% of the Lord's Resistance Army's soldiers." "Since the rebellion began in the 1980s, some 30,000 children have been abducted to work as child soldiers and porters, or to serve as 'wives' of rebels and bear their children" ("Uganda: Child Soldiers at Centre of Mounting Humanitarian Crisis," *Ten Stories the World Should Hear More About*, http://www.un.org/events/tenstories/story.asp?story ID=100). "UNICEF estimated that 8,400 children were abducted between June 2002 and May 2003. In July 2003 more than 20,000 child 'night commuters' were estimated to seek safety each night in Gulu, Pader and Kitgum towns, to reduce the risk of abduction" (CSUCS 2004a, 106).

10. For example, see BBC News (2004), IRIN (2006b).

11. For examples, see CNN.com (2005), IRIN (2003a).

12. See, for example, BBC News (2007).

13. See, as examples, Peter Singer (this volume); BBC News (2004); Associated Press (2005); IRIN (2006b).

14. See Hegre and Sambanis (2006, 508–535). Pooling all quantitative analyses of civil conflict, Hegre and Sambanis conducted a sensitivity analysis. They determined that nine factors (large population, low income, slow economic growth, recent political instability, illiberal democratic political institutions, small military, rough terrain, nondemocratic neighbors, and neighbors at war) were robustly associated with the onset of civil conflict. Ethnic differences were robustly linked to only low-intensity conflicts, not large-scale civil war.

15. A recent study by the Coalition to Stop the Use of Child Soldiers amply demonstrates that the 300,000 figure is wrong (CSUCS 2008).

16. In the interest of full disclosure, we should note that Simon Reich made reference to that figure (albeit somewhat ironically) in his coauthored chapter reprinted in this volume.

Chapter 1: Methodological Problems in the Study of Child Soldiers

1. Notable among single-country studies of ex-combatants in general in Colombia is Arjona (2006).

2. The group known as SWAY (Survey of War Affected Youth) is undertaking surveys in displacement camps in Northern Uganda, but their focus is on boys and girls abducted by the Lord's Resistance Army and living in these camps. See http://www.sway-uganda.org/.

3. This does not mean that any large-N statistical model is better than any small-N study; indeed, that is certainly untrue. But ultimately only statistical testing has the ability to disconfirm hypotheses by "holding constant" other predictors. In effect, statistical modeling is analogous to the "most-similar systems" design of Przeworski and Teune (1970). See also King et al. (1994).

4. This is the case for Achvarina and Reich (2006b).

5. Achvarina and Reich (2006b) note that the causal status of refugee camps is

particularly important, because policy interventions can reduce their vulnerability to incursions by irregular forces.

6. Roger Petersen's (1993) work on Lithuania in the 1930s is particularly useful here. Another example is David Laitin's analysis of rebellion in Catalonia and the Basque country (Laitin 1995).

7. Humphreys and Weinstein (2006a) do not focus on children, but their survey includes ex-combatants and noncombatants.

8. A good example of such comparisons is the work of SWAY in Uganda. See SWAY-Uganda (2006).

9. One significant group is perforce left out: the children who do not return from irregular armies. If the children killed in the bush are just a random sample of all combatant children, their exclusion does not matter. But if they are smaller, sicker, or malnourished, or if their attitudes affected their fighting behavior or their relationships with older combatants, then a problem of selection bias results.

10. Logit (or logistic) analysis is appropriate when the dependent variable is a dichotomous choice, such as voting Republican or Democratic, and can only take the values "0" or "1." If the dependent variable has multiple categories (stayed home, volunteered for rebels, volunteered for paramilitaries, abducted), then the multinomial logit is used. One of the categories becomes a reference or baseline, and the other categories are measured with respect to that baseline outcome.

11. If error is random, then the coefficient will be accurate, but the standard errors will be too large. We are thus likely to reject a hypothesis that should not be rejected. In most social science research, this is a lesser evil than accepting a false hypothesis. But in the case of child soldiers, where we hope to intervene in certain variables to change outcomes, the rejection of a true predictor is more serious.

12. Cf. Humphreys and Weinstein's (2006a, 14) description of the conflict in Sierra Leone. "The war . . . was long and complex. It lasted for over a decade and involved five primary factions, numerous sub-factions and various external actors. Over the course of the conflict, the government changed hands four times and two peace accords were negotiated and failed. Individual experiences of the fighting were also complex. Some ex-combatants were involved in the conflict for short periods of time, while others entered early in the conflict and stayed to the end. Some changed sub-faction or primary faction during the conflict and almost all moved locations."

13. This example comes from http://www.sociology.osu.edu/people/ptv/faq/missing/missing.htm.

14. An interesting case in point is the Naxalite rebellion in India. Though this conflict has been ongoing for many years, and though it is included in data fact books, the international press had essentially forgotten about it until *New York Times* articles appeared in the spring of 2006.

15. MI programs produce multiple data sets, each with different imputed values. After a multiple regression (or any other statistical technique) is implemented on each data set, the coefficients are averaged and the standard errors calculated by formulas known as Rubin's Rules.

16. Stata users can download a particularly good MI utility called ICE. Gary King has developed Amelia, and there are many other packages as well.

Chapter 2: An Ethical Perspective on Child Soldiers

I am grateful to Gregory Reichberg and Scott Gates for helpful comments on an earlier draft.

1. For representative statements of this currently orthodox view, see Anscombe (1981, 67); Finnis, Boyle, and Grisez (1987, 86–90); Fullinwider (1985, 90–97); Kenny (1985, 10); Nagel (1985, 69–70); and Walzer (1977, 136, 145).

Chapter 3: The Evolution of the United Nations' Protection Agenda for Children

1. CAAC is used as shorthand to denote children and armed conflict and children affected by armed conflict.

2. General Assembly resolution A/RES/51/77 of 1997 recommended that the secretary-general appoint for three years a special representative for children and armed conflict as a high-level independent advocate for war-affected children. The General Assembly has since extended the mandate of the special representative on three occasions, recently in resolution A/RES/60/231 of January 2006.

3. For a compendium of protection standards, refer to Human Security Network and the Office of the Special Representative of the Secretary-General for Children and Armed Conflict (2003).

4. See United Nations Peacemaker, United Nations Department of Political Affairs (http://peacemaker.unlb.org).

5. The 2004 Report of the Special Representative of the Secretary-General for Children and Armed Conflict to the General Assembly, UN document A/59/426, deals exclusively with the issue of mainstreaming CAAC in the UN system.

6. A case in point is the annual Arria Formula briefings of NGOs to the Security Council, preceding the annual open debates of the Security Council on CAAC.

7. See the Research Consortium on Children and Armed Conflict, established in 2002 under the auspices of the New York–based Social Science Research Council, which brought together nineteen academic and research institutions to discuss data collection on CAAC; research into changing trends in warfare that detrimentally impact children; and traditional norms, values, and practices that protect children in wartime and postconflict recovery. The special representative of the secretary-general for children and armed conflict has also outlined critical research priorities in her Strategic Plan for CAAC 2006–2008 (United Nations 2005b).

8. The secretary-general has made it clear that the focus of the CAAC agenda is not on situations of concern but rather on parties that commit grave violations against children. The mention of country situations is for the purpose of locating geographically these parties to conflict rather than to name specific countries as situations of concern.

9. According to the Security Council, an action plan should include the following elements: commitment by the listed party to immediately end violations; commitment by the listed party to release all children within its ranks; commitment by the listed party to cooperate with the DDR program; specific measures to prevent recruitment and re-recruitment of children; designation by listed parties of a high-level focal point to liaise with the UN team during the implementation of the action plan; agreed, time-bound benchmarks for measuring progress and compliance;

issuance of formal instructions by the political and military leadership of the listed party to their chain of command, reflecting commitments contained in the action plan; agreed arrangements for access by the UN team for monitoring and verification of the action plan.

10. Refer to letter dated 2 May 2006 from the Permanent Representative of France to the United Nations (chair of the SCWG-CAAC) addressed to the president of the Security Council, transmitting the Terms of Reference of the SCWG-CAAC, United Nations document S/2006/275.

Chapter 4: No Place to Hide

The authors wish to thank colleagues at the International Peace Research Institute in Oslo for their comments, especially Scott Gates and Håvard Strand. They would also like to acknowledge the suggestions of Jeffrey Checkel and Richard Higgott, in addition to Barry Ames, Davis Bobrow, Charlie Carpenter, William Keller, and Nita Rudra at the Ford Institute for Human Security at the University of Pittsburgh. Mark Hallerberg, now of Emory University, provided invaluable comments. They would like to express their gratitude to Sarah Lischer for providing access to her database of violence in refugee camps in Africa. Finally, two anonymous editors provided invaluable comments. Any remaining flaws are the authors' responsibility.

1. For a discussion on the use of child suicide bombers in the Israeli-Palestinian conflict, see Human Rights Watch (2002) and Defense for Children International (2004).

2. In this article we use the United Nations Children's Fund's definition of a child soldier: "any child—boy or girl—under 18 years of age, who is part of any kind of regular or irregular armed force or armed group in any capacity, including, but not limited to, cooks, porters, messengers, and anyone accompanying such groups other than family members." See also UNICEF (2004, 4).

3. The 1988 estimate was 200,000 child soldiers (UNICEF 1996; Human Rights Watch 2002d)

4. This claim is based on the figures discussed in detail elsewhere in this article for cases such as the Democratic Republic of Congo and Uganda. See, for example, Becker (2004).

5. Currently, the most important formal international conventions and protocols related to recruitment of children in armed conflicts are Geneva Convention, *Additional Protocol I (API)* (relating to international armed conflicts), Article 77(2); *Additional Protocol II (APII)* (relating to noninternational armed conflicts), Article 4(3)c; *Convention on the Rights of the Child (CRC),* Article 38; *Rome Statute for an International Criminal Court (ICC),* Article 8 (on War crimes), section 2(b) (xxvi); *Optional Protocol to the Convention on the Rights of the Child on the Involvement of Children in Armed Conflict* (OP-CRC-CAC), Article 4(1) and (2); and the *African Charter on the Rights and Welfare of the Child (ACRWC).* This list was provided in Coalition to Stop the Use of Child Soldiers (2002, 7–8).

6. Uganda is described in the literature as "a war fought by children on children," where "minors make up almost 90% of the Lord's Resistance Army's soldiers." "Since the rebellion began in the 1980s, some 30,000 children have been abducted to work as child soldiers and porters, or to serve as 'wives' of rebels and bear their children" (UN

2004). "UNICEF estimated that 8,400 children were abducted between June 2002 and May 2003. In July 2003 more than 20,000 child 'night commuters' were estimated to seek safety each night in Gulu, Pader and Kitgum towns, to reduce the risk of abduction" (CSUCS 2004a, 106).

7. These distributions were calculated on the basis of data found in UNHCR (1994), Callister (2003), and Amnesty International (2004b).

8. These figures were calculated on the basis of data drawn from CSUCS (2002, 2004a) and Human Rights Watch (2003a).

9. This number was derived by analyzing CSUCS (2002, 2004a) and Human Rights Watch (2003a).

10. Eleven countries in East Asia and the Pacific had child soldier participants (Barnitz 1999, 2–3).

11. Evidence to support this claim is extensive. Reportedly, child soldier numbers in Uganda and the Democratic Republic of Congo, for example, increased dramatically during 2002–2003 from previous years. See Becker (2004a, 219). Observers also claim that there was a massive increase in recruitment in the Ivory Coast in 2003 (CSUCS 2004b).

12. See Becker and Tate (2003, 7). The authors report that in Uganda the age of children being abducted had fallen from the thirteen to fifteen range to as low as nine or ten. When child soldiers were demobilized at the conclusion of hostilities in Mozambique, 4,678 of all officially demobilized children, or 18 percent, were younger than thirteen when recruited; 6,829 (27 percent) were fourteen to fifteen years old; and 13,982 (55 percent) were sixteen to seventeen years old (CBC 2004).

13. We observe that the relevant literature suggests that camps for internally displaced people really started appearing on a widespread basis in these conflicts in the late 1990s, whereas refugee camps were widespread many years earlier.

14. For example of a study on food aid delivery that does emphasize the importance of protection, see Frelick (1997) and Terry (2002).

15. One of the few examples is Barnitz (1999, 4).

16. Children constitute 57 percent of all inhabitants of UNHCR-mandated refugee camps (UNHCR 2001).

17. Confidential interview, UNICEF official, New York, 6 April 2005.

18. Confidential interview, Save the Children official, 25 March 2005.

19. Among our cases, we included some conflicts that commenced before 1975, provided that they concluded during or after 1975 and suitable data was available. Conflicts that concluded prior to 1975 were omitted due to a lack of suitable data.

20. The number of children being recruited was estimated from a series of reports with figures compiled by different operating field organizations, including Save the Children, Coalition to Stop the Use of Child Soldiers, Human Rights Watch, and UNICEF.

21. These seven conflicts were concentrated in five countries, with Niger being the location for three of them, and Mali and Senegal two each.

22. Although less reliable, the duration of a conflict may also serve as a proxy for the age distribution of a population as a possible explanation of child soldier rates. In principle, the percentage of child soldiers may rise as a war progresses because as adults die in conflict, children constitute a higher percentage of the population. We found no evidence to support that claim.

23. If the governmental forces were excluded from the calculation of child soldier ratios for the Ugandan conflict (1994–2002), the ratio would be 71 percent instead of the 22 percent that we have estimated. Lisa Sekaggya, the program coordinator for social protection at Save the Children in Uganda, estimates that the child soldier figure for oppositional forces is 90 percent. See Sekaggya (2004).

24. Poverty can be measured in several ways. Alternative methods are listed at the World Bank's Poverty Net, http://www.worldbank.org/poverty/mission/up1.htm; and the Human Development indicators, http://hdr.undp.org/reports/global/2003/pdf/hdr03_HDI.pdf. We have chosen percentage of population below the poverty line because this measure allows us to focus on income and consumption levels as indicators of the degree of economic need.

25. For our compiled data on poverty, please refer to appendix 2.

26. Whether such a distinction is significant, however, is a subsidiary hypothesis worthy of investigation as part of our ongoing research program.

27. Professor Lischer also provided us with her data set, on which we based our calculations.

28. Appendix 4 lists all instances of camp militarization and attacks in each case. The data on refugee militarization or attacks against them for the years prior to 1988 was unavailable, reducing the data points in our two historical cases of Mozambique (1976–1992) to five years from twelve and in Angola (1975–1995) to eight years from thirteen. We nonetheless include these cases in our sample. The values for the access variable in our nineteen cases, when compared with child soldier rates, are outlined in appendix 5.

29. With three missing values for poverty variable, we were able to calculate results for sixteen out of nineteen observations. We therefore recognize that the statistical reliability of the test might be limited due to the relatively small number of observations for which the data was available and hope to address the issue of a large N in further research.

30. In contrast to bivariate correlations, multiple regression coefficients capture the marginal effect of each independent variable on the dependent variable that is unique to the respective independent variable in the model. Hence, for example, the coefficient on the access variable expresses the rate of change in the child soldiers' variable, which could not have been associated with poverty or orphans. In this way, the multiple regression model controls for the effects of poverty and orphans.

31. If the independent variables are mutually correlated, it becomes harder to distinguish their individual effects on the dependent variable. Such cases usually result in lower precision of the coefficient estimates and hence higher standard errors.

32. For examples of human rights abuses by various rebel parties in Liberia, see Human Rights Watch (1990).

33. Of these, more than 500,000 were estimated to be located in Guinea; 318,000 in the Ivory Coast; 20,000 in Ghana; 6,000 in Sierra Leone; and 4,000 in Nigeria.

34. For selection of stories, see Human Rights Watch (1994, 29, 76); UNICEF (2002a, 23–31); Keairns (2002); and also see narratives regarding children compiled on the Coalition to Stop the Use of Child Soldiers Web site at http://www.child-soldiers.org/childsoldiers/voices-of-young-soldiers.

35. According to Human Rights Watch, "during the Octopus operation in 1992,

children were used by NPFL as cannon fodder. They were in the first wave of troops, and the older fighters were behind them" (Human Rights Watch 1994, 25).

36. The data was obtained from different organizations and sources. See, for example, Human Rights Watch (1994, 2004b), UNICEF (1996, 2000), and CSUCS (2001).

37. It is unclear from the literature whether the MODEL split from LURD in early 2003 or was operating as LURD's integrated force. Human Rights Watch, for instance, reported on the first version of MODEL origin (Human Rights Watch 2004b). Jean-Herve Jezequel argues that MODEL joined the LURD in 2003 (Jezequel 2004, 162). Other sources were allowed for both possibilities (e.g., GlobalSecurity.org Database 2005).

38. One report noted: "Since the upsurge of fighting in 2000, perhaps the most pressing concern about IDPs from the north of the country has been their total lack of protection from increasingly widespread human rights abuses carried out not only by Liberian security forces but by LURD combatants as well" (Norwegian Refugee Council 2005, 7).

39. The situation in Gbarpolu County, for example, deteriorated by December 2001 as fighting forced IDPs in a camp located in Bopolu to move south and northeast. Many sought shelter at Sawmill in Bomi County. But this camp was later attacked in January 2002, forcing IDPs to flee again. Likewise, in February 2002 incursions at Klay Junction forced IDPs to move toward Monrovia and Sinje in Grand Cape Mount county (Jezequel 2004, 25). But armed activities in Cape Mount and Bomi counties in May 2002 resulted in a high military presence in the Sinje camps, causing panic among both refugees and IDPs living there. (Jezequel 2004, 36). By then, the Sinje camps were home to approximately 11,000 Sierra Leonean refugees and a comparable number of IDPs (74). This pattern was repeated elsewhere: fighting in Bong County in April 2002 prompted IDPs to seek refuge near the central town of Gbarnga. Many of them sought refuge from the violence in the four camps established in the county. But the following month the civilians were forced to flee once again when local fighting broke out and three IDP camps were forced to close. About 75,000 IDPs resided in six IDP camps in Bong County and 7,000 in a camp in Buchanan. During the fighting in June and July, many of these camps and surrounding communities were attacked by both government and rebel forces. The camps were looted and many of the shelters were burned. Consequently, the majority of IDPs fled these camps. By the year 2002, villages and IDP camps in Lofa and Bong counties were emptied as their population fled to IDP camps closer to Monrovia (7, 25).

40. For details regarding this effort, see Norwegian Refugee Council (2005).

41. Kenneth Bacon, director of Refugees International, interview with authors, 23 September 2004.

Chapter 5: Recruiting Children for Armed Conflict

1. The outcome of this practice is frequently very harmful to the young women or girls who are abducted by force and exposed to various forms of sexual violence. The effects of societywide norms that allow or prescribe early sexual unions get perverted when embedded in organizations that rely on force. Forced recruitment of girls may cause an increase in the voluntary supply of boys, however, particularly in many of the

African countries where the traditional marriage markets have broken down, often due to increased scarcity of land. This illustrates how the surrounding social and economic institutions impact the forms of violence—and maybe also in this case contribute as a cause. In this chapter, however, we have chosen not to analyze systematically the gender aspects of the supply and demand for child soldiers. See Wessells's chapter in this volume for more on girl soldiers.

2. However, see Brehm and Gates (1997) on the general futility of the coercive model of supervision.

3. In the literature on civil wars, the terms "greed" and "grievance" are mainly used about different sets of causes of war. Greed is focused on economic factors that make it possible to finance rebel organizations and give them some chances to win military contests. Grievance regards political factors and forms of economic unfairness as explanatory mechanisms.

4. Nine percent joined because of fear. When one of the coauthors (Andvig) asked one of the scientific advisors of the ILO/IPEC study from Central Africa, Jon Pedersen (7 March 2006) why they had not asked their child soldiers (former and present) about what kind of punishment they had received when they were disobedient, Pederson replied that it was common knowledge that disobedience implied death (hence no one to ask).

5. Our analysis is limited to comparative statics. We will not explore the dynamic processes through which political motives and success in battle form a dynamic feedback. Such dynamic process-tracing would have to be more case-specific in nature.

6. Achvarina and Reich (2006) explore whether orphan rates have any statistically significant effects on the child soldier ratios in African conflicts and determine a negative result. This is not surprising. The orphan rates are not relevant when there is an excess supply of child soldiers (maybe partly caused by orphanage). It may not have any measurable impact on the aggregate ratio even if all child soldiers are orphans, since the number of child soldiers are so few compared to the total number of employable children. Because the number of orphans would be influenced by the conflict itself, we have also classical statistical problems of identification, particularly so since the variance of the child-soldier ratio is large compared to the variance of the orphanage rate. This is reflected in their range: while the child soldier rate in their cases varies between 0 and 50 percent, the orphan rate varies between 10 and 17 percent.

7. The ILO/IPEC (2003) reports on the impact of the mix of forced and voluntary recruits on the management of the organization. For example, in Burundi only the children who had volunteered were allowed to visit home.

Chapter 6: The Enablers of War

1. For more on the spread of child soldiers, please see Singer (2005, 9–34).

2. This rate is heightened for adult women. The AIDS death rate in Africa for women in their twenties is twice that of women in their sixties (Swarns 2001).

3. Some refugee experts think that this figure may be a high estimate, potentially exaggerated due to political reasons.

4. A typical example is the FARC in Colombia, which started out as a Marxist revolutionary group and is now a prime player in the international cocaine trade (Klare 1999).

Chapter 7: Child Recruitment in Burma, Sri Lanka, and Nepal

1. Gutiérrez Sanín's 40 percent statistic of child recruitment in Colombia is composed of 20 percent identified forced recruitment, 12 percent identified "conviction," and 10 percent identified fear or vengeance related to the army or paramilitaries.

2. Interviews were conducted near the Thai-Burma border from March to June 2002, in the east and north of Sri Lanka in August of 2004, and in Nepal in March and May 2006. Interviews with family members of children abducted by the Karuna Group in Sri Lanka were conducted in eastern Sri Lanka in October 2006. The names of the interviewees have been changed to protect them.

3. The largest number of children interviewed by the research team was participating in a rehabilitation program run exclusively for girls, resulting in a disproportionate number of girls interviewed for the investigation.

4. No girls are known to serve in Burma's national army, and the participation of girls in Burma's armed ethnic opposition groups is very rare.

5. Data supplied to Human Rights Watch by UNICEF Sri Lanka, 9 April 2007. This number represents only a fraction of the total number of children recruited, as some families may be unaware of the possibility of registering their children once recruited, may be afraid to do so, or may have difficulty reaching a UNICEF office. Of the children who have been released or returned from the LTTE, only 37 percent were previously listed in the UNICEF database.

6. After the March 2004 split, UNICEF recorded the return of approximately 1,800 children from Karuna forces to their homes.

7. Data supplied to Human Rights Watch by UNICEF, 9 April 2007.

8. For more information about these estimates, see Human Rights Watch (2002c, 103–106).

9. Human Rights Watch interview, 29 August 2006.

10. Human Rights Watch interviews, Batticaloa District, August 2006.

11. In one typical incident documented by Human Rights Watch, twenty-six people, mostly children, were recruited on 31 July 2004 from a festival at the Thandamalay Murugan temple in Batticaloa.

12. Although child abduction by the Karuna group was not unknown prior to 2006, it was relatively rare, with only nine cases documented by UNICEF during 2004 and 2005.

13. Interview, location withheld for security reasons, August 2006.

14. Interview with "Leela," Butwal, Nepal, 5 March 2006.

15. Interviews conducted near the Thai-Burma border, March 2002.

16. Boys who were trained in various training camps in each year between 1993 and 2001 gave similar accounts of such treatment, demonstrating that this is standard punishment for attempted escape. See Human Rights Watch (2002c, 68–71).

17. Interview with UN official, Batticaloa, August 2004.

18. Interview with "Arun," Kilinochchi, August 2004.

19. Interview, Trincomalee District, August 2004.

20. Of 6,098 cases of LTTE child recruitment documented by UNICEF since 2002, approximately 40 percent of cases were girls. In two of the nine districts monitored

(Kilinochchi and Mulaitivu), girls accounted for the majority of children recruited. Statistics provided by UNICEF, 9 April 2007.

21. Interview with "Kalawoti," Butwal, Nepal, 5 March 2006.

22. Interview with "Marudan," Kilinochchi, August 2004.

23. Interview with "Sivani," Batticaloa District, August 2004.

24. Interview with "Meh Reh," Thailand, March 2002.

25. Interview with "Saw Ler Wah," Karen State, Burma, March 2002.

26. Interview with "Kalawoti," Butwal, Nepal, 5 March 2006.

27. Interview, location withheld for security reasons, August 2006.

Chapter 8: Organizing Minors

1. I suspect that Collier's assumption is equally invalid when applied to many other countries.

2. The debate about whether an alliance between *narcos* and *guerrilleros* had taken place continues today.

3. The semantics of "dry the pond" to "catch the fish" refers to the known Maoist dictum that the guerrilla must act within the masses as a fish in the water.

4. The ELN was extremely brutal, but recruitment was voluntary.

5. Compared to other irregular groups, the participation of the ELN in the narco-economy has been rather restrained. At the height of the movement the ELN had as many as five thousand members.

6. "In the context of Berlin Operation, 38 uninterrupted days of combat have been completed in Soatá, Santander . . . 120 guerrillas deserted, among them 45 children. The FARC secretariat invested a billion pesos [approximately $500,000 thousand] in this offensive that tried to link the South and the North of the country" (*El Tiempo,* 3 January 2001, 3).

7. The example of Policarpa Salavarrieta is more remarkable considering that women were not given the right to vote until 1957.

8. The physical hardships of war have been largely overcome by technological developments. I imagine it is much easier to carry and manipulate an AK-47 than a musket.

9. A child may develop a knack for military activities, or the risk he incurs by supporting the guerrillas may become so high that the only way to avoid recruitment is to flee, or both.

10. Contrary to standard analyses, child recruits have at least two utility functions: one before and one after joining. When the transformation process is successful they can be very different.

11. More than 70 percent of the population of Colombia lives in cities. Regarding statistics on displacement, there is a wide disagreement between the figures of the government and the figures of NGOs; the criteria and methods that they use are very different.

12. ICBF is the Spanish acronym for Colombian Institute of Family Welfare. It is in charge of family and childhood problems. The database I am referring to is an extraordinary source of information; it gathers the essential characteristics of child combatants that join the ICBF reinsertion program from 1999 on. Though not a

representative sample, it is sufficiently big as to offer a good entry point to the universe of socioeconomic traits of Colombian underage fighters. See table 8.3.

13. Two reinserted boys said they had been recruited at age eleven.

14. Regarding gender, the problem is quite different. In the FARC, women fight on a par with men, and the fact of having so many females in the organization provides a precious cement to the organization, through in-organization mating.

15. The Ugandan Lord's Resistance Army probably has completely different reasons for hunting children.

16. Nothing of the sort appears in the case of women.

17. The Berlin operation was so publicized precisely because it was a rather extraordinary event. On the other hand, the average age of FARC members remains quite low (Gutiérrez 2006a, 2006b).

18. This section draws on Gutiérrez (2006b), which indulges in a detailed organizational analysis. I base the discussion on judicial proceedings, oral testimonies, field research, governmental reports, autobiographies, and literature about the Colombian conflict.

19. The exception to the nonpayment standard is when somebody is sent on a special mission—for example, terrorist—to the city. This happens very seldom, if ever, in the life of a fighter.

20. By individual looting (which is rare), I mean looting for individual purposes and without the authorization of the immediate superior.

21. Since there is a quantitative asymmetry, men complain when women find an extra-organizational mate. "Why should they look for men outside, if they have so much to choose here?" (Ferro and Uribe 2002).

22. For any army, but especially an irregular one with weak control mechanisms, having unhappy soldiers is very dangerous. During battle they can shoot their officers in the back.

23. The ELN relies much more on simple support, or at least benevolent neutrality.

24. The rules of the game are different in the militias; from now on I will concentrate on the FARC proper.

25. The standard practice is that each fighter eventually gets his or her family-sent gifts, but there is no guarantee.

26. My own count, from a database of political homicides from 1975 to 2002, built in the course of our research, gives a far worse ratio for the guerrilla: 1:2.5.

27. Geographical barriers will not prevent people intent on joining an illegal force from doing so. In reality, these barriers are not so strong. The FARC almost always coexists with other warlords and narcotraffickers. As the ICBF database reveals, departments like Antioquia, Guaviare, and Meta are a source of recruits for both the guerrillas and the paramilitary; surely also for the narcos.

28. No country counts minors as unemployed, because in theory they have not entered the labor market yet.

29. Here a "risky" life is defined as having a seventy times higher probability of being shot.

30. Kalyvas (2006) suggests that, after a certain level of conflict intensity, survival overrides any other motivation.

31. Of course, recruitment is full of examples of another key Tversky effect, framing.

As Kahnneman and Tversky (2000) warn, extrapolation from experimental results to daily life produces frequent errors.

32. Purely greedy agent B, who cares nothing about status, would be less prone to join the FARC. The high-risk population would be constituted by people with material *and* other interests.

33. Potential risks for nonjoiners in guerrilla-influenced regions are aerial fumigation of their crops, armed attacks by the guerrilla and/or its adversaries, economic crises, and general insecurity due to lack of social and state regulations.

34. However, the alternative need not be as strong as Lichbach states. As Wood (2003, 254) notes, the study of intrinsic other-regarding process-based and endogenous preferences may be as important to explaining quiescence as it apparently is in explaining insurgent collective action. Indeed, it is frequent that the same forces that fuel a war, bind it.

35. The same, of course, can be said of strictly economic explanations.

36. Incidentally, there are some marvelous descriptions of this effect in Tolstoy's "War and Peace."

37. Many oral testimonies by the paramilitary suggest that guerrilla deserters join the ranks of their former foes because they are searching for better economic horizons, and sometimes more individual elbow room. "Here he can choose the color of his shirt," claimed one paramilitary member about an ex-guerrilla who was now his comrade.

38. Inversely, nonjoiners may be characterized by longer time horizons, more risk aversion, and lower discount rates, which may act as a deterrent even in unfavorable conditions.

39. And adults do run away, not only when they are threatened personally but also when they fear that their children will be recruited.

40. The one-person, one-utility function would be a particular case, when $Ut_0 = Ut_1$.

Chapter 9: War, Displacement, and the Recruitment of Child Soldiers in the Democratic Republic of Congo

1. The standard definition of a refugee is found in the 1951 UN Refugee Convention. The convention defines a refugee as "[any person who] . . . owing to well-founded fear of being persecuted for reasons of race, religion, nationality, membership of a particular social group or political opinion, is outside the country of his nationality and is unable or, owing to such fear, is unwilling to avail himself of the protection of that country." Internally displaced persons (IDPs) have fled their homes but have not crossed national borders.

2. See, for example, UN General Assembly Resolution no. 56, par. 136, 19 December 2001.

3. See the *1951 Convention Relating to the Status of Refugees, Chapter 1*, General Provisions, Article 1, and the *Convention Governing the Specific Aspects of Refugee Problems in Africa*, Organization of African Unity, 1969.

4. The term "exiles" refers to people, including soldiers and war criminals, who left their country of origin but who do not qualify for refugee status. Exiles and refugees may live indistinguishably in camps, as they did in Zaire after the 1994 exodus from Rwanda.

5. The Organization of African Unity (OAU) Convention states that "Signatory States undertake to prohibit refugees residing in their respective territories from attacking any member state of the OAU" (OAU 1969). The Organization of American States (OAS) also urges the institution "of appropriate measures in the receiving countries to prevent the participation of the refugees in activities directed against the country of origin" (OAS, "Cartegena Declaration on Refugees," 1984). In a more recent document, the Security Council reaffirmed "the primary responsibility of States to ensure [refugee] protection, in particular by maintaining the security and civilian character of refugee and internally displaced person camps" (United Nations 1999b).

6. Singer notes that UNHCR initially set up housing for unaccompanied minors in separate areas of Sudanese refugee camps, making SPLA abductions even easier (Singer 2005, 59).

Chapter 10: Disaggregating the Causal Factors Unique to Child Soldiering

The author attended the Child Soldiers Initiative Working Group Session in Pittsburgh, 15–16 September 2006. The chapter is drawn from a data collection effort sponsored by the UNDP Liberia while the author was doing thesis research at the Joint Military Intelligence College. I'm deeply indebted to Dr. Scott Gates for helpful comments concerning this chapter and to Jamie Fuller for her keen editorial eye. The views expressed in this paper are those of the author and do not reflect the official policy or position of the Department of Defense or the U.S. government. The author takes responsibility for all errors and consistencies.

1. There are numerous recognized protocols and international laws. For details, see http://www.un.org/special-rep/children-armed-conflict/English/index.html.

2. See the UN Children an Armed Conflict Web site at http://www.un.org/children/conflict/english/index.html.

3. For more detailed information on Liberia's former fighters and factions, see Pugel (2007).

4. For more detail on operational activity modeling, see Humphreys and Weinstein (2005).

Chapter 11: Girls in Armed Forces and Groups in Angola

The author, who was technical advisor on the Angola research reported in this chapter, expresses his sincere gratitude to Vivi Stavrou, Mary Daly, Carlinda Monteiro, and the entire CCF/Angola team that conducted the research in Angola.

1. The methodology and findings are described in greater length in Stavrou (2005). Both the Stavrou report and this chapter cite some of the same narrative passages, which came from a set of inductively categorized field notes developed by the team.

Chapter 12: National Policies to Prevent the Recruitment of Child Soldiers

1. In this chapter, the term "education" will encompass not only formal schooling but also nonformal education and informal learning. Nonformal education is defined as structured and organized learning that mainly occurs in nonschool settings, such as adult literacy sessions in homes and tribal schools. Informal education includes culturally prescribed, fortuitous, and flexible learning experiences, such as apprenticeships, youth groups, military demonstrations, and traditional teaching stories. Estrada

Armas noted that in Guatemala, male Quiche speaking Indians who joined guerrilla and military groups gained Spanish language and literacy skills (Estrada Armas 2005).

2. With reference to Lao PDR and Vietnam, and as reported in an interview with Emmanuel Dolo (2007) regarding social policy development in the aftermath of fourteen years of war in Liberia.

3. Examples of illicit trades include arms, natural resources (such as diamonds, uranium, and gold), drugs, sex workers, and human trafficking.

4. Examples are provided in the Democratic Republic of Congo regarding push out circumstances leading children to flee home communities to become child soldiers.

5. For a valuable discussion on protection, security networks, and the importance of integrated services, see McClure and Retamal (2007).

6. Personal communication of Hernando Bernal Alarcón with reference to parent and community resistance in towns of the Department of Boyacá in Colombia.

7. Recommendation of Dr. Beverly Zweiben, formerly responsible for Multilateral Human Rights Affairs in the Bureau of International Organizations, U.S. Department of State.

8. See sections on UNICEF's program for Child Friendly Spaces.

9. This is the strong recommendation of Michael Southwick, former ambassador and former U.S. deputy assistant secretary of state, who assisted with the negotiation of the Optional Protocol.

Chapter 13: Wise Investments in Future Neighbors

1. The term "childhood" and its protection is used here in a very specific way. It means not only the protection of a child's physical being, but also the protection of a child's individual human agency. The goal of childhood protection is to ensure that children grow up normally in caring communities. UNICEF is the only large-scale, operations-oriented international agency of its kind. Its mission has also given rise to a unique operations structure particularly well-suited for the delivery of human security-based strategy through child-centered integrated services.

2. This chapter draws heavily from this report, which was written by a team headed by one of the authors.

3. This includes access to institutional documents such as assessments, plans, budgets, program materials, periodical reports, trip reports, evaluations, and coordinating structures.

4. In the early days of the Geographic Information Network in Europe (GINIE) project, considerable time was spent scanning and rehabilitating the formats of documents that already had been copied too many times.

5. UNESCO made the best efforts in education, working with national ministries, but they were hampered by chronic underfunding, due in part to the high costs of scanning and archiving already printed materials. Later, USAID took an early lead in making project documents publicly available online.

6. Gray or fugitive literature primarily consists of locally or internally generated documents, or documents printed in highly limited runs. Seth Spaulding was, for many years, the primary champion of fugitive literature collections in education. Frederico Major, then the director general of UNESCO and his special assistant, Gonzalo

Retamal, took the lead for the UN.

7. Confidential interview conducted in 1997, available at http://www.pitt.edu/~mmcclure/BiH/unescobih.html .

8. UNICEF and its NGO partners, with human security their operational core, stand in contrast with bilateral responses, such as USAID, with its weak center, and contractor-based NGOs that turn responses into strategy-free enterprise zones.

9. The IASC was established in June 1992 in response to United Nations General Assembly Resolution 46/182 on the strengthening of humanitarian assistance. See http://www.humanitarianinfo.org/iasc/.

10. The main objectives of IASC are to develop and manage systemwide humanitarian policies; to allocate responsibilities among agencies in humanitarian programs; to develop and agree on a common ethical framework for all humanitarian activities; to advocate for common humanitarian principles to parties outside the IASC; to identify areas where gaps in mandates or lack of operational capacity exists; to resolve disputes or disagreement about and between humanitarian agencies on systemwide humanitarian issues.

11. ISPs (internally stuck persons) are those who had wars break out in their neighborhoods and were unable to flee.

12. "Balkan Sunflowers brings volunteers from around the world to work as neighbors and friends in social reconstruction and renewal. By organizing social and cultural activities, we promote understanding, further non-violent conflict transformation, and celebrate the diversity of the lives and cultures of the Balkan region" (http://www.balkansunflowers.org/).

13. See also Canadian Cooperation Award 2004: The Education Renewal Project in Sierra Leone. Plan International. In 1999, drawing upon the experiences of earlier programs implemented by UNESCO in Somalia and Rwanda, Foster Parents Plan worked with Sierra Leone's Ministry of Education, Science and Technology and the Forum of African Women Educationalists (FAWE) to create the Education Renewal project.

14. The GINIE project sent out requests for information on new research on interventions related to trauma and learning. Within twenty-four hours several leading scholars (none of them net members) responded.

15. Reference is made also to the IRC experience in Northern Caucasus.

16. Almost 40 percent of the internally displaced have settled in and around the ten largest cities. Without official registration and proper identity documents, IDPs often face difficulty in accessing basic government assistance, employment, health care, and education.

17. For many years, both guerrillas and paramilitaries have depopulated rural areas and appropriated the land for political, economic, and strategic gain. Upon seizing control of an area, armed groups often kill or displace civilians they suspect of supporting the opposing side. Human rights defenders frequently suffer a similar fate. Although indigenous people represent only 2 to 3 percent of Colombia's total inhabitants, they make up as much as 8 percent of the county's internally displaced population.

18. Their incomes were not sufficient to meet basic market basket needs. Fifty-three percent of homes stated that their main survival strategy was assistance from neighbors, relatives, friends, the government, or some NGOs.

19. Colombia's Escuela Nueva was created in 1974 and has drawn from and combined various features of progressive education theory and practice. In 1985, the Colombian government adopted Escuela Nueva as a national policy for rural primary schools.

20. Quality of learning in the classroom is conditioned by the classroom climate. The variables constituting this indicator measure levels of violent or positive environment among students and the quality of teacher-student relations in the learning processes. This set of variables is more relevant than other aspects, such as physical conditions of the school. A UNESCO/LLECE (Laboratorio Latinoamericano de Evaluación de la Calidad de la Educación) study showed that against all predictions, Colombian rural schools showed better results than urban schools in the average of Latin America. This is mainly attributed to the quality factors and the school climate created by Escuela Nueva. See LLECE (2002).

21. Play dynamics help kids rediscover attachment. Games and recreational components with well-structured objectives as tools help to achieve psychological and emotional recuperation in children, significantly increasing the quality of children's communication.

22. In 1996, 2.7 million children voted to choose which of children's rights were most important in Colombia today. In the Children's Peace Movement, children help other children who have suffered from violence. Children also contact politicians and demand that, for example, schools and parks be designated as peace zones and that children be given protection when they walk home from school.

23. Most of this aspect of the report is based on Siegrist (2003).

24. The community has used the symbol of the human hand to show their commitment to protect the children from harm. Each finger of the hand is raised in protection and identified with a particular quality associated with peace. These actions have created a local movement that is linked with the broader Colombia Children's Peace Movement, combining psychosocial support with community-based actions for peace.

25. This is often the weakest part of international humanitarian intervention strategy. It cannot police itself very well and tends to create bubble economies that burst when the agencies pull out.

Chapter 14: Ending the Scourge of Child Soldiering

1. The Organization for African Unity, the Economic Community of West African States, the Organization of American States and the Organization for Security and Cooperation in Europe, and the European Parliament are among regional organizations that have denounced the use of child soldiers.

2. See papers from the conference "The Impact of Globalization from Above: The International Monetary Fund and the World Bank," June 2003, http://www.yale.edu/ycias/globalization/imf-wb.htm. See also Mosley and Hudson (2001).

Conclusion

1. Also see Paris (2001) and King and Murray (2002).

2. For a related dynamic, please see Polanyi (1944) and his discussion of the breakdown of the enclosure system.

3. Literally, *guerrilla* means small war; it is the diminutive form of the Spanish word

for war, *guerra*.

4. As reported in the 2006 annual data feature in the *Journal of Peace Research*, in 2005 there were thirty-one intrastate armed conflicts (involving at least twenty-five battle-related casualties), which were fought in twenty-two different countries. In 2004, there were thirty-two intrastate armed conflicts. These numbers constitute a significant drop since the early 1990s; in 1992 we recorded fifty-one active armed intrastate conflicts. See Gleditsch et al. (2002) and Harbom, Högbladh, and Wallensteen (2006).

5. This is becoming a common expression, but it should be noted that aspects of the First World War were fought between the British and Germans in German East Africa (Rwanda, Burundi, and Tanganyika, which is now part of Tanzania) and the bordering English colonies, and between South Africa and German Southwest Africa (Namibia).

6. See the Human Security Center (2005), where this position is persuasively argued.

7. See United Nations (2005c, sec. 1).

REFERENCES

Aborsangaya, Ozong. 2000. "Policy Dialogue to Advance the Process of Child Soldier Demobilization: Final Report for the Task Order, Educational Assessment: Demobilization of Child Soldiers in the Democratic Republic of Congo." Washington, DC: Creative Associates International.

Accra Declaration and the Plan of Action on War-Affected Children in West Africa. 2000. Adopted at a meeting of Economic Community of West African States (ECOWAS) in Accra, 27–28 April. http://www.essex.ac.uk/armedcon/story_id/000548.pdf.

Achvarina, Vera. 2007. "Effectiveness of the International Norm against the Use of Child Soldiers." Mimeo, University of Pittsburgh.

Achvarina, Vera, and Simon Reich. 2006a. "No Place to Hide: Refugees, Displaced Persons, and the Recruitment of Child Soldiers." *International Security* 31 (1): 127–164.

———. 2006b. "Why Do Children 'Fight'? Explaining the Phenomenon of Child Soldiers in African Intra-State Conflicts." Paper presented at the annual meeting of the International Studies Association, San Diego, CA, 22 March.

———. 2007. "Unpackaging Protection: Child Soldier Recruitment in Four African Conflicts." Paper presented at the annual meeting of the International Studies Association 48th Annual Convention, Chicago, 28 February.

Agence France Presse. 2006. "DRC Recruiter for Child Soldiers Convicted." *iafrica .com,* 19 March.

Aguilar, Pilar, and Gonzalo Retamal. 1998. *Rapid Educational Response in Complex Emergencies: A Discussion Document.* Geneva, Switzerland: UNESCO/IBE, UNESCO/UIE, UNICEF, and UNHCR.

Aird, Sarah. 2001. "Mozambique: The Battle Continues for Former Child Soldiers." Youth Advocate Program International Resource Paper. http://www.yapi.org/old/publications/resourcepapers/MozCS.pdf.

Alape, Arturo. 1989. *Tirofijo.* Bogotá: Planeta.

Allison, Paul. 2001. *Missing Data.* Thousand Oaks, CA: Sage University Papers.

Amnesty International. 2000. "Sierra Leone: Childhood—A Casualty of Conflict." http://www.amnesty.org/en/library/info/AFR51/069/2000/en.

———. 2002. "Liberian Civilians Face Human Rights Abuses at Home and Across Borders." http://www.amnesty.org/en/library/info/AFR34/020/2002.

———. 2003. "DR Congo: Child Soldiers Tell Their Stories." AI index AFR 62/038/2003.

———. 2004a. "Child Soldiers: Governments Failing Generations of Children. New Global Report Finds Child Soldiers in Over 20 Conflicts Worldwide." Press Release, 17 November. http://www.amnesty.org/en/library/info/ACT76/010/2004.

———. 2004b. "Liberia: Demand Justice for Child Soldiers." 17 May. http://web.amnesty.org/pages/lbr-170504-action-eng.

Anderson, John Lee. 1992. *Guerillas: The Men and Women Fighting Today's Wars.* New York: New York Times.

André, Catherine, and Jean-Philippe Platteau. 1998. "Land Tenure under Unendurable Stress: Rwanda Caught in the Malthusian Trap." *Journal of Economic Behavior & Organization* 34:1–47.

Andvig, Jens C. 1997. "Child Labor in Sub-Saharan Africa: An Exploration." *Working Paper No. 585.* Norwegian Institute of International Affairs.

Andvig, Jens C., S. Canagarajah, and A. Kielland. 2001. "Issues in Child Labor in Africa: Africa Region Human Development." Working Paper Series. Washington, DC: World Bank.

Andvig, Jens, and Scott Gates. 2006. "Recruiting Children for Armed Conflict." Paper presented at the Child Soldiers Initiative Working Group Session, Pittsburgh, 15–16 September.

Annan, J., C. Blattman, and R. Horton. 2006. *The State of Youth and Youth Protection in Northern Uganda.* Uganda: UNICEF.

Anscombe, G.E.M. 1981. "Mr. Truman's Degree." *Ethics, Religion, and Politics, Collected Philosophical Papers* 3:62–71.

Arjona, Ana M. 2006. "Local Life in War Zones: A Control Survey with Civilians for a Project with Demobilized Combatants in Colombia." Designing Research on the Micro-dynamics of Civil Wars Conference, Yale University, 14–15 April.

Armed Conflicts Events Data. 2003. http://www.onwar.com/aced/nation/lay/liberia/fliberia1989.htm.

Arnston, Laura, and Neil Boothby. 2002. "A World Turned Upside Down." *Child Soldiers in Mozambique: A Case Study of their Reintegration.* Washington, DC: Save the Children.

Asian Human Rights Commission. 2003. *Children and the People's War in Nepal.* Hong Kong: Asian Human Rights Commission.

Associated Press. 2005. "Minister: Suicide Bomber a Handicapped Child Iraq Police Say Attacker Seemed to Have Down Syndrome." 31 January. http://www.msnbc.msn.com/id/6889106/.

Azam, Jean Paul. 2002. "Looting and Conflict between Ethno-Regional Groups: Lessons for State Formation in Africa." *Journal of Conflict Resolution* 46:131–153.

———. 2006. "On Thugs and Heroes: Why Warlords Victimize Their Own Civilians." *Economics of Governance* 7 (1): 53–73.

Barnitz, Laura. 1999. *Child Soldiers: Youth Who Participate in Armed Conflict.* 2nd ed. Washington, DC: Youth Advocate Program International.

Bateman, Ian, Alisatair Munro, Bruce Rhodes, Chris Starmer, and Robert Sugden.

2000. "A Test of the Theory of Reference Dependent Points." In *Choices, Values, and Frames,* ed. Daniel Kahnemen and Amos Tversky, Cambridge, MA: Cambridge University Press.

BBC News. 2001. "UN Finds Congo Child Soldiers." 21 February.

———. 2004. "Child Suicide Attacks 'Must Stop.'" 3 November. http://news.bbc.co .uk/2/hi/middle_east/3979887.stm.

———. 2007. "Child Soldiers 'Are a Time Bomb.'" 5 February. http://news.bbc.co .uk/2/hi/europe/6330503.stm.

Beah, Ishmael. 2007. *A Long Way Gone.* New York: Sarah Crichton / Farrar, Straus and Giroux.

Becker, Jo. 2004a. "Children as Weapons of War." In *World Report 2004: Human Rights and Armed Conflict.* New York: Human Rights Watch. http://www.hrw.org/wr2k4/ download/wr2k4.pdf.

———. 2004b. "Living in Fear: Child Soldiers and the Tamil Tigers in Sri Lanka." *Human Rights Watch* 16 (13): 1–80.

———. 2006. "Child Recruitment in Burma, Sri Lanka and Nepal." Paper presented at the Child Soldiers Initiative Working Group Session, Pittsburgh, 15–16 September.

Becker, Jo, and Tony Tate. 2003. *Stolen Children: Abduction and Recruitment in Northern Uganda.* New York: Human Rights Watch. http://www.hrw.org/reports/2003/ uganda0303/uganda0403.pdf.

Beer, Jennifer. 1997–2003. *Communicating across Cultures: High and Low Context.* http://www.culture-at-work.com/highlow.html.

Bell, Coral. 2002. "Normative Shift." *National Interest* 70:44–54.

Bender, Christof. 1999. "Searching for a Strategy: Multiethnicity, Tolerance and National Stereotypes in the Educational Systems of Bosnia and Herzegovina." *Bosnia and Herzegovina Country Report.* http://www-gewi.uni-graz.at/csbsc/ documentary_report/Bosnia.html.

Bennet, T. W. 1998. "Using Children in Armed Conflict: A Legitimate African Tradition?" *Monograph,* no. 32 (Institute for Security Studies, Pretoria).

Berdal, Mats, and David Malone. 2001. *Greed and Grievance: Economic Agendas in Civil Wars.* Boulder, CO: Lynne Reinner.

Bergner, Daniel. 2003. *In the Land of Magic Soldiers: A Story of Black and White in West Africa.* New York: Farrar, Straus and Giroux.

Bergsmo, Morten. 2007. International Peace Research Institute (PRIO), Oslo, Norway, mimeo.

Bhalotra, S., and C. Heady. 2003. "Child Farm Labor: The Wealth Paradox." *World Bank Economic Review* 17 (2): 197–227.

Bhalotra, S., and Z. Tzannatos. 2003. "Child Labor: What Have We Learnt?" *Social Protection Discussion Paper Series no. 0317.* Washington, DC: World Bank.

Biggeri, M., L. Guarcello, S. Lyon, and F. C. Rosati. 2003. "The Puzzle of 'Idle' Children: Neither in School nor Performing Economic Activity." *Understanding Children's Work Project, ILO-UNICEF-World Bank.* http://www.ucw-project.org/ pdf/publications/idle_children.pdf.

Bisseker, Claire. 1998. "Africa's Military Time Bomb." *Johannesburg Financial Mail,* 11 December.

Blattman, Chris. 2006a. "The Consequences of Child Soldiering." Unpublished paper, Department of Economics, University of California, Berkeley.

———. 2006b. "The Logic of Forcible Recruitment and Child Soldiering: Theory and Evidence from Northern Uganda." Unpublished paper, Department of Economics, University of California, Berkeley.

———. 2007. "The Causes of Child Soldiering: Theory and Evidence from Northern Uganda." Unpublished paper, Department of Economics, University of California, Berkeley.

Blattman, Chris, and Jeannie Annan. 2007. "The Consequences of Child Soldiering." HiCN Working Paper, no. 22, University of Sussex.

Bonn International Center for Conversion (BICC). 1997. "An Army Surplus—The NVA's Heritage." *BICC Brief No. 3*, BICC, Bonn, Germany.

Boothby, Neil. 1992. "Displaced Children: Psychological Theory and Practice from the Field." *Journal of Refugee Studies* 5 (2): 106–122.

Brabazon, James. 2003. "Liberia: Liberians United for Reconciliation and Democracy (LURD)." Armed Non-State Actors Project, Briefing Paper No. 1, Royal Institute of International Affairs, Africa Program.

Brehm, John, and Scott Gates. 1997. *Working, Shirking and Sabotage: Bureaucratic Response to a Democratic Public*. Ann Arbor: University of Michigan Press.

Brett, Rachel. 2001. "Recruiting Child Soldiers." *Refugees* 1 (122): 19.

Brett, Rachel, and Irma Specht. 2004. *Young Soldiers: Why They Choose to Fight*. London: Lynne Rienner Publishers.

———. 2005. "Jóvenes soldados y combatientes: ¿Por qué van a luchar?" Organización Internacional del Trabajo-Oficina Internacional del Trabajo-Comité Andino de Servicios, Bogotá.

Brett, Sebastian. 2003. *You'll Learn Not to Cry: Child Combatants in Colombia*. New York: Human Rights Watch.

Broderick, Walter. 2000. *El guerrillero invisible*. Bogotá: Intermedio.

Broughton, B. 2003. *Study of the UNICEF Northern Caucasus Emergency Program: November 1999–December 2002*. Moscow: UNICEF.

Burnett, Nicholas. 2007. *EFA Global Monitoring Report: Strong Foundations, Early Childhood Care and Education*. Paris: UNESCO.

Cagoco-Guiam, R. 2002. *Child soldiers in Central and Western Mindanao*. Geneva: ILO/IPEC.

Callister, Fiona. 2003. "Liberia's child soldiers." *Tablet* (London), 4 October. http://www.thetablet.co.uk/cgi-bin/archive_db.cgi?tablet-00789.

Cardenal, Ernesto. 1999. *Vida Perdida*. Barcelona: Seix Barral.

———. 2004. *La Revolución Perdida. Memorias 3*. Madrid: Trotta.

Carpenter, Charli. 2007. "Protecting Babies Born in Captivity and Their Formerly Abducted Mothers: Existing Knowledge and Practice in Conflict Settings." In *Born of War: Protecting Children of Sexual Violence Survivors in Conflict Zones*, ed. R. Charli Carpenter, 210–225. Bloomfield, CT: Kumarian Press.

"Cayó Jefe De Finanzas Del Eln." *El Tiempo*. 2001. 3 January, p. 3. http://www.eltiempo.com.

CBC. 2004. "Africa: After the Wars." http://www.cbc.ca/afterthewars/childsoldier.html.

Center for Defense Information. 1997. "The Invisible Soldiers: Child Combatants." *Defense Monitor* 26 (4). http://www.cdi.org/dm/1997/issue4/.

———. 2001. "Children on the Front Line: Child Soldiers in Afghanistan." http://www.cdi.org/friendlyversion/printversion.cfm?documentID=2038.

Center for Emerging Threats and Opportunities (CETO). 2002. "Child Soldiers— Implications for U.S. Forces." Report from seminar, Quantico, VA, 23 September.

Chickering, Lawrence, Isobel Coleman, P. Edward Haley, and Emily Vargas-Barón. 2006. *Strategic Foreign Assistance: Civil Society in International Security.* Palo Alto, CA: Hoover Institution Press.

Child Workers in Nepal (CWIN). 2006. "Children in Armed Conflict." Factsheet.

"Children under Arms." 1999. *Economist,* 10 July, 21–23.

Christian Children's Fund/Angola. 2002. *Free to Play in Peace: Angola's War Seen through the Eyes of Its Children.* Luanda: CCF/Angola.

Cincotta, Richard, Robert Engelman, and Daniele Anastasion. 2003. *The Security Demographic: Population and Civil Conflict after the Cold War.* Washington, DC: Population Action International.

Clapham, Christopher. 1996. *Africa and the International System: The Politics of State Survival.* New York: Cambridge University Press.

———, ed. 1998. *African Guerrillas.* Oxford: James Currey.

CNN.com. 2001. "Sudan Protests UNICEF Child Soldier Airlift." 7 March.

———. 2005. "U.S. Commander: Taliban Recruiting Children." 23 July. http://www.cnn.com/2005/WORLD/asiapcf/07/23/afghan.taliban.ap/.

Coalition to Stop the Use of Child Soldiers (CSUCS). 2000. *The Use of Children as Soldiers in Africa: A Country Analysis of Child Recruitment and Participation in Armed Conflict.* http://www.reliefweb.int/library/documents/chilsold.htm.

———. 2001. *Child Soldiers: Global Report.* http://www.child-soldiers.org.

———. 2002. *Child Soldiers 1379 Report.* November. http://www.child-soldiers.org/document_get.php?id=740.

———. 2004a. *Child Soldiers: Global Report 2004.* London: Coalition to Stop the Use of Child Soldiers.

———. 2004b. *Child Soldier Use 2004: A Briefing for the 4th UN Security Council, Open Debate on Children and Armed Conflict.* http://www.hrw.org/reports/2004/childsoldiers0104/1.htm.

———. 2008. *The Security Council and Children and Armed Conflict: Next Steps towards Ending Violations against Children.* http://www.reliefweb.int/rw/lib.nsf/db900sid/SODA-7DP3ZS/$file/Full_Report.pdf?openelement.

Cobb, Charles. 2001. "Arms and Africa on UN Agenda This Week." *AllAfrica.com.* 9 July.

Cohn, Ilene, and Guy S. Goodwin-Gill. 1994. *Child Soldiers: The Role of Children in Armed Conflict.* Oxford: Clarendon Press.

Collier, Paul. 2000a. *Economic Causes of Civil Conflict and Their Implications for Policy.* World Bank Report, June 15.

———. 2000b. "Rebellion as a Quasi-Criminal Activity." *Journal of Conflict Resolution* 44 (6): 839–854.

———. 2003. "How to Stem Civil Wars, It's the Economy, Stupid." *International Herald Tribune,* 21 May.

Collier, Paul, Lance Elliot, Håvard Hegre, Anke Hoeffler, Marta Reynal-Querol, and
    Nicholas Sambanis. 2003. *Breaking the Conflict Trap: Civil War and Development
    Policy.* Oxford and Washington, DC: Oxford University Press and World Bank.
Collier, Paul, and Anke Hoeffler. 1998. "On Economic Causes of Civil Wars." *Oxford
    Economic Papers* 50:563–573.
————. 2000. "Greed and Grievance in Civil War." *World Bank Policy Research Paper,
    no. 2355.* Washington, DC: World Bank.
————. 2002. "On the Incidence of Civil War in Africa." *Journal of Conflict Resolution*
    46:13–28.
————. 2004. "Greed and Grievance in Civil War." *Oxford Economic Papers* 56:563–595.
Collier, Paul, and Nicholas Sambanis, eds. 2005a. *Understanding Civil War: Evidence
    and Analysis (Volume 1).* Washington, DC: World Bank.
————. 2005b. *Understanding Civil War: Evidence and Analysis (Volume 2).* Washington,
    DC: World Bank.
Cramer, Christopher. 2002. "Homo Economicus Goes to War: Methodological
    Individualism, Rational Choice and the Political Economy of War." *World Develop-
    ment* 30 (11): 1845–1864.
Dallaire, Romeo. 2004. *Shaking Hands with the Devil.* Toronto: Random House
    Canada.
Dallaire, Romeo, Phil Lancaster, Jacqueline O'Neil, and Sarah Spencer. 2007. *Children
    in Conflict: Eradicating the Child Soldier Doctrine.* Cambridge, MA: Harvard
    University Carr Center for Human Rights Policy. http://www.ksg.harvard.edu/
    cchrp/pdf/ChildSoldierReport.pdf.
Dao, James. 2002. "The War on Terrorism Takes an Aim at Crime." *New York Times,*
    April 7.
Defense for Children International. 2004. "Use of Children in the Occupied Palestin-
    ian Territories: Perspective on Child Soldiers." Palestine Section. July.
Deng Deng, William. 2001. *A Survey of Programs on the Reintegration of Former Child
    Soldiers 2001.* Ministry of Foreign Affairs of Japan. http://www.mofa.go.jp/policy/
    human/child/survey/profile7.html.
Derlyn, I., E. Broekart, G. Schuyten, E. De Temmerman. 2004. "Post-traumatic Stress
    in Former Ugandan Child Soldiers." *Lancet* 363:861–863.
Dolo, Emmanuel T. 2007. *Ethnic Tensions in Liberia's National Identity Crisis: Problems
    and Possibilities.* Cherry Hill, NJ: Africana Homestead Legacy Publishers.
Duffield, Mark. 1999. "Globalisation and War Economies: Promoting Order or the
    Return of History." *Fletcher Forum on World Affairs* 23 (2): 19–36.
————. 2001. *Global Governance and the New Wars: The Merging of Development and
    Security.* London: Zed Books.
Dufka, Corinne. 2005. "Youth, Poverty and Blood: The Lethal Legacy of West
    Africa's Regional Warriors." *Human Rights Watch Report* 17 (5A). http://hrw.org/
    reports/2005/ westafrica0405/index.htm.
Dyregrov, Atle, Rolf Gjestad, and Magne Raundalen. 2002. "Children Exposed to
    Warfare: A Longitudinal Study." *Journal of Traumatic Stress* 15:59–68.
Ellis, Stephen. 1999. *The Mask of Anarchy: The Destruction of Liberia and the Religious
    Dimension of an African Civil War.* New York: New York University Press.

Elster, Jon. 2000. "Rational Choice History: A Case of Excessive Ambition." *American Political Science Review* 94 (3): 685–695.

Erchak, Gerald. 1998. "Kpelle." Encyclopedia of World Cultures CD-ROM, Macmillan. http://www.sscnet.ucla.edu/anthro/faculty/fiske/135b/kpelle.htm.

Estrada Armas, Hugo. 2005. "Promoting Literacy and Women's Development in Mayan Communities in Guatemala." In *From Bullets to Blackboards: Education for Peace in Latin America and Asia*, ed. Emily Vargas-Barón and Hernando Bernal Alarcón. Washington, DC: Inter-American Development Bank.

European Union. 2003. "European Union Guidelines on Children and Armed Conflict." Council of the European Union document, adopted by the Political and Security Committee (PSC) at its meeting on 4 December.

Fearon, James. 2005. "Civil War since 1945: Some Facts and a Theory." Draft working paper, Department of Political Science, Stanford University.

Fearon, James, and David Laitin. 2003. "Ethnicity, Insurgency and Civil War." *American Political Science Review* 97:75–90.

———. 2004. "Neotrusteeship and the Problem of Weak States." *International Security* 28:5–43.

Ferro, Juan Guillermo, and Graciela Uribe. 2002. *El orden de la guerra. Las FARC-EP: Entre la organización y la política.* Bogotá: CEJA.

Finnemore, Martha. 1996. "Constructing Norms of Human Intervention." In *The Culture of National Security: Norms and Identity in World Politic,* ed. Peter J. Katzenstein, 153–185. New York: Columbia University Press.

Finnis, John, Joseph Boyle, and Germain Grisez. 1987. *Nuclear Deterrence, Morality, and Realism.* Oxford: Clarendon Press.

Frelick, Bill. 1997. "Assistance without Protection: Feed the Hungry, Clothe the Naked, and Watch Them Die." *Worldwide Refugee Information.* Washington, DC: United States Committee for Refugees.

Frey, Bruno. 1997. *Not Just for the Money.* Cheltenham, UK: Edgar Elgar Publishing.

Friman, H. Richard, and Simon Reich. 2008. "Human Trafficking and Human Security." In *Human Trafficking, Human Security and the Balkans,* ed. H. Richard Friman and Simon Reich, 136–154. Pittsburgh: University of Pittsburgh Press.

Fromm, Erich. 1997. *The Anatomy of Human Destructiveness.* London: Pimlico.

Fullinwider, Robert K. 1985. "War and Innocence." In *International Ethics,* ed. Charles R. Beitz, Marshall Cohen, Thomas Scanlon, and A. John Simmons, 90–97. Princeton, NJ: Princeton University Press.

Gates, Scott. 2002. "Recruitment and Allegiance: The Microfoundations of Rebellion." *Journal of Conflict Resolution* 46:111–130.

———. 2004. "Recruiting Child Soldiers." Paper presented at the CSCW Workshop on Techniques of Violence in Civil War, PRIO, Oslo, 20–21 August.

Gautam, Shobha, Amrita Banskota, and Rita Manchanda. 2003. "Where There Are No Men: Women in the Maoists Insurgency in Nepal." In *Understanding the Maoist Movement of Nepal,* ed. Deepak Thapa. Kathmandu: Martin Chautari.

Gleditsch, Kristian Skrede. 2007. "Transnational Dimensions of Civil War." *Journal of Peace Research* 44 (3): 293–309.

Gleditsch, Nils Petter, Peter Wallensteen, Mikael Eriksson, Margareta Sollenberg, and

Håvard Strand. 2002. "Armed Conflict 1946–2001: A New Dataset." *Journal of Peace Research* 39:615–637.

GlobalSecurity.org Database. 2005. "Movement for Democracy in Liberia." http://www.globalsecurity.org/military/world/para/model.htm.

Guichaoua, Y. 2006. "Why Do Youths Join Ethnic Militias? A Survey on the Oodua People's Congress in Southwestern Nigeria." Centre for Research on Inequality, Human Security and Ethnicity, Queen Elizabeth House, University of Oxford.

Gunaratna, Rohan. 1998. "LTTE Child Combatants." *Jane's Intelligence Review* (July): 32–37.

Gupta, Leila. 2000. "Psychosocial Assessment of Displaced Children Exposed to War Related Violence in Sierra Leone." Plan International Document, Freetown, Sierra Leone, 25 February.

Gurr, Ted Robert. 1971. *Why Men Rebel*. Princeton: Princeton University Press.

Gutiérrez, Francisco. 2004. "Criminal Rebels? A Discussion of War and Criminality from the Colombian Experience." *Politics and Society* 32 (2): 257–285.

———. 2006a. "Organizing Minors." Paper presented at the Child Soldiers Initiative Working Group Session, Pittsburgh, 15–16 September.

———. 2006b. "Tendencias del Homicidio Político en Colombia, 1975–2004: Una Discusión Preliminar." In *Nuestra guerra sin nombre: Transformaciones del Conflicto en Colombia*, ed. María Emma Wills and Gonzalo Sánchez, 475–504. Bogotá: Norma.

Gutiérrez, Francisco, and Mauricio Barón. 2005. "Re-Stating the State: Paramilitary Territorial Control and Political Order in Colombia (1978–2004)." *Crisis States Research Centre Working Paper 66*. London: London School of Economics.

Guzmán, José Luis. 2005. "Educational Reform in Post-War El Salvador." In *From Bullets to Blackboards: Education for Peace in Latin America and Asia*, ed. Emily Vargas-Barón and Hernando Bernal Alacrón, 43–62. Washington, DC: Inter-American Development Bank.

Guzmán de Luna, Eduvigis Auxiliadora. 2005. "Reintegrating Ex-Combatants into Society in El Salvador." In *From Bullets to Blackboards: Education for Peace in Latin America and Asia*, ed. Emily Vargas-Barón and Hernando Bernal Alacrón, 159–174. Washington, DC: Inter-American Development Bank.

Harbaugh, W. T., and K. Krause. 1999. "Children's Contributions in Public Good Experiments: The Development of Altruistic and Free-Riding Behaviors." Working Paper Series, University of Oregon Department of Economics.

Harbaugh, W. T., K. Krause, and L. Vesterlund. 2001. "Risk Attitudes of Children and Adults: Choices over Small and Large Probability Gains and Losses." Working Paper Series, University of Oregon Department of Economics.

———. 2004. "Learning to Bargain." Working Paper Series, University of Oregon Department of Economics.

Harbom, Lotta, Stina Högbladh, and Peter Wallensteen. 2006. "Armed Conflict and Peace Agreements." *Journal of Peace Research* 43:617–631.

Harden, Blaine. 2000. "Africa's Gems: Warfare's Best Friend." *New York Times*, 6 April.

Hegre, Håvard. 2004. "The Duration and Termination of Civil War." *Journal of Peace Research* 41 (3): 243–252.

Hegre, Håvard, Tanja Ellingsen, Nils Petter Gleditsch, and Scott Gates. 2001. "Towards a Democratic Civil Peace?" *American Political Science Review* 95:33–48.

Hegre, Håvard, and Nicholas Sambanis. 2006. "Sensitivity Analysis of the Empirical Literature on Civil War Onset." *Journal of Conflict Resolution* 50 (4): 508–535.

Hill, R. Carter, William E. Griffiths, and George G. Judge. 2001. *Undergraduate Econometrics*. 2nd ed. New York: Wiley.

Hogg, Charu Lata. 2006. *Child Recruitment in South Asian Conflicts: A Comparative Analysis of Sri Lanka, Nepal and Bangladesh*. London: Royal Institute of International Affairs and the Coalition to Stop the Use of Child Soldiers.

Høiskar, A. H. 2001. "Underage and Under Fire: An Enquiry into the Use of Child Soldiers 1994–98." *Childhood: A Global Journal of Child Research* 8 (3): 340–360.

Homer-Dixon, Thomas. 1994. "Environmental Scarcities and Violent Conflict: Evidence from Cases." *International Security* 19 (1): 5–40.

———. 2003. "Synchronous Failure: The Real Danger of the 21st Century." Presentation, George Washington University, Washington, DC, 1 December.

Honaker, James, and Gary King. 2006. "What to Do about Missing Values in Time Series Cross-Section Data." http://gking.harvard.edu/files/pr.pdf.

Honwana, Alcinda. 2006. *Child Soldiers in Africa*. Philadelphia: University of Pennsylvania Press.

Hovil, L., and E. Werker. 2005. "Portrait of a Failed Rebellion: An Account of Rational, Sub-Optimal Violence in Western Uganda." *Rationality and Society* 17 (1): 5–34.

Howe, Herbert. 2001. *Ambiguous Order: Military Forces in African States*. London: Lynne Rienner Publishers.

Hultman, Lisa. 2005. "Killing Civilians to Signal Resolve: Rebel Strategies in Intrastate Conflict." Paper presented at the Annual Meetings of the American Political Science Association, Washington, DC.

Human Rights Education Institute of Burma (HREIB). 2006. *Despite Promises: Child Soldiers in Burma's Armed Forces*. Chiang Mai: HREIB.

Human Rights Watch. 1990. *Liberia: A Human Rights Disaster. Violations of the Laws of War by All Parties to the Conflict*. New York: Human Rights Watch.

———. 1994. *Easy Prey: Child Soldiers in Liberia*. New York: Human Rights Watch.

———. 1995a. *Children in Sudan: Slaves, Street Children and Child Soldiers*. New York: Human Rights Watch.

———. 1995b. "Liberia." In *Human Rights Watch World Report 1995*. New York: Human Rights Watch.

———. 1999. "The Use of Child Soldiers in the Democratic Republic of Congo." http://www.hrw.org/campaigns/crp/congo.htm.

———. 2001. "Democratic Republic of the Congo, Reluctant Recruits: Children and Adults Forcibly Recruited for Military Service in North Kivu." *Human Rights Watch Report* 13 (3): 1–19.

———. 2002a. *Erased in a Moment: Suicide Bombing Attacks against Israeli Civilians*. New York: Human Rights Watch.

———. 2002b. *Liberian Refugees in Guinea: Refoulement, Militarization of Camps, and Other Protection Concerns*. New York: Human Rights Watch.

———. 2002c. *"My Gun Was as Tall as Me": Child Soldiers in Burma*. New York: Human Rights Watch.

———. 2002d. "UN Cites Child Recruiters but Omits Leading Offenders." *Human Rights News*, 16 December. http://www.hrw.org/press/2002/12/childsoldiers1216.htm.

———. 2003a. *Forgotten Fighters: Child Soldiers in Angola*. New York: Human Rights Watch. Available at http://www.hrw.org/reports/2003/angola0403/.

———. 2003b. *We'll Kill You If You Cry: Sexual Violence in the Sierra Leone Conflict*. New York, NY: Human Rights Watch.

———. 2003c. *You'll Learn Not to Cry: Child Combatants in Colombia*. New York: Human Rights Watch.

———. 2004a. "Child Soldier Use 2003: A Briefing for the 4th UN Security Council Open Debate on Children." New York: Human Rights Watch.

———. 2004b. *How to Fight, How to Kill*. New York: Human Rights Watch.

———. 2004c. *Living in Fear: Child Soldiers and the Tamil Tigers in Sri Lanka*. New York: Human Rights Watch.

———. 2005. *Clear Culpability: "Disappearances" by Security Forces in Nepal*. New York: Human Rights Watch.

———. 2007a. *Children in the Ranks: The Maoists' Use of Child Soldiers in Nepal*. New York: Human Rights Watch.

———. 2007b. *Complicit in Crime: State Collusion in Abduction and Child Recruitment by the Karuna Group*. New York: Human Rights Watch.

———. 2007c. *Early to War: Child Soldiers in the Chad Conflict*. New York: Human Rights Watch.

Human Security Center. 2005. *Human Security Report 2005*. New York: Oxford University Press.

Human Security Network and the Office of the Special Representative of the Secretary-General for Children and Armed Conflict. 2003. *Children and Armed Conflict: International Standards for Action*. http://www.unicef.org/emerg/files/HSNBook.pdf.

Humphreys, Macartan, and Jeremy Weinstein. 2004. "What the Fighters Say: A Survey of Ex-combatants in Sierra Leone." Working Paper no. 20, Center on Globalization and Sustainable Development, Earth Institute, Columbia University, New York.

———. 2005. "Handling and Manhandling Civilians in Civil War: Determinants of the Strategies of Warring Factions." Unpublished paper, Department of Political Science, Stanford University.

———. 2006a. "Who Rebels? The Determinants of Participation in Civil War." Paper presented at the Midwest Political Science Association Conference, Chicago, 20 April.

———. 2006b. "Handling and Manhandling Civilians in Civil War." *American Political Science Review* 100 (3): 429–447.

———. 2008. "Who Fights? The Determinants of Participation in Civil War." *American Journal of Political Science* 52 (2): 436–455.

Ignatieff, Michael. 1998. *The Warrior's Honor: Ethnic War and the Modern Conscience*. New York: Henry Holt and Co.

ILO/IPEC. 2003. *Wounded Childhood: The Use of Children in Armed Conflict in Central Africa*. Geneva: ILO/OPEC.

Integrated Regional Information Networks (IRIN). 2003a. "Afghanistan: Eight Thou-

sand Children under Arms Look for a Future." 8 August. http://www.irinnews.org/
InDepthMain.aspx?InDepthId=24&ReportId=66989&Country=Yes.

———. 2003b. "Africa: Too Small to Be Fighting in Anyone's War." December. http://
www.irinnews.org/IndepthMain.aspx?IndepthId=24&ReportId=66280#top.

———. 2003c. "Liberia: New Rebel Group Pushes Closer to Capital." 28 April. http://
www.irinnews.org/report.aspx?reportid=43260.

———. 2006a. "DRC: Security Situation in North Kivu Remains Precarious." 8
August. http://www.irinnews.org/Report.aspx?ReportId=60049.

———. 2006b. "Iraq: Insurgents Using Children to Fight US-Led Forces." 2 November. http://www.irinnews.org/report.aspx?reportid=61917.

Inter-American Commission on Human Rights (IACHR). 2000. *Annual Report 2000.*
Colombia. Washington, DC: IACHR.

Internal Displacement Monitoring Centre (IDMC). 2006. "Democratic Republic of
Congo: Some 40,000 Flee Ongoing Fighting Every Month. A Profile of the Internal
Displacement Situation." *UNHCR Refworld,* 1 March. http://www.unhcr.org/
refworld/docid/4451e9544.html.

International Criminal Court (ICC). 2002. *Rome Statute of the International Criminal
Court.* The Hague, The Netherlands: International Criminal Court.

———. 2006. "Decision to Unseal the Warrant of Arrest against Mr. Thomas Lubanga
Dyilo and Related Documents." Public Document no. ICC-01/04-01/06, 17 March.

Iversen, V. 2002. "Autonomy in Child Labor Migrants." *World Development* 30:817–834.

———. 2005. "Segmentation and Rural Network Multipliers in Rural-Urban Migration." *Working Paper T9.* Development Research Centre on Migration, Globalisation
and Poverty, University of Sussex, UK.

Jacobs, Dan. 1991. "Protecting Children from the Scourge of War." *Consultative Group
on Early Childhood Care and Development* 10:1–27.

Jaramillo, Ana, M. Ceballos, and Villa Marta. 1998. "En la Encrucijada." *Corporación
Región* (Medellín), 1–27.

Jepperson, Ronald L., Alexander Wendt, and Peter Katzenstein. 1996. "Norms, Identity,
and Culture in National Security." In *The Culture of National Security: Norms and
Identity in World Politics,* ed. Peter J. Katzenstein, 35–47. New York: Columbia
University Press.

Jezequel, Jean-Herve. 2004. "Liberia: Orchestrated Chaos." In *In the Shadow of "Just
Wars": Violence, Politics and Humanitarian Action,* ed. Fabrice Weissman. Ithaca, NY:
Cornell University Press.

Kahneman, Daniel, and Amos Tversky. 2000. *Choices, Values, and Frames.* Cambridge,
MA: Cambridge University Press.

Kaiser, David. 1990. *Politics and War.* Cambridge, MA: Harvard University Press.

Kaldor, Mary. 1999. *New and Old Wars.* Stanford , CA: Stanford University Press.

———. 2001. *Las nuevas guerras. Violencia organizada en la era global.* Barcelona:
Tusquets.

Kalyvas, Stathis. 2001. "'New' and 'Old' Civil Wars: A Valid Distinction?" *World Politics*
54 (1): 99–118.

———. 2003. "The Ontology of 'Political Violence': Action and Identity in Civil Wars."
Perspectives on Politics 1 (3): 475–494.

———. 2005a. "The Ontology of Political Violence: Action and Identity in Civil Wars." *Perspectives on Politics* 1:475–494.

———. 2005b. "Warfare in Civil Wars." In *Rethinking the Nature of War,* ed. Isabelle Duyvesteyn and Jan Angstrom, 88–108. Abington: Frank Cass.

———. 2006. *The Logic of Violence in Civil War.* Cambridge, UK: Cambridge University Press.

Kaplan, Robert D. 1994. "The Coming Anarchy." *Atlantic Monthly,* February, 44–76.

Kaufman, Stuart J. 2001. *Modern Hatreds: The Symbolic Politics of Ethnic War.* Ithaca, NY: Cornell University Press.

Keairns, Yvonne. 2002. *The Voices of Girl Soldiers: Summary.* New York: Quaker United Nations Office.

Kelso, Casey. 2004. In *Child Soldiers: Global Report 2004.* London: Coalition to Stop Child Soldiers.

Kenny, Anthony. 1985. *The Logic of Deterrence.* London: Waterstone.

Khapoya, Vincent B. 1998. *The African Experience: An Introduction.* 2nd ed. Upper Saddle River, NJ: Prentice Hall.

Kielland, A., and I. Sanogo. 2002. *Burkina Faso: Child Labor Migration from Rural Areas.* Washington, DC: World Bank.

King, Gary, James Honaker, Anne Joseph, and Kenneth Scheve. 2001. "Analyzing Incomplete Political Science Data: An Alternative Algorithm for Multiple Imputation." *American Political Science Review* 95 (1): 49–69.

King, Gary, Robert Keohane, and Sidney Verba. 1994. *Designing Social Inquiry: Scientific Inference in Qualitative Research.* Princeton, NJ: Princeton University Press.

King, Gary, and Christopher J. L. Murray. 2002. "Rethinking Human Security." *Political Science Quarterly* 116:585–610.

Kingma, Kees. 2002. "Demobilization, Reintegration and Peacebuilding in Africa." *International Peacekeeping* 9 (2): 181–201.

Klare, Michael. 1999. "The Kalashnikov Age." *Bulletin of the Atomic Scientists* 55 (1): 18–22.

Lachanthaboun, Sengdeuane, Khamla Phomsavanh, and Anne Thomas. 2005. "Teacher Training in Remote Areas of Lao PDR." In *From Bullets to Blackboards: Education for Peace in Latin America and Asia,* ed. Emily Vargas-Barón and Hernando Bernal Alacrón, 63–82. Washington, DC: Inter-American Development Bank.

Lacina, Bethany Ann, and Nils Petter Gleditsch. 2005. "Monitoring Trends in Global Combat: A New Dataset of Battle Deaths." *European Journal of Population* 21:145–165.

Laitin, David. 1995. "National Revivals and Violence." *Archive Européennes de Sociologie* 36:3–43.

Lara, Patricia. 2000. *Las Mujeres en la Guerra.* Bogotá: Planeta.

Lazarsfeld, Paul, Bernard Berelson, and Hazel Gaudet. 1968. *The People's Choice: How the Voter Makes Up His Mind in a Presidential Campaign.* New York: Columbia University Press.

Levi, Primo. 1989. *The Drowned and the Saved.* New York: Vintage.

Levitt, Jeremy I. 2005. *The Evolution of Deadly Conflict in Liberia.* Durham, NC: Carolina Academic Press.

Lichbach, Mark. 2005. "How to Organize Your Mechanisms: Research Programs, Stylized Facts, and Historical Narratives." In *Repression and Mobilization*, ed. Christian Davenport, Hank Johnston, and Carol Mueller, 227–243. Minneapolis: University of Minnesota Press.

Lischer, Sarah Kenyon. 2000. "Refugee Involvement in Political Violence: Quantitative Evidence from 1987–1998." *Working Paper no. 26*, Center for International Studies, Massachusetts Institute of Technology.

———. 2005. *Dangerous Sanctuaries: Refugee Camps, Civil War, and the Dilemmas of Humanitarian Aid*. Ithaca, NY: Cornell University Press.

———. 2006. "War, Displacement, and the Recruitment of Child Soldiers." Paper presented at the Child Soldiers Initiative Working Group Session, Pittsburgh, 15–16 September 2006.

Little, Roderick, and Donald Rubin. 1987. *Statistical Analysis with Missing Data*. New York: Wiley.

LLECE. 2002. *First International Comparative Study (Language Mathematics and Associated Factors*. Santiago de Chile: UNESCO/OREALC.

Lock, Peter. 1998. "Military Downsizing and Growth in the Security Industry in Sub-Saharan Africa." *Strategic Analysis* 22 (9): 1393–1426.

Loescher, Gil, and James Milner. 2005. "The Significance of Protracted Refugee Situations." *Adelphi Papers* 45 (375): 7–12.

Machel, Graca. 1996. "The Impact of Armed Conflict on Children." *United Nations Document A/51/306 and Add.1. 1996*. New York: United Nations.

———. 2001. *The Impact of War on Children*. Cape Town, South Africa: David Philip.

Makarenko, Tamara. 2003. "A Model of Terrorist-Criminal Relations." *Jane's Intelligence Review* (August): 6–10.

Mazurana, Dyan, Susan McKay, Khristopher Carlson, and Janet Kasper. 2002. "Girls in Fighting Forces and Groups: Their Recruitment, Participation, Demobilization, and Reintegration." *Peace and Conflict: Journal of Peace Psychology* 8 (2): 97–124.

McClure, Maureen, and Gonzalo Retamal. 2007a. "The Goat Stays." In *Wise Investments in Future Neighbors: Recruitment Deterrence, Human Agency, and Education*, 1–34. Pittsburgh: Ford Institute.

———. 2007b. "Youth Security in Refugee Camps: Using Humanitarian Education to Turn Them from Recruitment Centers for Soldiers to Child-Friendly Spaces." In *Wise Investments in Future Neighbors: Recruitment Deterrence, Human Agency, and Education*. Pittsburgh: Ford Institute for Human Security and University of Pittsburgh.

McKay, Susan, and Dyan Mazurana. 2004. *Where Are the Girls? Girls in Fighting Forces in Northern Uganda, Sierra Leone and Mozambique: Their Lives during and after War*. Montreal: International Centre for Human Rights and Democratic Development.

Médecins Sans Frontières. 2006. "Food, Nutrition, and Mortality Situation of IDPs in Dubie, Katanga." 23–25 March, Médecins Sans Frontières. http://www.msf.org/source/countries/Africa/drc/2006_dubie_report.doc.

Medina Gallego, Carlos. 1990. *Autodefensas, paramilitares y narcotráfico: Origen, desarrollo y consolidación. El caso Puerto Boyacá*, Bogotá: Documentos Periodísticos.

———. 1996. *ELN: Una historia contada a dos voces*. Bogotá: Rodríguez Quito Editores.

Mehlum, Halvor, and Karl Ove Moene. 2006. "Fighting against the odds." *Economics of Governance* 7 (1): 75–87.

Mertler, Craig A., and Rachel A. Vannatta. 2001. *Advanced and Multivariate Statistical Methods: Practical Application and Interpretation.* Los Angeles: Pyrczak Publishing.

Mesquida, Christian, and Neil I. Weiner. 1999. "Male Age Composition and Severity of Conflicts." *Politics and Life Sciences* 18 (2): 181–89.

Metz, Stephen. 2000a. *Armed Conflict in the 21st Century: The Information Revolution and Post-Modern Warfare.* Carlisle, PA: U.S. Army War College, Strategic Studies Institute.

———. 2000b. *Refining American Strategy in Africa.* Carlisle, PA: U.S. Army War College, Strategic Studies Institute.

Misser, François. 2006. "Democratic Republic of the Congo: Prospects for Peace and Normality." *Writenet,* March 2006. Available at: http://www.unhcr.ch.

Model United Nations of the University of Chicago. 2003. *Reintegration of Child Soldiers.* Chicago: MUNUC.

Molano, Alfredo. 2001a. *Trochas y fusiles.* Bogotá: El Áncora.

———. 2001b. "La justicia guerillera." In *El caleidoscopio de las Universidad de los Andes,* ed. Bonaventura de Sousa Santos and Garcia Mauricio, 331–388. Bogotá: Universidad Nacional de Colombia, Siglo del Hombre.

Morin, Richard. 2001. "Boy Trouble." *Washington Post,* 24 June.

Mosley, Paul, and John Hudson. 2001. "Aid, Poverty Reduction and the New Conditionality." Paper presented at the Aid Impact Forum, Centre for Development Research, Copenhagen, October 22.

Mueller, John. 2003. "Policing the Remnants of War." *Journal of Peace Research* 40 (5): 507–518.

Mwepu, Francis. 2006. "Ituri: The Congo's Own Rwanda." *Institute for War and Peace Reporting,* July 27. http://www.iwpr.net/?p=acr&s=f&o=322577&apc_state=henpacr.

Nagel, Thomas. 1985. "War and Massacre." In *International Ethics,* ed. Charles R. Beitz, Marshall Cohen, Thomas Scanlon, and A. John Simmons, 53–74. Princeton, NJ: Princeton University Press.

Napoleon. 1999. *On the Art of War.* Selected, edited, and translated by Jay Luvaas. New York: Simon & Schuster.

National Transitional Government of Liberia, United Nations, World Bank. 2004. "Joint Needs Assessment, February 2004." http://www.lr.undp.org/needs_assessment.pdf.

NCDDRR Joint Implementation Unit (JIU). 2006. *Status Report.* 2 October. Austin: NCDDRR/JIU.

Neild, Robert. 2000. "Expose the Unsavory Business behind Cruel Wars." *International Herald Tribune,* 17 February.

Ngowi, Rodrique. 2003. "War Has a Baby Face in the Congo." *Star* (South Africa), 10 July.

Nichiporuk, Brian. 2001. *The Security Dynamics of Demographic Factors.* Santa Monica, CA: Rand.

Nichols, Johanna. 2000a. *The Ingush (with notes on the Chechen): Background Information.* Berkeley: University of California.

———. 2000b. *Information on the Chechen Refugee Situation in Ingushetia.* Berkeley: University of California.

Norwegian Refugee Council. 2005. "Profile of Internal Displacement: Liberia." *Global IDP database*, 25 August. http://www.humanitarianinfo.org/liberia/mediacentre/press/doc/Liberia%20-August%202005.pdf.

Olson, Mancur. 1971. *Logic of Collective Action: Public Goods*. Cambridge, MA: Harvard University Press.

Oluwaniyi, Oluwatoyin O. 2003. "The Phenomenon of Child Soldiers in Liberia and Sierra Leone." *African Journal of Peace and Conflict Studies* 1 (1): 140–157.

Organization of African Unity. 1969. Convention Governing the Specific Aspects of Refugee Problems in Africa ("OAU Convention"), 10 September. *UNHCR Refworld*. http://www.unhcr.org/refworld/docid/3ae6b36018.html.

Ospina Serna, Hector Fabio, and Sara Victoria Alvarado Salgado. 2001. *Los niños, las niñas y los jóvenes recuperan su voz en la construcción de procesos de paz: Experiencia en 32 instituciones educativas oficiales e instituciones de protección en Colombia*. Bogotá: CINDE.

Otis, John. 2001. "Rebel Held: Child Soldiers." *Houston Chronicle*, 3 August.

Otunnu, Olara A. 2003. *Rights of the Child: Annual report of the Special Representative of the Secretary-General for Children and Armed Conflict*. Submitted in accordance with General Assembly resolution 51/77* United Nations Economic and Social Council General, E/CN.4/2003/77, 3 March. http://www.hri.ca/fortherecord2003/documentation/commission/e-cn4-2003-77.htm.

Pais, Marta Santos. 1999. *Human Rights Conceptual Framework for UNICEF*. New York: UNICEF.

Pape, Robert. 2005. *Dying to Win: The Strategic Logic of Suicide Terrorism*. New York: Random House.

Paris, Roland. 2001. "Human Security: Paradigm Shift or Hot Air." *International Security* 26:87–102.

Pedersen, J. 2005. "What Should We Know about Children in Armed Conflict and How Should We Go about Knowing It." Fagforeningenas Forskerorganisasion MS.

Peters, Krijn. 2004. *Re-Examining Voluntarism: Youth Combatants in Sierra Leone*. Pretoria: Institute for Security Studies.

Petersen, Roger. 1993. "A Community-Based Theory of Rebellion." *European Journal of Sociology* 34:41–78.

Pinto, Borrego María Eugenia, Vergara Ballén Andrés, and Percipiano Yilberto LaHuerta. 2002. "Diagnóstico del programa de reinserción en Colombia: Mecanismos para incentivar la reinserción voluntaria individual." Document 211, Archivos de Macroeconomía Departamento Nacional de Planeación.

Pizarro, Eduardo. 2004. *Balance y perspectivas del conflicto armado Colombiano*. Bogotá: Norma.

Platteau, J. P., and C. André. 1996. "Land Relations under Unbearable Stress: Rwanda Caught in the Malthusian Trap." Paper presented at the Center of Research in the Economics of Development, University of Namur, Belgium.

Polanyi, Karl. 1944. *The Great Transformation: The Political and Economic Origins of Our Time*. Boston: Beacon Press.

Polgreen, Lydia. 2006. "Violence Forces U.N. to Evacuate Darfur Camp." *New York Times*, 8 May.

Population International. 2003. Briefing Notes, March. http://www.population institute.org/index.php.

Posada-Carbó, Eduardo. 2006. *La nación soñada*. Bogotá: Norma-FIP.

Profiles. 1999. "Natural Born Killers." May.

Przeworski, Adam, and Henry Teune. 1970. *The Logic of Comparative Social Inquiry*. New York: Wiley-Interscience.

Pugel, James. 2006. "Key Findings from the Nation Wide Survey of Ex-combatants in Liberia: Reintegration and Reconciliation, February–March 2006." Report for the UNDP Liberia.

———. 2007. *What the Fighters Say: A Survey of Ex-combatants in Liberia*. Report for the UNDP Liberia.

Punamäki, R. L. 1996. "Can Ideological Commitment Protect Children's Psycho-Social Well-Being in Political Violence?" *Child Development* 67:55–69.

Refugees International. 2005a. "Democratic Republic of the Congo: Demobilization of Rwandan Soldiers Going Slowly." *Refugees International Bulletin*, 16 December. http://www.refugeesinternational.org.

———. 2005b. "Democratic Republic of the Congo: Internally Displaced Unable to Return Require Alternative Resettlement Possibilities." *Refugees International*, 23 June. http://www.refugeesinternational.org.

———. 2005c. "Refugee Voices: Child Soldiers in the Democratic Republic of the Congo." *Refugees International*, 22 June. http://www.refugeesinternational.org.

———. 2005d. "Refugee Voices: One Female Child Soldier's Story in the Democratic Republic of Congo." *Refugees International Bulletin*, 7 November. http://www .refugeesinternational.org.

Renner, Michael. 1998. "The Global Divide: Socioeconomic Disparities and International Security." In *World Security: Challenges for a New Century*, ed. Michael Klare and Yogesh Chandrani. New York: St. Martin's Press.

Reuters. 2001. "To Child Soldier, 14, War Was 'Shoot or Be Killed.'" 12 June.

Reynolds, P. 1991. *"Dance Civet Cat": The Tonga and Child Labor in Zimbabwe*. London: Zed Books Ltd.

Richards, Paul. 1996. *Fighting for the Rainforest: War, Youth and Resources in Sierra Leone*. Oxford: James Currey.

Romero, Cesar. 2002. *Cuestionario Atención Psiocosocial: Respuestas a Questionnaire on Psychosocial Support Intervention(s)*. Bogotá: UNICEF.

———. *Atención psicosocial a niños y niñas afectados por el conflicto armado*. Bogotá: UNICEF.

Romero, Mauricio. 2002. *Paramilitares y autodefensas, 1982–2003*. Bogotá: Iepri-Planeta.

Salazar, Alonso. 1990. *No nacimos pa' semilla*. Medellín: Corporación Región.

———. 1993. *Mujeres de fuego*. Medellín: Corporación Región.

Salopek, Paul. 2002. "The Guns of Africa: Violence-Wracked Nations Are Dumping Grounds for World's Arsenals." *Seattle Times*, 27 February.

Save the Children. (n.d.). *Child War Database*. http://www.savethechildren.se// programme/childreninarmed/childsoldiers/.

———. 2000. "Children of the Gun." *Children in Crisis* project report, September. http://www.savethechildren.org/crisis.

———. 2005. *Forgotten Casualties of War: Girls in Armed Conflict.* London: Save the Children.

———. 2006a. "Congo Case Study: Aimerance, Girl Soldier." *Reuters AlertNet,* 7 July.

———. 2006b. "Congo Case Study: Furaa, Girl Soldier." *Reuters AlertNet,* 7 July.

Save the Children Fund UK. 2000. *War Brought Us Here: Protecting Children Displaced within Their Own Countries by Conflict.* London: Save the Children Fund UK.

Schelling, Thomas. 2003. *The Strategy of Conflict.* Cambridge, MA: Harvard University Press.

Schugurensky, Daniel. Forthcoming. *Colombia Escuela Nueva.* A work in progress edited by Department of Adult Education, Community Development and Counseling Psychology, Ontario Institute for Studies in Education of the University of Toronto.

Scott, Colin. 1998. "Liberia: A Nation Displaced." In *The Forsaken People: Case Studies of the Internally Displaced,* ed. Roberta Cohen and Francis M. Deng. Washington, DC: Brookings.

Sekaggya, Lisa. 2004. "Ugandan Children Born in Captivity and Their Human Rights." Paper presented at the Conference on War Babies, Pittsburgh, 13 November.

Shaw, Martin. 2000. "The Contemporary Mode of Warfare? Mary Kaldor's Theory of New Wars." *Review of International Political Economy* 7 (1): 171–180.

Shepler, Susan. 2004. "The Social and Cultural Context of Child Soldiering in Sierra Leone." Paper presented at the PRIO workshop, Techniques of Violence in Civil War, Oslo, Norway, 20–21 August.

Siegrist, Saudamini. 2003. *Colombia Case Study.* New York: UNICEF/EMOPS.

Singer, P. W. 2001. "Caution: Children at War." *Parameters* 4:40–56.

———. 2002. "AIDS and International Security." *Survival* 44:145–158.

———. 2004. "Talk Is Cheap: Getting Serious about Preventing Child Soldiers." *Cornell International Law Journal* 37 (3): 561–586.

———. 2005. *Children at War.* New York: Pantheon Books.

———. 2006. "The Enablers of War: Causal Factors behind the Child Soldier Phenomenon." Paper presented at the Child Soldiers Initiative Working Group Session, Pittsburgh, 15–16 September.

Slim, Hugo. 2008. *Killing Civilians: Method, Madness and Morality in War.* New York: Columbia University Press.

Smith, Chris, and Alex Vines. 1997. *Light Weapons Proliferation in Southern Africa.* London: Centre for Defence Studies.

Smith, Daniel, and Rachel Stohl. 1999. "Small Arms in Failed States: A Deadly Combination." Paper presented at Failed States and International Security Conference at Purdue University, 8–11 April.

Smith, Deborah. 2001. "Children in the Heat of War." *Monitor on Psychology* 32 (8). http://www.apa.org/monitor/sep01/childwar.html.

Somasundaram, Daya. 1993. *Child Trauma.* Jaffna, Sri Lanka: University of Jaffna.

Special Court for Sierra Leone. 2003. Case No. SCSL-2003-01-I. The Prosecutor against Charles Ghankay Taylor, Amended Indictment.

Stavou, Stavros, and Robert Stewart. 2000. "The Reintegration of Child Soldiers and Abducted Children: A Case Study of Palaro and Pabbo Gulu District." In *Act*

Against Child Soldiers in Africa: A Reader, ed. Elizabeth Bennett, Virginia Gamba, and Deirdre van der Merwe. Pretoria, South Africa: Institute of Security Studies.

Stavrou, Vivi. 2005. *Breaking the Silence: Girls Forcibly Involved in the Armed Struggle in Angola.* Luanda: Christian Children's Fund/Angola.

Stedman, Stephen John, and Fred Tanner. 2003. "Refugees as Resources in War." In *Refugee Manipulation: War, Politics, and the Abuse of Human Suffering,* ed. Stephen John Stedman and Fred Tanner. Washington, DC: Brookings Institution Press.

Stichick, Theresa, and Claude Bruderlein. 2001. "Children Facing Insecurity: New Strategies for Survival in a Global Era." Harvard Program in Humanitarian Policy and Conflict Research Policy Paper.

Stichick, Theresa, Rebecca Winthrop, Wendy Smith, and Gillian Dunn. 2002. "The IRC's Emergency Education Program for Chechen Children and Adolescents." *Forced Migration Review* 15:28–29.

Stohl, Rachel. 2002. "Targeting Children: Small Arms and Children in Conflict." *Brown Journal of World Affairs* 9 (1): 281–292.

Swarns, Rachel. 2001. "Study Says AIDS Is Now Chief Cause of Death in South Africa." *CNN.com,* 16 October.

SWAY-Uganda. 2006. http://www.sway-uganda.org/.

Taylor, Michael. 1988. "Rationality and Revolutionary Collective Action." In *Rationality and Revolution,* ed. Michael Taylor. Cambridge, MA: Cambridge University Press.

Terry, Fiona. 2002. *Condemned to Repeat? The Paradox of Humanitarian Action.* Ithaca, NY: Cornell University Press.

"They'd Make You Kill Your Parents." 2000. *Toronto Star News,* 23 July.

Tualeka, Baihajar, Sondang Irene Erisandy, and Livia Iskandar-Dharmawan. 2005. "Early Childhood Development for Refugee Children in Indonesia." In *From Bullets to Blackboards: Education for Peace in Latin America and Asia,* ed. Emily Vargas-Barón and Hernando Bernal Alacrón. Washington, DC: Inter-American Development Bank.

Twum-Danso, Afua. 2003. "Africa's Young Soldiers: The Co-Option of Childhood." *Monograph no. 82,* Institute for Security Studies, Pretoria. http://www.iss.co.za/Pubs/Monographs/No82/Content.html.

UNAIDS-UNICEF. 2002. *Children on the Brink, 2002.* New York: United Nations. http://data.unaids.org/Topics/Young-People/childrenonthebrink_en.pdf.

UNESCO Institute for Education/Plan International. 2000. Building a Rapid Educational Response, Joint UIE /Plan International Project, Freetown, March.

UNICEF. 1996. *State of the World's Children: 1996.* New York: UNICEF.

———. 1999. *Child Friendly Spaces Initiative.* Albania, internal document, UNICEF.

———. 2000. *Progress of Nations.* New York: UNICEF.

———. 2001. *National Strategy for Children.* Republic of Albania. http://www.unicef.org/albania/nationalchildstrategy.pdf.

———. 2002a. *Adult Wars, Child Soldiers.* Bangkok: UNICEF. http://www.unicef.org/evaldatabase/files/EAPRO_2001_AdultWars.pdf.

———. 2002b. *Children Affected by Armed Conflict: UNICEF Actions.* New York: UNICEF.

———. 2004a. *Child Friendly Spaces/Environments (CFS/E): An Integrated Services Strategy for Emergencies and Their Aftermath.* New York: UNICEF.

———. 2004b. "Fact Sheet: Child Soldiers." http://www.unicef.org/emerg/files/ childsoldiers.pdf.

———. 2007. *The Paris Principles: The Principles and Guidelines on Children Associated with Armed Forces or Armed Groups.* Available at http://www.unicef.org/protection/ files/ParisPrinciples310107English.pdf.

UNIFEM. 2004. *Getting It Right, Doing It Right: Gender and Disarmament, Demobilization and Reintegration.* New York: UNIFEM.

United Nations. 1999a. *Security Council Resolution 1261.* UN Doc. S/RES/1261 (1999).

———. 1999b. *Security Council Resolution 1265.* UN Doc. S/RES/1265 (1999).

———. 2001a. "Consolidated Inter-Agency Appeal 2002: Liberia Internet." http:// www.reliefweb.int/appeals/2002/files/lib02.pdf.

———. 2001b. *Security Council Resolution 1379.* UN Doc. S/RES/1379.

———. 2003a. *Report of the Secretary-General on the Situation in Liberia.* UN Doc. S/2003/582.

———. 2003b. *Security Council Resolution 1460.* UN Doc. S/RES/1460.

———. 2004a. *Security Council Resolution 1539.* UN Doc. S/RES/1539.

———. 2004b. "Uganda: Child Soldiers at Centre of Mounting Humanitarian Crisis." *Ten Stories the World Should Hear More About.* http://www.un.org/events/ten stories/story.asp?storyID=100.

———. 2005a. *The Fifth Report of the Secretary-General to the Security Council on Children and Armed Conflict (2005).* UN Doc. A/59/695-S/2005/72.

———. 2005b. *Report of the Special Representative of the Secretary-General for Children and Armed Conflict to the General Assembly.* UN Doc. A/60/335.

———. 2005c. *Security Council Resolution 1612.* UN Doc. S/RES/1612.

———. 2006a. "Humanitarian Efforts in Darfur Jeopardized by Aid Workers' Deaths." United Nations Press Release, 6 August.

———. 2006b. *6th Report of the Secretary-General to the Security Council on Children and Armed Conflict, October 2006.* UN Doc. A/61/529-S/2006/826.

———. 2006c. *Second Report of the Panel of Experts Established Pursuant to Resolution 1591 (2005) Concerning the Sudan.* UN Doc. S/2006/250. Rec. 11.

UN Country Team in Colombia (UNCT). 2003. UN Humanitarian Situation Room, Colombia Report, March, UN OCHA Reliefweb. http://www.reliefweb.int/rw/ rwb.nsf/db900SID/SODA-6288JP?OpenDocument.

UN Department of Peacekeeping Operations. 2006. Confidential Code Cable no: 396, 28 November 2005; Code Cable no: 151, 4 May 2006.

UN Fund for Population Activities (UNFPA). 2003. *State of World Population: Making 1 Billion Count.* New York: UNFPA.

UN General Assembly. 1951. *Convention Relating to the Status of Refugees, 28 July 1951.* United Nations, Treaty Series, vol. 189, p. 137. http://www.unhcr.org/refworld/ docid/3be01b964.html.

———. 2001. *General Assembly Resolution no. 56,* par. 136, 19 December.

UN High Commissioner for Refugees (UNHCR). 1994. *Liberia: What Hope for Peace?* http://www.unhcr.ch/cgi-bin/texis/vtx/print?tbl=RSDCOI&id=3ae6a6bc0.

———. 2000. *Background Paper on Refugees and Asylum Seekers from the Democratic Republic of the Congo*. Centre for Documentation and Research. Geneva: UNHCR.

———. 2001. *Refugee Children in Africa: Trends and Patterns in the Refugee Population in Africa below the Age of 18 Years*. http://www.unhcr.org/statistics/STATISTICS/3b9378e42d.pdf.

———. 2002. *Prima Facie: The Newsletter of UNHCR's Department of International Protection* (April). Geneva, UNHCR.

———. 2003a. *2003 UNHCR Statistical Yearbook, Democratic Republic of the Congo*. Geneva: UNHCR.

———. 2003b. "Turning Refugees into Gunmen." *Refugees* 131:18.

———. 2004. *2004 Global Refugee Trends*. Geneva: UNHCR.

———. 2005. "Life Is Precarious, Unpredictable, and Sometimes Deadly." *Refugees* 2 (139): 9.

———. 2006. *State of the World's Refugees. 2006*. Oxford: Oxford University Press.

UN Human Settlements Program. 2003. *The Challenge of Slums*. New York: UN-HABITAT.

UN Mission in the DRC (MONUC). 2006. "Statement of UN Mission in DR Congo's (MONUC) Mandate." http://www.monuc.org.

UN Office for the Coordination of Humanitarian Affairs (UNOCHA). 1998. "Refugees and IDPs in the Democratic Republic of Congo." http://www.reliefweb.int.

———. 2001. "DRC, Affected Populations by Province, Refugees and Internally Displaced." Map prepared by UN OCHA Great Lakes Regional Office, Nairobi, September.

———. 2002a. "Affected Populations in the Great Lakes Region." UN OCHA Regional Support Office-Central and East Africa, 31 July.

———. 2002b. "Humanitarian Briefing Pack—Democratic Republic of the Congo" and "Access and Vulnerability in the DRC" (map).

———. 2003. "DRC Affected Populations by Province Internally Displaced." http://www.reliefweb.int/rw/fullMaps_Af.nsf/luFullMap/327A0E3B63609642C1257069003681F3/$File/ocha_AFC_cod150605.pdf?OpenElement.

U.S. Department of Labor. 2003. Bureau of International Labor Affairs. See http://www.dol.gov/ilab.

U.S. Department of State, Office to Monitor and Combat Trafficking in Persons. 2006. *Trafficking in Persons Report 2006*. Washington, DC: U.S. Department of State. http://www.state.gov/g/tip/rls/tiprpt/2006/65983.htm.

Universidad de Ibagué and Universidad del Rosario. 2006. *Escuelas que Educan y Sanan: Evaluación Intermedia*. Bogotá: Universidades del Ibague and Rosario.

University Teachers for Human Rights (UTHR). 1995. "Children in the North East War: 1985–1995." *University Teachers for Human Rights Briefing Document No. 2*. Jaffna, Sri Lanka: UTHR.

Vargas-Barón, Emily. 2005–2006. *Planning Policies for Early Childhood Development: Guidelines for Action*. Paris, Geneva, and Bogotá: UNICEF, UNESCO, ADEA, CINDE and Red Primera Infancia.

———. 2007. *Formative Evaluation of Parenting Programmes in Belarus, Bosnia and Herzegovina, Georgia and Kazakhstan*. Geneva: UNICEF.

Vargas-Barón, Emily, and Hernando Bernal Alarcón, eds. 2005. *From Bullets to Blackboards: Education for Peace in Latin America and Asia.* Washington, DC: Inter-American Development Bank.

Vargas-Barón, Emily, and Maureen McClure. 1998. "The New Heroics of Generational Commitment: Education in Nations with Chronic Crises." In *Education as a Humanitarian Response*, ed. Gonzalo Retamal and Ruth Aledo-Richmond, 271–289. London: Cassell Press and UNESCO's International Bureau of Education.

Veale, Angela. 2004. *From Child Soldier to Ex-fighter: Female Fighters, Demobilisation and Reintegration in Ethiopia, ISS Monograph no. 85.* Pretoria: Institute of Security Studies.

Veale, Angela, and Aki Stavrou. 2003. *Violence, Reconciliation and Identity: The Reintegration of Lord's Resistance Army Child Abductees in Northern Uganda, ISS Monograph 92.* Pretoria: Institute of Security Studies.

Vélez, María Alejandra. 1999. *FARC-ELN: Evolución y expansión territorial.* Bogotá: Tesis de grado de la Facultad de Economía de la Universidad de los Andes.

Verhey, Beth. 2001. "Child Soldiers: Preventing, Demobilizing and Reintegrating." In *World Bank Africa Region Working Paper Series No. 23.* Washington, DC: World Bank.

Vick, Karl. 2001. "Small Arms' Global Reach Uproots Tribal Traditions." *Washington Post*, 8 July.

Vitoria, Francisco de. 2006. "On the American Indians." In *The Ethics of War: Classic and Contemporary Readings*, ed. Gregory M. Reichberg, Henrik Syse, and Endre Begby. Malden, MA: Blackwell.

von Clausewitz, C. 1976. *On War.* Ed. and trans. Michael Howard and Peter Paret. Princeton, NJ: Princeton University Press.

Walzer, Michael. 1977. *Just and Unjust Wars.* New York: Basic Books.

Watchlist on Children and Armed Conflict (WCAC). 2003. *The Impact of Armed Conflict on Children in the Democratic Republic of Congo (DRC).* New York: WCAC.

Weinstein, Jeremy. 2002. "The Structure of Rebel Organizations: Implications for Post-Conflict Reconstruction." *Research Dissemination Note 4, Conflict Prevention and Reconstruction Unit.* Washington, DC: World Bank.

———. 2005. "Resources and the Information Problem in Rebel Recruitment." *Journal of Conflict Resolution* 49 (4): 598–624.

———. 2007. *Inside Rebellion: The Politics of Insurgent Violence.* Cambridge, MA: Cambridge University Press.

Wessells, Michael. 2006. *Child Soldiers: From Violence to Protection.* Cambridge, MA: Harvard University Press.

West, Harry. 2004. "Girls with Guns: Narrating the Experience of War of FRELIMO's 'Female Detachment.'" In *Children and Youth on the Front Line: Ethnography, Armed Conflict and Displacement*, ed. Jo Boyden and Joanna de Berry, 180–194. New York: Berghahn.

Wiles, P.J.D. 1977. *Economic Institutions Compared.* New York: Wiley.

Williamson, John. 2006. "The Disarmament, Demobilization and Reintegration of Child Soldiers: Social and Psychological Transformation in Sierra Leone." *Intervention: International Journal of Mental Health, Psychosocial Work and Counselling in*

Areas of Armed Conflict 4:185–205.

Williamson, John, and Malia Robinson. 2006. "Psychosocial Interventions, or Integrated Programming for Well-Being?" *Intervention: International Journal of Mental Health, Psychosocial Work and Counselling in Areas of Armed Conflict* 4:4–25.

Wilson, Scott. 2003. "Colombian Fighters Drug Trade Is Detailed." *Washington Post*, 25 June.

Women's Commission for Refugee Women and Children. 2001. "Against All Odds: Surviving the War on Adolescents." *Women's Commission for Refugee Women and Children.* http://www.womenscommission.org/pdf/ug.pdf.

Wood, Brian, and Johan Peleman. 1999. "The Arms Fixers." *PRIO Report.* Oslo: PRIO.

Wood, Elisabeth. 2003. *Insurgent Collective Action and Civil War in El Salvador.* New York: Cambridge University Press.

World Bank. 2004. Annual Report. Washington, DC: World Bank.

———. 2005. *Poverty Manual.* Washington, DC: World Bank. http://siteresources .worldbank.org/PGLP/Resources/povertymanual_ch3.pdf.

World's Children's Prize for the Right of the Child. 2008. "Prize Laureates: The Children's Peace Movement." http://www.childrensworld.org/page.html?cid=589.

Young, Crawford. 1998. *Ethnic Diversity and Public Policy.* New York: St. Martin's Press and United Nations Research Institute for Social Development.

CONTRIBUTORS

Vera Achvarina is a Ph.D. student at the Graduate School of Public and International Affairs, University of Pittsburgh.

Barry Ames is chair of the Political Science Department and Andrew W. Mellon Professor of Comparative Politics at the University of Pittsburgh.

Jens Christopher Andvig is a senior researcher at the Norwegian Institute of International Affairs (NUPI).

Jo Becker is the children's rights advocacy director for Human Rights Watch.

Tonderai W. Chikuhwa is a program officer in the Office of the UN Special Representative for Children and Armed Conflict.

Scott Gates is a co–principal investigator for this project, research professor and director of the Centre for the Study of Civil War (CSCW), International Peace Research Institute, Oslo (PRIO), and professor of political science, Norwegian University of Science and Technology (NTNU).

Sarah Kenyon Lischer is assistant professor of political science at Wake Forest University.

Andrew Mack is the director of the Human Security Report Project and a limited-term professor at the School for International Studies, Simon Fraser University.

Maureen W. McClure is the chair of administrative and policy studies in the School of Education at the University of Pittsburgh, senior research associate in the Institute for International Studies in Education (IISE).

Jeff McMahan is professor of philosophy at Rutgers University.

James B. Pugel is currently a doctoral student at the Institute for Conflict Analysis & Resolution (ICAR), George Mason University, and is a research associate with the Centre for the Study of Civil War (CSCW), International Peace Research Institute, Oslo (PRIO).

Simon Reich is currently director, Division of Global Affairs, Rutgers, Newark, and former director of the Ford Institute at the University of Pittsburgh.

Gonzalo Retamal is the senior education advisor for Humanitarian Assistance, IBE/UNESCO.

Francisco Gutiérrez Sanín is a researcher at the Instituto de Estudios Políticos y Relaciones Internacionales—Universidad Nacional de Colombia.

P. W. Singer is a senior fellow in Foreign Policy Studies and director of the Project on U.S. Policy toward the Islamic World at the Brookings Institution.

Emily Vargas-Barón directs the Institute for Reconstruction and International Security through Education (the RISE Institute).

Michael G. Wessells is senior advisor on child protection for Christian Children's Fund, professor of Clinical Population and Family Health at Columbia University, and professor of Psychology at Randolph-Macon College.

INDEX